**Ib Melchior
Man of Imagination**

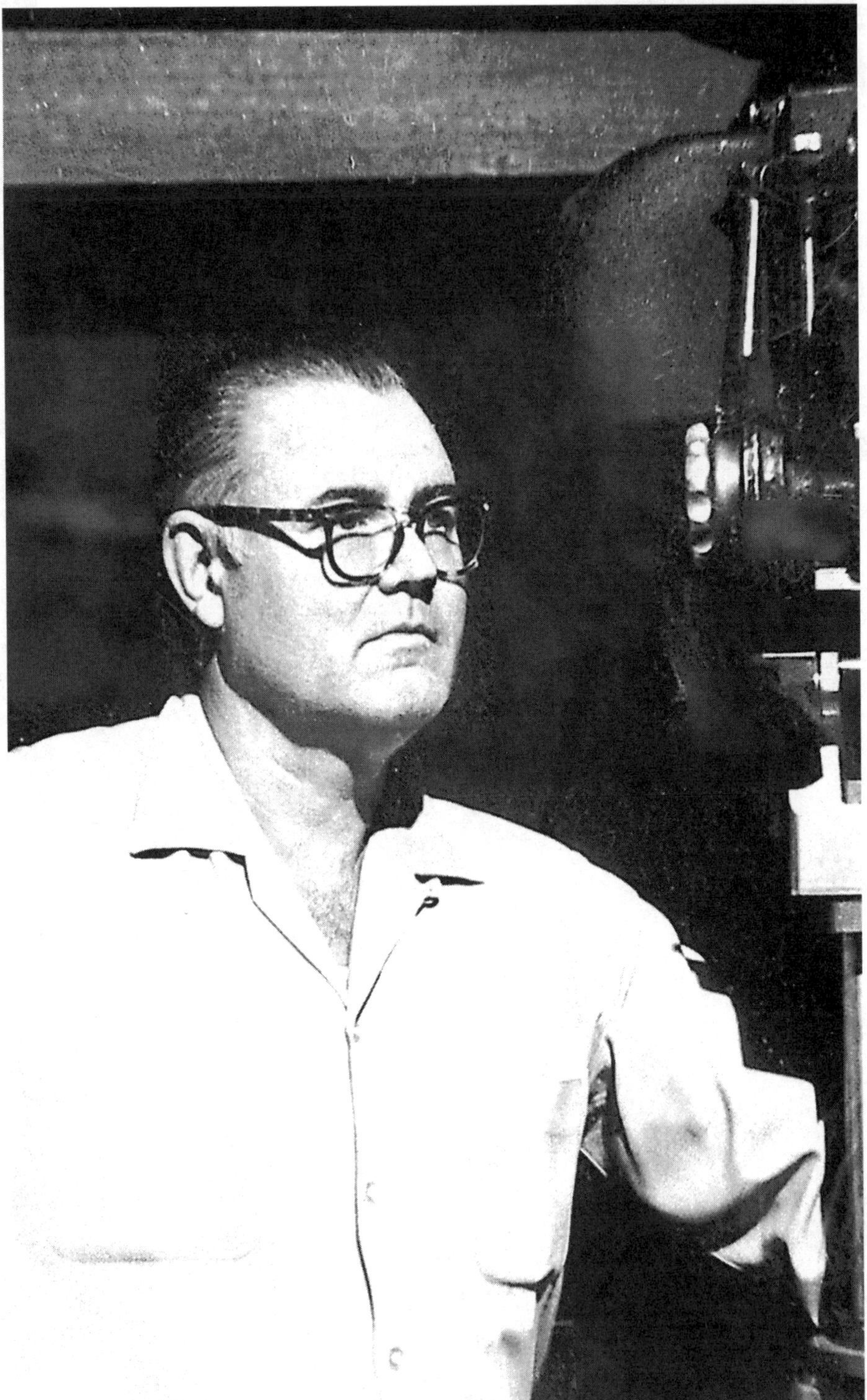

Ib Melchior
Man of Imagination

Midnight Marquee Press, Inc.
Baltimore, Maryland

Copyright © 2000 Robert Skotak
Cover Design: Susan Svehla

Without limiting the rights under copyright reserved above, no part of this publication may be reproduced, stored in or introduced into a retrieval system, or transmitted, in any form, or by any means (electronic, mechanical, photocopying, recording, or otherwise), without the prior written permission of the copyright owners or the publishers of the book.

ISBN 1-887664-41-6
Library of Congress Catalog Card Number 105432
Manufactured in the United States of America
Printed by Kirby Lithographic Company, Arlington, VA
First Printing by Midnight Marquee Press, Inc., July 2000

Acknowledgments: Scott Nollen

To Dennis, Sue and Jeff with love.
To Dennis, especially,
who helped in so many ways
to see this project through.
And, of course, to Ib and Cleo.

TABLE OF CONTENTS

8	Introduction
12	Foreword
14	A Small Country, a Large Wilderness
20	Forget About the Fat Lady Singing: What About the Man Who Laughs?
25	"Oh wonder! How Beauteous Mankind is! O Brave New World..."
31	Rita Hayworth, Toothbrushes and Houses of Horror
37	War
42	The Bell Tolls at Noon
48	Into the Airwaves
52	Cool Your Jets, Corbett!
62	Making Write Turns
64	Taking an "A" World Through the Alphabet
72	Hollywood, Japan, the Moon and Beyond
82	Off Into Space
89	*The Angry Red Planet*

TABLE OF CONTENTS

122	*13 Demon Street*
127	The Danish Films: *Reptilicus* and *Journey to the 7th Planet*
153	*Hour of Vengeance*
158	*Reptilicus* Returns
160	*The Time Travelers*
191	*Robinson Crusoe on Mars*
211	Space Family Robinson
217	*The Outer Limits*
226	*Planet of the Vampires*
248	*Cyborg XM-1*
257	From Laser Beams to Vietnam
260	Real Monsters and Weapons of Destruction
279	Stories and Histories in a Box
283	*Death Race 2000*
290	How the Robinson Family Got *Lost in Space*
295	A Three Letter Word
299	Acknowledgments
300	Appendix A
304	Appendix B
315	Index

INTRODUCTION

If you are only interested in reading about old science fiction movies, then this book is not for you.

For this book contains a lot of dull stuff about a man who touched the beating heart of another; stepped into the cold of outer space; witnessed the horrors of Dachau; directed some of the first TV shows; called one of the most famous opera singers of the century "father"; became a war hero; was knighted; had himself arrested for drunk driving; worked with laser beams; jumped out of airplanes; "infiltrated" an American city; broke a 400 year-old cipher; wrestled lions; had the fangs of a leopard at his throat; picked up a prostitute; learned how to kill with a pencil; rode an African elephant; sorted 50,000 beetles; stage-managed ice shows; worked with rockets and the Rockettes. A man who was a spy and counterspy, an actor, stage manager, singer, set designer. He speaks six languages; is a novelist and has been a gourmet chef; helped sail a tall ship and... and—incidentally—wrote or directed a bunch of science fiction movies that many of us have enjoyed! Several of which have become both cult movies and earned a respectable place among mainstream viewers.

So perhaps you'll want to read this book after all.

The man who's done all the above things—among many others—is Ib Melchior. The operative word for this man of many faces—or minds—is *imagination*. In all of its forms.

His wife, Cleo Baldon, an accomplished lady in her own right, suggests that a more apt word might be "intrepid." Leo Handel, a friend for 60-some years, offered yet another word to describe him: "Positive."

Perhaps it is the imagination that allows—empowers—a person to become intrepid—and being positive frees up the use of the imagination. In any case, they're enviable qualities all.

For our purposes, however, "imagination" will do just fine.

I discovered Ib Melchior simply by noticing the unusual quality of the name itself when it first began to be mentioned in Forrest J Ackerman's magazines over four decades ago. I saw "Melchior" usually in conjunction with some new "space" film, or odd-titled project like *The Multiple Man*, *The Micro-men* or *The Angry Red Planet*. And all of these projects seemed to be about amazing "things to come," things that would somehow change the old-fashioned world in which I felt we were living at the time.

I have been around long enough to remember President Truman and an era in which parents still asked their children to "gas-out" the lights at night. I remember carry-overs from World War ll, like city-wide "black outs," and air raid sirens on Saturday mornings. I recall listening to radio dramas in the dark before TV came along. And I remember how, only a few years later, "radio cowboys" were overpowered by sudden video images heralding what was to come: radioactivity and atomic weapons. One of the earliest images I remember seeing on TV was the first live broadcast of an atomic bomb test. It was both beautiful and frightening—and all new. I remember seeing the last dirigibles passing overhead with their passengers waving down to my brother and I standing atop a hill in Detroit, and it felt like they were going away and would never come back. Indeed, the last of the "old" was everywhere: While in grade school, I had the chance to shake the hand of an ancient man who'd fought in the Civil War as a child. He told us, "Now you can tell your children that you shook the hand of a man who shook Abraham Lincoln's hand," which he had. The "past" was very much a fading part of our lives.

My brother and I were terribly interested in those exciting things the future promised. We saw the George Pal film *Destination Moon* in June 1950 at the Kramer Theater on Michigan Avenue—one of those plush old theaters that exist now only in memories. Suddenly, the idea of other worlds beyond our own triggered something in both of us. A passion for space. The planets. We searched out libraries, and soon discovered Chesley Bonestell's wonderful "interplanetary art"—and more science fiction movies.

Those movies were the best of all: Science fiction movies at the time meant movies in which a crew of brave souls got aboard a giant "Roman candle," blasted off for outer space, dodged meteors—always the meteors—and stepped out onto the surface of some strange world.

Seeing a space movie was enough to keep us in a state of rapture for weeks, even if we recognized that the science was usually wrong. But we were more than willing to overlook some of that in exchange for a glimpse of any world that would take us away from our old-fashioned world for 90 minutes on a Saturday afternoon.

We—children of those times—believed in space, and the promise of science. We believed it even when the adults insisted space travel was, quite literally, impossible. A joke. "Buck Rogers stuff" was the familiar term of dismissal they used. There wasn't even a bona fide space agency to write to. Nothing. But while the adults laughed, we knew somewhere in some desert—wherever "White Sands" might be—things called "V-2's" were going up into the sky. And they certainly didn't look like airplanes. They were real rockets!

It was a dream coming true that nobody seemed to notice—except the kids. Because the kids watched *Tom Corbett, Space Cadet* and the parents didn't. We all knew this space stuff would come to pass. We knew that a great age of exploration was dawning. It would all come to pass because the movies and TV said so.

Then came Sputnik. In 1957. Suddenly it was important for our country to get into space, and that's all that the newspapers wrote about, it seemed, for the next several years... '57... '58... '59.

Eventually the adults and parents stopped laughing.

Unknown to us, thousands of miles away from our home in Michigan, a man with the unique name of Melchior, had had the same fascination with space travel and science—among many other interests, and had not only worked on *Tom Corbett*, but was beginning to write scripts and direct science films very much in tune with the space age.

For several years his little group of films filled my youthful Saturdays with images of wonderful, exotic worlds out there. I knew the films he made were shot on low or, at most, moderate budgets, and I knew how much more creativity and resourcefulness was often required in working that way. My brother and I knew he didn't have a big studio behind him, as did Jack Arnold and George Pal. Perhaps we knew this because we watched through the eyes of young filmmakers, for, by this time, we were making our own films in 8 and 16mm. Studying how films were put together gave us a real appreciation for how difficult even seemingly simple things could be when you had little money with which to work. You'd have to do a lot more as a director on these films. Our parents certainly found that out, once we started tearing up their basement to make our first movies.

Somehow, in spite of the budgetary compromises, Melchior's films had a quality, a flair for creating colorful worlds, ingenious challenges, science mixed with adventures and a feel for the romance of time and space. His stories were/are never about complicated or neurotic characters who angst over their own importance or the meaning of their lives. That always seemed refreshing.

It took a few years before I realized that Melchior had become something of a hero to me: With so few positive voices in the world, his was refreshingly optimistic.

In the early 1970s I decided to contact Ib Melchior. He turned out to be everything one could hope for in a hero: He was courteous, kind, gentlemanly, erudite, intelligent, upbeat, optimistic and sweet. That last word was more often than not used to describe the man by friends and colleagues. I learned a lot about him and the very extraordinary life he'd led. The science fiction stuff, as fun as it was, comprised but a small part of an even more amazing and accomplished life. He never evaluated his life, his value, by Hollywood standards, as had many others. He had avoided the pitfall of measuring his worth with movieland's crooked yardstick, and thereby managed not only to keep sane in that crazy town, but maintain his good graces—two things Hollywood has seldom been able to manage.

Over the quarter century I have known Ib Melchior, I have found myself returning to his little group of movies again and again, even as time, special effects and budgets long ago moved fantastic films to whole new levels of visual spectacle. Melchior's movies fit together like a neat "set." Side by side, they seemed to form an opus, or an opera of sorts. Whatever it was, I, simply, enjoyed them.

I have written about Melchior's life and films from time to time, updating now and then, correcting errors, adding new information. This book is a culmination of all my research, which I've conducted on and off over several years between projects. It represents the most complete assembly of materials to date on his life, his adventures, his films. In searching for new material, I have availed myself of various archives and other sources in Los Angeles, New York, England, Rome and Denmark. I have interviewed over 65 individuals either connected with the making of Melchior's films, or his life in some way, in the hopes of putting together the most comprehensive collection possible under one cover. I have tried at all times to find unpublished images and much additional information to mix in with older material. Also, I have made every effort humanly possible to correct past mistakes.

This is a book about a writer, primarily, and I have therefore made very extensive use of actual quotes from Melchior's books, scripts and short stories. Some of the excerpts here are from projects that, for one reason or another, never saw the light of day. Because of this, they offer an intriguing glimpse at "what might've been" in some alternate universe where they actually did get produced; an alternate universe where intelligence and imagination get projects made instead of hustlers and promoters. Featured are summaries of science fiction films "announced" in *Spacemen* and *Famous Monsters* magazines decades ago but never filmed; a look at several unrealized *Star Trek*, *Science Fiction Theater* and *Outer Limits* stories, and a view into the origins, and difficulties of staging *Tom Corbett, Space Cadet* on live TV. We'll also get an extremely rare glimpse at a 1938 stage version of *Brave New World*, and visit one of the first "cosmic" plays ever written, originally presented in 1946.

But the bulk of this book consists of extensive, retrospective sidebars on each of Ib Melchior's motion picture projects, each greatly expanded from any previously printed material on these subjects and updated for accuracy. The chapter on *Planet of the Vampires*, for instance, features the first interviews ever published—to our knowledge—with the Italian crew members who actually helped make the film. In addition, two appendices present documents, records and references in support of the films discussed.

With few exceptions, there are no personal scandals, or Hollywood tell-alls on the following pages. The only catastrophes are those witnessed by Mr. Melchior during his war years. It is only fair to warn the reader that certain shocking and disturbing things could not be left out if truth is to be served. They are part of the life experiences of our subject, as well as the life experience of the world.

This then is our unsensationalized, no-gossip, upbeat—we hope—tribute to a man who has lived life to its fullest; who has made his life one long flight of imagination.

Robert Skotak
May 2000

FOREWORD

The solving of seemingly impossible problems, the struggle for survival, man's ultimate strengths and weaknesses—these themes frequently appear in the writings of screenwriter-director-novelist Ib Jorgen Melchior. They are stories of—usually—a group of men undergoing supreme tests of their abilities on alien and hostile worlds of space and time, in the battlefields of World War II or even in the scorching deserts of the American Southwest.

His science fiction stories range from the sturdy adventures of *Robinson Crusoe on Mars* and *The Time Travelers* to the bizarre, satirical projections of *Death Race 2000* and "The Winner and New...," a short story in which the election of a new president occurs under outrageous, but no longer unbelievable, circumstances. In "The Premonition," an episode in the *Outer Limits* TV series, events detail not only man's ability to surmount a mind-boggling scientific riddle, but speculate at the possible nature of phenomena-like ghosts, coincidences and premonitions.

Some of his titles are well-known works within the genre, titles that include such colorfully weird space operas as *Planet of the Vampires*, *The Angry Red Planet* and *The Time Travelers*. Less well known are projects that include his ambitious attempt to "Americanize" the first *Godzilla* sequel, his screenplay work for the supernatural / mystery series *13 Demon Street* with Lon Chaney, Jr., and a number of unproduced projects like *Crater Base One*, *The Micro-Men* and *The Multiple Man*. And just coming to light is his role as the actual creator of genre favorite *Lost in Space*, parallels between his *Starship Explorers* and the first *Star Trek* TV series, and his influence on a Nebula Award-winning novel. Some of his most noteworthy work, however, would fall in an area separate from his genre stories, such as his over one dozen World War II novels and his acclaimed "pre-Hamlet" version of Shakespeare's *Hamlet*, titled *Hour of Vengeance*.

"In the area of feature motion pictures and television writing, my work has mostly been with science fiction and adventure themes," Melchior stated. "Science fiction—good science fiction—is one of the most stimulating and provocative literary and cinematographic fields of inventive and imaginative endeavor.

"I feel that science fiction films must be visually captivating and awe-inspiring to be successful. It is, however, important that the ideas and concepts used are plausible; taking a trend, for example, and running with it into the future, such as *Death Race 2000*, a story meant to condemn peoples' lust for violence.

"Adventure-action films, of course, afford opportunities of effective pacing and excitement, but it is vital that the adventures happen to real people with whom identification is possible. For my own approach to a story, I like to bring a little more to a script than a good story line and character developments. Perhaps *Robinson Crusoe on Mars* was the best example of this approach—man's indomitable spirit winning out over insurmountable odds." And this is certainly true of his war novels and his own life

Melchior prepares the next sequence for *The Time Travelers*. The principal photography for the complex film was completed in 15 days.

experiences as a wartime counter intelligence agent. In these cynical times, his "don't give up/can do" philosophy has proven inspiring.

His work as a decorated war hero, actor, writer, director, then, finally, novelist, reveals a panorama of the century's history. For fans of the genre, his work in the field paralleled and contributed much to the eventual acceptance of science fiction and "fantastic" entertainment in our culture. His films epitomized that adventurous, spirited era when men truly first reached into outer space, with the support and best wishes of the entire country behind them: Melchior was the only filmmaker in Hollywood—with the exception of George Pal—to have made extensive use of outer space as a background for motion pictures, and while one would be severely limiting his life's accomplishments by overemphasizing his work as the first "Space Age Film Maker," it would not be an inaccurate description. For this alone he deserves consideration, in addition to his many other contributions to the worlds of science, supernatural stories, military adventure novels, technical invention, documentaries and television direction—to say nothing some of the contributions he made toward ending the Nazis threat in World War II.

A SMALL COUNTRY, A LARGE WILDERNESS

Outlined by the cold North Sea on one side, and the vast Baltic on the other, Denmark was, and remains, primarily an agricultural country, one dotted by farms, meadows and woodlands steeped in colorful Scandinavian history: The very land itself could probably tell tales, if properly tilled, of great, worldwide Viking conquests, explorations and achievements. Many of the land's streets and towns retained their ancient cobblestones and red brick, wood and stone structures well into the 20th century, as if reluctant to yield up to changing times the paths and ways of those who'd walked there before; unwilling to let the footsteps of its history-makers and later storytellers—such as that weaver of tales and invisible clothes, Hans Christian Andersen—become paved over by any myopic architects of less fanciful, more modern worlds .

Denmark is a small country—somewhere in size between that of Maryland and West Virginia. A small piece of land that, perhaps to some alien visitor, might seem insignificant because of its size.

What determines the true size of anything after all? A big man may be weak, and therefore thought to be small. And the human brain, while a mere seven inches in diameter—a "seven-inch wilderness" as described by one doctor—can hold within it the idea of the entire universe and have room left over; in some way, could the brain be the larger thing? Is it that the size of a thing is determined by how it extends beyond itself and influences the surrounding world? A people, a land, a country—large or small—expands its size to the size of its explorers, its heritage, its dreamers.

Considering its link to Viking history, Denmark has good reason to brag of its ancient adventurers, some of the earliest, boldest and most influential explorers the world has known. The tales they'd brought back from the "outer regions" they explored were of strange new lands, of great storms and battles with enemies and the elements, of

Ib Melchior with parents Inger and Lauritz

thunder gods, and of heroic deeds. Sagas. It was a tradition that inspired Wagner, that gave rise to tales of dragons and monsters, to Beowulf... to sources later storytellers could—and did—recount, expand and embellish upon.

In its influence then, Denmark would not at all be seen as a small country. It had given the world a large piece of colorful and lasting lore. Its ancient tales of fanciful adventures and bold heroes would be carried on by one of its own into the 20th century, into other countries by another storyteller: one who would transpose many of the ancient tales into modern terms, who would champion first and foremost the ability of the human imagination to range far and wide, from the forests of rural Denmark to the outer edges of the solar system. His name: Ib Jorgen Melchior.

Early Years

Ib Melchior was born in Copenhagen, Denmark, on September 17, 1917.

Ib's father was an imposing man named Lauritz. His mother was named Inger. Lauritz and Inger were both involved with the theater, which is how they'd met. Ib was one of their two children; he had a sister named Birte. For a short time they all lived in an apartment in Copenhagen.

But it was only for a short time that they all lived there together...

Soon after Ib was born, his father divorced and remarried. The year was 1923. Lauritz moved from his apartment in Copenhagen to a new home in Germany. Young Birte stayed in Denmark. As did Ib.

Over the years, the young Melchior did not see much at all of his father, who spent a great deal of

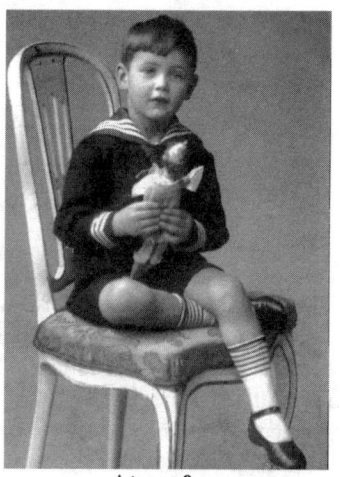

At age four

time on the road: The senior Melchior traveled mostly because he was a singer. No ordinary, everyday singer, mind you, but a Wagnerian opera singer. Indeed, Lauritz Melchior was to be most frequently described as being, perhaps, the greatest Wagnerian tenor of the past century. He had a voice, according to one who'd heard him sing in later years, "that'd fill a room and rattle the windows!" His operatic engagements took him all over Europe where he was much in demand. The opera was considered one of the most popular forms of entertainment in those years.

Ib's mother, Inger, was to experience much illness in the years that followed her divorce from Lauritz. Her son would often be turned over to the care of several housekeepers in her absence.

From a very early age, having been left very much alone a great deal of the time, the young Melchior quickly learned to be self-sufficient, to expand his mind through study and to entertain himself by exploring the world around him—the natural world with its plants and animals and insects. A love of nature was formed early in his life—especially animals:

> My first vivid memory was at the age of close to three. I had strayed from view during a summer

> stay in the country, and was finally found playing blissfully with a huge, 'vicious' English bulldog kept chained in a neighbor's yard, pulling his ears and generally making a nuisance of myself. They had a most difficult time getting me away from my playmate, who growled menacingly at anyone trying to get near enough to retrieve me. I had a ball.

To a great extent, he learned to keep himself company with his own thoughts—by exploring his own imagination. He recalled:

> It always had to be linked with imagination. At eight to 10 I drew storyboard adventures in comic-strip style, and colored them vividly. I also drew and cut out settings and characters for a puppet theater. At 11 or 12, I wrote short skits and other entertainments, and, with my sister, performed them for my father and the family on special occasions.

Storytelling in some form was clearly in his future.

With the death of his mother in 1929 when he was 11 years old, Ib was enrolled at Stenhus College—a boarding school—where he was to spend much of his youth. And no matter that he'd been left to fend largely for himself young Melchior even then seemed determined to live a life—as many friends and acquaintances were later to emphasize—in the "affirmative."

Stenhus was one of the strictest boarding schools in Denmark. There were only a little over 100 students, and the school was run partly as a farm; the boys grew much of their own food. They dug potatoes, gathered berries, took care of the chickens, cleaned the pig pens and kept the grounds, all done in the early morning and during special work hours after school. Ib was somewhat of a nonconformist and had formed a close friendship with four other kindred souls. Through their years at the school they were often in trouble with the rector, frequently being disciplined when they overstepped their bounds. Then, only weeks before graduation, they took their revenge for all the perceived injustices done them.

It was the practice of the rector occasionally to award a class with the permission of going to town to see a movie. Such permission was given Ib's class, but Ib and his four friends were told they could not join their classmates; they were not allowed to go as punishment for another one of their infractions. When the appointed hour for the class departure arrived, the entire group rode their bicycles off the campus—Ib and his four friends with them—right past the office windows of the rector, who always watched such events. And when the class returned a few hours later, there were Ib and his friends, full of "that was great" enthusiasm as they bicycled past the rector's windows. It was only a matter of minutes before the five were called on the carpet. This time they had gone too far; this time their punishment would be more severe. The parents of one of the boys, who lived nearby, were summoned to the office, and the rector explained to them that even though it was just before graduation, he had decided to expel the boys for direct and flagrant disobedience.

According to Melchior:

> And now it was our turn. With affronted innocence we denied having done as the rector said. We had indeed left the campus, but we had gone only a little way down the road to our Latin teacher, because we had some difficulty with a lesson. We had spent a few hours there and then gone back to the campus. It so happened that the rest of the class had returned from their pleasure trip at the same time. A quick telephone call confirmed our story. The embarrassment of the rector was the sweetest revenge we could ever have prayed for.

Only years later did Ib realize and appreciate the lessons of Stenhus Boarding School and its strict discipline. He stated:

> If you are not taught discipline when you are young, how are you going to function with self-discipline when such becomes a necessity for your success.

After the war, when Melchior visited Denmark, he looked up his old rector and they became good friends, a friendship which lasted for years. The five friends, inseparable during their school years and united in their rebelliousness, had about as divergent adult lives as imaginable: one became the pastor of one of the oldest and most important provincial churches in Denmark; one was gay and became a window dresser for a London department store; one turned Nazi during the German occupation of Denmark; and one was executed by the Nazis as a freedom fighter. Ib was the fifth.

Osa Jensen had, by the year 2000, known Ib Melchior for almost three-quarters of a century, ever since the summer days they'd spent together as youngsters in Denmark—another time, another world. Osa—at the time Osa Peterson—recalled memories of those times as if they'd happened yesterday:

> Ib lived at the boarding school—Stenhus—in the city, a very strict boarding school. He had only one sister—it was a small family. His father, being a famous opera singer, of course, was traveling all over, singing throughout Europe. He wasn't a bad father, by any means—quite the contrary—but that was his living and you just had to respect that. His father was very demanding though. Everything had to be perfect.

> Ib's sister, Birte, lived in the same city I did, Hillerod, a medium-sized city about 30 to 40 minutes north of Copenhagen. It was a very beautiful area. I knew his sister. I was about 10 or 12 years-old, and Ib came several times a year to visit with his sister on school vacation. Ib was, of course, older, and very much admired by us.
>
> He liked to talk—Ib wasn't particularly quiet—and so we talked about many things. I wrote short stories—mostly about animals—and it seemed to me we exchanged stories between us—either by mail or when he came. And he'd say, "I wrote a great story—do you want to hear it?"

On Sundays, many of the local people went out to picnic by the private lake nearby:

> It was lovely. The lake had an old castle from the 14th century in the middle of it, surrounded by water. It was a lovely view. And we'd go out on that lake, and Ib would be rowing and rowing and rowing. He was a big, husky guy—tall like his father. Strong. And his father would come out on the boat as Ib rowed, and his father would just lean back, singing away with this big voice. It was a small lake, and so people all around, sitting along the shore, and in their gardens, could hear him sing. So Ib would be rowing while his father sang. It was very dramatic. That was very exciting for me, naturally—and I thought that it was all very special.

At the time, Lauritz Melchior primarily sang at Covent Gardens in London, and the Berlin Opera—although in later years he was to perform at the New York Metropolitan Opera House. Ib seldom saw his father in those years, other than on the occasional holiday. He didn't see his father perform until he was 13 years old:

> The first time I ever heard my father sing on the stage in person was in 1930 in Bayreuth in Bavaria; It was a performance of [Wagner's] *Parsifal*. And the opera lasted for eight and a half hours! And then I thought *all* operas would last that long, and I was puzzled how they could do a matinee and evening show in the same day if each one was eight and a half hours long! Then, of course, I found out they weren't all that long. But Bayreuth—that was the first time.

"That man was on stage hours at a time," related Cleo Baldon, Ib's wife-to-be many years later. "Wagner just goes on and on—and Ib's father would be standing there like a *typhoon* the whole time... He was a such a hero to the students that at Bayreuth on the last night of the season, the young men in the town unhitched the horses from his carriage and pulled him physically through the streets to his hotel! I mean, wow!—*That*'s your father?!"

Indeed, it could prove a hard act to follow—if one chose to do so!

According to Cleo, Lauritz, despite his bigger-than-life image, "had the intelligence of *humor*—or the humor of intelligence—whichever—and was always able to capitalize on moments. Once he was on the stage with Brunhilda, and the horse she leads in was not supposed to be fed or watered for some time before the performance. Well, somebody had goofed and during the performance it raised its tail and dropped its lunch on the stage! There was a hushed moment— and then Ib's father just shrugged and said, *'everybody's* a critic!'"

True to his interest in the performing arts, the younger Melchior, while still at Stenhus, had joined the drama department and appeared in three school plays between 1930 and 1934, the final one as Count Anslo in *The Victorious Might*. His notices read, "Melchior demonstrates that he knows how to act a part, and his acting merits much praise." He was off to a pretty good start. And then—perhaps as a nod to his parental tradition—at the age of 18, he sang the part of the teacher in the modern Kurt Weil opera *The Boy Who Said Yes*. The reviews were excellent, *Politikens Magazine* commented that the performances of the three leads—of which Melchior was one—"was an extraordinarily fine effort." Another reviewer similarly stated, "...the leads carried out their far from easy tasks extraordinarily well."

The Boy Who Said Yes was his first operatic performance. An appropriate one for someone who's attitude was always positive!

It was not until several years later, when the young Melchior has emigrated to the USA that he began to study singing in earnest. He had been told that it was a good way to strengthen and add depth to his stage voice. His teacher was the illustrious Austro-Hungarian Metropolitan Opera Bass-Baritone Friedrich Schorr. Soon it was clear that the young Melchior was an above average tenor with great potential. But his tutoring did not last long. He explained:

> The more I sang with Schorr, the higher my voice became until it became a high lyric tenor, and I did not cherish going through my professional life sounding like the lead in a boys choir.

Melchior also began to have other doubts about a singing career. After all, he was becoming increasingly aware of being recognized more for being someone's *son* than himself. Perhaps the struggle to establish his own independent identity was a big enough challenge without running the risk of constant comparison with his father's near-legendary voice. The decision to give up lessons put an end to what might've been an entirely different kind of career. The training in enunciation and projection, however, stayed with him.

FORGET ABOUT THE FAT LADY SINGING: WHAT ABOUT THE MAN WHO LAUGHS?

Although the opera was extremely popular at the time, a huge draw throughout Europe, Melchior had his eyes already set on something that was rapidly overtaking all the other arts, including opera. *The* choice in mass entertainment—even as far back as the 1920s—had been motion pictures.

Osa Jensen recalled that young Ib accompanied her and her friends most often to the movies during his summer visits. The movies were a special treat for them. An important and exciting event—although their exact tastes in movies were quite different:

> At the movies Ib loved to see things like *Count of Monte Cristo*. I think we saw it two or three times with him. It scared me. I'd just close my eyes during the scary parts, but he *loved* it. And then he'd take us girls to see a musical and just *sit* there.

Osa sighed in exasperation and laughed:

> He was *so* bored! These musicals were very different from what he was raised with: He'd been raised with the classics. *Classical* music... But Ib was a very easygoing fellow and very nice. He *always* brought chocolates when we went to the movies—not hard candy because I didn't like that. He was thoughtful—and a gentle person. A big Teddy bear. He'd take you by the hand when you crossed the street when most boys didn't.

The excursions to the movies were indeed extra-special events in Melchior's formative years. There was a connection there. Was it in the storm and thunder, the love of things bigger than life—a kind of modern version of Wagner's magic and power—that the motion picture shadow-play promised? Whatever it was, it was not an idle interest, but a pull, an excitement—a compelling force that had him return to the theater over and over again:

I was fascinated by films and theater. I saw my first motion pictures when I was maybe 10 years old. One of them was *The Man Who Laughs* with Conrad Veidt. And I never forgot it. It was—it *is*—hard to say what the exact appeal of *The Man Who Laughs* was—except to say that the whole damned thing was so new to me. It was a whole different world. First of all, it was a period piece, so it was like a fantasy, and I got very caught up with the character—the tragedy of this man who had his lips cut off so that he always laughed.

As a boy, it really got to me, and I was also fascinated by *how* it was made: I found out most of these pictures were made not in Denmark, but abroad, most of them in Hollywood specifically. When I got a little older I saw every film that was ever made, a lot of them German and American films; some Danish ones too, of course. And there was something called the "director" who made these things. So I said, *"This* is what I want to do!" And this is when I got interested in wanting to become a Hollywood director. I also decided that being a director meant that you had to know *everything*: You had to tell everybody what to do—or at least be able to. That meant you had to know about things like sets and editing and so on.

Melchior approached the task of becoming a director very scientifically: If one wanted to become a doctor, one needed to know everything about medicine. If one wanted to become a director...

It all made sense. But where does one begin to practice the "medicine" of film making?

Directing is what I wanted to do, but, being a little kid in Copenhagen, I realized that was almost impossible. It was like a dream. It *was* a dream. And it was not until I was studying medicine—I was going to be a doctor and had been studying medicine at the University of Copenhagen—that a group called The English Players came into town, and I saw my chance. They put on performances in English. Now I knew enough English from school that I could follow the plays and enjoy them. And I read in their program about what The English Players were. They had their own theater in Paris, and they spent at least two seasons traveling

The English Players, based in Paris, created quite a stir throughout Europe, at places like the Royal Szinhaz in Budapest, shown above.

around all over the world, especially in Europe, and I got fascinated by that. I said to myself, if I wanted to be a director in Hollywood, I've got to be an *actor* first, because I'll have to be able to tell the actors what to do: I need to know everything there is to know before I can become a director. Now if I could become a member of this troupe, I could, number one, improve my English, number two, I could learn the theater, and, number three, I could *act*. I could see the world—and get *paid* for it. So I thought, "That's it!"

So with all the chutzpah of a 19 year old, I made an arrangement with the director of the troupe, Edward Stirling, to audition for him. One early, early morning, after the performance was over and after everybody had had their dinner and so forth—about three o'clock in the morning, all the maids were cleaning up the auditorium—and I auditioned for him in the theater on the stage; for

A teenage Ib Melchior as Louis Dijon in *Oscar Wilde*, a play produced by The English Players.

> Stirling and his wife. I remember that I did one very dramatic scene from *Peer Gynt*—Osa's death. The death scene is very dramatic. I did that in Norwegian. I did one piece from an English play—Shaw's *Arms and the Man*, I think—in English, and then one piece in Danish. And they were very kind and they said something I'd never heard before; "Don't call us, we'll call you." And I was *delighted* because I expected a call from them any day!
>
> They left and went down to the Riviera and while they were down there, their stage manager got appendicitis—a very bad case—and he was flown back to England. So the assistant stage manager became stage manager and their prop boy became the new assistant stage manager. Now they didn't have a prop boy. Where do you get a prop boy in France on the Riviera? And somebody obviously said 'Hey, how about that crazy guy up in Denmark? He'll do anything. Why don't you call him? So they did call me and said, "Now if you can get here within the week, you have a job." So I went to the University of Copenhagen and they gave me a special examination so I could get my degrees, which was very nice.

It wasn't long after that Melchior took off and joined The English Players and became a prop boy. In a remarkably short time he became, first, assistant stage manager, then started acting. And not long after starting to act, he became the stage manager and eventually co-director of the troupe.

So his Danish *chutzpah* not only landed him exactly where he wanted to be, but accelerated his schooling. He graduated from the University of Copenhagen with the degree of Candidatus Philosophiae—called philosophicum, a study in philosophy, logic and physiology.

> My debut was in a play called *Oscar Wilde* by L. and S. Stokes and I played Louis Dijon. And I [actually] met the man whom I portrayed, which was very interesting. I had dinner with him. It was fascinating knowing this was the man I had portrayed—of course, he was a lot older at that time. He was one of Wilde's boyfriends... This was my first good part.

Others would follow, other "good parts"—one after another... even into the future.

"OH WONDER!
HOW BEAUTEOUS MANKIND IS!
O *BRAVE NEW WORLD*..."

It was during his tenure with The English Players that the ambitious young Melchior had his very first brush with a comparatively "young" cultural phenomenon—one that would increasingly come to impact upon the modern world, as well as Melchior himself: Science Fiction. The term itself meant nothing to most people. Yet.

The occasion was The English Players' ambitious production of Aldous Huxley's satiric novel of the far-but-near future, *Brave New World*.

The novel would go on to become one of the century's seminal works; required reading in school, influential and frequently quoted. But it was a mere six years after its publication that the troupe decided to make it one of their productions. Its unwieldy, fragmented, sometimes meandering structure made it a problematical story to adapt, but adapted it had been, by a Russian playwright named Louis Walinsky: An appropriate enough circumstance in a way, since *Brave New World* had been inspired by the Russian author Yevgeny Zamyatin's classic novel, *We*.

The English Players' production would be supervised by Edward Stirling. It was September 1938. Melchior recalled:

> One of my shows was *Brave New World*. The book hadn't been out long at the time. It was very new. I played the character Foster in it. But, my idea was again, in order to become a film director, that I had to be able to do *everything*, including sets.

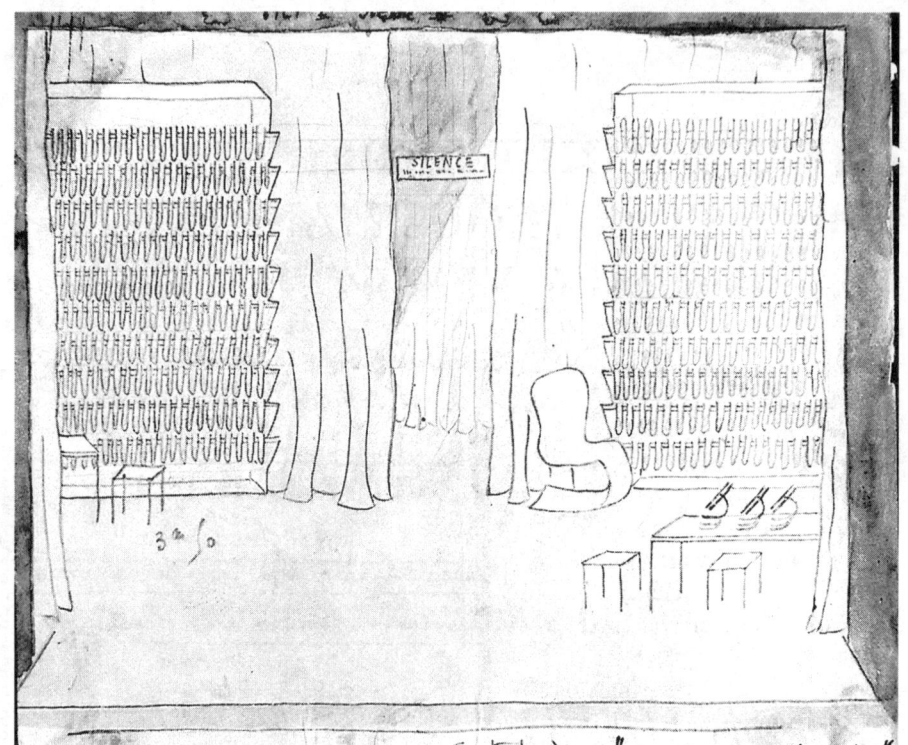

Melchior's sketch for the Hatchery in the 1938 production of *Brave New World*.

> Scenery. So I talked the director, Edward Stirling, into letting me design the scenery for the production, and I did and they used it. In fact it got special mention in some of the Paris papers. It was a small theater and all, but it worked.

In many ways—technically and dramatically—*Brave New World* was a daring undertaking. From a thematic standpoint, the play had had its share of controversy—the same as the novel—in its focus on unattached sexual relationships, and prophesies of test-tube breeding and controlled genetics. The play's subject matter proved too strong for the British censors, and it was banned from that country.

Technically, *Brave New World* was one of the troupe's most difficult undertakings and yet it would be entrusted to Melchior. By this time, they had willingly placed quite a bit of faith in him. He didn't let them down. Melchior was tasked with creating 10 different settings and 13 scene changes. Those were a greater number than in most plays, and they all had out-of-the-ordinary requirements. Act One featured "The Central London Hatchery," "The Girl's Dressing Room," "The Roof of the Center," "The Director's Office," "Bernard Marx's Room" and "The Savage Reservation in New Mexico"; Act Two featured "A Hospital for the Dying," "Outside the Hospital," and "The Office of the World Controller." The final act was set in "the English countryside in the year 2500."

Melchior's production design for *Brave New World* included perspective views of a city in the future.

Melchior designed and produced walls lined with hundreds of test tubes, a city of the future in perspective, a section of rocky countryside, glass benches—and many other stylized settings:

> I do not remember exactly how much time we had to build—mostly paint the sets—but it was probably a matter of *days* since we did things very fast. The future sets—which now look like today!—were mostly painted backdrops with light holes for the skyscraper windows. The countryside set called

for a ruined tower where the savage hangs himself. That was built, as was the wall next to it. The backdrop behind it was the regular forest backdrop [we used]. As I remember, we had a few fake rocks and some greenery, though I cannot remember if the greenery was live or artificial. Much depended on the lighting of the set, which had to be dramatic and which I also did. At the end we saw the legs fall down in the doorway, as the savage hung himself. It was very effective.

All on a tiny budget, and designed to fit on a small stage.

Melchior did manage to simultaneously prepare for his role of Foster—a bland conformist in the novel who helps define the very inertia of the social status quo. An ironic bit of casting for the anything *but* status quo actor.

The play was well-received and drew special notice for its imaginative settings and designs of the future. According to the *Paris Daily Mail*:

> *Brave New World*, dramatisation of Mr. Aldous Huxley's widely read and much discussed or controverted [sic] novel about... re-Creation, is Mr. Edward Stirling's latest production with his English Players at the Paris Theatre de L'Oeuvre... The repertory of the L'Oeuvre and the Players is world-famous. It comprises, in both cases, an enormous mass of dramatic masterpieces. *Brave New World*, this most recent addition to the number, is most remarkable... To transfer such an apocalyptical vision to the stage, condensing Mr. Huxley's book, all imagination and scientific hypothesis, stirring adventures interwoven with psychological, even Shakespearean, subtleties, into a drama that shall be clear to average intelligence and reasonably short—though with changes of scene taking place every few minutes—all that is a formidable enterprise. ..The *Brave New World* of Messrs. Huxley and Walinsky, plus Mr. Edward Stirling and The English Players, shows us our planet and the human race as they may be some six or seven centuries ahead of the present era; as it may be in, say the year 2500. Then, so it appears, mankind no longer will be born. It will be, like the calf of which the British Association talked gravely last week, of test-tube parentage. Or modifying the simile, it will be cultivated by scientific manipulation much as trout spawn is "raised" in hatcheries...

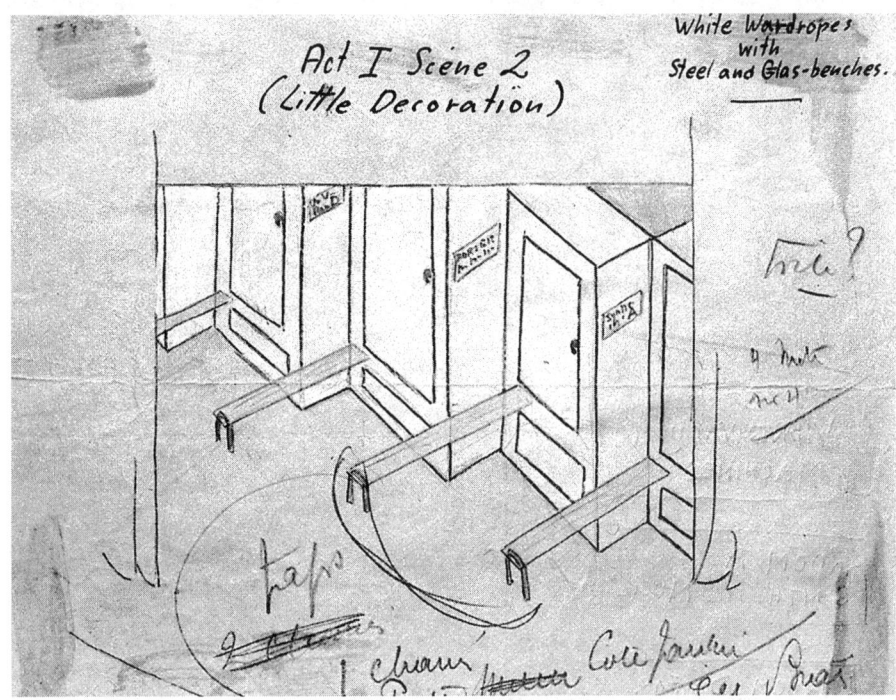

Melchior's sketch for the locker room in *Brave New World*

The reviewer, Percy Mitchell, summarized some of the play's high points with a special mention of Melchior's art direction: "The Huxley-Walinksy play is ingeniously staged with fantastic decorative effect. And, it is excellently interpreted with a semi-realistic semi-unearthly power."

The New York Herald Tribune also praised the undertaking:

> Paris had its first look into the world of 2500 Thursday evening when the ultra-civilization envisaged by Aldous Huxley in his *Brave New World* was portrayed at the Theatre de L'Oeuvre by Edward Stirling and his English Players... Such lines as "When the individual feels, the community reels," and "The trans-Atlantic plane is 13 minutes late, the service is getting terrible," are samples of the thought and conversation in the *Brave New World*.... In keeping with the streamlined plot, the settings are ultra-modern, with the exception of the reservation scene, where the wildness of the countryside is well presented.

With the first of an eventual four production design jobs with the troupe behind him, Melchior could check off another item on the list of "have-to-have" skills he felt required to learn before he could direct motion pictures.

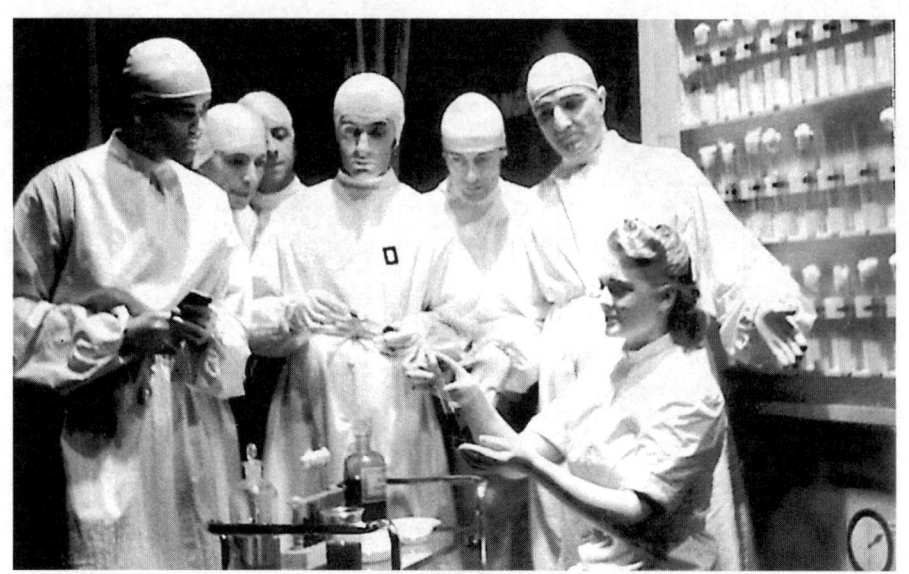

The actual set for the Hatchery in *Brave New World*.

There had been a growing sense for some time, however, that even as the group traveled and enjoyed successes across Europe with their dramatic presentations, another drama was looming, dark and threatening, over all. The sense of it came from news articles of quiet revelations and rumored troubles with aggressive forces in Germany. Sometimes such information came not in the shape of a sheet of newspaper. Sometimes revelations could arise from seemingly inconsequential things, in a seemingly pastoral setting...

As much as three years before *Brave New World*, knowledge of this looming danger was conveyed to Melchior in a most disarming way. Cleo Baldon remembers:

> Ib often traveled with friends through Europe, and in the summer they would go get jobs with the farmers and make enough to go on to the next place. And at one of the farm families, the job there was to go out to collect the eggs. So Ib brought them in and gave them to the farmer's wife, and she said "that's one for us and two for the war," and she dropped them into "water glass"—it was a gooey, gelatinous substance that was used to preserve eggs. So they were preserving eggs: The farmers knew the war was coming and were preparing for it, and that's how Ib learned the war was coming. But as he looked around, he saw all these *other* people who didn't know war was imminent.

The danger was building, unseen, under their very noses. What a difference a couple of years were to make.

RITA HAYWORTH, TOOTHBRUSHES, AND HOUSES OF HORROR

Just prior to World War II, Ib Melchior finally realized a long-held dream and came to the United States. He'd come with The English Players to do a Broadway show, arriving in the New York in December 1938. His Viking ancestors may have arrived first in their long ships and discovered the New World years before Columbus, but Melchior's travel was aboard the *S.S. Washington*—a lot more comfortable, if a slightly more mundane way to cross an ocean!

When the Players completed the show, they returned to Europe, minus a key person, Ib Melchior, who had become their technical director. Having come this far, he decided to stay and follow his dreams, wherever they might take him.

Melchior made a trip to Los Angeles in 1939, in search of Hollywood—and a job in the motion picture business. His stay was not long, but gave him an inkling of how quirky the business could be. He got himself a job with the Henry Rogers publicity agency where his work entailed, among other activities, assisting on photo shoots. And how did he know he was *really* in Hollywood? When right off the bat his first task was to buy some black underwear for Rita Hayworth! It was for a photo layout for the actress—then known as Marguerite Cansino—for a prestigious magazine. So Melchior, with his doctorate degree and all, was summoned to purchase the needed item. Fortunately, the vital item *fit*! Perhaps he had a future in Hollywood after all! But, Melchior mused, while this might be a pleasant pastime, he figured he couldn't do that for long without creating a lot of talk!

Eventually Melchior moved on from the agency and returned to New York as new opportunities in theater were opening up. Shortly upon returning, he became a stage manager at the famous Radio City Music Hall and Center Theater. Between April 1941 and June 1942 Melchior worked in their Stage Managing Department. It proved anything but dull—a hectic 18 month period during which he was kept on his toes keeping the complex stage shows flowing without a hitch: The backstage was a world unto itself, a veritable maze of elevators, trap doors, turntables, gears, fog and steam machines, lights and other machinery. The shows were indeed some of the most demanding—mechanically as well as choreographically—ever attempted on stage. "Actually," Melchior stated just after the war, "it's a very smooth-working establishment. During my term of office there, none of the Rockettes got jammed in the turntable, and..." (he probably said with a twinkle in his eyes) "not a single ballerina fell down the elevator shaft." He somehow also managed to keep everybody else—including himself—from getting ground up in that churning complex of mechanical "paraphernalia" that was the Music Hall's entertainment machine.

All in all, a far cry from the Shaws, Wildes and Shakespeares of his European days!—and it was followed, in 1942, by a stint as stage manager on an enterprise even further removed from the "masters": At the Center Theater he oversaw ice shows for their ongoing *Stars on Ice* production.

It was shortly after his arrival in the United States that Melchior really discovered a great new field of interest—science fiction—which he'd first encountered working on *Brave New World*:

> When I came to this country in 1938, the only science fiction I had ever read was Jules Verne's stories, and H.G. Wells's *Things To Come,* and I'd found them very interesting. Then I picked up a science fiction magazine and I got hooked. It was fascinating. One story series was "The Grey Lensmen" by E.E. 'Doc' Smith... I said "Hey, this is terrific! This is great!" And then I met a few writers, like Theodore Sturgeon and, eventually, one of my heroes, Curt Siodmak, who was writing films, short stories, books and directing motion pictures, and I got even more interested... And I became a fan of reading science fiction... *good* science fiction: There's good and bad like everything else. So I was now pretty much an expert on *reading* science fiction, but I hadn't written any.

In light of his later career as a director of films mixing factual scientific research with occasional flashes of wild "space opera" adventure, it made perfect sense his first attraction to the genre was E.E. Smith, often referred to as the "father of space opera!"

With Germany's invasion of Poland several years earlier, the war—the first humble signs of which had been glimpsed with those farmers' eggs—had finally, fully broken out in Europe. His father, Lauritz, living in Germany at the time, was forced to abandon his sizable estate, taking with him only what he and his wife could pack in a few hours. Although Lauritz was a Danish Lutheran, the Germans saw to it he was listed as a Jew in the "Sigilla Veri"—the handbook they used to "out" all German Jews. His property was confiscated and, in fact, was never to be returned to the rightful owners— the Melchior family—over a half-century later.

Ib Melchior found he couldn't do much in the war effort initially, because he couldn't go back to his native Denmark, to which he was still a subject. However, with the bombing of Pearl Harbor on December 7, 1941, the U.S. was finally entering the war. Over the next several months he grew determined to find a way to do his part—this in spite of the fact he had, in March, just married an American girl—an actress—he'd met several years earlier, Harriet Hathaway Kale.

Melchior wrote a letter to the Armed Forces War Department. It was May 1942 and the horror of the bombing was still fresh in his mind when he composed the letter that read, in part:

> My name is Ib J. Melchior, son of the Metropolitan Opera singer Lauritz Melchior. I am 24 years old and arrived in this country on Dec. 9, 1938. I have my First Naturalization Papers, being a Danish subject, and I am working on my final papers now, to which I am entitled, having been here more than three years.
>
> I would like to know if it would be possible for me to get into the Army Intelligence Service. I think I could be of the most value to America, my new country, there, inasmuch as I possess knowledge that might be of value along those lines... I have done a lot of traveling in Europe myself, mostly on foot or bicycle, and I have a good knowledge of these countries, especially Denmark, Germany and France. I speak English with a slight accent and furthermore I speak (read and write) Danish and German perfectly. Also French, having worked in that country almost a year, and Norwegian and Swedish, which are similar to my own native Danish. I have had a thorough education, finishing college in Denmark with a first degree and getting the degree of Candidatus Philosophiae from the University of Copenhagen, also with a first degree. Besides that, I have studied premedical chemistry, physics and anatomy...

Receipt of his letter was acknowledged. Then nothing. Several weeks went by. He noticed he was getting strange looks from friends. Peculiar. Then one day while having his hair cut his barber suddenly asked "What've you been up to? The FBI was around asking questions about you."

It hit him. He was being investigated!

Not long after, he was asked to meet two officers at a seedy hotel. If it had been a scene in a movie it couldn't have been much weirder. He was drugged, and asked questions like, "Tell me, Melchior, how would you feel about sticking a knife in a man's back?" He lost all memory, and, later, all knowledge of the incident was disavowed.

He was then asked to report to Temporary Building Q in Washington, DC. The officer there told him, "Melchior, you realize that when you stepped across that threshold you lost your identity?" According to Melchior: "I was told 'Sign this.' It was a note that said, 'I hereby volunteer for hazardous duties. No questions asked.' I signed it."

He was then told, "Take off all of your clothes. All of them. Everything."

"So I did," Melchior continued. "And I stood there stark naked, with only the toothbrush I had been told to bring!" Melchior was given a new name—MEL G-8—

Melchior writing reports of his latest investigation during his WWII service.

and was instructed to go into another room. There he found himself in the company of a whole room full of naked men, all holding toothbrushes! "I had no idea what I had gotten myself into—and it is not easy to stand around with a bunch of naked guys with toothbrushes!"

For the next two months he underwent the kind of grueling tests that one only reads about in the most far-out fiction. He was shot at with live rounds, had inkblot tests, had TNT detonated under him, crossed tightropes above mined riverbeds, faced seemingly impossible obstacle and intelligence tests, endured a pitch-black military version of the "house of horrors" and got to learn more about just how excruciatingly painful tear gas could be than he ever cared to know. He was taught cryptography, "dirty" hand-to-hand combat and learned how to operate every conceivable weapon and vehicle from a half-dozen European countries. And that was basic training:

> I finally found out that I had joined the OSS (the Office of Strategic Services), America's first wartime spy organization.
>
> At the end of the first month I said I've had it. I'm going to fall flat on my face and never get up again. But after the second month I got up and said, "Bring on Germany and Japan and I'll lick them single-handedly!" That's the way they worked. They tore you down and built you up again.

Melchior pauses on a bridge in Luxembourg during the war.

At the end of the training, only six of the original 36 volunteers were left.

His "graduation exercise" had him sent into an unidentified American town as a foreigner bearing "mediocre" papers—this was during the height of the war and suspicions of anything out of the ordinary ran high—and asked to carry out a subversive espionage mission, a mission which neither the local authorities nor the FBI were informed of. He passed the test.

It was around this difficult time that Melchior first encountered a man to whom he immediately took a dislike. The man was Leo Handel, an Austrian, who was also going through basic training. He'd come to the United States upon viewing a documentary screened in his native country titled, *America, Land of Unlimited Opportunities*. Right then and there he knew he had to leave his native country and involve himself in this wonderful country. Little did either one of them know their lives would become linked for the rest of their lives! At the time, the first impressions boded not well at all. Handel recalled:

> One day—I can still remember it —down some stairs came a fellow very cocky and supercilious— and it turned out it was Ib! And, it further turned out he'd had the same impression of me!"

Ib Melchior: Man of Imagination

Melchior agreed:

> I thought he was the most stuck-up man I'd ever met, and he thought the same thing about me!

Handel concluded:

> Actually, both of us were very unhappy and out of place and sort of covered it up by appearing very self-confident—neither of us was. And it turned out we had a little bit in common.... My father, in his earlier days, was a pianist, and so the common denominator was *music*.

They decided to stay in touch.

> Ib [though] was transferred—to England's staging area—and I was sent to Italy, but we kept in touch.

Melchior added:

> When we were sent to different areas, we constructed a code; of course, I could not just say I'm in Germany attached to such and such a unit, doing such and such, but, I did it by saying in letters, "*Dear* Leo"—which meant I was in Germany, or "*Hi* Leo," which meant I was in France, and so on.

The chance meeting and continued communications proved fortuitous. The two men not only maintained a lifelong friendship, but shared professional fortunes—and misfortunes—over the next half-century.

Nonetheless, the gain of such new friends occurred under circumstances that would take Melchior far from home. There would be unanticipated rewards—new skills obtained and once-in-a-lifetime experiences—but it did not come without the kind of great sacrifices made by all the men who've ever marched off to war. For one, he had to leave behind his new wife, Harriet, and his child, Leif—born just a few months earlier. Harriet would rise to the occasion, taking over her husband's post in the Center Theater to support the little family during the war.

WAR

Melchior's subsequent experiences as an agent of the OSS and, later, of the CIC (Counter Intelligence Corps) in Europe during one of the most violent eras known to man made him a true eyewitness to history at its most extreme. He made a hair-raising excursion all alone deep into enemy territory with little to disguise him but an ability to bluff; learned firsthand of frightening Nazi experiments with atomic weapons, ghastly "psychological experiments" performed on human "lab animals," and a terrible machine of destruction—a 1,000 foot-long German super-cannon called the "millipede" that could have turned the tide of the war; He entered into the concentration camp at Dachau where the bodies—the vast majority of them Jews—lay stacked in heaps, some alive and some dead, but all tortured and starved. He'd witnessed the development of weapons and technologies that a couple of years earlier had been pure science fiction. All put toward the application of killing people.

Throughout the war Melchior drew upon and expanded an apparent deeply inbred resourcefulness that later was utilized for entirely different purposes in the entertainment world. Melchior was that rare being in the military establishment—an artist, not militant by nature, who applied the creative mind to avoid brutality as often as possible.

He met one survivor—a Jewish woman named Wanda from Poland—who'd undergone just about as much horror as the human mind could possibly endure. He learned of the level of degradation visited upon her, the Jews and other undesirables, not as a bit of distant history, but as events that had occurred but weeks or days earlier.

He described his encounter with Wanda in his autobiographical book, *Case By Case*:

> ...[S]he had been the subject of a medical/psychological experiment carried out under the Nazi Applied War Research Program, an experimental offshoot of the program spawned by the Section R experiments conducted at Dachau under the Chief Physician, Dr. Siegmund Rascher, who used the camp inmates for his hideous research experiments. Among them were the low-pressure chambers, designed to test how much depressurization an unprotected human being could stand flying at high altitudes. The human guinea pigs, placed in a vacuum chamber, were subjected to an ever-increasing vacuum until they screamed in agony and tore their hair out in an attempt to relieve the excruciating pressure in their heads; they tore at the

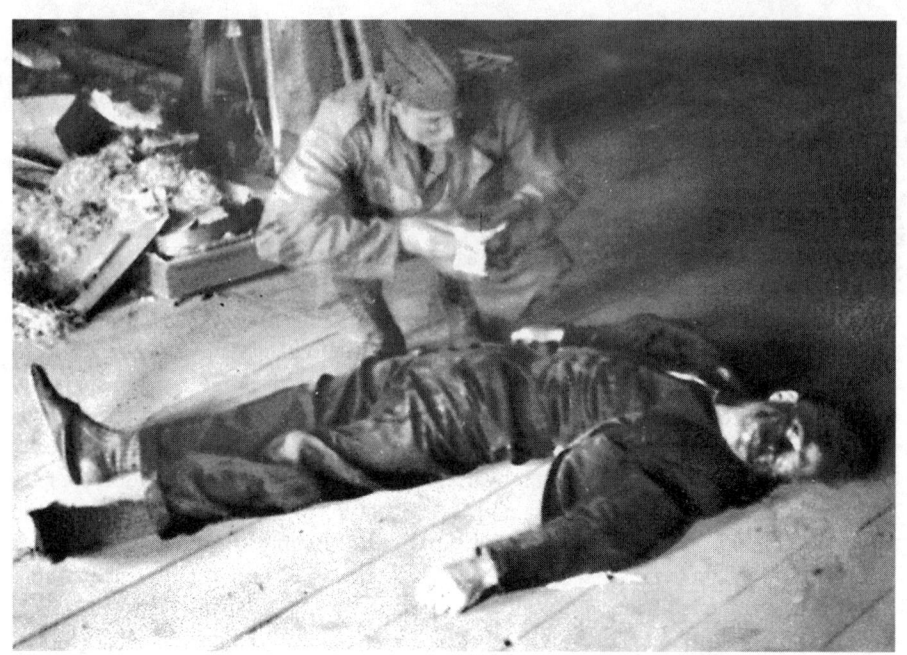

Melchior holds the suicide note of Reichsamtsleiter Anton Eckl, moments after Eckl had taken his life.

seats restraining them and shrieked until their lungs burst. Another was the experiment of being subjected to freezing cold, to learn what would happen to pilots downed in Arctic waters. The subjects were submerged naked in icy water until their abject screams of pain were silenced as they lost consciousness. Attempts at revival were done by using the warm, naked bodies of women prisoners placed close to the frozen man, the women instructed to stir sexual arousal in the victim to see if that would induce a more rapid recovery. Most of the victims died under these macabre manipulations. The Nazis had forced Wanda to watch the execution of her father and the subsequent grisly disassembly of his body, then made her do the same to her brother.

Melchior experienced a world only those who were there could possibly grasp—and even then that was impossible. It was a world gone crazy. He did whatever his skills, his education and his imagination would empower him to do to as a CIC agent to unwind the Nazi war machine. One incident—uncovering the highly secret Nazi "Werewolf" underground terrorist organization—came about by his ability to note small, seemingly insignificant details. In another instance his insistence upon investigating a seemingly insignificant occurrence—a single gunshot in the woods—led to the retrieval of German records pertaining to the waging of World War III. Those abilities allowed Melchior, and others like him, to ferret out a variety of spies, saboteurs and war criminals:

One example of Melchior's ability to avoid violence—and perhaps to prove that problems could be solved with the imagination rather than bloodshed—is contained in the story of one of his postwar intelligence gathering missions: On a secluded estate in the thick forests outside Regensburg had been located the Administrative Headquarters of the ruthless Waffen SS, the crack combat branch of the Nazi Elite Corps. When Allied troops arrived after the war, the staff and all paperwork was gone. Knowing that some of this information was probably buried on the estate, Melchior questioned Major Maximilian, a Deputy Chief of the Gestapo in the area, about the missing information. "Max" was finally intimidated into bringing to them a terrified secretary who had worked at the elite headquarters. She admitted that she had helped bury the "loot" of a German officer but knew nothing of records or other paperwork. The caretaker, a formidable older woman still proud of her Nazi connections, had refused to cooperate, saying she knew nothing. The Germans, of course, in a similar situation, would have no doubt resorted to various tortures in extracting such

Melchior had just finished interrogating a suspected saboteur after a bombing in Luxembourg when this photo was taken.

information. So might many a less civilized American interrogator. Melchior tried to find another way.

With the girl's information, Melchior and his men took a group of German POWs with shovels to the estate along with "Max" and his trusty German Shepherd, Rolf. To the dour caretaker Melchior said,

> "You see, we will *not* search aimlessly. We will *not* dig without method. Rolf will show us where to dig. He has been carefully trained by the Gestapo to *smell out* anything touched by human hands, even though it may have been buried for months."

Ib Melchior: Man of Imagination **39**

For his role in capturing Nazi General Paul Krueger, Melchior was decorated by major General S. Leroy Irwin in the latter stages of WWII.

Melchior being awarded the Knight Commander Cross by Grand Master Prince Vincenzo Abbate Castello Orleans in 1965.

The caretaker didn't believe him, but when the dog zeroed in on a spot and started wildly digging, she became afraid. When Melchior ordered the men to start digging and warned the woman that would be her last chance to admit what she knew, she finally broke: "The dog is right," she said. Melchior demanded, "How many other places are there?" "Twelve," she said tonelessly. "No. Thirteen. Thirteen." She showed Melchior all the burial sites on the property, and the boxes contained personnel files, war activities and casualty losses—achievements that qualified as war crimes and other important data on the Waffen SS—a treasure trove for the Nuremberg war crimes trials to come!

But, in actuality, all the stuff about the dog's abilities had been a bluff! Melchior, in reality, was relieved that there hadn't been occasion to dig deeper in the spot Rolf the dog had singled out, because just one foot deeper Melchior had buried a long, arm-thick Bavarian *sausage*, after dragging it all over the estate, laying a trail for Rolf to follow to his prize to the *one* file cabinet the location of which they already knew about, unbeknownst to the obstinate lady! Melchior related:

> The dog had turned in an Academy Award performance. The last hoard we dug up was the steel cabinet with the commandant's loot. We insisted that the caretaker be present. The look on her face when she saw the sausage and finally realized she'd been had was worth the price of admission.

Years of thinking creatively, indeed, had made, with Melchior, a different sort of force in the war: a man who sought out new ways to solve problems and obtain information, ways that would employ a faculty of Man's he would repeatedly cite over the years as one of the greatest assets available to every person on Earth—the "human imagination." And it didn't matter if that imagination gave rise to rather unorthodox solutions. In Melchior's case he would use magician-like misdirection and trickery in the war far more often than brutal interrogation. Sometimes it was a matter of finding another way—one nobody else had considered.

Cleo Baldon would recall numerous tales of this type of resourceful thinking:

> In Luxembourg, there was an incident in which Ib was trying to get the troops across a river. [The problem was] they didn't know how deep it was. So Ib went to the local fishing clubs to find out how they could get across the river, because they knew where the fords were. They knew where the shallows were because they knew the bottom of the river. So he got them together and they mapped the river and he got them across... *That* encapsulates his kind of creativity.

Melchior reflected on the potential for such "unorthodox" approaches and their potential for problem solving in peace, but especially during times of conflict. "What I did in the war was really quite unmilitary," Melchior pointed out:

> I used my ability to act many, many times. Just like a lawyer has to act in order to convince the jury, you had to convince these people you had more information than they did. There wasn't that much difference between what I did in the war and what I did as a performer in the arts.

In recognition of his heroic services during the war, Melchior received a Bronze Star and five combat stars in the U.S., and was decorated by the King of Denmark. Years later he was awarded the Knight Commander Cross of the Militant Order of St. Brigitte of Sweden and the Medal of Merit by the Old Guard Veterans Organization.

Cleo Baldon said of Ib:

> I know this with Ib. If you could put him in a big box with a whole bunch of people and shake it all up, when you spilled it all out, Ib would come out first. On top. He's going to be the leader.

THE BELL TOLLS AT NOON

Melchior returned to New York immediately following the war. After years of adventures overseas, he was actually ready for more:

> When I got back after the war, I didn't want to pick up at the Radio City Music Hall. That wouldn't have been any progress.

He had, by this time, developed a strong command of the English language and spoke, as mentioned by more than one acquaintance, "a fluent, scholarly English." With his knowledge, special training and soft-spoken gentlemanliness, he could have taken on just about any of dozens of jobs in a country suddenly uplifted and propelled to prosperity after the war. In spite of everything that had happened overseas, in spite of his incredible experiences as a CIC agent, it didn't take him long to realize that truly, the movies still held a special place in his heart. One way or another, he was determined to express himself in motion pictures. One of the first things he did was get back in contact with his many colleagues, both old and new. Among them, the young Austrian he'd thought so arrogant at their chance meeting during training, Leo Handel. Both Melchior and Handel were anxious to get something going. But how would they do that? Melchior chuckled:

> After the war, we both wanted to make films, but we didn't even know what those little holes in the side of the film were!

Somehow the two managed to pool their resources and produce several documentary shorts:

> One 16mm film we did was called *Summer Theater*, and it was about an actress working in summer theater getting her experience. An interesting little sidelight on that was that we narrowed it down to two actresses. One was named Ann Sorg—and she's the one we finally selected; she was just right for the part: The other one we rejected was named Grace Kelly!

Their second effort—in 35mm—documented how a real-life news story makes its way to the printed newspaper page. It was called *City Desk Item*.

They may have been little films, but at least, at long last, Melchior was in the movies! They were also beginning to work for some of the big guys: Leo Handel was working at that time for MGM in New York as their public opinion surveyor, and hired his friend to help. Melchior was able to put some of the skills he'd gained as an interrogator to peacetime use, taking highly scientific opinion polls for Handel—certainly a much more pleasant application of that particular talent!

It was the fall of 1946. Melchior had just turned 31—a time in life when many a young man would be seeking to settle down to some secure and predictable life. He'd successfully completed his college degree, traveled throughout Europe, mastered a half-dozen languages; he had been an actor, prop boy, scenic designer, stage manager; he rose to hero status in the war; come back to make films, and been a publicity agent, among other things. Yet...

To Melchior anything was still possible. There were a lot of worlds yet to explore. An imagination to be used.

An opportunity arose in October for Melchior to take on something new and challenging—directing the revival of a 1927 play once considered fantasy. A play about atomic war.

Melchior had been working in New York for over a year when he was summoned to Toronto to handle direction of the somber-themed *Wings Over Europe*, written by Maurice Brown—who later produced the prominent play *Journey's End*—and Robert Nichols. *Wings Over Europe* had caught the attention of Toronto native and local star, Norman Roland. Roland was living in New York building an international career—primarily as a singer—though he'd earlier built a reputation as a stage actor in his home town. During a brief vacation from a tour in Tokyo, he came across the old play and quickly realized its new importance: It dealt with a young scientist, David Morrow, who makes a world-shaking discovery, a discovery which will make "Prometheus triumphant" or, perhaps just as likely, destroy mankind: Nuclear fission. An atomic bomb! Clearly, with the terrifying aftereffects of the devastation of Hiroshima and Nagasaki fresh in the public's mind, *Wings Over Europe* was no longer the Jules Verne fantasy it was thought to be in the 1920s, when the idea of splitting the atom seemed a distant possibility at best.

Ib Melchior: Man of Imagination   **43**

Even back then, in spite of its unbelievability, the play had elicited excitement: Indeed, local critics recalled that *Wings over Europe* had created, 20 years earlier, an even bigger stir than had a presentation of *Dracula* at the same theater. *The New York Journal* reminded readers it had once described *Wings over Europe* as "a completely fascinating play—as engrossing as a detective mystery, as searching and provocative as a telescope, and as interesting as no play in this town has been in many months."

With his interest in the Civic Theater in Toronto, Norman Roland booked the topical property for the opening presentation at the just reopened Hart Theater. It was to be performed in November. In September he summoned Ib Melchior to Toronto to direct. The play was in three acts, all confined to one famous room—10 Downing Street in London—and focused on the interactions of a cast of 17 men, most portraying members of the British Cabinet. The dramatic thrust of the play centered on the reactions and measures a fantastic power such as the atomic bomb might provoke when its reality is suddenly thrust into the midst of an austere group of Lords and Admirals. Finding capable actors to portray such figures proved a difficult casting challenge.

Melchior spent two arduous weeks amidst Toronto's drama centers ferreting out any and all the available acting talent in an effort to find a physically suitable cast. He needed to find actors who were also up to the dramatic demands of the play, filled as it was with bigger-than-life men of high reputation dealing with bigger-than-life issues. Intensive interviews and readings resulted in—according to one paper at the time—"a cast that is one of the most imposing ever assembled for a single production locally."

Weeks of difficult rehearsals were—as Melchior commented on October 5, several weeks before the premiere—"somewhat of a challenge to the abilities of the group." By the third week of October, Melchior was encouraged that "rehearsals are making satisfactory progress... The time spent on assembling a suitable cast already is showing promise of dividends." One reporter charting the production's progress was impressed:

Melchior kiddingly threatens to end it all if the actors don't shape up during rehearsals for *Wings Over Europe*.

A posed shot from the 1946 play *Wings Over Europe* directed by Melchior.

> The Civic Theater has been fortunate... in being able to get Ib Melchior to come up from New York to produce the play, for this young director has the fire and vision necessary to bring out the latent drama of the script.

Melchior could be found in off hours in his hotel moving chess pieces, representing the actors, across a flattened blackboard, carefully plotting their position changes on the stage. The complex choreography was like any other complication Melchior had come across in his life. Just another problem to be solved. In this case, a bit of imagination to sort out what he regarded at the time to be "a straight problem in stage mechanics." Seven days before the play's opening, he felt things were going smoothly. Finally. There had been times when the soft-spoken director had been known to put a toy gun to his temple in a threat "to end it all" if the rehearsals didn't shape up!

Even now, with many accomplishments behind him, the image, the reputation of his father—the "great Wagnerian tenor"—once charioted to his hotel on the strength of his fans, loomed large. Such a dazzling image could—and often did—blind those who stood best to recognize the son's own expanding powers. As often as not, Melchior's name would be prefixed or tailed by mention he was the son of Lauritz—as if that was sufficient and the only "accomplishment" to his claim. On several occasions during pre-production of *Wings Over Europe*, Melchior found himself viewed under the narrow beam of that light. "You know," he replied as patiently as he could to one reporter who asked about his father one time too many:

> That is a very annoying question. I can tell you that my father, naturally, has been able to intro-

duce me to many important people of the theater. But once I've got a job, I've had to prove myself the same as any other man. In the theater, it's your personal record that counts, not whom you know, or to whom you're related.

If Melchior thought these friendly corrections might take care of it, he was wrong. Throughout his many successes over the years, whose *son* he was often came in with him at the beginning of the day and went home with him at night. A shadow that had been cast large ahead of him. A foregone perception to some. The young Melchior, however, was perfectly capable of moving through the landscape with his own imagination, goals and ideals. But perception can stick like glue. In a way, moving beyond the shadow of that great Wagnerian tenor would be another test for the young Melchior, another problem to solve. A battle to engage—a quiet one no doubt—but a battle nonetheless.

Wings Over Europe itself was considered a success. Much of its power was owed to a gambit on the director's part: To the threatening roar in the closing moments of incoming planes overhead, Melchior added the long, drawn-out but deathly 12-tone toll of Big Ben, chiming the noon hour. A number of people on the production team warned Melchior that the two-minute tolling—with the actors all silent on stage—would not work, would not at all have the dramatic impact he imagined it would. But Melchior stuck to his guns, and when the bell began to toll in the very first performance, the audience grew terrified and silent, afraid that any minute the entire place might explode. As the viewers held their breaths, Melchior sighed in relief: He'd stretched the dramatic moment to the breaking point—and it had worked exactly as he predicted! It was a real gamble, done against everyone's opinion, but it had worked like a charm.

The reviewers covering this, the first staging of "atomic drama" in America, were also caught in the spell—even if they had had difficulty describing it. *The Evening Telegraph* commented:

> When *Wings Over Europe* was first played in Toronto—was it not in 1929?—the atomic bomb was still for the man-in-the-street in the realm of fantasy—so that it is in a world sharply differentiated from that of the earlier decade that the play is revived by The Civic Theatre Association... Be-

fore the final curtain has fallen upon the play the drone of *Wings Over Europe* is heard (planes at 60 an hour!), but the bombs have not fallen. Last night's audience must still have had, on the other hand, freshly in mind the incidents of Hiroshima. And planes have attained a speed of over 600 miles an hour! It is therefore within a framework completely revised in terms of scientific achievement, of psychological argument as conditioned by our own times, that the present revival of the play is presented. The emphasis shifts then from time to time in relation to the two performances separated by a quarter of a century, but the emergence of a "Prometheus triumphant" still poses a problem seemingly insoluble. And there the interest of the play is concentrated.

The *Daily Star* labeled it a "Cosmic Play," and reiterated its sudden topicality:

The Civic Theatre took a dive off the deep end, reviving this cosmic drama of the '20s—in 1946. When some English troupe did this super Shaw thriller, people were as quaky about planes as they were blissfully ignorant of the atomic bomb. Since Hiroshima, that mystery drama of the romantic '20s has blazed into the headlines and burbled in radio sets. Familiarity breeds contempt; but when last night Norman Roland staggered into a death-leap from an old-fashioned bullet fired by an English cabineterian at 10 Downing, and another elective-democracy minister examined the bomb in his hand, even the audience caught the jitters—as though, in a jiffy, to the roar of backstage planes, the theatre under the Quad might blow up.

The realistic hocus-pocus was actually no more mystery than the human animated statues on stage; but the trick of Melchior, producer, his corps of aides and the all-male troupe was to make the atomic bomb of headlines feel like an earthquake or an electric storm.

The *Globe*'s Roly Young was far more to the point: "Director Ib Melchior... has whipped up a most striking production."

Wings Over Europe was Melchior's second direct foray into the realm of science fiction, albeit of the social variety. Clearly, this might be a road to travel. After all, it was one of the purest ways to indulge the imagination he'd yet come across.

INTO THE AIRWAVES

Melchior's years in New York were to pay off. The city in the late 1940s and early '50s was hopping with that rapidly expanding new entertainment technology, television. It was an exciting time for people from a variety of backgrounds—technical, dramatic, administrative, literary—to jump in to this grand experiment in electronic communications. It was the "cyberage" of its time.

Melchior related:

> Television had become popular enough that there were now several stations around. I decided the next thing to do to really become a Hollywood director was to become a television director. But how to do that?

He had an idea that acting might be the best route into this new medium and worked to keep his performing skills finely tuned. Melchior joined a summer theater during 1948, the Windham Playhouse in New Hampshire. Here he played Professor Baehr in *Little Women*, a dramatization of Louisa May Alcott's famed book. The critics were most kind to him. *The Lawrence Evening Tribune* wrote: "He captured the audience almost immediately with his portrayal of the lovable German professor. His was a sparkling performance." He also played Inspector Belsize of Scotland Yard in Emlyn Williams' chilling *Night Must Fall*. To account for his Danish accent, a line was inserted into the play which explained that his character was a Danish Police Inspector transplanted to the London police force. Again the *Tribune* lauded him: "The leads may have been provided with the stage most of the evening, but it remained for Ib Melchior in a bit part to give some punch to the production. He did it without effort." One of those leads was Melchior's wife, Harriet Hathaway Kale, an accomplished and seasoned actress. She never did forgive her husband for this review; it may indeed have contributed to their divorce years later.

In 1947 Melchior had gone to several networks, including CBS in New York, to check it out. He found that he liked the way the CBS directors worked best since they could deal directly with the crew and not through a technical director (TD). If he were to realize his goal of becoming a director himself, this is how he wanted to be able to work. Now was the time to play the acting card:

> I went to the CBS people and asked for anything with an accent—German, French, whatever. In one year I did 30 parts, nothing big, but a lot of work on live drama shows like *Studio One*, *Suspense*, etc.. What I did was follow the AD [associate

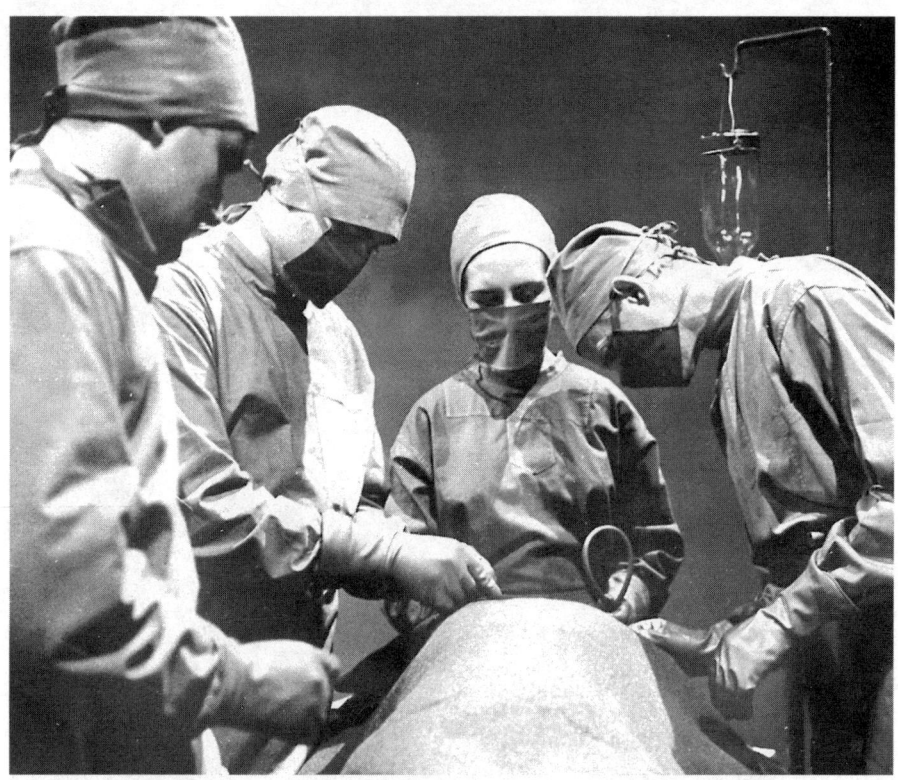

Melchior (far left) during a dramatic scene on *Studio One* in 1950.

director] around and after a year I knew more about what an AD does than he did. I then went to the network people again and they made me an AD.

For the next few years, between 1947 and 1953, he worked as an AD, then as a director. He worked 12 hours a day, on as many as nine different shows a week. At one time or another he directed *TV's Top Tunes*, *The Perry Como Show* and *The Eddy Arnold Show*. Before long, he'd chalked up hundreds of directorial credits. He had even begun to leave a bit of his signature behind: He was the one who thought, for instance, that Perry Como looked better sitting on a stool, rather than standing while he sang. That one touch of casualness became not only an icon of the era, but set the tone for the hugely popular show itself.

The live work became second nature to Melchior:

> I remember once when I was directing *The Perry Como Show* that for some reason there wasn't an AD and I had to do it all. I had to do the presetting and work with the cameras all at the same time. And it just so happened that John Huston was in the control room. Afterward he was impressed and

Ib Melchior: Man of Imagination

Perry Como and director Melchior—The relaxed atmosphere Como provided propelled the show to top ratings for years.

said, "I don't know *how* you did it!"—and that was one of the biggest compliments I've ever had.

One of the shows, Melchior recalled, featured Frank Sinatra as a guest. The scene was with two bums sitting in an open freight car sharing a sandwich, and singing "Friendship." Melchior said:

> Here I had two of the most accomplished performers and I was supposed to tell them what to do. After all, I was the director. Then I had one of the more brilliant ideas I ever had. "Wing it," I told them. "Do whatever comes into your minds. Have fun. Play off each other." They were delighted, and they put on a show to beat them all. Best of all, my reviews as a director were terrific.

Those were also the days of the infancy of color television. Two rival siblings were slugging it out—CBS' mechanical color wheel system, and NBC's electronic system, the ultimate winner. But while the battle was still going on, it was imperative

Melchior (center) at work directing activities on live-action television in the early years of broadcasting.

to transmit the best possible color picture during the few hours of color broadcasting per week. Melchior was in on this TV adventure, and told the following story:

> At CBS the video technicians—or vidiots, as they were commonly called—had found that the best system of obtaining the truest color was to focus a camera on a bowl of fruit and had painted all the oranges a bilious, outlandish green. Twisting, twiddling and swearing over their dials the vidiots valiantly tried to color-correct the entire bowl. Finally we, in the control room received a call from one of them. "Well," a voice said wearily, "we've got your oranges orange, but your bananas are blue."

Before that, however, he was involved as an AD on *The Jack Benny Show* and *The Ed Sullivan Show*, as well as on the groundbreaking granddaddy of televised science fiction, *Tom Corbett, Space Cadet*, a show that was to become an icon of the genre for many years to come: Such was its legacy that a half-century later, the term "space cadet" would continue to be used in reference to someone who's a bit far out.

COOL YOUR JETS, CORBETT!

Tom Corbett, Space Cadet was one of the first manifestations of space-age pop culture in the country—or the world—the *Star Trek* of its time. Following the public's exposure to amazing new technologies developed during World War II, science fiction was finally beginning to make ripples among the populace. Things once thought too fantastic to be taken seriously were no longer so fantastic. At the same time, science fiction's potential to overtake the Western as a mainstay of entertainment had been given a tremendous boost by the huge box-office success and publicity surrounding the release of two pivotal motion pictures in 1950, *Rocketship X-M* and *Destination Moon*.

While *Captain Video* came first to TV, it was *Tom Corbett* that really began to burn up the airwaves.

Melchior managed to land in the right place at the right time. He remembered:

> When the show began, they had another AD on, but he was not particularly interested in doing it. We went to the guy who assigned the ADs and I said that I would very much like to do *Tom Corbett*, and as I remember it, I got the AD-ship on the show by agreeing to do another show somebody else didn't want to do!
>
> Tom Corbett was a young cadet in the Earth Space Academy in the year 2350. He was being prepared to enter the Solar Guard, whose job it was to maintain universal peace. They had atomic-powered spaceships and ran into all sorts of problems. *Tom Corbett, Space Cadet*, the show, was the only science fiction show on CBS, and one of the few on TV at the time.
>
> *Tom Corbett, Space Cadet* ran 15 minutes a day, three days a week... originating from Liederkranz Hall Studios... [My job was to] make sure all the actors' marks were correct, and all the cameras had their angles, preset the cameras and keep it all flowing. It was all done continuously without a break. We rehearsed everyday, just like, later on, we did *The Perry Como Show*. Then we had one dress rehearsal and then did it. Everything was done at one time, the effects and all, and it was all done on the stage. We had another stage— a black stage—where we put the miniatures in, but

it was all done at the same time. George Gould was the director—a brilliant man. He invented the matting amplifier on that show in order to create the special effects.

THE MAKING OF TOM CORBETT

Although Melchior stayed with the show for many episodes, he was not there the first few weeks. The show actually had its origin with a man named Mort Abrahams, later to produce *The Man from U.N.C.L.E.* and co-produce the *Planet of the Apes* films, among many other endeavors. The idea of the show was, in Abrahams' words:

> To present, as accurately as contemporary knowledge allowed us, a scientific sketch of where we were with relationship to space travel and space science in general; and to do it in a way that was primarily, of course, entertaining. The entertainment factor was designed to keep young audiences' attention to the program, so they absorbed the material. We tried to do it with some humor and, of course, to attain as wide an audience as we could. We realized we had a responsibility to kids, so we tried to avoid violence. The little we had was justified, always justified. The kids themselves—the space cadets—were very moral. We modeled them in essence after the idealized concept of a West Point cadet, and our ambition was to serve and entertain.

Abrahams had met Stanley Wolf, who'd owned a recording studio in New York in 1947. At the time, Abrahams was working for a large bank involved in estimating the eventual revenue from the new television market. About a year after the two men met, Wolf called Abrahams and said, "How would you like to produce a television show?... I just sold a television show, and I'd like you to produce it." Abrahams protested that he knew nothing about producing TV. At that time, no one did! Since Abrahams had been estimating TV revenue, he'd made a few contacts both in the technical TV area and advertising. He absorbed what he was shown and took it from there.

Ib Melchior: Man of Imagination

According to Abrahams:

> I said to Wolf, "What is this show about?" He said, "It's a kids' show, and I'm gonna call it *Tom Corbett, Space Cadet*"... It's based on a book [called *Space Cadet*]." So I said, "Okay, I never heard of it, but—fine." I looked at Scribner's as I passed by, and the entire window was full with a display of *Space Cadet*, whose author was Robert Heinlein—a very prominent science fiction writer. So I went in, bought a copy of the book, went up to Wolf's office and I said, "Is this what you're talking about?" He said, "Exactly." I said, "Well, what's the story?" He said, "Well, I'll tell you what it is. Two weeks ago, I came home one evening, and my son, who's 11, was reading a book, and he was so absorbed in it that he didn't even acknowledge my coming into the house. So I walked over to him, and I said, "What is so interesting?" and he said, "I'm reading something that is so great, Daddy. It's called *Space Cadet*." And he explained that it was basically about a school for training what they called astronauts. Wolf then said, "Two weeks [ago] I had lunch with the Kellogg company and their ad agency, and they told me they had just bought a children's series to be put on the air in three months. And they told me what it was, and I said to them, "'You made a terrible mistake. You should have bought a property that I own called *Tom Corbett, Space Cadet*. [So] by the time we finished lunch, I had convinced them to cancel the show they had bought and buy *Tom Corbett*.'"

Abrahams thought that was marvelous:

> I said "That's a great piece of salesmanship." He said, "Well, here it is. Do you want to do it?" And I said, "Sure, I want to do it." He said, "Well, they're negotiating for time on—I think we started on CBS or NBC and then moved over to ABC—three 15-minute segments a week, 7:00 to 7:15 (PM)." We made a deal between us and I started organizing the show.

And that, in a nutshell, is how it all began.

Space Cadets Tom Corbett (Frankie Thomas) and Joan Dale (Margaret Garland)

"Tom Corbett was played by Frankie Thomas," recalled Melchior, "and Tom Poston was one of the other guys. He played a Mercurian whom everybody insisted on referring to as the Mercurichrome!" Other regulars in the cast were Jan Merlin as the rather volatile Roger Manning, Al Markim as the subdued Astro, radio actor Carter Blake as Commander Arkright, Margaret Garland as Dr. Joan Dale and Edward Bryce as the forceful—if obviously named—Captain Strong. Guest stars, who often had to hustle to keep up with the clockwork timing of the seasoned regulars, included Jack Klugman, Jack Lord, William Windom and Frank Sutton.

Mort Abrahams discussed the casting sessions:

> Frankie Thomas had done some work before and Jan [Merlin] had done a little. They all had done some work. We saw a lot of people. I didn't even know how to start casting, so I got a book that listed all the agents and figured if they're an actor, they'll probably have an agent, so I called every agent in town and I said, "Here's what I want. Clean cut. Between 20 to mid-20s. Strong personalities. Some acting experience—but I don't want polished actors. I want personalities I can build characters around." Lord knows how many people we saw— maybe a couple hundred. And most of it was just,

Ib Melchior: Man of Imagination   **55**

An aerial view of the Space Academy from *Tom Corbett, Space Cadet*—a photograph of a miniature retouched to add more realism.

"Come in, please. Sit down. Let me tell you, this is about young boys who are training to be—and so forth—and their adventures both in space and at the Academy. So tell me something about yourself. You know, where you were born, your family situation"— and we just let them talk to see if George and Albert got a sense of something in there that we could build on. We didn't start off by saying, "Well, we want one short, fat guy and one stupid guy and one smart." We thought we'd go the reverse way. We would find the actors and build on their own idiosyncratic personalities—hoping that they *had* idiosyncratic personalities. And that's really the way we went about casting.

Captain Strong [Ed Bryce] was obviously a command figure. First of all, he was tall and slender; and he had a very graceful kind of walk. It was easy to see him in a position of authority. Thomas was just a little off-center, as was Jan Merlin. Jan had, I recall, a brush haircut and was sort of on the Dead End Kid side. There was a little tough edge to him, a little hard edge. Frankie had a sympathetic streak to him. So they had individual characteristics that were very usable; and we were able to build on them, and yet they all merged with each other. It was, in a sense, a buddy picture.

But there was, on this show, a whole new aspect beyond dramatic presentation: heavy-duty technical requirements mixed with split-second timing. Shows such as these were on the air long before the advent of video tape, so they had to be performed, photographed and broadcast *live*. There was absolutely no room for mistakes or redos. This work demanded extreme professionalism, tight planning and a quick intelligence to make rapid, think-on-your-feet decisions. When something went wrong, millions of people were watching. There was no room for error. If nothing else, Melchior's military training and experience with tense, potentially explosive situations in the war arena proved invaluable in this new medium, as would the live TV experience later provide him with the on-the-spot resources needed for short-scheduled, low-budget filmmaking.

Melchior stated:

> Since the show was done live, we naturally had to come up with some way of making spaceships, alien terrains and all sorts of machinery. So what we were able to do was to take the actors and photograph them against black, then take a miniature spaceship, for instance, which maybe was only a foot long and through this matting amplifier we could have our actors actually walk on the outside of that spaceship to make repairs or whatever needed doing. Naturally that meant very exacting camerawork, but it was a fascinating show to work on.

It was through the aforementioned matting amplifier that all the compositing was handled. [The device underwent further refinement in later years at ABC at the hands of engineers Dave Fee and Rolf Drucker.] A forerunner of the later chroma-key matting technology, the amplifier generated a matte for any object or performer at the same time as it was being captured by the TV camera, allowing for real-time compositing. Among the effects Melchior helped realize with this "gizmo" were non-gravity floating and jumping effects, planetary approaches, asteroids visible through the porthole and even an attacking dinosaur on a jungle planet.

For floating effects an actor would be suspended on blackened wires in front of a black backing, or would lie atop black cloth laid out on the stage floor. The

A model of the rocket seen on *Tom Corbett, Space Cadet*.

Ib Melchior: Man of Imagination

Tom Corbett, Space Cadet **Viewmaster Reel**

black would be electronically dropped out so that some new background could be put in its place. An actor could be made to tumble by rotating an optical prism on the front of the lens. A high jump and "flip" was accomplished by quickly tilting the camera down on the isolated-against-black actor, rotating the prism and quickly tilting up again to return the actor back onto the ground. On one show a dinosaur was created by using a baby alligator with a paper fin attached with tape along its spine shot against black and combined electronically with a photograph of a jungle. A third element involved an actor matted into the foreground, necessitating a third camera.

Jan Merlin, as one of the frequently "matted" cadets, had much firsthand experience with the process:

> We were aware of the kind of experimental thing that it all was. We were *all* excited about it... It was fascinating because none of us had ever been in the position of acting in front of a black screen... It was confusing and odd, because we would sometimes have a color material draped over [a shape], and we'd put our foot on it, for instance, but when you saw it on the screen, it would look like we were in a jungle and we had just put our foot on a great big rock, or a beastie or something. It was marvelous, just fabulous to us. We'd float around, walk up sides of spaceships.

Merlin laughingly recalled how they met dinosaurs on postcards, and crossed vast fields of boiling oatmeal and fought with gigantic three-inch crocodiles and stuff like that. "It was fabulous then—but, of course, it's so primitive today...."

Part of Melchior's job was to keep the timing of the miniature backgrounds and the actors in sync without adding to the ordinary problems an actor would have staying in character. Occasionally off-screen monitors were placed around the set for the actors' discreet use, though this too presented its own problems. Merlin remembered:

> If it was possible to see a monitor we would [have one]. But they seldom used it because it distracted from our look. You'd be apt to be looking at the monitor rather than playing the scene the way it should be played, so most of the time we didn't have the monitor. We were given very definite places to walk and to move to, and to look at. And it was eerie, it was weird to be *acting against nothing*.

Often the actors' only guide would be from Melchior's commands from the booth. According to Merlin:

> With us, the pressure we usually got would be the *time*. Sometimes, if the show would slow down, they'd have us speed up. You'd get Ib sending out directions like "speed it up," or whatever, but never in a frantic kind of way. This was the most steady, easy, gentle man who could possibly be. I don't think they ever had a problem on that show that we could ever be aware of, because it was kept so quiet. They held a very firm and gentle hand on all that."

Melchior remembered:

> After I'd been working in live TV for a while, I got to the point where five *seconds* seemed like a lifetime! It's amazing how you get used to working with time in a situation like that.

Merlin responded:

> I'd never met Ib before, and the moment I heard his name I thought, "Oh my God, That's a very unusual name..." And I was really, really quite in awe of the man. But he fitted in with everything else. It was *all* so overpowering to all of us.
>
> I think it very likely that Ib came up with quite a few [solutions] on the show. I remember when we started with the rocket and we had this piece of set standing up there that was supposed to be the base of the rocket —-and they were going to shoot

Moments before going on the air the cast and crew of *Tom Corbett, Space Cadet* run through a final rehearsal.

>it taking off. You wonder who came up with the idea of saying, "Hey, we got a fire extinguisher over on the side wall over there." You wonder where that originated? —Well, it originated right inside that control room.

The blast-off effect was one of the show's recurring effects—a fiery exhaust from the tail of the spaceship. Melchior's little fire extinguisher trick was one he remembered first using in a children's stage play.

While the show's special effects have been far surpassed by today's sophisticated digital technology, it was painstaking, groundbreaking work upon which current technology was built—all done live by a nerves-of-steel crew. There were a few things, however, nobody had anticipated that caused unintentional laughs. Abrahams recalled, for instance, the first go-round on the space suits:

>[The suits] looked like the Michelin Man. They looked fabulous. The only problem was that on the first show, the actors put them on, and they couldn't move in them. They were like, really, having *tires* all over you!... Nobody could walk in them. And as a matter of fact, two of the actors

fell down—one of them, fortunately, off camera. But they were all experienced actors and they ad-libbed their way through it.

Needless to say, a new set of redesigned suits was ordered up!

But the technical crew was top-notch, and most problems were minor, as Abrahams recalled:

> Ib was a member of the technical crew. He was like the audio man or the cameraman—but he was very effective in his work—a very pleasant man... I'd heard his father sing many times. Our relationship was based more on music than it was on the show itself. He did not have any aspirations to be a singer, but he *did* talk about wanting to write. When I asked him if he wanted to write science fiction, thinking he might possibly want to write a couple scripts, he said he wasn't sure. He didn't think that was his area, that he wasn't sure. And I never pursued it because I didn't want to press him.

That doubt about science fiction would not last forever.

A holiday greeting to Melchior from the cast and crew of *Tom Corbett, Space Cadet* drawn by Jan Merlin.

Ib Melchior: Man of Imagination   **61**

MAKING WRITE TURNS

Up to the late 1940s, Melchior had not, in fact, yet taken up any kind of writing:

> I didn't start writing until years after the war. I wasn't at all interested in writing. I didn't think I *could* write. That was *not* one of my things—English was not my native language, and I'd always thought how can I compete with people who've spoken this language all their lives?.... But I recall I was again at my barber—I must've spent a lot of my time at the barber, obviously—and I was reading a magazine called *True* and it was full of stories, a lot of them war stories. And I thought, my story's better than these! So I went home and wrote my first story, which was the story of the Nazi Werewolves. It sold immediately. And I said, hey, this is great! I'm rich. I can keep doing this—*except*, the next one took 20 submissions before it was sold!
>
> But that was my beginning as a writer. I started as a magazine writer. I got to know several of the editors of men's adventure magazines like *Stag, Blue Book, Argosy*, etc., and wrote many stories for them.

Still, he had not attempted science fiction, although the field was a growing interest of his.

Melchior continued working out of New York at this time, dividing his efforts between writing and television directing. Between 1952 and '53, he got involved as an associate producer at the documentary production company G.L. Enterprises and did a variety of films, including an underwater short entitled *Main Street Undersea*. This documentary about life in a coral reef required Melchior to spend weeks underwater with a meticulous set of storyboards he'd designed to maintain continuity in storytelling among thousands of unfamiliar sights and teeming fish. Melchior, who always emphasized the importance of friendships and relationships, even here in the alien world undersea, made friends—in this case, with a gentle octopus and a particular Angel fish he named "Helen" who came to visit and flirt with him repeatedly. Years later, when Melchior was courting his wife, Cleo, Homer, as the octopus was nicknamed, helped win her over. In telling her the story of how it felt to have this creature explore him, he gently pinched her bare arm to simulate Homer's sucking cups. It was a very imaginative bit of flirtation she would never forget.

During 1955 and '56, after directing several hundred shows for CBS, he went over to NBC to direct episodes of a documentary series about the medical world called *The March of Medicine*. It was immediately apparent that working in film was where he wanted to be. Melchior soon became one of the show's most intelligent, well-researched directors, his background in science and the arts a valuable asset for a series both informational and dramatic. His December 1955 episode, "Alcoholism: The Revolving Door" drew exceptional notices: "An engrossing and valuable glimpse into the problem of alcoholism," declared *The New York Times* reviewer. "The show packed much interesting and worthwhile information into its 30 minutes." The C-C News, also out of New York stated, "Those bar room scenes which gave such excellent atmosphere and immediacy to *The March of Medicine*'s... show on alcoholism... were directed by Ib Melchior."

Melchior's interest in rocketry and space travel extended to his work on documentary films such as *Hot Run*, which told an *October Sky*-like story of a teenager who developed new rocketry techniques that caught the attention of military officials. (See page 258 for other information)

The following year, critics fell over themselves with praise over *Monganga*, a feature-length documentary about a medical missionary in Africa named John E. Ross. Dr. Ross had steadfastly dealt with extremes in medical conditions among the Congolese natives—from leprosy to arthritis, sleeping sickness to elephantiasis. Melchior directed all the U.S. portions of the film.

"As absorbing and inspiring an hour I've ever spent by the home screen," stated *The N.Y. World, Telegram and Sun*: "A color film of surpassing beauty... It was, in every sense, an inspiring film." *The New York Post* felt that "television can be justly proud of this hour." *The New York Times* was equally enthusiastic: "*The March of Medicine* presented an absorbing hour-long documentary on the work of a missionary doctor... the presentation was both graphic and informative." *Variety* added: "All hands... rate a low bow for putting together [a show] that gripped the viewer throughout."

These projects, shot on film instead of live television, were slowly bringing Melchior closer to his ultimate goal of directing and writing for feature films. They also brought him recognition in the form of several national awards for documentary production.

In spite of his documentary successes, within a short time Melchior would move from "what is" to "what if...?"

TAKING AN "A" WORLD THROUGH THE ALPHABET

My first science fiction piece was "The Racer," for *Escapade*. It has been republished many times, because it is a story that still holds true: Man's love of violence...

I remember, I had gone to the Indianapolis 500. I knew one of the racers whom I had met in 1939 in Muncie, Indiana. He had invited me to the race and I sat in the box next to his wife, when there was a terrible accident right in front of our box. The juxtaposition of the horror of the woman who sees her husband burning to death on the track versus the absolute elated fascination of the rest of the crowd was amazing. *This* is what they came to see—"Wow! Look at that!"—and it hit me so strongly I wrote this story... It was a protest against the love of violence for violence's sake.

"The Racer" took place in the near future and detailed a hyped-up cross-country road race between various colorfully named race drivers who not only have to cross the finish line in the best time possible, but run over and kill as many people as they can along the way. Every person hit counts for points, the more infirm or disabled the victim is, the higher the score. Cleo Baldon observed:

> A lot of Ib's thinking is taking something that's just an "A," and then extending it on through the alphabet—taking an idea and running with "what if." That's what "The Racer" is—our inclination to gamesmanship taken to "Z." Taken to crazy.

It is an angry satire aimed at a sick streak in society. After witnessing firsthand the horror and bloodshed of war, Melchior was revolted by the display of unabashed bloodlust in a peacetime setting presented as entertainment.

"The Racer" depicted a contest that, were it to be broadcast in the new millennium, would merely resemble one of the endless stream of real TV's high-speed car chases transposed from city streets into a paying venue. The entertainment value of these police chases parallels those of "The Racer": The viewer can't wait for someone to crash or die at the end. The popularity of such bloodlust would become apparent with the growth of actual consumer services available in year 2000 that, for a fee, would alert a customer by beeper when a car chase was in progress on TV.

This story would turn out to be an accurate prediction of an array of such violent "sporting events" of modern times, and would encompass things like pro wrestling, with its super-hyped, colorfully costumed heroes and villains wallowing in the most extreme forms of pseudo-violence and vitriol as entertainment; violent outbreaks between team members at legitimate sporting events; and the unabashed parade of brutality, anger, murder and destruction piped into 21st century homes daily via "reality programming" and the local TV news. Unarguably, the story predicted the evolution of the "Era of Violence" in the entertainment world.

Another one of Melchior's stories published at the time did not wax optimistic about the American body politic—"The Winner and New..."—in which the next President of the United States is elected to office by winning top prize on a televised quiz show. Again, from the viewpoint of today—in an era that cherishes the hot political sound bite that scores points with viewers in place of substance, and finds the populace glued to high-stakes quiz shows—Melchior's story seems on its way toward being proven unerringly, disturbingly accurate.

Will humankind be able to curb such bloodlust in the future? Is this a problem that can be solved, or is he ultimately cynical? Melchior commented:

> [After what I've seen] I shouldn't be, but I *am* still an *optimist*. I think there is going to be an awful lot of wrong things done before things improve. But all-in-all, I am an optimist, because I think we all have within us a strength, or the ability to weather things that seem insurmountable. Our own minds are probably our own biggest safeguards, because our minds will safeguard us against despair, if you want.

As an example of this "power," Melchior relates a frightening story from the war years. There was a vital map that had to be secured from an abandoned house in a bombed-out town, near the Moselle River in Germany. Enemy machine gunners had the area pinpointed, but Melchior figured if he made an unexpected run for it, by the time the gunners saw him and re-aimed, he'd be at the house. Melchior made the run. Unfortunately, his theory turned out to be wrong! The gunners started to fire immediately. Melchior suddenly found himself in a broken run under heavy gunfire:

> Now, if I had stopped to *really* think, to *comprehend* that here are one or two machine-gunners shooting at *me* and me alone, I don't know what I would've done. Instead of that, my mind totally disregarded that, and became suddenly interested only in the *sounds* that the bullets made when they hit wood, or bricks or stone or metal! Now I find that interesting. My mind had immediately seized

> upon something else, something that was perfectly solid, and perfectly healthy and perfectly safe. Had I started thinking they're going to hit me any second, I might've faltered or done something stupid. Now this is what I mean by saying your mind can save you. I feel the same way if you're in any really bad situation: Your mind will come up with a solution. I believe very strongly in something I call the third way out.

The "third way out" was something that went back to Melchior's childhood. He'd read a story as a youngster about a boy in Lapland who, with his horse pulling a sled with a big vat on it, is returning home in the snow at night. Suddenly, a group of wolves start to chase him. Whatever he might do—he can't outrun them, he can't fight them—whatever he does, he's dead! "Except," Melchior explained, "there is always that *third way out*. In his case, he stopped the sled, turned the vat over and crawled *under* it. He'd let the horse go because the horse, alone, could outrun the wolves. And when the horse arrived at the boy's home by itself, the family knew to send a search party. The boy meanwhile, was safe under the vat."

The story had a profound effect on the young Melchior:

> My entire life, I've always looked for that third way out—and it was always there. And I think that's an ability we all have within us.

A way to look at things from a different perspective. Beyond either-or thinking. A means to find solutions.

Melchior, encouraged by the acceptance and good reception of his science fiction satire, began to write more stories in the genre. Among them—"The Vidiot"—a story based on his experiences with the matting amplifier on the *Tom Corbett* TV show. It dealt with a studio technician who, in attempting to create a complex video composite on a fictional show called "The Planeteer," gets a very different effect: He stumbles upon a means to see through solid matter at any distance desired. Although the story was fantasy, Melchior filled it with accurate details that came directly from his days on the *Corbett* TV show.

Another piece, more of an experiment than anything he'd written up to that point, was a successful attempt to reveal to the world that William Shakespeare was, in fact, actually a science fiction writer! Written in verse form (and bylined, "by William Shakespeare, assisted by Ib Melchior! Here's Sport Indeed!") fully revealed Melchior's enthusiasm for and extensive knowledge of the Bard's works. In the piece Melchior sent up Shakespeare's writings by cutting and pasting lines from many of his most famous plays to create a free-verse trip through the solar system:

> Shall I abide in this dull world?
> There is nothing left remarkable beneath the visiting moon,

> Therefore devise with me how we may fly,
> With ships made cities,
> A space for further travel.
> Then must thou needs find new heaven, new earth!
> We'll to our ships,
> Which ten times faster glide than the sun's beams...

The above excerpt, utilizing lines from *Antony and Cleopatra, As You Like It* and *Romeo and Juliet,* was just the beginning of a complete journey among the planets, and comprised an impressively fresh notion of where one might find material for space adventure!

The mid-1950s remained a fertile time for Melchior as *author*—a man who'd just, a few years earlier, hesitated to write in what was still, to him, a "second language." By now he'd written and sold a long list of true-life stories and specialized articles to a wide variety of publications. With that challenge behind him, his interests in television and motion picture writing—*fictional* writing—was increasing. So was his awareness of the frustrations those media could provide: He'd been paid to write 13 treatments for an ambitious Biblical series for Amis Films—a huge amount of work—that'd failed to go into production.

He experienced similar frustration with a new ZIV-TV anthology show in 1955 that seemed to dovetail perfectly with his developing taste for science fiction—the aptly-named *Science Fiction Theater.* He submitted a treatment that, like the Biblical series, failed to get produced: "Waste Product" was a story that anticipated the kind of environmental issues regarding toxic waste with which science fiction had yet to deal. Against such a background he explored the mysterious notion of the community mind.

The story is simple enough: A father and his son set out for a week of hiking, hunting, fishing and camping in a forested area which, unknown to them, has been contaminated by nuclear waste from the chemical separation plants up the river. Isolated from civilization, the two gradually become witness to a

Melchior examines the Shakespeare plaque set in the wall of Elsinore Castle. He'd conducted years of research into the history and legends surrounding *Hamlet,* tracing its origin to early Viking history.

Ib Melchior: Man of Imagination   **67**

strange evolution in the natural life around them: Fish in the river grab at minnows on the fishing hooks and carry them away, apparently in an attempt to heal the wounds of the tiny fish in a small pool, rather than eat them! The father and son shoot and kill a jack rabbit and its cry of pain is so much like that of a human baby—and so loud—as if inside their very heads—that they cannot bear to kill another one. The sound haunts them long afterwards. "Something is happening here in the forest that I don't understand—that I don't like," says the father. Overhead, buzzards circle. The insects work in concert to get at their food supplies. Bees attack them. All about, the forest is terribly silent and still. Controlled? The father has no explanation.

Later, they use their rifles to kill a group of bobcats that have surrounded them. The bloody battle that follows convinces them to flee for civilization. As they run to find the highway, they grow aware that all the animals in the forest are following them. The father and son halt, cut off by the animals from the highway. They prepare for an all-out battle for survival against the creatures of nature, but it remains a standoff. The boy and his father are unable to bring themselves to fire. They begin to sense a strange, calming *peace*. They lower their weapons—and the animals begin to disperse, leaving the two humans to hitch a ride back to civilization.

The prodigious radiation which had soaked into the vegetation that the animals had fed upon had apparently amplified the strange, inexplicable phenomenon observed among ants, called the "community mind"—a kind of controlling force that organizes their activities. Perhaps that power exists in all things; perhaps it is a form of natural radiation, which can be amplified and extended by doses of nuclear radiation. When the humans showed up with their guns and fishing lines, they were regarded as a dangerous threat to all the animals, who then began to act together in order to expurgate that threat. In the end, even the father and son tuned into the community of life which desired, after all, only peace.

The story had been inspired by a scientific experiment Melchior had come across:

> I had never forgotten an experiment that was done on wanderer ants. Wanderer ants move, sometimes, in a mile-long column. They are all very, very organized. In the center of all, the workers are carrying the eggs, and so on, and then they're flanked by soldiers—army ants—and every once in a while there's a war battalion. It is almost like Roman phalanxes.
>
> What they did in the experiment was position two men a hundred yards apart. Up front, one man was given a signal and just swept a branch across them. Within seconds the other man reported that soldier ants, a hundred yards away, started rushing to the front.

How did the information travel so fast? Scientists were baffled: "So this is what I say is the community mind. The ants all *knew* the same thing at the same time. But, even if that was not strictly true, it was enough of a truth for me to say there exists the community mind. And then, I elaborated on that."

Melchior's treatment ended, as did every episode, with host Truman Bradley:

> He is standing next to the display ant hill and the radiation counters; he says: "Our story was fiction. But it is fact that already today scientists are confronted with the problem of disposing of atomic waste products. If these wastes are not efficiently destroyed—no one can foresee how in the long run they might affect life on earth..."
>
> Again we see the busy ants—their inexplicable community mind regulating their every activity.
>
> "Is their way of communication a form of radiation? And could continued exposure to certain radioactive waste products induce this same community mind in other animal life?
>
> "Perhaps science—some day—will tell..."

In the intervening years since Melchior's story, scientists have come a long way to understanding the community mind, especially as it relates to the insect world. Pheromones—minute, information-carrying chemical "scents"—rather than atomic dispersal— have shown evidence as to the true cause of communal communication among the lower life forms. It is now referred to as "swarm intelligence," a kind of chemical internet.

It is, in retrospect, not that hard to imagine why "Waste Product" was rejected, in spite of standing imaginatively head and shoulders above the average series episode: It certainly must have been perceived as being too difficult to film, with too much animal action. More significantly, it was written at a peak time of male machismo in the country, manifested in its most naked form by hunting. Surely a story that projected the sheer pain of the wounded quarry into the very minds of the hunter himself would have been anathema.

Melchior did, however, two years later, sell the treatment as a short story to *Fantastic Universe* magazine. Its real significance to Melchior's later film career rested in the fact that it would prove to be, essentially, an Earthbound version of *The Angry Red Planet*—a film that was to become one of his most famous projects.

Mental processes, self-hypnotism, intelligence stimulation and ESP were all subjects which—like the mental empathy of "Waste Product"—Melchior found compelling at the time.

For instance, Melchior picked up a thread of his "Waste Product" in an unpublished, vaguely Wellsian short story titled "Improvement." In an attempt to isolate and eliminate the human ability to "dislike" things—including people—a scientist inadvertently eliminates *fear* from all the life on a Pacific island. Lacking caution, the entire populace engage in a riot of dangerous activities and feats of daring that result in the violent death of everyone involved!

Throughout his career, Melchior would toy with endless variations and combinations of his story ideas: Elements discarded or unproduced from one story or script would be updated and blended into a new project. In this way, even a non-science fiction piece of fiction might manifest seeds of science fiction ideas from prior projects. The real world, seen from a fresh perspective, could be just as fantastic as a made-up world, the colossal plans of destruction of World War II, and as fantastic a phenomenon as *The War of the Worlds*; or the communication abilities of a particular earthly creature—snake, insect, cat, spider—as weird as any off-world entity. *If* shown in the light of imagination.

Melchior recalled:

> Years ago in the 1950s, I wrote a story called "Alien Property," the idea being that the universe is divided up into many different areas including our solar system, each owned by a different race of beings. And we don't even know it. We're just like ants on a farmer's field... If I belonged to a colony of ants in a field, I would be totally unaware that there was a farmer who owned me because he owned the field. It could be that we are just little, insignificant things that nobody really gives a hoot about!... Then maybe there are these alien expeditions that come out to explore, to see what's going on in the lower 40s. Who knows, maybe that's the way it really is!

The 1950s was a time when humankind was just beginning to probe outer space. It may've also been that "space" was just starting to probe humankind: It seemed for a while like the Earth was suddenly being visited by someone from out there—at least that's what was conjectured about the mysterious lights—the Unidentified Flying Objects—that invaded the skies in the early '50s. In later years, at least one conspiracy writer actually claimed that because of their status within the military or with high-ranking officials, Melchior—along with directors like Robert Wise and Joseph Newman—may have been privy to secret inside information about the UFO phenomena. In turn, they were supposedly incorporating these secrets in their films to educate the public as to the truth about UFOs! Melchior would shake his head in slight amusement by the absurd notion:

> The gentleman is sadly in error. I certainly have no direct knowledge of UFOs, or any special information... My own opinion is that it is quite obvious that there *is* and *must be* life on other planets. It would be ridiculous to think not. Whether they have come here or not is still open for debate. I would like for them to come here: They're welcome to land in my garden if they want! Frankly,

I would have to be totally convinced before I could say, yes, they have come here already. There is a lot of evidence for it, but there is also a lot of evidence against it. Unfortunately, when people make absolutely ridiculous claims, it destroys reports that might be real ones. I am the kind of guy who says, okay, show me, and then show me again before I'd believe in anything like UFOs. I'd look for other explanations first.

Once, I was trying to peddle another story idea which asked, "Why don't we try to get a dozen people together—scientists, science fiction writers, mathematicians, linguists, etc.—and develop a program on what to do if we *were* contacted by an alien race?"—because at the moment we have nothing. The military would try to shoot them down, others would worship them and so on. There is no plan. And that still holds true. I think it would make an interesting story which I still might develop, because I believe there *are* other civilizations out there. It would be ridiculous not to think so. Whether or not they come here in flying saucers...?

He'll only believe it when they land in his garden.

HOLLYWOOD, JAPAN, THE MOON AND BEYOND

By 1956 there was a growing trend for television shows to be shot on film, and a resultant general migration to West Coast production facilities to handle the work. The writing, so to speak, was on the wall. Melchior knew he needed to follow the film work westward. He hooked up with Leo Handel again and, in 1957, moved to Los Angeles, where he slept on Handel's couch until he could find a place to live if he did decide to stay. He did: Los Angeles was his new home.

While he continued to produce and direct documentaries and public service films, he also continued to look for any means to get into feature films.

In early 1957 such an opportunity presented itself when American Broadcasting-Paramount Theaters Pictures Corporation purchased *Gojira No Gyakushyu*—a.k.a. *Godzilla Raids Again*—the first in what was to become an endless series of Godzilla sequels for U.S. release.

Melchior was hired to alter the first sequel to *Godzilla*, *Godzilla Rides Again*, to create a more American film—*The Volcano Monsters*.

Ib Melchior: Man of Imagination

Since they had not acquired the rights to the Godzilla name of the first release, or the American rights to the "character," AB-PT chose to circumvent the problem by extensively doctoring the feature. They envisioned altering the film to create the impression of a new monster. This would entail shooting new sequences with American actors, producing new special effects and eliminating such identifiable Godzilla traits as his glowing back plates and his nuclear-fire breath.

Melchior was commissioned by Ed Barison and Harry Ryvnick of AB-PT Pictures to come up with a version of the film that would seemingly take place primarily in the U.S. After a long session of copious note-taking at the movieola, selecting all the usable shots, Melchior conceived the story of a joint US-Japanese scientific team's discovery of the perfectly preserved remains of two dinosaurs in a cavern at the base of a newly erupted volcano. One of these is Godzilla—or Gojira, in the original version—but is here identified as a female Tyrannosaurus Rex. The other is an Anklyosaurus.

The dinosaurs are shipped to San Francisco on board an aircraft carrier. En route, a storm topples the poorly secured Tyrannosaurus into the sea. Upon arrival in the city, the Anklyosaurus revives—just in time to encounter the Tyrannosaurus who surfaces nearby.

The two "volcano monsters," as the media has dubbed them, duke it out all around San Francisco. Ultimately, the Anklyosaurus is vanquished. The Tyrannosaurus wanders back into the sea, to be later sighted moving about a valley of snow and ice on an island in the north. There, the hero contrives a means to create a wall of fire by setting up and igniting a ring of oil-filled drums nearby, which melts the ice and buries the monster alive. A final aerial assault by fighter jets completes the task.

Melchior's script was an attempt to make a silk purse from a sow's ear, and he nearly succeeded in doing so. He wove distinctly Western character complications that tied the fate of one of the scientists—Professor Carlysle—to that of the Tyrannosaurus. If the critter is destroyed utterly, Carlysle—hanging on for life by a thread—will die of despair, his potential for once-in-a-millennia research gone for good. So the hero must stop the creature without totally destroying it.

Melchior selected only those shots from the original footage that wouldn't betray their Eastern origins. Oriental landmarks were not used, except in one sequence where they could be identified as the "Chinatown" district of San Francisco. He also ordered up a half dozen new shots of the "Tyrannosaurus" in the city and a number of matte shots and split screens of the creatures being hoisted off the volcanic island aboard the aircraft carrier, and wide shots of the supposed dinosaurs being transported into San Francisco past the Golden Gate Bridge. He planned additional rear-projected shots of crew members in front of the Anklyosaurus aboard the carrier, as well as the construction of the full-sized front foot of the Tyrannosaurus and large plates of the Anklyosaurus for interaction with the American actors.

Melchior's proposals and script, had they been followed, would've produced a far from classic film—the source material being extremely weak to begin with, including terrible special effects—but one superior to the eventual all-Japanese version that got released, minus any additional work, as *Gigantis, The Fire Monster*, when AB-PT Pictures folded soon after, and Warner Bros. reacquired the project.

Melchior's first effort at World War II action, *When Hell Broke Loose,* **starring Richard Jaeckel (left) and Charles Bronson.**

Melchior recalled:

> Ed Watson, who was my roommate at the time, worked with me on *The Volcano Monsters*. There was a lot of new footage we had to write into it and that sort of thing. Nothing became of it after all the work. But the people I worked with on it, Barison and Rivnick, later did the first film that I did work on, *When Hell Broke Loose*. It was based on my story of the Nazi Werewolf terrorist organization and their attempt to assassinate General Eisenhower. I worked as technical director/consultant and dialogue director. It was shot at Producer's Studio and was very much a "B."

Oscar Brodney wrote the script from Melchior's story, and Kenneth Crane directed. Melchior stated:

> I think it was his first film as director. He had been an editor.

When Hell Broke Loose is noteworthy as one of the very first films of later superstar Charles Bronson. It was released in 1958 by Paramount Pictures.

The same year also saw Melchior's involvement, surprisingly out of character, with a film produced by Universal-International titled, *Live Fast, Die Young,* starring Mary Murphy and Michael Connors. Melchior's script, *Girls on the Loose,* from a story written in conjunction, once again, with Ed Watson, was far removed from his by now trademark stories of brave acts and science fiction adventure, but its themes of corrupted youth, juvenile delinquency and the "morally-challenged" members of society was typical of the Beat Era.

Girls on the Loose described a teenage girl runaway's pinball ricochets through a California landscape littered with fast-buck artists, fronts, con men and motorcycle gangs. The story proper is told from the viewpoint of the girl's older sister as she follows her younger sister's trail, sometimes days, sometimes hours away from finding and rescuing her from these corrupt forces. Eventually, of course, the older sister is in danger herself of falling prey to the very same forces.

Melchior's script presented a surprisingly long, meandering trail full of the sub-genre's peculiar visual and aural icons: lots of neon and peeling paint; roadhouses, low-life joints, bus stations, seedy bars, alleys and back rooms. To everybody on the run, everyone else is a "sucker." The women say things like "simmer down, sister," and view their male customers as "creeps." The men drink, chew toothpicks and ogle the women. Gang members hurl challenges and dowse rivals in gasoline, while a narrator intones concern over this "cancer in our society."

Melchior's script was no doubt a reaction to the rise in juvenile crime and the first signs of a newer, amoral culture developing in the folds of the postwar United States. His script was an attempt, not entirely successful, to illustrate as many "easy-street" rackets possible that were going on in the country at the time.

Interestingly, Melchior's script was cinematically more stylistic than usual—his scripts tending, on average, to be more visual than stylistic—in that every scene in the story ended with a specific visual or sound link to the scene that followed it. There wasn't quite a stream-of-consciousness flow or an *On the Road* sensibility to the story, but it was at least vaguely attuned to both. "I had put some very good ideas into that film, which they took out for some reason," mused Melchior. "I remember I was angry about it at the time."

The revised screenplay, *Seed of Violence*—a classier title—by Allen Rivkin and Melchior, managed to both slick it up and water it down. The new storyline could not help but result in a routine film, *Live Fast, Die Young*: Not surprisingly, it is little known today.

In 1957, the boom in science fiction motion pictures was still alive, and Melchior was once again given the opportunity to write in the genre. He was commissioned by producer Vic Satinsky to write two science fiction-themed screenplays, *The Micro Men* and *The Multiple Man,* based on Melchior's ideas, as well as a jungle film, *The Savage Trap.*

Written in conjunction with a man named Pete Purcell, *The Multiple Man*, in tone, lay somewhere between an elaborate episode of *Science Fiction Theater* and a "creature-less" story—if one can imagine such a thing— from the later *Outer Limits* series: A scientist—Dr. Kenneth Rogers—is experimenting with radioactive isotopes at a top secret government lab in Los Angeles. His goal: Develop a new type of rocket fuel. A terrible accident occurs, and he is exposed to a deadly dose of radiation. Although the exposure unquestionably should have killed him, he remains, unbelievably, unharmed, until suddenly—briefly—he seems to see his wife from two different angles at the same time!

Although he doesn't know it, the atomic exposure has affected his physical being on a molecular level. As he walks down a corridor at the lab, he suddenly blacks out for a moment and falls to the floor. When he opens his eyes, the corridor no longer looks the same. Everything is old, run down. He opens a door to what he thinks is his lab— only to find a high school gymnasium!

As his head clears he realizes he is no longer at the lab at all, but in a high school corridor—in San Francisco. Dr. Rogers calls the lab back in Los Angeles—only to find no one believes he is who he claims to be: Dr. Rogers, it seems, is right there with the lab personnel in Los Angeles! Dr. Rogers soon finds he has become a pursued man, having been identified by authorities as a possible "impostor" who may've been privy to classified government secrets. As Rogers makes his way back toward Los Angeles—all the while being hunted by the police—he notes a strange phenomenon: His hands have begun to age at a faster rate than the rest of his body!

Eventually it becomes clear there are, in fact, two identical "Dr. Rogers" in existence. One, the original; the other a sort of atomic "clone" created when his molecular structure was split in two by the exposure to fissionable matter. It had occurred the moment he'd hit the ground after blacking out: The impact jarred a second Dr. Rogers into existence, and dislocated it dimensionally several hundred miles away from the original. Now it's as if the two Dr. Rogers are living up their lives at *twice* the normal rate, aging at a highly accelerated pace.

Finally, after a prolonged chase, the second Dr. Rogers is able to confront his doppleganger and reemerge as one normal person once again. Weirdly, the recombined Dr. Rogers manifests the total of all the minor bodily injuries—a cut to the forehead, bruises etc.—each had gotten separately.

Unfortunately the script, which might have generated an intriguing, if modest, motion picture, failed to find funding. Likewise, *The Micro-Men*, Melchior's tale of an ancient meteor containing microscopic spores of pure intelligence that, through the means of viral infection, begin to subjugate the wills of those exposed to them.

With the launch of the Russian satellite, Sputnik, the late 1950s continued to be a time of great interest in space travel, missiles, satellites and moon colonies, sparked especially by the media-fueled notion of the US "race for space" with the Russians. Many movies, news specials, radio and television shows were daily documenting the fascination and progress of man's conquest of space. The fascination was easy to understand. As the last frontiers on Earth came to be discovered, explored and conquered, men would feel the increased need to find, quite literally, new worlds to conquer. Outer space provided the new frontier and, along with it, challenging, even frightening prospects: a realm in which humans, indeed, would be in mortal danger almost every step of the way while attempting even simple tasks like eating, breathing, maintaining atmospheric pressures and body temperatures. The Russian director of Popular Science Films in the Soviet Union, Pavel Klushantsev, had made several motion pictures about space travel and its impact upon the human body and spirit. He succinctly described the challenge, as well as, by implication, the appeal of space exploration:

> Man is a very delicate and fragile being. It requires the same amount of care to launch him into space as to send [for instance] a valuable live fish to a zoo on the other side of the world. [A fish would have to be] put in a jar of water, fed and carefully watched so that the water does not splash, overheat or become polluted. A spaceship is a "jar of air" for man and more trouble is involved with a person in this "jar" than with a fish. That's why, from the very start, scientists tried only to send a man into space in extreme cases and automatic devices whenever possible.

With interplanetary exploration a national priority, it was a natural time for writers—such as Melchior— and producers to try to bring some sense of reality to their space productions. It was in this atmosphere that *Crater Base One*—a proposed TV series—was conceived.

Melchior was also commissioned to write three scripts for a "scientifically accurate" 30 minute-per-episode weekly series. According to Melchior,

> *Crater Base One* concerned the activities at a base on the surface of the moon. It was produced by Pine-Key Productions under producers T.L.P. Visigood and James B. Dougherty for Warner Bros. Some of the other writers were A.E. van Vogt, Robert Heinlein, Mark Cliffton and Edmond Hamilton. This was in 1959. They sent us drawings of the base layout so we knew where everything was supposed to be, etc., and I wrote several scripts for them.

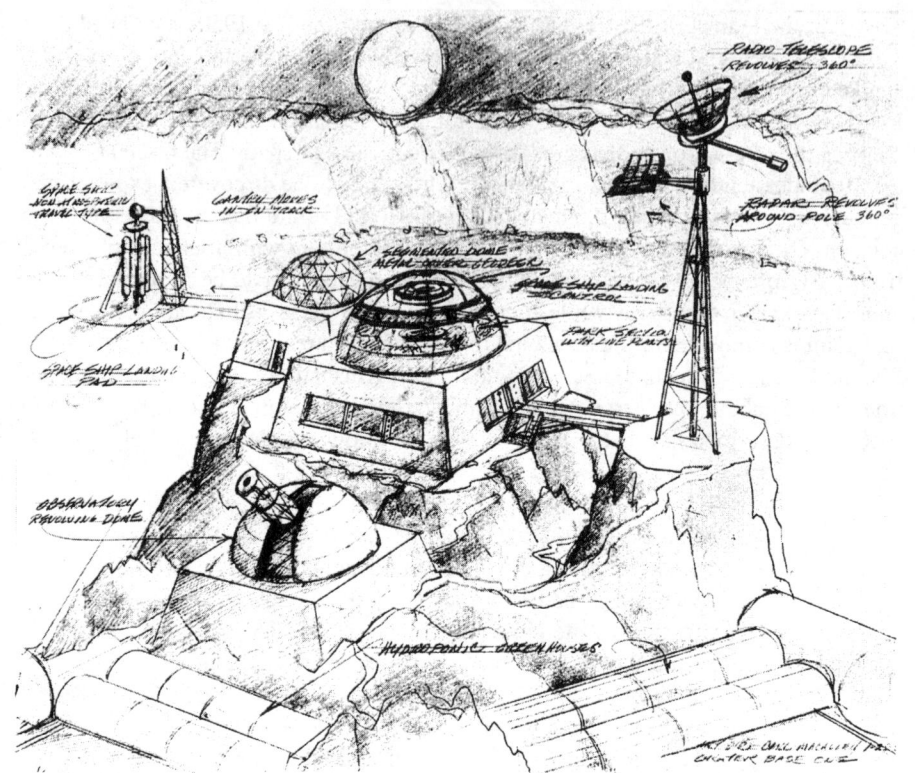

The producers of *Crater Base One* supplied its writers with illustrations depicting the moon base.

According to the notes supplied to the writers by the producers at the time:

> Earth's bleak, beautiful moon has stirred man's imagination since long before the beginning of recorded history. Close—but always out of reach—the moon has been the cause of countless tales of mystery and myth in all cultures at all times. Now—at last—science is about to catch up with myth. The hour is near when man himself shall first sail out into space. And very soon, his destination will be the ever-tantalizing moon.

The producers were very clear as to the kind of audience to which they were appealing. The stories were to be set in the future of 1988—a real world, not one from *Flash Gordon*:

> *Crater Base One* is a new kind of television format," the producers stated. "It is not a detective

story in a moon setting. Nor is it a hide-and-seek cowboy story which is doctored up by placing the hero inside a space suit and sending him off to get the bad guys... Rather, *Crater Base One* is the story of intelligent pioneers in a very hostile world, living only in the minds of men with *imagination*.

So, briefly, this is what we want: Imaginative stories of real, well-paid, clear-thinking individuals in a probable world where these individuals must do a job while living in a confined society, continually adjusting to an environment which makes every normal function become something new and challenging.

The Crater Base facility itself was to be built down in solid lunar rock, near the Mare Imbrium with only a portion visible; to be equipped with a radio telescope, radar, radio and observatory, television broadcasting equipment and hydroponic greenhouses. Women and men would be housed, military-style, in separate quarters. Along with scientific research, many base personnel would be occupied with maintaining oxygen regeneration and air-conditioning equipment, power supplies, water recovery systems and providing for medical care, photographic needs, food preparation, laundry—even movie projection. (One backward-looking guideline in an otherwise imaginative proposal, insisted that women were to do all the cooking.)

The format was very much in line with Melchior's interests, right from the start. After some discussion with the Pine Key executives, he was put on the writing roster. He quickly developed three stories which were accepted for production: "Moon Blight," "A Handful of Life" and "Eclipse."

"Moon Blight" suggested the extreme fragility of the ecosystem within the base: a small bag of pine cone kernels, innocently smuggled into the base, is discovered as the catalyst behind rampant, gigantic growth of a dangerous fungus originating in the hydroponic gardens. Ingenious, scientific "sleuthing" is the resource drawn upon by Melchior's base personnel in saving the day. The story bears some of the characteristics of the later film *Mutiny in Outer Space*, also about a mutating fungus on a space station.

Melchior did extensive research for "A Handful of Life," a tense adventure story and best of the *Crater Base One* treatments. Two astronauts—series character regulars Superintendent Scott McCall and Chief Mining Engineer Gordon Farrell—take on exploration of a distant, hazardous ring wall in the base's lunar crawler. Disaster occurs when Farrell is seriously injured attempting to climb the steep wall. He is bleeding inside his suit. The crawler is too far away to reach—and their oxygen is limited. Yet Farrell must get out of his suit to stem the bleeding. The two men—formerly at odds—begin to work together. They break their way into an igloo-like "lava bubble" not far away, big enough to fit two men; by quickly polishing the concave surface of a metal container with the pumice-like lunar dust, they create a solar mirror which they use to heat the rock inside to human-survivable levels. They seal themselves within, then fill the bubble with oxygen from their life-support cylinders, thereby creating a tiny refuge

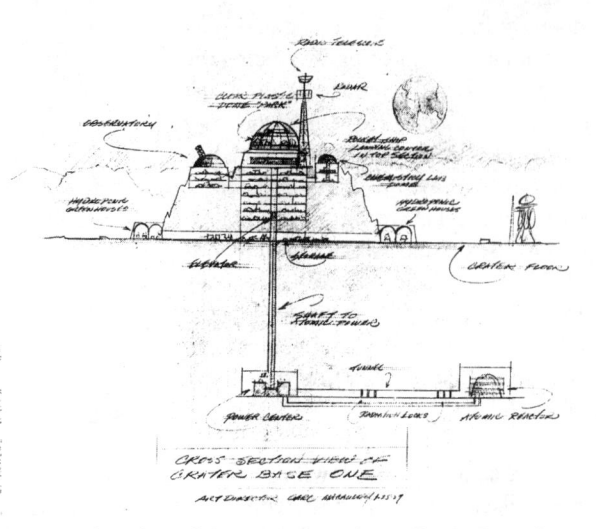

An elevation view of the moon base from *Crater Base One*.

for human life in the otherwise deadly realm. Thus protected, they are able to remove Farrell's suit and take care of his wound.

"A Handful of Life" represented Melchior's wartime survival training projected to the lunar wastes: The situation appears totally hopeless—even if the men *don't* panic! Their ingenuity quickly helps them find the a way to convert everyday objects into survival tools. The story required Melchior to study heat-retention factors of rock in a vacuum, melting and evaporation temperatures of solid oxygen," the gaseous point of nitrogen, etc., as well as lunar geology to establish the likelihood and characteristics of lava bubbles, pumice and crater-wall formations on the moon.

At the time, Melchior had grown increasingly attached to parallel storytelling, relating two seemingly unrelated but analogous events. In "Eclipse," the base personnel are planning a recreational event, a play which will humorously recall Christopher Columbus's famous—or infamous—ploy of convincing the Indians he had the power of shutting off the light of the sun; the claim, of course, was timed to his awareness of an impending solar eclipse.

The play in Melchior's story, likewise, is scheduled to coincide with a real solar eclipse. At the same time, a senator has arrived, threatening to cut off funds to the base. He believes the difficult and stressful living conditions on the base are not conducive to scientific research. His actions, if taken, will have the same result, metaphorically, as the eclipse and plunge the base into darkness. But the ability of base personnel to rescue the senator's son when he becomes lost out on the lunar surface, and continue to maintain their work, while having some fun with the play all at the same time, convinces the senator that men could indeed live up to the challenges of lunar life: He was wrong about pulling the plug.

Crater Base One, in its premise, represented an attempt at dramatizing the toll that nuts and bolts practical concerns would take on humans attempting to establish themselves on the moon. Its premise was definitely of an era devoted to the headlines of the day. Highly conceptual speculation it was not; though, its unproduced stories were not far off in depicting how human imagination would be taxed in the *near* future: A little over a decade later, the Apollo 13 disaster occurred. That event—like Melchior's stories of the time—required finding a "third way out."

Melchior was again discouraged that yet another science fiction project did not see production. Following the disappointments of *The Volcano Monsters*, *The Multiple*

Man, *The Micro-Men*, and *Crater Base One*, but he was not ready to give up yet. It was just a matter of finding the right producers at the right time.

But why persevere? After so many near misses? As many other creative people in Hollywood could attest, for every project that got made, a half-dozen others got turned down and lay gathering dust. Yet, the obstacles were not enough to discourage most. Why not? How important after all could it be to make a movie, see a script sold, create an "entertainment"—to produce drama? Was it about glamour and money, or more than that?

One of Melchior's former colleagues, Jan Merlin, experienced an event that helps provide some insight into the pervasive nature and importance of drama: During World War ll, Merlin had been active in the Pacific where his bravery and actions as a torpedo man won him numerous honors. Within days of the atomic bombing of Hiroshima, he and his fellow crewmen were sent to the devastated city to survey the damage:

> I got put in a group—a shore party. They gave us side arms and sent us in... I've since tried to describe it, but nothing can approach how ghastly it was to be there. There's no way to tell it. Pictures don't tell it because they're just pictures... But to be there, and to have that dust rise up at you and to see the people looking at you, and the whole horror of it...

But he was to encounter something that would attest to man's ability to survive:

> On the perimeter of Hiroshima, when you went beyond the hills, there, of course, the blast had been kept away from the villages because of the hills. I encountered a Japanese theater there, and spent some time watching the family that lived to one side of it. Obviously, the whole family acted in this theater, and I watched parts of their performance—and it changed my life. I felt that if it was still worth it for them after such a terrible experience to perform before people, then this was something *meaningful*... and as I came away from that, that's what triggered me into pursuing [my acting career]. It was a romantic way of thinking about it, I suppose...

The impulse even in the midst of a great catastrophe to tell stories, enact dramas, perform entertainments was perhaps not just an idle thing to pass the time, but a vital part of human culture itself. A need. Part of human nature.

Reason enough to keep plugging away.

OFF INTO SPACE

Finally, with *Men Into Space*, a prestigious new CBS series similar in principal to the unrealized *Crater Base One*, Melchior was to not only have his science fiction scripts purchased, but filmed. Melchior explained:

> *Men Into Space* was a series that showed man's first steps into space... the construction of the first satellite, the first trip to the moon, etc. But, of course, actual science caught up so fast with it that the series ended before it was finished. It was, however, a very good show and completely scientifically correct.

A ZIV Production supervised by producer and former art director Lewis J. Rachmil, *Men Into Space* early on secured the assistance of the Department of the Defense, the United States Air Force and the dean of astronomical artists, Chesley Bonestell, to

William Lundigan rehearses a scene for "Voice of Infinity" for *Men Into Space*.

insure accuracy, production values and believability. It also enlisted the aid of Studio Film Services, headed by veteran visual effects men Jack Rabin, Irving Block and Louis DeWitt, men who were used to producing a lot for little money.

According to Melchior:

> I got involved in *Men Into Space* because one of the producers I'd worked with the previous year on *When Hell Broke Loose*, Sol Dolgin, was also involved with the show. They called me in to see if I had any ideas. I always have ideas and I have many, many sources. Everything interests me. Everything I read gives me ideas. I have a "what if" mind. I read a little snippet and I immediately think, who is it? and what happened? and what could happen? and so on. And before you know it, you have a story.

For the series, Melchior wrote two scripts. The second of the two, entitled "Voice of Infinity," was directed by Alan Crosland, Jr. and aired April 20, 1960, and starred, besides series regular William Lundigan as Col. Edward McCauley, Ralph Taeger and Myron Healey. The network synopsis reveals a storyline close to Melchior's heart, a story about man's greater strengths:

> McCauley believes that men and women possess untapped, indefinable reserves of physical and mental strength which will carry them through any crisis, but an electronics expert who has devised a device for measuring stability under stress disagrees. Their respective opinions are suddenly put to the test when an accident causes the space station to spin on it's axis at ever increasing speed.
>
> The artificial gravity begins to increase to intolerable levels, at the same time rendering useless the instruments necessary to correct the fatal damage, making the situation utterly hopeless. Cruelly weighted down both by the torturous gravity pull and his grim responsibility, McCauley still finds deep within himself a fount of strength that transcends even the supposedly infallible equipment's capabilities and enables him to cope with the crisis and save the space station.

Melchior explains:

> I came up with an idea and presented it to the producers—in other words, talked the whole thing out,

A dramatic moment from Melchior's episode for *Men Into Space*, "Water Tank Rescue."

and gave them a page or two of what I wanted to do, and they hired me to do it. I did the same thing for *The Outer Limits*. Unfortunately, those were the days when the story editor invariably put his name on every script, even if he did very little.

Melchior was less happy with the outcome of the second of his stories to be filmed, "Water Tank Rescue," which aired October 28, 1959. As he recalled:

> I had a terrible experience on that one which, in essence, got me out of television writing. I wrote the script about an astronaut who is going to the moon with two others. The three descend from the mothership in orbit to the moon's surface. What they had done was sent up materials in robot planes and these three men were supposed to go there and gather things up and start to build a moonbase. What happens then is that one of them suddenly gets an attack of appendicitis, which, you know, can happen to anyone at any time, even if you're the healthiest guy around. So now he's dead unless they can get him back. They can't operate on

> him, and if they try to re-enter the Earth's gravity, the force he'd have to withstand would kill him. Except in those days scientists were doing some experiments with what they called the "Iron Maid," which was a container full of liquid in which you submerged the person and he could withstand up to 30 gravities. So my story was that they jury-rig, from one of the tanks, an "Iron Maid" and bring him back.

Melchior made sure every detail of his story conformed to a logical flow. Potentially, astronauts would be people who had undergone stringent physical and psychological testing, and whatever problems that developed after such careful planning would have to arise from unpredictable turns of events.

> Whenever I do a story whether it's a book or a script, I have to first know my characters. I make a character study, and I may even go so far as to say he went to such and such school, etc., so I have an idea of what this person is like. It may not even show up in the script, but *I* know it, and therefore he *acts* according to who he is, what he has become. Once I can *see* through the eyes of my characters, then I can begin to build the skeleton on which I hang everything else. That may change, but I always have a "continuity" to start.

In the case of "Water Tank Rescue," Melchior was careful to create a dangerous situation for his astronaut that would make sense under conditions projected by various space agencies at the time. For instance, no one with a *known* heart condition would be allowed to undertake such a dangerous thing as a flight into outer space. But not everyone was as logical, as proven by what happened while working on that episode:

> Everybody liked the concept. It was a new idea. The sponsor took it home. He liked it. His wife read it and thought it was a good story... "But," she said, I just don't like this appendicitis business." She apparently once saw a submarine movie or something in which someone had to be operated on with a spoon and it bothered her! So she had an idea: Instead of appendicitis, he has a heart condition! So he is an astronaut with a bad heart!! And he has a heart attack. And I said, "Oh, come on! An astronaut with a bad heart!? I will not stand for it!" But they'd already bought it. I tried, but couldn't get them to take my name off it.

Melchior did find room for some "heart" within the rather straightforward story: The launch of the spacecraft is revealed not in a scene at the actual launching site, but in the kitchen of the astronaut's home. As his concerned wife goes about her household chores trying to keep a stiff upper lip, her son, aware of the exact launch time and not fully aware of her worries, watches the seconds ticking down on the kitchen clock while excitedly counting down the familiar technical routines that are taking place many miles away. The countdown continues to zero—a torturous experience for her, an exhilarating one for the boy, and a fresh approach to the typical countdown scene of the genre. Melchior remembered:

Moon base cargo begins to arrive in "Water Tank Rescue."

> It was a little better way to show the humanity of the guy, that they're a family and are all concerned. Otherwise, it would've been just a special effects scene. So, I decided to integrate their concern into the actual space launch.

Melchior had been asked to make a few changes along the way. One change involved having the base commander come up with the idea for the water rescue rather than McCauley. As originally written, McCauley was to have gotten the idea at the last minute from a casual comment made by one of his men. The rescue would then have been thought up by the show's main character, and would have to be implemented under greater pressure. The change requested by the story editor not only made the hero seem less heroic, but also lessened the dramatic tension, especially since the rewrite telegraphed the solution by having the characters start to discuss the idea much earlier. Otto Lang's direction lacked the critical energy needed to convey the excitement of the last-minute rescue—and what should have been a nerve-wracking wind up.

Melchior pitched several other ideas for *Men Into Space*, continuing with the series' dictate that stories deal with men encountering, becoming dramatically entangled with and solving the practical problems of space exploration. Among the stories he outlined were "The Methuselah," "Stress," "Saboteur!" and "Blind Faith."

"The Methuselah" told of events surrounding an attempt to capture an "ancient" Earth satellite—the "Methuselah" of the title—in order to study long-term effects of meteors and cosmic radiation on the metal of which it was constructed. The drama pivots around a certain Major David Wayne who is to accompany Colonel McCauley on the mission. He once exhibited a moment of hesitation—which reads as "cowardice" in his mind—during a parachute jump with McCauley, and now manifests his inner demon as hostility toward the Colonel. Ultimately, his moment of hesitation at the jump point is replayed in outer space terms, as he is forced to leap "into the void" to rescue McCauley during a disastrous link-up attempt with the satellite. The rescue proves cathartic for the Major, and he and McCauley are able to be friends again.

Of particular interest in the story, in retrospect, are the uncanny similarities in the details of the link-up with latter-day shuttle missions, including scenes staged in an unpressurized shuttle bay, use of an extended grappler arm and satellite rendezvous procedures. The details only falter in that McCauley employs a *hand-held* portable jet to maneuver, which would—and does—prove easy to lose.

"Stress" recounted the disastrous effects excessive mental tensions might cause in space, as a pilot—Kincaid—goes on a critical mission with extra worries on his mind: His wife back on Earth took ill just before his mission. Ultimately McCauley is forced to launch Kincaid and his copilot to safety in escape capsules after Kincaid breaks down and smashes a critical electrical circuit. McCauley, the last man out, saves himself by tapping into the power of an emergency flashlight in order to release his own escape capsule.

A third story, "Saboteur," foreshadowed the film *Project X* (1987) in recounting the events that occur on a space station when "Sam," a small, trained monkey being used in weightlessness experiments, learns how to escape and begins traveling through the air ducts and hidden passageways of the station. A serious problem arises when it is learned Sam has stolen and stashed chemical vials somewhere on the station that will soon explode. McCauley and his men must trick Sam into revealing where he has hidden the chemicals. Melchior put a warning in his story pitch that no animals were to be mistreated in any way in filming the episode.

"Blind Faith" dealt with the serious dramatic tension that grows between the new Moon Base chaplain, Tom Ward, and an antagonistic base crew member named Steve Harmon. Gradually, Ward begins to view the antagonism as his personal failure and soon begins to question his own faith. Seeking an answer as to why this stumbling block has been put in his way, he takes a stroll onto the lunar surface to the edge of a high cliff, meditating on the heavens for insight. Suddenly, the cliff gives way and he is plummeted deep into a crevasse. He lies unconscious, unaware that his face—though protected from the airless vacuum by his space helmet—is exposed to the searing rays of the sun. In a short time, he will be rendered blind, right through his eyelids. Ironically, it is Harmon—the only one familiar with the safe points of the dangerously crumbling cliff—who can rescue the chaplain. Somehow McCauley's words are persuasive and Harmon makes an all-out, successful effort and rescues the chaplain. But he is too late in one sense, because Chaplain Ward has been rendered blind by the sunlight. Yet, Ward is at peace, for he no longer is blind to God's way. This was meant to happen in

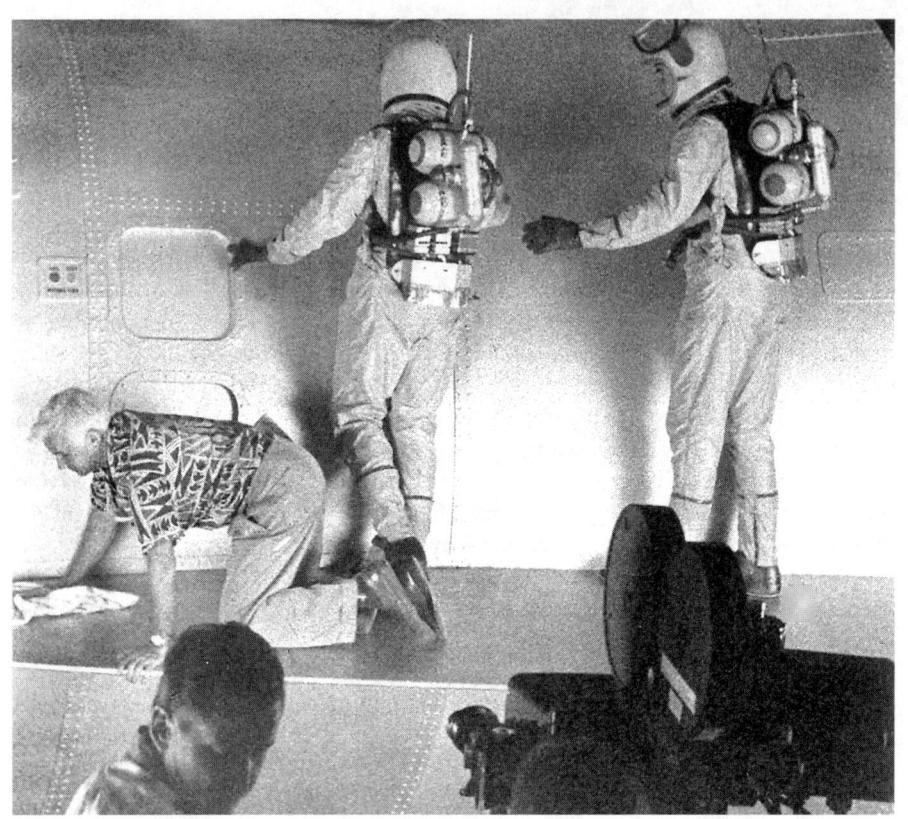

Final preparations are made to film the EVA sequence in *Men Into Space*.

order to bring Harmon—a man full of ill will—back to care for his fellow man. The chaplain's blind faith is restored.

The episodes were never filmed, since *Men Into Space* was to cease production soon after Melchior submitted the stories. But each story in its way brought home the same theme of men somehow finding an imaginative solution to a seemingly impossible situation.

Melchior commented:

> I like to put people in the kind of jeopardy that seems to have no solution, because I believe we all have a strength within us that will come forth in situations like that, and triumph. So this is what I've done in all my stories... for my *Men Into Space* stories, and all the rest: The triumph of the inner person over outside forces.

Around the same time as *Men Into Space*, another project was in the works that eventually led to one of the more popular cult films in the science fiction realm, *The Angry Red Planet*.

THE ANGRY RED PLANET

Without Ib Melchior, it seems highly unlikely that Sid Pink's idea for *The Angry Red Planet*—a tale of monsters on Mars—would ever have seen the light of day: Melchior took the seed of basically a very simplistic, pulp science fiction situation which contained several visually attractive images—a tranquil sea, a spired Martian city, etc.—enhanced it, created a real story from its raw materials and added numerous ideas of his own. Though Pink in recent years has written of his dissatisfaction with Melchior's screenplay, he appeared to be quite happy with it 20 years ago when he told this author, "Ib did a fine job of putting the script together."

Added to the film's creative mix was talented artist-inventor Norman Maurer. He added immensely to the practical realization of the project.

Between Pink's ability as a promoter able to get "deals" and "freebies" in exchange for screen credit, Maurer's ability to render visuals and organize much of the physical production, and Melchior's decades of writing and extensive directing experience with actors and cameramen, the rushed, low-budget little picture that resulted, *The Angry Red Planet*, wound up having quite a bit more going for it than one could reasonably expect.

Melchior was to become the target, many years after the film's production, of extensive, overtly hostile criticism about his contributions to the making of *The Angry Red Planet,* on the part of Sid Pink, his onetime producer and, later, occasional "collaborator." Pink made claims that Melchior's dialogue was, essentially, awful, and had to be rewritten, and that he, not Melchior had actually directed, substantially, the picture, and so forth. Over the years, Melchior refrained from commenting to any extent on the charges, other than to express surprise and confusion over the statements, and "pity" for the man who made them, a man who had once confessed to him that he found it difficult to tell the truth—about *anything*. None of the people contacted among the cast and crew seemed to concur with Pink's statements. In fact, they universally expressed diametrically opposite viewpoints. As well, many of the statements contained in Pink's writings are contradicted by the surviving paper records—shooting schedules, photographic proof sheets, sketches, etc. Most of all, Melchior's camera angle sketches have survived, and provide strong physical evidence of his careful pre-planning of virtually every setup in the film.

Almost 41 years after the film went into production in 1959 Melchior commented:

> As you know, I have declined to say anything about Sid Pink as a man or as a professional, [so when I] comment on my involvement with *The Angry Red Planet*, I will talk about my *work* with Mr. Pink.

It's not difficult to understand Melchior's reluctance to speak about this man, when one refers to just one incidence when Pink—in a book written and published by him—claimed credit for producing, writing *and* directing *The Angry Red Planet* in *Denmark* when all the records show that the film was entirely shot in Hollywood at the Hal Roach Studios by Melchior. The film's titles credit Melchior as both writer and director of the film, not Sid Pink, who simply took that credit for himself. Why did Melchior never respond to Pink's outrageous statements? "We have a saying in Denmark," Melchior commented. "What can you expect from a cow but a *moo*? Pink's utterances did not need the dignity of a reply. All you had to do was consider the source."

It all began in early 1959. A striking and intelligent actress named Naura (then billed as Nora) Hayden, who had worked with Sid Pink on several projects around that time, had been given a script titled *Invasion of Mars*. He had written it, with the idea of producing a film based on the material, to star Hayden. Pink had, at the time, been away from motion picture production for some years. In the early 1950s he'd been involved with films like *Five* and *Bwana Devil*, the latter the film that launched the first big 3-D craze. But certain problems arose that led him to leave the business for a number of years. It was not until 1958 that the producing bug bit him again. Drawing upon his early interest in science fiction, he conceived a story for possible production that was to utilize numerous elements of the early pulp era: space travel, monsters, alien landscapes and stalwart adventurers.

Pink wrote his story, "Invasion of Mars," in five days. Explained Pink:

> I thought that there had been so many stories of invasions of Earth from space, that it would be novel to do the reverse, where we are the invaders of somebody else's realm.

Again, going back to early readings, Pink dreamed up outlandish monstrosities, including a gigantic spider creature and huge water-dwelling amoeba.

But, neither Hayden, when she read his pulp epic, nor Pink—by his own admission—felt it ready for production. The story needed much work if it was to ever attract the serious consideration of investors.

Hayden had by then become acquainted with Melchior through their mutual friend, Leo Handel. Hayden had recommended that Pink consider giving it to Melchior to put it into filmable shape. Under those circumstances, the script was, indeed, offered to Melchior. He commented:

> I met Mr. Pink socially, and he told me he had written a screenplay, but could find no distributor for it since it needed work, and could find no one who could write a script following his storyline which was acceptable to him. I was new in Hollywood, having just arrived there from New York, where I had been directing hundreds of TV shows, including *The Perry Como Show* and *The March of Medi-*

cine. I was hoping to direct feature motion pictures in Hollywood, only to find out that I belonged to the wrong union, the RTDG, the Radio and Television Directors Guild, rather than the DGA, the Directors Guild of America, and therefore could not be employed as a director. The only way for me to break into the right guild was to find a producer who would insist to the guild that only I could direct his film. Being an unknown in town, I had about as much chance of doing that as I had of buying up MGM and Paramount, with Warner Bros. thrown in for good measure; so when I heard Mr. Pink lamenting about his troubles in finding someone to write his script for him, I saw my chance. I told him that I would write his script for scale, and that he only had to pay me for it if he liked it, provided that I also direct the motion picture, also for scale. Mr. Pink, seeing that he had nothing to lose, agreed. I wrote the script. He liked it. And I became the director, and, subsequently, was accepted into the correct guild.

The script Mr. Pink gave me had the title *Invasion of Mars*, it was marked "Shooting Script," and came with the credit, "An Original by Sid Pink." Reading it, it at once became apparent why no distributor would touch it. The script was hopelessly inept and amateurish. You cannot fault Mr. Pink for that, since he had no knowledge of motion picture writing at all. But, in addition, the "science" in this sci-fi film betrayed an astonishing lack of common knowledge and was so at odds with fact as to be ludicrous; the dialogue dilettante, and the characters stock and totally unbelievable. One of the most glaring examples: One of the astronauts selected to go on this, man's first landing on Mars, was a man in his late 60s with a bad heart condition!"

Melchior had already run into the irritation of being forced to include an astronaut with a heart condition in his *Men Into Space* script, and certainly wasn't keen on having that mistake foisted on him again.

Numerous other scientific misconceptions continued to add up. Melchior made a list of problems with the Pink original, and recently reviewed it:

A scientist, who believes that man coexisted with the dinosaurs, despite the fact that the earliest pos-

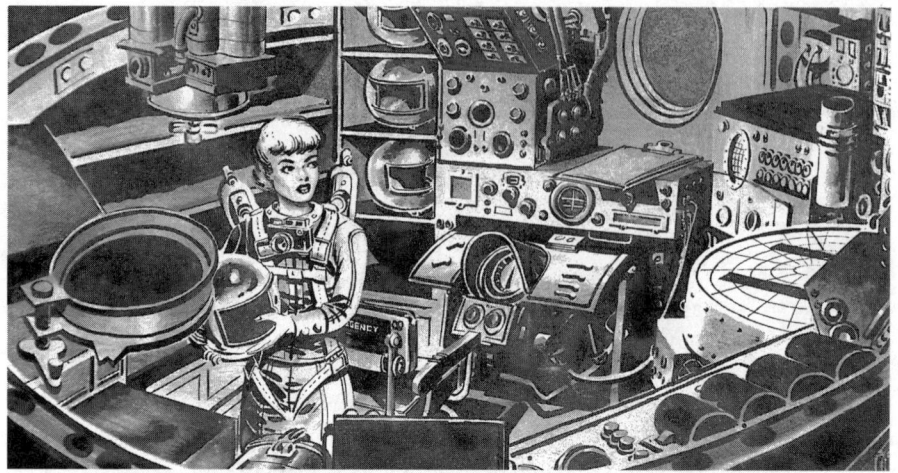

A rare Maurer sketch depicting Iris in fear of being observed by Martians.

> sible hominid dates back 5.5 million years, while the end of the dinosaurs occurred some 65 million years ago! Thus, ignoring the tens of millions of years that separated them, he has man triumph over the awesome creatures! An astronomer who, when the ship encounters a comet, 80,000,000 miles into space, he gauges it to be so hot that: "For a few seconds the ship got hot." He—the astronomer—says that "the temperature of the comet was immeasurable." Truly a unique comet; all others have no heat or light of their own but consist of frozen gasses and dust particles around a nucleus in various configurations.

Melchior eliminated all of these elements from his new *Invasion of Mars* script—including the glowing comet shooting through space. Later, some of them would be put back into the film during post-production—including a red-hot glowing meteor that nearly collides with the ship.

There was no end to the science problems. Melchior recalled:

> Admittedly we knew less about Mars then, than we do now, but that did not seem to justify the opinions of the other scientist aboard, a young woman (Dr. Iris Ryan) who is an expert zoologist, who states that the atmosphere on Mars is so *thick* that even radar beams cannot penetrate it. An opinion agreed with by the Earth Base authorities, who caution the explorers not to go out without their space suits. Never leave home without it! They

A scene with Nora Hayden shows the actual ship interior from *The Angry Red Planet*.

hear no sounds on the planet. "With this heavy atmosphere perhaps there is no sound possible," states this scientist, who also believes that an amoeba cannot be frozen, and that reptiles "have no susceptibility to extreme cold!" But then, according to our hero, she is nigh unto infallible: Her mother got the Nobel Prize—in *entomology*. The Nobel Prize? For the study of insects? The Nobel prizes are awarded in physics, chemistry, physiology, medicine, literature, economics and peace. Not bugs!

As for the dialogue, the hero, our space pilot, [made comments] like an inane chauvinist, even for those days, constantly addressing the woman scientist, as "Hi, luscious!" or "Hello, beautiful!," and tells her, "I always thought a dame was a dame and one with brains, well, they (sic) were the worst kind."

The fourth member of the expedition is Sammy, a technician supposed to render comic relief, with such lines as, "I can blast an ant at 16 paces," "Fee, Fi, Fo, Fum—Martians, Martians, here we come" and, after seeing a three-eyed monster, "Three eyes—boy, what a headache for my

Ib Melchior: Man of Imagination

Norman Maurer's sketch of the three-eyed Martian creature patterned after the work of Noel Sickles.

eye doctor!" But he *is* good; he has a way of communicating by radio between Mars and Earth *instantaneously*—never bothered by the distance time-lag in communication!

Often the language in the script was so stilted and convoluted that it was difficult to understand, such as this sentence [spoken by the Martian Being]: 'We require your full attention so that there need be no opportunity for your not having completely understood us." I think [we] know what is meant—but, it was quite a mouthful.

The main problem, however, was the fact that there was no story. It was simply an account of four people going to Mars, having some encounters there and going home. They all survive except one, the 60-something astronomer, who dies of—[of course] a heart attack.

My task was obvious. First, I had to come up with a story; I discarded *Invasion of Mars* and, using the gist of some of the encounters on Mars that Mr. Pink insisted upon retaining, I wrote a new script... The result was at least good enough for AIP to undertake the distribution of the film, the first of five films I did with them.

Pink's original version of *Invasion of Mars* hardly qualified, at 59 pages, as a script at all. And, indeed, the writing was that of an amateur. It did tell essentially the same tale as the film as far as the scenes on Mars were concerned—the same basic

Special effects cameraman Lloyd Knechtel prepares a shot of the Martian, later cut. Note the original title on the slate.

creature encounters, with the addition of a one-eyed, hypnotic serpent seen on the shore of the Martian lake—but in a shapeless manner full of some of the worst dialogue ever committed to the scripted page.

It was a colorful, cheerfully unabashed fantasy, though not remotely filmable by any professional standards: For one thing, as Melchior was keenly aware, the story consisted merely of a blast-off to Mars, an uneventful trip through space, a landing on Mars showcasing encounters with strange monsters and an escape to Earth with a warning from the Martians never to return. Some of the images, admittedly, were original—at least in the context of filmed science fiction, if not in the history of the "pulp science fiction" tradition that so obviously inspired those images: A motionless sea on Mars with its spired city—an "ancient city" called Darlanva, incidentally, in Pink's story—was a noteworthy flash of imagination. But, it all added up to little, and lacked any sense of dramatic, scientific or structural sophistication.

To the otherwise lackluster-to-nonexistent plot, Melchior added a dangerous, remote-controlled attempt to land a "dead ship" back on Earth, a case of amnesia complicating the recall of what happened on Mars and the entire framework of a series of events told in flashback that foreshadowed, from the start, a potential crisis—an unknown disease that may spread and infect untold numbers of people on Earth. The crisis—introduced early—is only resolved at the climax. Melchior did not concern

Maurer's pre-production sketch of the carnivorous plant based on Melchior's description.

himself with the unlikelihood of Martian creatures as depicted in Pink's story, and later Norman Maurer's sketches. Melchior stated:

> We did not know at the time whether there was any life at all on Mars. I thought that there might be, not intelligent life, but some reptilian life and some vegetation—like mosses or lichens, that sort of thing. But Mars was still unknown.

Rather than overanalyze that aspect of the project, Melchior simply decided to have some fun with it.

Unfortunately, while he was able to alter and improve most of the dialogue Pink had put in the mouths of the pilot, heroine and requisite professor, he retained—either by Pink's insistence, or in an effort to meet Pink "halfway"—much of Sammy Jacobs's inane comedy relief. And it is that dialogue that would later do the most damage to the completed film. It was the same sort of character that had cropped up in and damaged a whole run of space-themed films of the 1950s—*Conquest of Space*, *Destination Moon* and others, with but few, ironic exceptions, like *Flight to Mars*. Fortunately Melchior did manage to cut quite a few of these lines, such as the professor's aping of "Sammy-speak": "Sammy, in your own vernacular—how'm I gonna take it easy with worms, jelly beans and fuzzy wuzzies outside?"

The film worked better with the exit of the Sam character, courtesy of one giant amoeba:

> I *had* to kill off Sam once I put a story into the script—that Tom was infected on Mars and Iris was the only key to his survival. First, she had to be

made to remember; then she had to concoct the cure. If Sam had been alive, this dramatic situation—one woman having to save one man—would have been diluted, because there would've been *two* people to work with. And that would have negated the dramatic effect. So, once there was a story to be told, Sam *had* to die, or the story would have been weakened.

If nothing else, what was to become known as *The Angry Red Planet* would eventually shape up to be—greatly aided by Melchior's screenwriting thoroughness—science fiction cinema's first mega-planet: plenty of everything in all shapes and sizes—life envisioned as big and tentacled and available in zero, one, two and three-eyed varieties. They came by land and from under the sea. Critters insectile, botanical, unicellular— and all quite angry—from cities a half mile high, from beneath placid mirror seas and from out of jungles overripe and dangerous. The overall effect was described by one critic as "an extreme example of '50s outer space paranoia. Four spacemen effect a landing on Mars and, as if in punishment for their temerity, are constantly threatened by a variety of menaces bent on their termination." It certainly was, as another critic put it, "the product of a fertile imagination."

O'Banion (Gerald Mohr) and Sgt. Sam Jacobs (Jack Kruschen) gaze out the porthole of their spaceship. Sam would meet his doom on Mars. Notice the rough set construction and coffee cup.

A woman doctor, Dr. Iris Ryan (Naura Hayden) is in a state of shock upon her return to Earth from Mars in a tragedy-struck experimental rocket. Doctors use sodium pentothal to jar her memory of the journey's events since she has apparently experienced things so terrifying on the planet that she now suffers from trauma-induced amnesia. They administer the drug, even though they know that it will probably distort her recollections of anything out of the ordinary—which is virtually everything on Mars. She tells of their encounters on a planet where humans are little more than troublesome parasites. The story's conclusion brings a warning pointing a finger at Man's spreading violence... a kind of outer space "Yankee Go Home." A surrealistic quality was imparted to the images, motivated by Melchior's setting of the story in a flashback format. It provided a *raison d'être* for a visual process called Cinemagic—which made images appear something like drawings rendered in red—the resultant weirdness representing the taint of memory's distortions.

Melchior's atmospheric early draft of the script emphasized the mental stresses of entrapped human beings dealing with an enemy whose physical appearance and motives were unfathomable. Their ship was to be held fast to the planet's surface by an inexplicable force, a force they cannot understand. As their isolation continues to grow, the crew begins to draw comparisons between their growing ennui and sensory deprivation experiments in which the subjects, cut off from stimuli and information, eventually went "stark, raving mad." In the earlier version of the script, the planet itself apparently cast an almost hypnotic spell of fear over the entire crew, even at the ship's first approach far out in space. The source of this hypnotic fear was implied to be the deliberate work of the unseen Martians. But in the end, Melchior was constrained to use more of Pink's comedy relief, and many of these aspects were deleted.

The sense of "something in the air" derived from Melchior's earlier story, "Waste Product," with its father and son trapped in the woods by the coordinated actions of "lower life forms" in silent communication—i.e., the notion of the "community mind." While it is only hinted at in his Mars screenplay, the professor's sudden, almost irrational sense that they are in danger no doubt was meant to read as his ability to "tune in" on the dangerous intentions of the Martians: It is a point that—had it been emphasized—might have answered critics who felt the professor was jumping to some pretty big conclusions.

Melchior's actual final shooting script, dated August 11, 1959, was an intricately detailed expansion of Sid Pink's original idea. Every shot in the script was described in much greater detail than in screenplays typical of the era—everything from specific technical information such as space orbital procedures to the clothing worn by all of the characters. Likewise, the camera setups, uses of color, character movements, etc., were all carefully plotted, in an attempt to work out problems in advance of actual shooting. Even a simple transitional shot was used to convey atmosphere. "The Universe. In all it's grandeur and splendor it stretches into infinity." Among other details that survived in the final draft: a dust-devil that springs up for an instant when a giant amoeba comes up on a Martian shore; the presence of scattered reptilian bones inside the mouth of a huge Martian "fly-trap"; and a tiny airship moving past the massive skyscrapers of the Mars city. Melchior further tried to suggest a kind of threatening sensualness to the Martian animal life: "Huge, vine-covered leaves hugging the earth, half-opened, glisten moistly in the faint light under the trees... the leaves open up wide to receive Iris—quivering moistly in anticipation."

Other qualities distinguished it from the rash of similar such films—*Fire Maidens From Outer Space*, *Missile to the Moon*, *Queen of Outer Space* and *Twelve to the Moon*—produced at the time: its hero is a female professional who pilots the ship home once all the males are incapacitated and then saves the life of the male lead through her knowledge as a biologist; the consistent matching of the stock footage of the Atlas missile with new miniature footage at a time when most film producers carelessly mixed shots of models from other movies with mismatched, grainy, out-of-date V-2 and other stock footage; the use of exterior ship "distressing" visible on the tail of the rocket suggesting the effects of heat on the ship, one of the first examples of miniature "aging"; the appearance of a small deformation crater at the base of the ship upon landing—a detail usually ignored; believable details of the design of the ship, including it's double hull meteor-bumper, the use of porthole shields to avoid meteoric dust

A quiet moment between takes on the set of *The Angry Red Planet*. Note the "Marscape" in the background.

scratches, the dimming of instrument lights prior to landing and the visible presence and use of scientific instruments (microscopes, chemical and radiation analysis, cameras, exterior sound microphones, etc.); the introduction of everyday activities into space flight, like shaving, filing, cleaning, using perfume, reading, etc.; the use of realistic hand-held, newsreel-style camerawork to introduce the crew; ongoing radio transmissions to Earth and tape logging; an unusual flashback story structure; first use of computers aboard a movie spaceship; accurate landing procedures; and the then-rare use of a variety of recognizable names such as Burroughs Computers plainly visible at several points in the film—largely due to producer Pink's promotions—lending a note of reality. The more fantastic elements that follow the fairly scientific buildup are partially the result of the "seen-through-drug-haze" premise, and were not quite as much a fantasy in 1959 when *The Angry Red Planet* was made, especially since the question of whether or not there were lakes, plants and/or animal life on Mars was far from settled.

Most of these details and nuances were Melchior's contributions, and a far cry from the more typical "just throw it together because no one will know the difference" attitude of many writers at that time.

THE MAKING OF *THE ANGRY RED PLANET*

The entire film was originally going to be shot in anaglyph 3-D, with meteors, monster-plant tentacles and a Martian's three bulging eyes popping out of the screen. But that proved too expensive. A new technique called Cinemagic, invented by co-

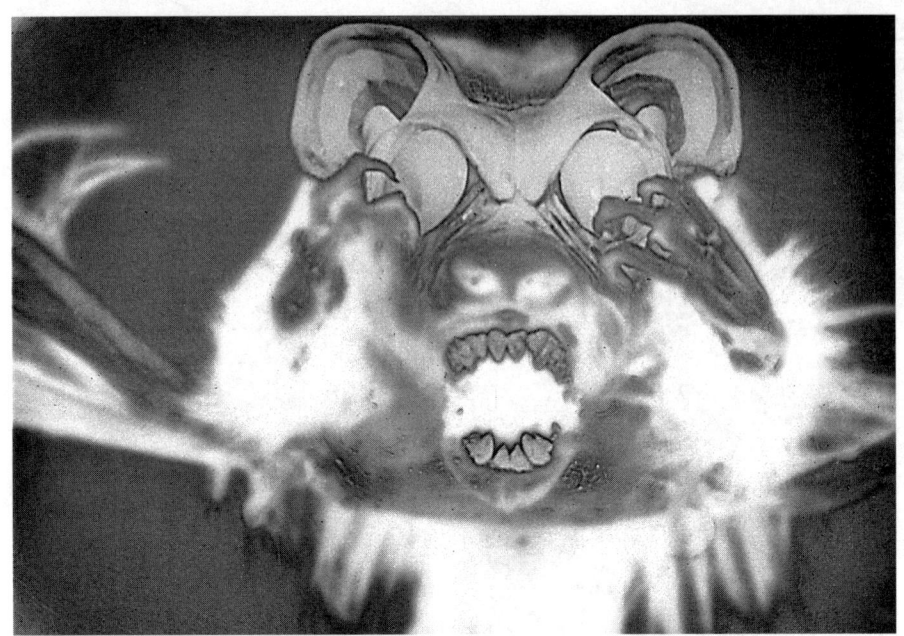

The Martian batratspider howls in pain and in Cinemagic.

producer and former comic book artist/innovator Norman Maurer was utilized instead. The basic idea was to create a stylized, deliberately nonrealistic look based on illustrations for the dream sequences on Mars. And although the technique wasn't perfected in time to be used successfully in the film, it imparted an abstract look to those sequences. A few scenes would not look out of place in an underground film of that era, and in some instances anticipated the feel of the Saturday morning cartoon fare of the '80s and '90s.

No one would underestimate Maurer's contribution to the making of the film. Melchior concurred:

> One thing: If it had not been for the support, the talent and vision of Mr. Pink's co-producer, Norman Maurer, the film would never have been done.

Maurer was an exceptionally fine commercial artist and comic illustrator who had worked on such titles as *Boy Comics*, the original *Daredevil* and *Dennis the Menace*. His work with the highly regarded illustrator Joe Kubert on the prehistoric tales of Tor was an instant classic. By coincidence, Maurer had also been a pioneer, like Pink, in 3-D, as one of the developers—along with Kubert and Norman's brother, Leonard—of anaglyphic stereo comic books. Their 3-D versions of *Tor* and *The Three Stooges,* published by St. John Comics, were quickly recognized as being the finest work ever done in the dimensional graphics field. [Maurer, incidentally, was married to head-Stooge Moe's daughter, Joan.]

According to Pink, at the time they met:

> Norman had developed a graphic process he called Artiscope, which he demonstrated to me. I told him if we could develop something on the same lines, but with a more practical use, I would be interested in doing something with it. And this is how Cinemagic was born.

Maurer's Artiscope experiments were an attempt to convert photographic images to graphic line. Assisting him was his brother, Leonard —who was an electronics expert—and Norman's wife, Joan. Pink's offer was straightforward, as Maurer recalled:

> Sid just wanted to make a modest-budgeted science fiction picture and needed an effect for the Mars sequence. I was called in to invent and develop this process, which I did with Pathe Laboratories, and to co-produce. I did everything a producer would normally do since Sid was then a theater owner with no production experience.
>
> When I came onto the project, the script was already done. I did rather large, detailed drawings on each monster based on what was in the script. I designed the batratspidercrab and the rest of the creatures, and designed most of the sets, the shrubbery, trees, the man-eating plant, etc. Sid took care of the business end.

Maurer, his brother, Leonard, and Pink were concurrently developing the new film process, a task which took 10 months. Conceptually, Maurer's intent was to alter a photographic image in a manner similar to Eastman's tone-line technique in order to approximate the look of line drawings. Cinemagic, as the process was eventually dubbed by Pink, involved several printing stages. Maurer explained:

> A positive 35mm black and white and a negative were sandwiched together, printed on a third film through a specially built and designed pair of small Lucite lenses to bend the light. The film was then exposed in red onto color film.

Pink saw in Cinemagic the potential to realize his ambitious science/fantasy/horror tribute to the old pulps. Pink emphasized:

> The idea was to render the backgrounds as cartoon illustrations. We could then project whatever we wanted behind the actors and Cinemagic would blend them right into these backgrounds. We could

The batratspider, its eyes frozen, staggers away as the actors are blended with the monster.

use drawings, puppets, miniatures, whatever and everything would blend perfectly. That would allow us to go totally wild, take the audience into a whole different, weird world and it could be as fantastic as we could imagine.

Alex Toth's storyboard for the above scene.

Although Cinemagic used black and white film printed on color stock, it was far more expensive than simply shooting in color. Still, the pictorial advantages of "motion picture illustration" was the factor that would allow them to carry out such a wildly ambitious project with as little money as they had to work with.

Prior to actual production, Pink's Cinemagic Productions, Inc., issued a fact sheet that hyped the technique as "a revolutionary new process for motion picture making. Performed optically... no pen or pencil drawings. Cinemagic adds a new ingredient to the screen, 'the miracle of man's imagination.' This is the first time anyone has dared to change the photographic image since the days of Edison..."

While not anywhere near the innovation it was promoted to be—and certainly not by a long shot the first attempt to alter the look of the filmed image—Cinemagic *did* allow some of the film's weirder excesses and highly uneven special effects to slip by less objectionably. Melchior found it a mere novelty. He felt it necessary to have one of his characters, Professor Weiner, attempt to "explain it all" to the audience as an effect caused by the sodium pentothal on Iris's mind:

> The only thing I remember from the producers was them telling me about that Cinemagic effect. There were to be a lot of monsters in it—and I wasn't particularly interested in that—but at that time I took what I could get. They wanted as many effects on Mars as I could put into it, and the rest of it was kind of confined to the interior of the ship.

With a budget of a mere $190,000, $54,000 of which would be needed for special lab costs alone, Melchior, Maurer and crew were faced with a tremendous challenge. Filming would require 18 sets, many of which needed constant redressing; the schedule was a near-impossible 10 days, with only five days scheduled for inserts and additional miniature effects; numerous mechanical and other special effects would have to be dealt with during principal photography, including still and motion picture background projection. But at least, most of the story was confined to indoor shooting:

> Everything was shot on a stage at Hal Roach, except when they're waiting for the rocket to come down. That, I think, was the studio's film vault in the background.

Maurer played a large role in getting the project underway:

> I was in full charge of physical production, as well as all the production design. Sid took care of the cast—most of it—writer, director, cameraman and editor. I commissioned the balance.

Among those selected by Maurer was a storyboard artist to produce detailed sketches that would help solve some of the problems, at least on paper. Maurer chose talented friend and one of the graphic world's greats, Alex Toth.

Toth had a longtime interest in cinema and cinematic design. His comic book panels were unusual and bold in composition, possessed a film editor's approach to action sequences and reveled in simple but dramatic use of light and shadow. Toth had become an acquaintance of Maurer's during the latter's days on the old *Daredevil* comic series. When Toth arrived in Los Angeles in 1957, he looked up Maurer and renewed their friendship.

Alex Toth storyboarded a number of sequences, including treks through the Martian jungle.

As it became imperative to break down the more complex sequences in *Invasion of Mars*, Maurer called upon Toth. Together with Melchior, they designed the special effects sequences, and the related live-action shots. Toth recalled:

> I didn't storyboard the entire film, just the three Mars sequences... Norman's effect on the film was quite strong: He was the real art director. Everyone was nonunion practically. The resources were very limited, a shoestring affair. It was for me a quick, slapdash bit of boarding.

Through composition, Toth's boards focused attention on Iris: The haunted expression that blazed in her eyes in many panels pictorially centralized her importance to the story. Other boards were used to establish the characters' size relationship to rear-projected images and horizon lines and helped inspire odd, but obtainable camera angles.

The cinematographer chosen to realize many of the boarded images was Stanley Cortez. By 1959, Cortez had built up quite a reputation, one which had been bolstered immensely by his stylized work on Charles Laughton's *Night of the Hunter* (1955). According to Melchior:

> Cortez was selected by Pink, and the reason, I think, that he did the film was to prove he could get the same quality with a low budget in 10 days as he could in a multimillion dollar production. And he did.

To help expand production values, the producers offered screen credit in exchange for free or reduced rates on services and equipment—one of Hollywood's first films to embrace that later commonplace practice. Most conspicuous was the extensive use of Burroughs computers and electronic equipment, with the company logo clearly visible in virtually every shot aboard the MR-1. Other deals were made with Bulova (for wall clocks), Ford (for a variety of vehicles) and Hasselblad (Iris' camera on Mars.). A credit in all the initial ads hyping "Eastman's new 5250" film stock also seemed to indicate a price break on film costs in exchange for ad lines.

The film was a pretty way-out space opera for 1959. Its use of the occasional "composed" shot, backlot crane shots, a fairly impressive blockhouse set, carefully dubbed first-generation stock footage and montage sequence gave the film more of an "A" look than could be expected from a film shot in nine days. The nine days also included one day for all of Bill Hansard's process photography, totaling 24 scenes in all! Normally such work would be scheduled for an entire week.

A basic problem remained: Melchior didn't have the means to use standard split-screens, traveling mattes and opticals to expand the alien world. All those effects were too costly. Melchior instead had to settle for simple full-sized mock-ups and monsters along with the imaginative and obvious rear-projected artwork done by Norman Maurer. Melchior emphasized:

> In order to employ the many effects we did we had to cut the special effects budget and use imagination instead of dollars. I prefer it that way, as a matter of fact.

Shooting began on Thursday, September 10, 1959, and wrapped on Friday, the 22nd. Each day required the shooting of an average of 12 scripted pages and up to as many as 17. By comparison, today, five pages a day is considered a good pace. Melchior's years directing live TV kept the schedule moving forward at a brisk rate.

Filming began first on the non-Cinemagic sequences—the airfield, control block, a city street, the hospital, interior spaceship cabins, etc. Melchior made lists of various functions he needed to see activated on the walls of computer equipment supplied by Burroughs: Warren Lewis, a man sent by the company to "baby-sit" all their donated electronics, kept everything running smoothly, from simple meters and magnetic recorders, to the more complex diagnostic panels with their familiar rows of tiny blinking lights.

Melchior remembered in particular trying to get through a scene in the hospital early in the production. It could've been done in short order, *if* the actor had just known his lines!:

> I had a fairly complex hospital scene. There were some five dollar words in it, and there were two doctors. One had two lines and that was it. And the other one had a lot of lines. And we shot it and [the one with all the lines] blew it, then blew it, then blew it again. And he kept doing that. And I'm seeing my budget going down the drain. I mean one day over and we wouldn't have been able to finish the picture! Finally the actor who had only the two lines came over when we broke for the other actor to go over his lines again. His name was J. Edward McKinley. He came over and said, "Look, sir, why don't you switch us. We haven't shot anything else with him. Let me do his part." I asked, "Well, how long will it take you to learn those lines?" and he said, "Oh, we can do it right now." I said okay. So we

The mountain peaks of Mars are projected behind the actors.

Process re-photography for the lake sequence begins.

switched. And we got it in one take! So he saved me... and he's been in everything I've done since then!

Some of the scenes were shot in color; some—the scenes on Mars—were better shot in black and white for the Cinemagic effect. These sequences were a bit more complex, since they involved filming a giant man-eating plant, as were scenes on an 18-by-30 foot lake built on the stage. Actor Les Tremayne recalled:

> The shot with the four-person raft was done on a pond that was just a rolled up plastic thing with propped up sides to hold water. It was only a foot or two deep. We kept paddling faster and faster but we weren't getting anywhere. We were dragging on the bottom. I was on the aft end sitting on my butt. I felt my feet falling asleep. After the take, I was the last one out. I took two steps and fell over. Two young guys on the crew came running over and caught me: They thought I'd had a heart attack. But my feet had just fallen asleep.

Melchior recalled the problems with the infamous lake:

> Mr. Pink was told to make the tank—it had to be built on the stage—three feet deep. He saved money by making it only two feet deep. So, now, they get into that rubber boat—four people—and

A giant creature intrudes on the space travelers attempting to study a Martian city.

> go absolutely nowhere! They're sitting on the bottom. They're going like crazy [paddling] and going nowhere. So it was rebuilt to three feet.

Dealing with mechanical effects on such a minuscule budget became the source of much grief. The six-foot-long crab claw of the batratspidercrab, for instance, was to be brought into frame and pinch Les Tremayne between two rocks, timed to match rear-projected footage of the miniature creature. Initially $13,000 had been allotted to build an overhead track support mechanism to actuate the claw. Melchior was rather dubious about the whole thing, but was assured it would be no problem. During production, however, money began to run thin, and the mechanism was never built. Melchior recalled:

> We had no more money when it came time to shoot the batratspider claw grabbing the character of Gettel. They were going to cut it out. So I said, if you do that, then all the rest of what we shot wouldn't make any sense. How can you do that? I mean, Gettel is dying. Why? So I took two long two-by-fours and put the two claws on them and put them in a scissors position and mounted them on a little cart and just wheeled them in and crushed him. It cost nothing, but it worked.

The Mars scenes also required the actors to wear dead-white makeup that, according to Naura Hayden, "made me look like Helen Twelvetrees." Likewise, the set had to be lit in a slightly stylized manner; and the props, plants and creatures had to be selectively airbrushed to enhance their tone values. Foreground set pieces had to be lit in balance to projections of miniatures and Maurer's artwork.

McKinley recalled that, all in all, the production went quite smoothly. This was his first feature film after years of television work, and he had a chance to stick around the set and watch Melchior work:

> It [all] went pretty fast—except for the guy who couldn't say his lines. I saved them half a day on that 'cause this guy would've still been there... Ib Melchior was a good, decent director. He knew what he was doing because, as a former actor himself, he knew how to direct actors. Some of these people have never been on both sides of the fence, so they don't know really how to get the best out of an actor. Ib did... We'd run through a scene once or twice and, if there were any corrections, Ib would make them at that time. This film was like TV—two, three takes.

McKinley had less fond recollections of one of his co-stars:

> I recall Gerald Mohr always played cops. When they put [the space helmet] on him, he went crazy. He didn't like the head gear. He was claustrophobic. He really couldn't stand it, so they took the faceplates off.

He recalled another instance where Mohr was "a pain in the ass":

> Naura Hayden was playing a scene soothing Mohr's forehead as his character had become feverish from alien infection, and Mohr said, "What the hell you trying to do?—you trying to give me a Marcelle?" [an old-fashioned hairstyle] when she was up there trying to bring him to, rubbing his forehead. He said, "Look, I don't want a permanent wave!" He down played Naura a lot.

Hayden agreed that although Mohr did have a "good side," he could be full of himself. He would play up to her. She recalled:

> I told Gerry, "You eat little girls for breakfast"—that was his type. And he could be two-faced after his flirtations: In the boat, that raft, we were filming in this little, itty-bitty pond. Gerry's wife was

on the set, keeping her eye on him. And he'd be waving to her, throwing her kisses, saying, "I love you, I love you!" and we all thought, oh, come on!

Melchior got along well with Mohr. The casting of Mohr had proven a good move in that he physically had a "look" very much like some of those famous seven, real-life astronauts chosen for the first space missions.

Melchior later considered him for the lead on his proposed *Space Family Robinson* series.

Hayden too agreed that filming of *Invasion of Mars/The Angry Red Planet*, contrary to Pink's later claims, went relatively smoothly. Even some of the trickier scenes, such as with the foam-rubber, tentacled plant:

> The filming of the tentacle went smoothly. There was a lot of pre-planning between Sid and Ib. Sid was a good producer. And Ib was sweet and adorable. He did a good job. He was open to suggestions. No ego problems. Ib was very detailed, well-rehearsed and prepared...

Hayden had been involved with the production from the outset—it was her suggestion to Pink to bring Melchior aboard in the first place. Later, during post-production, she would sit in meetings and offer useful suggestions for cutting the film. For instance, a close-up of Iris's boot as the tentacled plant begins to move. The scene was shot by Melchior per her suggestion and helped overcome the mechanical plant's plentiful "inadequacies" in the sequence.

The miniature work and rear-projection plates, which were needed for re-photography with the actors on the last day of the schedule, were shot simultaneously on another stage on the Roach lot. Herman Townsley, who had been associated with big-budget effects projects, including George Pal's *Destination Moon* (not *The War of the Worlds*, as per Pink's recollection), was in charge of building the miniature spaceship, the monstrous tentacled plant, the three-eyed Martian, the bizarre batratspidercrab puppet, the giant one-eyed amoeba and the models representing the jungles and Martian sea. His model crew consisted of Howard Weeks and Herb Switzer.

An impressive Maurer rendering of a Martian skyscraper in *The Angry Red Planet*. The Martians in the earliest screen treatment revealed the name of the city–Darlanva.

The illustrious batratspider puppet built by Howard Weeks.

Known for his invisible wire work, Townsley had solved the problem of visible strings on the batrat puppet by casting the critter in the lightest weight resin known, allowing him to use superfine wires coated with a patented acid he'd developed, which eliminated metallic reflections. Even though the whole thing—complete with monkey fur—hardly weighed a couple ounces, Townsley had faced knotty physics problems in working out the delicate weight-to-support ratios: His special acid was a factor since, while it made the wires more invisible, it also weakened them.

Howard Weeks, who had created the effects for the low-budget *The Man from Planet X* in the early '50s, employed a double "flying T" rig to operate the creature, but, unfortunately, found the nearly weightless marionette had a bouncy quality that was difficult to eliminate in only one or two takes—a task made all the more difficult by the number of joints that had to function: six legs and claws, tail, two arms and jaw. He hired marionette maestro Bob Baker to help operate it. Baker, who'd many years earlier created the wonderful marionette operetta at the opening of Edgar Ulmer's PRC film *Bluebeard* and later designed one of the aliens seen in *Close Encounters of the Third Kind*, worked the loose-jointed, featherweight puppet as best he could. It was not an easy task.

The amoeba was a whole new problem. Townsley had it sculpted, then cast in Ken-plastic (polyvinyl chloride) to give it a deep skin look. The three-foot model was attached to an underwater track along with a cluster of air hoses which were used to achieve bubbling and churning effects. The breathing and tentacles were rigged to operate hydraulically, but only the breathing function ever worked properly. The entire rig was situated in a tank that was custom-built for the film. It was fed by a constant

This never-before-seen still shows the amoeba covering the spaceship. The scene was mercifully redone to better effect by Maurer and Melchior in Maurer's garage.

flow of water which ran off over the edge into a retainer-circulator system. This provided the "endless horizon" required. The water could only be photographed when dead still in order to appear mirror-like.

The lake itself was not a standard studio tank, but a small, plastic-lined affair approximately 20-feet wide, set in front of a translucent, evenly-lit screen. It was just deep enough—two feet—to hide the amoeba's mechanics.

The amoeba faired pretty well surrounded by churning water, but on land the amoeba model—which more resembled a Portuguese Man-of-War—was mounted on a small tractor-like mechanism that nobody seemed particularly happy with.

A particular source of amusement for the film's detractors and a constant irritation to those who worked on it was the now famous rotating "eyeball" effect. Melchior had described the giant amoeba as having "two roughly circular nuclei, almost like 'eyes' in its center, which revolve constantly." Melchior was definitely not happy about that:

> What I had in mind was that what you could see inside of it was a vague shape—a nucleus. The special effects people were working on this while I was doing something else, so this is the sort of thing you have no control over. I was told, "Don't worry, they're working on it." I was shooting already, and they still hadn't completed it. Now, finally, here comes the amoeba, and it turns out to be a crazy thing with that damned eye on it. They had taken the evocative description literally.

Pleased with his accomplishment, one of the effects men beamed, "Oh, but it revolves!" and proudly turned it on. Immediately the eye began rotating, accompanied by a horrible grinding noise. Melchior was aghast. "Oh, come on!" he cried. "Stop! If we have the eye at all, I don't want it to revolve!"

But Melchior was overruled. The money had already been spent on it. "So here comes this thing," Melchior sighed—"a ridiculous, nonsensical thing... I remember I was furious with what they'd done with the amoeba. My description of it had been totally misunderstood."

Longtime special effects supervisor Howard Anderson, Jr. had been the one hired to provide all the high-speed photography of the miniature monsters. He was given all of four days to shoot. His crew included Bob Ryder, Lloyd "Goldie" Garnell and miniature cameraman expert Lloyd Knechtel. Anderson photographed all the scenes of the batratspidercrab, and the amoeba rising out of the water, the city and mountains along the lake shore and the amoeba coming up onto the beach. Knechtel filmed all the scenes of the three-eyed Martian—rising from behind a mountain, looking through the porthole, and a later-deleted scene of it alongside the spaceship—as well as the infamous scenes of the amoeba traveling through the jungle and approaching the spaceship with its ridiculous rotating eyeball. At least Anderson had had the sense to shut the eye mechanism off for his scenes. Anderson recalled:

> I don't think we even had a chance to view the dailies on that film. Ib had a storyboard and very much wanted it to turn out a certain way. He came down to our stage. He was very close on that one, very hands on. He helped with moving stuff around and "let's do this, etc." He was very much hands on with the effects.

The 18 effects plates required of the batratspidercrab were shot early in the schedule, on September 2nd. The amoeba scenes on the lake, however, were shot on September 21, the day immediately before they were needed for live-action re-photography. There would be no room for error with these scenes: One mistake and there wouldn't be a seaworthy monster to project behind the actors. Fortunately, Anderson managed to pull it off without a hitch. Knechtel's scenes of the Martian and remaining land scenes of the amoeba attacking the spaceship would be shot on the first two days of October.

The three-eyed Martian intelligence itself was built large enough to be worn like a hood by a midget. In this instance it was Billy Curtis, best remembered as one of the Munchkins in *The Wizard of Oz* (1939). Although the Martian was seen only briefly, it remained perhaps the screen's eeriest alien until H.R. Geiger came along, and certainly, for its time, one of the best crafted. However, it did not please Melchior:

> I didn't really like the three-eyed Martian, [even though] it *was* well-done. I don't know anything about making monsters, but I remember my objection to this one was what does it all mean? Why

Extremely rare portrait of the elusive three-eyed Martian, one of the most surreal creatures created at that time.

does he have three eyes? Why does he have these two other mouths? It looked great, but it didn't have *plausibility*: I cannot see *why*. I can see, for instance, how *we* have evolved. I can see how our fingers have come to be very important. In that case, you have a monster with 10 appendages—fingers—extending from another appendage—but it makes sense. This [Martian] did not make sense. What were all those things hanging over his arms for? What did they do? I could've made up a whole backstory explaining all these things, but it would've been a whole new story... I mean, it *was* imaginative, but I preferred things to make more sense.

Melchior elaborated:

To me, if you design a creature that lives on a world that is bathed under two suns, and you design a creature with huge eyes—it's nonsense. Its eyes would be tiny. Now this is just one example. It

> seems most people just design these monsters which don't bear any relationship to where they come from. Same thing if you design a creature that comes from a planet with 10 times the Earth's gravity and you give it long, spindly legs. You don't do that. They would be squat. This is what I object to in monster design, that there is no relationship between what they [look like] and their environment. They're too arbitrary.

Another problem lay in the fact that the Martian's supposed hundred-feet-tall stature is never made clear in the film, since it was always shown without scale reference. Two shots of the creature that would have established its size—one of it towering above a tree, and another of it alongside the MR-1—wound up altered, in the one case, so that the tree was unnoticeable. The other was simply cut.

Eventually Melchior himself wound up pitching in to create some of the miniature effects with Maurer when money problems arose:

> By the time we got to that whole scene of the amoeba slowly oozing up on the ship, there was no money left. No more money! But it was something we had to have. That entire special effects scene eventually cost about $2.50! We did it in Norman Maurer's garage. We got a lot of Jello of various consistencies and put poster paint in it. And then we built a box, which was simply a piece of glass with sides on it, and we stuffed all that jello down in there and put it up on two ladders. We put a camera under it shooting up at it, and I crawled up on the ladder and stood there kneading that damned stuff with my hands, and Norman was down there shooting it. That became what we matted into the porthole. It was a rather good effect, I thought.

Another shot—of the amoeba fully engulfing the spaceship—had been shot by Lloyd Knechtel, but was so bad it was unusable. That too had to be redone:

> We bought a toy spaceship which was about a foot long, and we took the same kind of stuff [used in the porthole] and froze it in the refrigerator until it became nice and hard. Then we stuck that spaceship down in the middle of it, put it on a hot plate and melted it, shooting in reverse!
>
> Now they were acceptable shots, but they weren't what they should've been. But at least we

were able to finish the picture. And we paid for these things ourselves. There was no more money. This was the kind of crap we had to put up with! We *had* to shoot. We had deadlines.

It was around the same time as the effects redo's—October 19—about a month after the production had wrapped and a rough cut of the film had been made, that Naura Hayden and Jack Kruschen were brought in for miscellaneous inserts and close-ups, the only live-action filming done beyond the original nine days. Melchior had drawn up his own list of inserts he felt were needed, and added to them some notes provided by the editor John Hoffman, Pink, Maurer and Hayden. Contrary to Pink's later claims, Melchior stated he directed these inserts and pickups, which included a few routine line retakes. Pink was only involved to help, but not direct: According to Melchior and surviving records, no "upper ship" scenes of any consequence, despite Pink's claims, were shot in post-production. They had all been shot during principal photography. All in all, it was remarkable that so few pickups were required; all the more so considering that virtually every shot had to be achieved by the first unit: "There was no second unit on this picture," Maurer emphasized, "only some insert work done afterwards. It was a mad, rat-race rush to get it done. Sid had a release date for Thanksgiving, and we had to be done by then."

During post-production, it was discovered that the lab could not control the Cinemagic process to produce a refined effect. Some scenes worked perfectly, but most failed completely to achieve the "visual motion illustration" look touted in pre-production publicity releases. "All we really got was that glowing effect," commented Pink. "We never got that nightmarish quality we wanted."

Maurer stated:

> Pathe Labs never succeeded in controlling my process under production pressures. We created some optical parts and they lost them, so we had to redo them. It could've been far better if Sid allowed just a bit more time. He advertised a release date long before the process was perfected, and we were forced to use what we had, even if it wasn't right.

Although the producers were disappointed, what they wound up with resembled another photographic technique called solarization. This, fortunately, imparted a suitably eerie quality to many scenes.

Paul Dunlap's musical score, consisting of oppressive rumblings and electronic chord-bleeps, helped sell the surreality of the Martian environments: The recording sessions utilized a nucleus of eight to 10 musicians Dunlap had culled from the Fox orchestra, to which he added a lead trumpeter, borrowed from Nelson Riddle, for several tracks. He stuck with a basic core of instruments, with an emphasis on French horns. He created the background tone by means of mixing kettle drums with sustained chords on an organ, all the while trying to avoid, with the latter instrument, any sounds that—in his words—"betrayed its humble origin." To this he integrated electronic to-

Nora Hayden, Gerald Mohr and Les Tremayne—the stars of *The Angry Red Planet*.

nalities and plinkings generated by one of the forefathers of such music, Jack Cookerly. Melchior stated:

> The music served its purpose. I don't like music in films when it no longer is background to the action. I always let the composer do his job, unless I was really unhappy about something. I'd tell them I want excitement, or chase music, or a certain mood, but I wouldn't tell them how to do that.

Melchior recalled the cast:

> Naura was a natural, and she played herself, in a way. I enjoyed working with her to no end. She took direction. I'd tell her what to do, she did it. I liked her a lot. And Gerald Mohr was a prince. With me, he was terrific. He was great. I thought he was good-looking... and fit the part. Norman was around on the set and helped out a lot. He was very supportive, and I had a lot of respect for him. He knew what he was doing. Stanley [Cortez] was

A member of the crew stands in the miniature lake on the set of *The Angry Red Planet*.

great. Of course, I let him handle the photographic aspects of it... He was receptive to the angles I'd sketched. ... I simply said, "I want a man walking from here to here, and I want to end up with a tight close-up on him"—and he'd set it up. And I'd tell him I want this angle, because I need to see this and I need to see that, and Stanley never had a problem working that way. The lighting and all that were all his. I just told him the mood I wanted, the action I wanted in it and how I wanted it covered. I didn't tell him what lenses to use, what the lighting should be, etc... I left that up to him.

You know, I had to work like hell to get the damned thing done. It would've been better with a longer shooting schedule. It was really, truthfully, a matter of just trying to get it in the can, without it being terrible. I mean you get what you can, but you do not have the time to fix anything or fine-tune it at all.

Melchior remembered that he'd experienced a lot of interference from Pink during the making of the film, a lot of "Why don't you shoot it this way?" and "Why are you...?" and so on. Such behavior only made his job more difficult:

> Sid [had had] no experience in motion picture making other than as an exhibitor and as the partner of Norman Maurer on *The Angry Red Planet*. Norman was the working producer on the film. At the time it seemed that Pink's efforts were mostly in the promotion department. He is an excellent promoter. Unhappily, I know that Pink has badmouthed practically everybody who was involved in that film—including Norman and me—pitiful attacks and claims in his writings, and has claimed credit for every positive achievement for himself. For a long time that was one of the more scornful jokes around town—especially among those in the know. The truth is that Norman and I pulled Pink's effects chestnuts out of the fire and saved the day for him, and that is, of course, a hard thing to forgive.

Leo Handel was a visitor to the set during principal photography and related some of the problems that had arisen during the production:

> I visited the set and everything was fine. [But] I still remember—as a filmmaker it seemed absurd to me—they [needed] to move to another set, but there was no set. And then they found Sid Pink somewhere, and he was negotiating with a company about—as I recall, although it may have been something else like it—a free razor! I mean, you just don't do that: You make sure the set is ready [because] so many people are depending on it! But Sid was [trying to get something for free], and there were people waiting.
>
> [Sid Pink's claims about Ib] are pure fantasy. I know that Ib wrote the thing and directed it. I was on the set and I *know* that Ib made it... [Pink's] a very charming guy: That's the ammunition of con men. They're very charming. I mean you meet them and you're their best friend... We cannot explain why he acted the way he did. I mean, everything was there and he could've done beautifully, without problems, and made lots of money. But he had to go through all those business contortions...

Naura Hayden—she later changed her name back to that from Nora— who at one time partnered with Pink, was also puzzled by Pink's claims against Melchior:

> I don't understand Sid's attitude and why he [would say] these things. Sid was a frustrated director, I think, and he'd always look over Ib's shoulder and try to second guess him. He really wanted to direct. Perhaps that's why.

During post-production it was decided by Pink that a better title was needed. At the suggestion of an exhibitor, he used a descriptive phrase Melchior had injected to describe their destination: *The Angry Red Planet*. It was a good choice, and put the film on a short list of notable 1950s titles, alongside *When Worlds Collide*, *World without End* and *This Island Earth*.

The Angry Red Planet premiered at the 4-Star Theater on Wilshire, and was attended by a host of show people, including Hedda Hopper, Barry Sullivan, Ester Williams, Debbie Reynolds, George Pal... even the Three Stooges. Melchior recalled:

> One of the people attending was the actor Don Taylor and he behaved very badly, very unprofessionally. He laughed at all the wrong times. He was really the only one. Perhaps he'd had one too many. I remember very little about it except that it got a good reception. There was one thing, which I found funny and had them take out. When Gettell dies, Iris shoots him out into space because, of course, she can't have a dead body on the ship. When she did it, it sounded like she had flushed the toilet. And I said, "You can't do that," and they cut it out.

Alex Toth remembered how hard his friend Norman Maurer had toiled on the film, and considered its experimentation in the face of a zero budget:

> For what was available, the effect came across all right [although] some animation art was used for the city on Mars that was obviously a strip of art pulled past on an animation stand...

Toth was more impressed with some of Melchior's live-action sequences than the special effects: "the opening shots on the airfield with the police escort, the man with the fungus on his arm were done very well and built up tension."

Young fans and space film enthusiasts with a taste for the weird loved the film when it was released widely in the summer of 1960. It was not a great favorite with critics, though a few found it "remarkably spectacular," or commented on its eerie effects and "fertile imagination." However, as time went on, the film was increasingly reviewed as one of the most novel space films of its time. Certainly a toll was taken by some of the hapless animation turned in by Ray Mercer's company in post-production: When the plot required a shot of the rocket in space, or a meteor zooming by, they

Assistant director Lou Perloff (left) and Ib Melchior on a brief break during production.

provided blatant cell animations. It was one thing to show a stylized semi-realistic creature in a surrealistic sequence, and quite another to try to pass off second-rate animation in a realistic setting.

But in the final analysis all the problems were academic: *The Angry Red Planet* went on to be a big hit for American International, who acquired it for release from Sid Pink and Norman Maurer's Sino Productions.

For Melchior, *The Angry Red Planet* would become a film closely linked with his name. He would look at it—a major accomplishment if only from an organizational standpoint—with a certain philosophy:

> It was kind of fun. I would like to have done it with a little bit different of a story, but I had fun with it, and it was a fun film. The same thing with *Robinson Crusoe on Mars*. It was in the same timeframe, within a couple of years, and we still didn't know about conditions on Mars... We were just beginning to play ball in space, so to speak...

More importantly, Melchior was now in the Directors Guild. His boyhood dream of being a Hollywood director had finally come to pass.

13 DEMON STREET

In the months prior to the release of *The Angry Red Planet*, Melchior spent time outlining plans for other space projects, including a film story that would eventually be produced by Paramount Pictures called *Robinson Crusoe on Mars*. It was, however, announced as "in preparation" for Hertz-Lion Productions in early 1960. Until then, Hertz-Lion kept him busy with current projects of their own.

Hertz-Lion was a company responsible for a number of very low-budget, low-quality efforts like *The Brain from Planet Arous* and others. In late 1959 they raised additional capital and were in the process of upgrading their product. Early in 1960, they announced a $4,000,000 dollar slate of features and TV projects for the year, among them Leo Handel's *Inside the Moon*, and a proposed TV series of "action stories from the Bible" titled *The Sword*, with Melchior to story edit. Also on their slate was *Killer Secret*, a feature adaptation of Melchior's *Life* magazine story about the search for Shakespeare's handwritten manuscript for *Hamlet*, based on Melchior's real-life experiences. But first they approached him to develop stories for their current television series, *13 Demon Street*.

The concept of the series was to fuse the mystery and ironic plotting of *Alfred Hitchcock Presents* with horror-supernatural elements. Its host was an unnamed, doomed arch-criminal played by Lon Chaney, Jr. When Melchior got involved, the show was already in production in Stockholm, Sweden, as a co-production with Svensk Filmindustri, with four episodes in the works, several under the direction of famed novelist-screenwriter Curt Siodmak. Gus Unger was the producer.

Melchior developed three half-hour tales, two of which were filmed. A review of them reveals a side of Melchior's writings that had never come to light: His penchant for short stories of the macabre. He completed the first installment, "A Gift of Murder," on February 2, 1960, It told the story of Jim Duncan, an American advertising executive recently relocated to a small town in Sweden. He is a "go-getter" who has come to set up a live-wire American-style advertising department at the growing Vikstrom Boat Yards.

Jim is angered by the brazen advances made on his wife, Betty, by young Carl Vikstrom—son of the boat yard's owner—at their 7th wedding anniversary party.

Jim finds among the anniversary offerings a peculiar gift—a "Do-It-Yourself Voodoo Kit." The instructions read, "performance guaranteed. If you want to revenge yourself on some enemy of yours by injuring him or her, follow these instructions. So simple a child of five can do it! Just paste a picture of the face of your intended victim over the blank one on the doll. Stick one of the pins into whatever part of the person you want to injure. If you want to kill, stick the pins squarely through the face itself!"

Needless to say he avails himself of the offer—in order to get rid of his boss' son.

He tests it first by damaging the younger Vikstrom's hand, then makes the fatal pin-strike to the doll's face: The result—Carl Vikstrom looses control of his car because of his voodoo-damaged hand and plunges to his death in a river.

Jim is promoted, but now finds himself attracted to Jana, the new secretary hired by the senior Vikstrom to help with the work load caused by his son's death. He finds himself plotting to kill Betty, his wife, to clear the way for a relationship with Jana. But Betty—already suspicious—swaps her photo with Jim's on the voodoo doll by scratching out and thereby eliminating the likeness of her image on the front side—leaving her silhouette only—and pasting Jim's image on the unseen back side. In the darkness of the candle-lit ritual Jim sees what he believes is Betty's image and plunges the needle squarely into it, which kills him instantly.

Lon Chaney closes the show with: "a diabolical murder in league with vile and hellish rites of voodooism—and all for personal gain and desires. Well, he'll never learn now that so often when you want to hurt someone else, you really hurt yourself!"

Voodoo was the subject of a number of similar shows of the era. Melchior's episode is distinguished by a classic construction that is both tight and ironic. Jim first damages Carl's hand, and it's the damaged hand that causes the fatal loss of control while driving near the river. Carl's death precipitates the hiring of temptation in the person of Jana, and his "putting the make" on Carl's fill-in mirrors Carl's advances on Betty earlier, the very behavior which started the whole series of events. Putting Jim's picture on the "mirror side" of hers on the voodoo doll closes the cycle.

Melchior's next offering, delivered March 21, 1960, was "Black Nemesis," a tale with a twist of humor. Again the Lon Chaney character opens up the show from within his creaky, timeworn house on 13 Demon Street: "Come, let me show you a crime in which the misbegotten criminal world violated not only the laws of the world—but also the laws of the unearthly world beyond!..."

This is the story of a phony mystic, Monsieur Aramit, "your guide to the World Beyond." Aramit fleeces the gullible elder citizens of London with his French affectations and cheap parlor tricks that seemingly conjure up ghostly apparitions of the dearly departed. But business is falling off, and his gambling debts are piling up. He must raise $1,000 by a certain deadline to pay off an obnoxious, cigar-smoking gambling house proprietor named Bernie Hawkins—or else!

Aramit targets the skeptical Mrs. Claire Standish, wife of the wealthy Doctor Robert Everett Standish. Aramit kills the doctor, then goes to work on Claire, manufacturing misty, ectoplasmic "ghosts" of her late husband and charging her a fortune to continue contact with him.

Aramit barely collects the amount needed by midnight from Claire to begin to pay his debts. Alone, the room is still dark from the seance as he turns to regard Hawkins' two "enforcers" who've shown up to collect. Aramit freezes as he sees behind them a ghostly ectoplasm begin to materialize—with a pale face starting to emerge within it. Is it Standish? Terrorstruck, he reaches for a gun. Before he can fire, the two henchmen, unaware of the apparition behind them, react more quickly and gun Aramit down, killing him instantly.

Seconds later, Bernie Hawkins steps forward. The "apparition' was Hawkins himself, stepping in out of the darkness. The ghostly "ectoplasm" was nothing more than billowing smoke from his cigar, backlit by the street light outside.

Aramit's guilt—like the famous "Tell-Tale Heart"—conjured a ghost in his mind's eye where there was none.

Especially interesting in this amusing tale is a ruse Aramit uses to help convince Claire of his powers. He makes a cryptic prediction supposedly from beyond: "When the fruit of man's labor, meant to be up high, is underfoot, you, the doubter, shall walk with regret on hallowed ground!"

Puzzling over this, she and her friend Helen are walking down the street minutes later when they come across a poor London street artist making a chalk drawing of a graveyard on the sidewalk. They are unable to go around it, so Claire reluctantly, walks over it. Helen is thunderstruck, realizing that Aramit's prediction just came true. She explains that Claire just walked on the artist's work, "the fruit of man's labor—underfoot. And a picture certainly is meant to be 'up high' ...And a grave is hallowed ground, you'll admit... and you didn't want to walk on it—you did it 'with regret'! How can you doubt Aramit now!?"

Aramit, of course, had paid the artist handsomely to set the whole thing up ahead of time in order to make his prediction come true.

Melchior's final entry, delivered April 15, 1960, was titled "Shadow from Beyond." The setting: Copenhagen.

Erik is a young artist-photographer involved in crime scene recreations. He has eyes on the fortune his model, Nita Hass, will inherit upon her marriage. Standing in his way is her violent-tempered stepfather, Otto, who sees through Erik's pretenses of romance.

As tempers flare, Erik bludgeons Otto with an ashtray, then quickly sets about to stage his death to appear accidental. He props the dead man so his head hangs over the edge of an elevator shaft at the rear of his studio: The elevator car is known by many to be defective and in need of repair. He sets up a scene so that it appears that the older Hass—known also for fits of fainting—has passed out and fallen near the elevator shaft. The car, it has been previously observed, always overshoots it's floor. This then will appear as if the car, in correcting it's overshoot, came down on the old man's head after he fainted!

Erik seems to have gotten away with the perfect murder. He continues his scheming romance with Nita and his photographic work. But camera work requires lighting, and lighting creates shadows. Now Erik suddenly finds himself haunted by an unwanted shadow whenever he is shooting. It is the shadow of a man—a man without a head! It drives him to near madness. Desperate, he stakes out a trap for the shadow creature: a ring of lights. When the shadow again appears, he will blast it with light from all angles, creating a trap for it in which there can be no shadows!

But the lights are accidentally triggered, temporarily blinding Erik. In a panic, he accidentally stumbles toward the elevator shaft in which he murdered Otto and plummets to his own death.

Erik's cover-up makes perfect sense: He is a photographer for a crime magazine, experienced in setting up props and actors in death reenactments. His attention to detail is painterly: He even goes so far as to reset Otto Hasse's wristwatch back in time, then smash it to establish the moment of death. He then goes to a tobacconist immediately thereafter, at the "adjusted" time of death, to set up his alibi.

Karen Kadler, Michael Hinn and Lon Chaney, Jr. in *The Devil's Messenger*, a film made from three episodes of *13 Demon Street*.

A particular macabre touch is the actual moment of beheading which recalls the earlier film *The Fly*: Erik must trigger the head-crushing elevator car from several floors below. The only indication of the grizzly occurrence above is the "subtle change of pitch of the elevator machinery, as if the car above had an obstruction to overcome in it's downward journey."

Thirteen episodes of the series were actually filmed, including two of Melchior's teleplays, "Black Nemesis" and "A Gift of Murder." The latter was directed by Curt Siodmak, the former by Jason Lindsey. The production values and direction, even being generous, were perfunctory to low-grade. And Lindsey rewrote the ending of "Black Nemesis," completely missing the point of the story. It was a totally wasted effort. "A Shadow from Beyond," the best of Melchior's stories, didn't make it to the production stage. More than that, Hertz-Lion had run into cash flow and other problems during production, and ultimately *none* of the episodes shot—including Melchior's stories—were ever aired in the U.S.

The series was not well-produced by any standards, and the low budgets undermined each of the episodes in different ways: lack of proper lighting, set dressing, camera coverage, etc. The production's very thinness, however, occasionally insinuated a frosty bleakness that lent the shows the kind of semi-underground mood common to non-Hollywood production of the era. Curt Siodmak shed some light on the less than ideal events surrounding the production:

> It was a television show of 13 pictures I shot in Sweden under terrible circumstances. The whole series was [then] called *Number 13 Demon Street*. They then edited some of the episodes in the U.S. without asking my opinion and that became the

film *The Devil's Messenger*. I asked my name to be removed. The company who did that could not sell it... but CBS saw it and liked it. They then did a whole series afterwards with Boris Karloff, using most of the stories from my 13 episodes. I had nothing to do with the film version, although I am credited as the [episode] director.

In the film version of the series, Lon Chaney's scenes were reworked so that his "arch-criminal" character became Satan himself bent on destroying the Earth with a nuclear bomb. The reedit was a desperate measure at best.

If his involvement on *13 Demon Street* didn't turn out so well, that was not the case with another "involvement" that came up around the same time, a chance meeting with a woman named Cleo Baldon—a woman of great intelligence and artistic sensibilities, already on her way to becoming a noted environmental designer. Melchior had recently been divorced when Cleo entered the picture. She recalled:

> Ib and I met at a party across a crowded room. We were sitting kitty-cornered across a coffee table. I had never heard of him. As a matter of fact, I just *hated* his tie! [But] he started telling a story and I kept moving closer. The story was so good I kept moving closer to him and it ended up in a one-to-one conversation." One thing led to another—including the exchange of phone numbers.

For Cleo, several things were immediately apparent at that first encounter: Aside from being a good storyteller, this man was intelligent, and seemed to have kept some difficult things in perspective—or at least he knew how to handle them. She recalled:

> The night I met Ib, somebody asked him about his father and he handled it so well. I could see a certain pain. Ib's one of those people, you know, block him one way and he goes the other way; he happens to be very smart. This thing of having a famous father set him aside. It didn't open any doors for him, even though people always thought it had done a lot for him. But that wasn't the case, and that kind of perception could get to be painful. I thought he handled this so brilliantly that I was attracted to that too...
>
> He said later the thing he thought was interesting was that as I was listening to him, I put my hand up and my earring just fell into it, so he thought I must be pretty sensitive if I could just *sense* my earring slipping!

THE DANISH FILMS: *REPTILICUS* AND *JOURNEY TO THE 7TH PLANET*

In early 1960, several months before the release of *The Angry Red Planet*, Melchior was again quickly involved in familiar territory: outer space—and a trip to a new planet. He would also revisit the type of material he'd worked with a few years earlier, *The Volcano Monster*. The situation?: AIP—impressed with the outcome of *The Angry Red Planet*—had created an opportunity for Sid Pink to make a couple of new science fiction films. Intent on directing them himself in Denmark, his Cinemagic Productions contracted with Melchior to develop screenplays for the proposed films from two verbally delivered story ideas of his. Ironically, by the time *The Angry Red Planet* was unreeling across the U.S., Maurer and Pink, the partners who'd originally started Cinemagic, Inc., with an eye toward producing a number of films, had split over profit and other disputes, and "newcomer" Melchior had, by circumstance, now become Pink's unofficial new partner.

One of the ideas was a straightforward monster project titled *Reptilicus*. The other was *Journey to the 7th Planet*—a space adventure intended as a follow-up to *The Angry Red Planet*, complete with giant serpent and insect creatures providing challenges to a small crew of space explorers.

Sid Pink, according to Melchior, got in contact with him in the early part of 1960 to discuss the two movie ideas. If Pink had any misgivings, as he later claimed, about Melchior's capabilities as a writer, they were—again according to Melchior—never made known to him, or to anyone else, as far as he was aware. Pink always treated him well.

Melchior, however, felt that it was essentially Jim Nicholson and Sam Arkoff who'd suggested him as a writer for the proposed projects. Melchior explained:

> AIP, I believe, wanted me. I would venture to say, Pink knew that I could deliver, even if he later said I was terrible, or believed that I didn't know what I was doing. Therefore, he knew that his investment, at least to that degree, was safe. I was a known entity, rather than someone he had not worked with before. He knew I could do this. Also, AIP had suggested to Pink that he use me again. I don't think they said to him he *had to* use me, but I think Pink realized—he *knew*—I could deliver.

Mid-March 1960: A meeting was held in the offices of American International between Melchior, Pink and various parties at the company. Pink talked about the two projects he had in mind. At a time when kids were lining up to see all manner of giant monsters—from the Tokyo variety to the King Brothers' just-released spectacle, *Gorgo*, AIP thought it wise to make a film of their own in the genre. Pink had agreed with the suggestion, and came in to the meeting with an idea for his own giant monster-on-the-loose story, *Reptilicus*. (This title was suggested by Melchior at the story session that followed.) The other idea discussed at the meeting was *Journey to the 7th Planet*, not quite a remake, but very much in the mold of *The Angry Red Planet*. Why mess with success?

Various ideas were exchanged. Melchior had been working on a story idea of his own about a serum that causes an organism to regenerate any body part, creating, when distributed among people, in essence, an indestructible society. He'd gotten the idea from reading about how reptiles and certain aquatic creatures such as starfish could regenerate entire limbs. He felt it might have applications to the monster story. What if a chunk of some ancient animal—a reptile in this instance—were found frozen deep below the ground and hauled up, say in a core sample or—borrowing a scene from the opening of his own 1958 script, *The Micro-Men*—caught in the drill bit of an oil well rig?

The story would, of necessity, be set in Denmark, since that was where the film was to be shot. Melchior, of course, was the perfect screenwriter from that standpoint. Being among the few Danish screenwriters in Hollywood, he could map out the creature's travels and the landmarks to be destroyed with relative ease and authority. Pink requested two other things: First, that the script feature a lot of military action, since he expected to get the cooperation of the Danish army and navy. Secondly, that the story should have two love interests—an American and a Danish one to provide a salable distribution angle for both the U.S. and abroad. One of the female leads, the prim American Connie Palmer, a representative from the United Nations, was to be played by Naura Hayden.

Melchior wrote up the thoughts that were discussed into a brief 95-word—more or less—story format. With this bare-bones summary, an agreement was drawn up and signed on March 14, 1960, and Melchior went off to develop the full screenplay. He was given 10 weeks to complete both *Reptilicus* and *Journey to the 7th Planet*, which was also briefly outlined in similar manner at the meeting.

Melchior recalled how the ideas came about during their discussion:

> The original idea for *Reptilicus* was just here's this big monster—where he came from, nobody knows; he just shows up, and now he's going to destroy the city. And I asked, how do you get a big monster today? I thought the story needed something. Regeneration was my idea. And I came up with the idea of finding a frozen piece of a creature that could *regenerate* itself. There are many creatures that can regenerate themselves, even from a small part. We all regenerate to some extent. Everyone

> knows about a lizard losing its tail and regrowing another one. A worm you can cut into several pieces and it will regrow itself and a starfish can regrow its entire body from just one arm. This is regeneration. There is a scene in the film where that is all explained. Now supposed you have a huge monster doing the same thing—that's where I got the idea —and it gave me a wonderful ending.

The ending, which would show a bit of the blown-off creature—it's claw—beginning to regrow at the bottom of the sea, was, as hard as it is to believe, unique and new at the time. Most stories ended with the monster clearly destroyed. The implication of a creature coming back to life again was just beginning to occur in films; even in the case of sequels, the preceding film never provided the "set up."

After the meeting, Melchior went off to work on the screenplay, arming himself with maps of Copenhagen to remind him of street names and locales he could destroy with his typewriter. Melchior recalled:

> I knew Copenhagen and obviously I used that knowledge so I didn't go from one place that was six miles away to another in one second. And I just began to do a lot of [other] research. Research is a wonderful thing. And I found out more about starfish... And I found out about other organisms, where even a *small* piece can regrow the entire organism. And I thought, "Why not?"—If this is *science*, if this is not just something made up of thin air, *it exists*—all you do is run with it a little further... And this, at least, made sense as to how that damn monster came about.

Melchior wrote the entire script himself based on the agreed-upon verbal storyline, contrary to Pink's later assertion that he wrote the script. In any event, Pink was, by all accounts, very happy with it. Melchior stated:

> I always tried to do one thing: to have *logic*. I do not think it's good to simply drop something in. I tried in everything I wrote to not have any loose ends. It's got to make sense. If anything, that's what I tried to do in my science fiction films. I've not always been successful, but we're not always successful in everything we do anyway.

But, after all, what was most important for the studio was that the story feature massive destruction, scenes of the monster trampling through the city and a lot of military action. Melchior had that last count sewn up pretty well too, given the personal war experiences he could draw upon. Not surprisingly, the tactical maneuvers, military dialogue and strategy in the screenplay were strong and authentic. Melchior made the monster as much of a war machine as a giant reptile; a true juggernaut, able to fully regenerate itself, heal even its most catastrophic wounds, take to the air, move across the land and live under the sea.

Reptilicus had a greater shot at immortality than most screen monsters—blow him up and each and every little piece would regenerate into a whole new *Reptilicus*. With enough attempts on his life, the entire planet would be buried beneath his descendants. As one of the characters says near the opening, "Never know what you'll run into when you drill holes in old mother Earth. Sometimes she resents it, and you're apt to find yourself smack in a mess of trouble."

On paper Melchior's script became a lively enough war adventure—man vs. this one-monster army. The scenes of destruction came easy, a combination of those real-life experiences in World War II, as well as his earlier work on *The Volcano Monsters*, where the extensive use of miniatures suggested a lot of possibilities to Melchior. It was only later that he fully realized how much more experience the Americans and Japanese had acquired over the Danish technicians in the area of special effects.

Reptilicus itself was described by Pink as a serpent with a bat's head. Melchior retained mostly the serpent idea, and described the creature as a composite being with "characteristics of the giant dinosaurs and a colossal flying Pteradon." He is descended from an era of experimentation in nature, making him "one of nature's ill-fated attempts to take the important, evolutionary steps from reptile to mammal."

The creature—at least on paper—read impressively:

> In the center of the meadow, *Reptilicus* is drawing himself up to his full gigantic height... and for the first time the men see the hellish, noisome creature they are hunting... *Reptilicus* is nearly full grown, towering 80 feet into the air! His body is long and slender, almost evilly snake-like—with a long pliable tail; he is covered with huge, overlapping, bony scales. Big tufts of coarse, black hair stick out from between the scales—especially around the neck; the rear legs, on which he stands, are sturdy and squat; his forelegs are grotesquely small—but with long, sharp, cruel claws. From his sides sprout a pair of huge, long, tapering wings, almost like giant bat wings; not as yet developed enough for flight, they are folded against his sides. On his long neck sits a hellish abomination—the head of *Reptilicus*... His head seems to be a deformed cross between the ugly, triangular head of a rattle snake, and the malicious features of a vampire bat! Huge, slit-pupiled eyes gleam coldly and cruelly; venom-dripping fangs menace from the

Reptilicus roars in pain as his outer armor and wings are burned away by a flamethrower. The Danish technicians managed to keep the wires from burning during the sequence.

slimy, gaping maw, and bony, scaly protuberances give the whole misbegotten creation a savage, demoniac appearance...! The monster roars with rage.

Later, when caught in a flamethrower's inferno, he is roasted, blinded and sent fleeing into the sea near death, only to return good as new two days later ready for more trouble. He now secretes an oily substance that protects him from any further use of fire. The scientists realize that the creature's body learns how to build up protections against any weapons. Now *Reptilicus* unfurls his wings and takes to the air, destroying huge areas of countryside and parts of Copenhagen with impunity. Heavy artillery can't be brought into play against him for fear of scattering his parts everywhere. His destruction must be carefully planned. The military sits by, almost at a standstill.

THE PRODUCTION

Two versions of *Reptilicus*—one American and one Danish—were shot in and around Copenhagen simultaneously over the greater part of three months in the summer of 1960—an 86-day shooting schedule, according to Pink. Pink directed the English version, and the veteran Poul Bang the Danish version. Denmark's well-known Saga Studios provided four stages, personnel and a portion of the equipment.

Behind the camera for both versions was one of Denmark's top cameraman, Aage Wiltrup, a capable cinematographer, who at 44 years of age was a veteran in the business—and handsome enough to have been an actor himself. He recalled that he shot the very first sequences undertaken on the film—the depth-bombing of the submerged *Reptilicus* by Coast Guard cutters—on June 23, 1960, adding that the scenes were shot without Pink's involvement. Pink was overjoyed—according to Wiltrup's son Thomas, speaking for his father—and commented that if the rest of the footage was as good as the first, the film would be a great one.

One of the film's visual selling points—among the few, actually—were the huge scenes of panic in the streets of Copenhagen—involving about 2,500 extras—arranged for by Pink, truly second only in numbers to those organized for the much bigger film, *Gorgo*. Multiple cameras—five in all—were set up above, below and alongside the Knippelsbro [a bridge] to capture the action of stunt bicyclists taking a tumble into the river below when the panic-stricken engineer opens the draw bridge. Wiltrup was again involved in the capacity of unofficial second unit director working to capture the sequence. Unfortunately, there were problems with a couple of the cameras, by Pink's account, and not all the action was fully covered. Especially unfortunate in that the stunt work was very daring—and *very* dangerous.

Wiltrup's frustration with the bridge scene, as with many other shots in the film, related to what he felt to be poor editing. The editor had failed, for instance, to eliminate such glaring errors as a man laughing and staring at the camera in the middle of the supposedly frightened exodus on the bridge.

Wiltrup thought the Melchior script had potential that was not directed to best advantage by Pink. He and his crew pitched in as best they could. The Danes, however—though experienced technically—had had little exposure themselves to science fiction, as this horror movie was labeled there, and some of the specialized equipment simply was not available. Added to that was Pink's own lack of experience as a director.

Throughout the production, Wiltrup kept his camera with him wherever he went, even on days off, in an effort to catch various bits and pieces described in the script. For instance, he ventured out one rainy evening amidst a terrible thunderstorm to capture flashes of lightning needed for the stormy night scenes of the monster's escape. *That*, according to Wiltrup's son, was his father's level of dedication.

Pink was somewhat handicapped by the loss of his onetime associate/right-hand "man," Naura Hayden, originally slotted to star in the film. She had decided to drop out of the production when she refused to share, by Pink's account, equal billing with the German actress Ann Smyrner. According to Hayden, she did not really like the project—a monster movie—and had decided to move on to other things.

Danish-born Mimi Heinrich played young Karen Martens—the requisite professor's daughter and love interest of Svend, the man whose drill brought up the bloody flesh of the creature. Heinrich had had a successful career as both a comedienne and actress in that country, with almost 20 feature credits in several countries to her name when the film was made. According to her:

> [*Reptilicus*] was the first science fiction made in Denmark. I'd been playing a lot of dramatic parts, not all comedy. I thought it was kind of fun that somebody wanted to make a sci-fi picture in Den-

Carl Ottosen, Ann Smyrner and Marlies Behrens—the Danish stars of *Reptilicus*.

mark. There was an American and a Danish version shot at the same time. I remember I was called out to where they made the film—I'd made a lot of films in Denmark—and they asked me if I would be interested in coming out to talk to Sid. I read some for him. He asked me a lot of questions, and I got the part.

I thought it was kind of a crazy idea really, because we were not used to it [science fiction]. But also, *because* of that, I thought it was a very good idea... I saw Ib's name on the script, and that made the whole difference. So, of course I wanted to be in the film. It was Ib's script, and I liked Ib very, very much. I'm still very fond of him. He's such a gentleman. You feel comfortable and happy about things when you're around him.

Once live action wrapped, there was the matter of the miniatures to be shot. Pink had hired a man named Kai Koed, an experienced model builder, to construct a miniature version of portions of Copenhagen, along with a lightweight marionette to repre-

Reptilicus may have run out of time in his quest to destroy Copenhagen.

sent the creature—the same, semi-reliable technique that had been employed to motivate the batratspidercrab critter in *The Angry Red Planet*. The problem with the new film was that the creature would have to be on screen about 10 times longer! Though there were later claims that Denmark's animation specialist, Bent Barfod, had been brought in by Pink to redo the *Reptilicus* creature via stop-motion photography, no evidence exists that anything of that nature was ever done on the film.

Built at a cost of, reportedly, 50,000 kroner, the mini-city had to be constructed mostly of various types of card stock atop wood framing. The project was ambitious to say the least, and if the results looked like what it was—with some exceptions—the fault lay in the lack of money and real expertise in the area of miniature effects—a difficult art.

Aage Wiltrup was called upon to film the miniature sequences. That alone was unusual in films. Such specialized work was ordinarily assigned to technicians specifically trained in the field. His job was complicated by the very smallness of the scale, and the fact that most of the scenes with the monster would have to match the unforgiving demands of the daylight sequences shot with the actors. It would've been prudent on Pink's part, perhaps—had he thought that far ahead—to have set his destruction scenes at night instead.

Melchior's script called for numerous miniature shots; extremely ambitious by any standards. There were many, many scenes to be shot with the *Reptilicus* puppet being operated on wires. Wiltrup consulted with a famous musician friend of his—a guitarist—in order to get his hands on the finest piano or guitar wire available for the puppet. He did this even though he observed—after viewing two screenings of an

American horror movie that employed a creature on wires—that the vast majority of filmgoers were too distracted by other things in most scenes even to notice the wires. Still, he attempted to hide them as best he could. He shot the scenes, looking for two to three second moments in which everything worked perfectly. He never dreamt the editor would leave in entire shots—essentially his outtakes—in which wires had become visible and backgrounds had gone out of focus. He was much happier with the later American cut of the film supervised by Melchior and editor Anthony Carras, with its faster cutting and optical enhancements.

Wiltrup's real complaint, according to his son, were with Pink's *laissez-faire* approach to directing. He recalled how Pink would show up, look at the miniatures and comment, "The models are too small; they should be this big," then disappear for a week or so having provided nothing more than hand-gesture approximations but no drawings as an indicator of what he had in mind. When Pink came back, according to Wiltrup, he said, "No, no—the houses are still too small"—and expect the models to be redone without paying for them.

Obviously if the recollections are accurate, as they appear to be, Pink would've been better off sticking to producing instead of directing.

Mimi Heinrich recalled:

> [*Reptilicus*] was quite difficult to film. People were not used to this kind of movie. And Sid was difficult to work with because he didn't understand what was going on all the time. Not to put him down, but he might not have been the best director in the world... He didn't let us know this was the first film he was directing.

American International was not happy with *Reptilicus* as it had been turned in by Sid Pink. But for all the work that'd been done on paper, the film had some degree of production values—including the crowd scenes—and several very attractive female stars. There was also the nicely photographed, if superfluous and badly edited, travelogue footage of Copenhagen, an effective opening sequence in which the oil-drilling team dredges up a bloody chunk of *Reptilicus*'s tail and a creepy end shot of the monster's severed claw returning to life on the ocean floor. But the rest of it...?

The list of problems was long. The monster itself appeared to exist in its own world separate from the actors, and much of it was obvious puppet work. The film suffered the lack of a discerning hand in staging actors and setting up sequences, as well as in the handling of post-production decisions. Carl Ottosen's performance was mannered and stilted to

Rare behind-the-scenes shot taken on location during filming of *Reptilicus*.

the point of caricature, and some of the other actors, who were of several nationalities, spoke with unacceptably thick accents, and had apparently been instructed by Pink to speak very deliberately to accommodate dubbing. And the special effects had proved to be beyond the means of the budget and resources available. Kai Koed's models were extremely ambitious, but hardly convincing, cardboard-like constructions. They might have slipped by with less screen time.

The actions of the creature itself—operated by two to three people—were severely limited to begin with, and further hurt by the sloppy editorial supervision that failed to cut shots short—as had been Aage Wiltrup's recommendation. He'd shot the material expecting that two or three second cuts of the puppet would work all right, if the right pieces were used: Pink and his editor insisted on holding on many shots, even as the puppet veered completely out of the operators' control. With more careful editing the marionette quality would've been much less of a problem. As it was, the editing only served to give marionettes a bad name.

Journey to the 7th Planet

And what would one ultimately find on Melchior's version of the seventh planet—Uranus—millions of miles from the Earth? Probably not a dense forest with a trickling stream, a village complete with a blacksmith shop, barns, and thatch-roofed, candle-lit cottages, a windmill near two tall birch trees and the Queen of Light! But this was, at least, what his international crew of five found instead of the expected atmosphere of poisonous, ammonia and methane gasses frozen at -200°. At least until they discovered they'd landed in a piece of world constructed of pure thought made solid.

Journey to the 7th Planet owed its beginnings to the same March 1960 meeting at American International that gave birth to *Reptilicus*, but was, by far, the more interesting concept. Sid Pink brought in an idea very much like *The Angry Red Planet*, in which explorers tangle with dangers on a distant planet.

His story ideas were discussed verbally at the meeting—nothing had yet been written down at that point—and Melchior put together an 83-word storyline based on their discussion: A landing is made on Uranus, where some kind of super-intellect creates an Earth-like area to test the spacemen's abilities prior to the creature's planned relocation to Earth. According to the original meeting notes, the intellect creates a robot man and woman and various [not described] monsters for the men to encounter. The men find a way to destroy the intellect and escape. The robot woman, who they try to take back with them, disappears once they leave the planet.

Melchior remembered:

> Pink just had some thoughts about a universal mind... The stories for both *Reptilicus* and *Journey to the 7th Planet* you could write on the back of an envelope. First of all, I didn't select Uranus. Pink did. Venus we knew was impossible. First of all, it was too damn hot—we knew that a long time

> ago. Same with Mercury. We did not know everything about Mars, but we felt it *might* sustain life. But we didn't know what kind of creatures, if there were any, might be there. The places I selected for my stories were Mars and Titan: Titan had an atmosphere. Most of the planets outside of Mars though are un-landable if you will...
>
> The seventh planet, Uranus—well, we didn't really know anything about it, not much at all. I just decided if you go up there and find nothing but gasses, where does that leave you? So, never mind what the *exact* truth is about this planet. I decided to just invent something that would work. But the idea was Sid's of going there—the idea of somebody—some*thing*—using people's minds to create things.

The last point apparently was interposed later by Melchior, since the notes from the story meeting gave no indication that the intellect was extracting thoughts from the humans.

As far as the question of the great distance that would have to be traveled, and the use of stock footage and miniature shots of a one-stage rocket to get there, Melchior felt, though a fudge, it was a reasonable one for the time:

> That was the kind of thing that was universally accepted. The same idea that everybody in the universe spoke English: It is ridiculous, it is nonsensical... but it worked for a certain kind of story.

The basic idea Pink clearly derived from *The Angry Red Planet*. The lineage reveals itself in an earlier draft of *The Angry Red Planet* in which Melchior described the idea of the planetary force as a kind of "super brain... a great power in control of all the forms of life on Mars." In that draft, the word "good!" appears in what is apparently Pink's handwriting next to this description. *Journey* expanded on that seed of an idea, which gave it a coincidental surface resemblance to Ray Bradbury's 1948 story "Mars is Heaven."

Melchior's basic plot involved a crew of five astronauts who take off in the year 2001 to investigate puzzling signals coming from the planet, only to be overcome by the mental power of an alien thing—a huge brain-like creature that lurks beneath the surface of Uranus. They are subjected to beautiful and horrifying material reconstructions projected out of the very substance of their memories. They revisit places from their childhood that magically appear, and fight monsters representing their own subconscious fears. Finally they face and destroy the creature that has taken command of their thoughts.

As with *Reptilicus*, Melchior went off to write the screenplay—writing it concurrently with the monster movie—in April and May 1960.

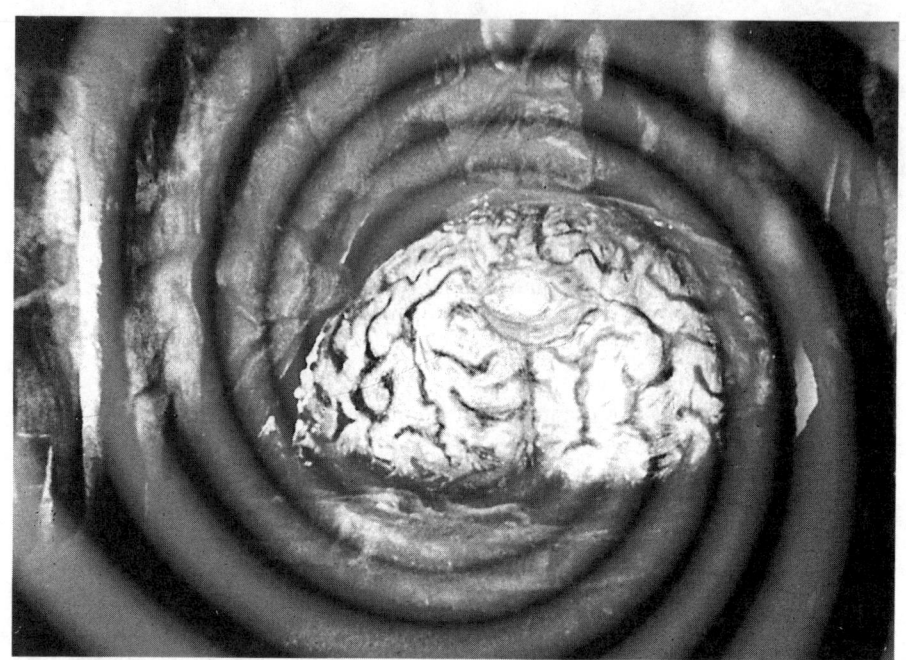

Literal visualization of brain-like mass in a sub-Uranian cavern, resembling a human brain, had to be optically disguised with spirals and floating colors in *Journey to the 7th Planet*.

What I had in mind at that time was that when the [alien] picks your mind for information, it would only see what you see. It did not realize that there were, for instance, *roots* under the trees; It didn't really know there were other things to it, which is, I think, a fun idea. It's just the surface it's aware of. The apple tree, for instance: It stands to reason: When you visualize it in your mind, you don't see the roots. You know that they're there, but you don't see them. You don't see inside of things...

Journey to the 7th Planet is about the next step in what I *do* believe in: I do believe we have a capacity, however very limited, of things like ESP. I believe that we can occasionally do things with our subconscious minds that we cannot do consciously. As an example: At UCLA a doctor there let me watch a hypnosis session. The subject wore a short-sleeve shirt, and the doctor took a pencil and told him, "See, this is a hot poker"—and he touched it to his arm. The man thought he was being burned, and the pencil raised a *welt* right on that spot. His *mind* had told him his body that he'd been burned. Now, I saw this with my own eyes

> under controlled conditions. All the body's defenses had come to the forefront and raised that welt. I believe we might be able someday to do the reverse of that and *heal*.
>
> It was really the mind, totally the mind that did this. Is it not possible that somebody—or something—in the future may have other powers, to be able to read your mind, to actually visualize what is in your mind. From doing that to *recreating* it, is another step. So, in essence, this alien had simply a way-in-the-future ESP ability.

Melchior's belief in the powers of the mind extends to the writing process itself. Long ago he'd developed methods of accessing the mind's deep, creative centers:

> When I write, a lot of my writing is done when I'm asleep. During the day there are all kinds of things that intrude on your thinking: The light coming from the window, a noise in the corner... these are all things that intrude. When you're asleep, nothing intrudes except your own mind. I keep a pencil and a little note pad next to my bed. I don't wake up. I just scribble on it and in the morning the notes are just strewn all over the place. But that's where I get ideas. Your subconscious mind never stops working, even when you're asleep. It keeps thinking, What about this? and How about that?—and suddenly you get ideas. It is a problem-solving thing. I've come to rely on my subconscious mind *enormously*.

That process was particularly appropriate for a story about a creature that sucked out the subconscious thoughts of its victims.

It was up to Melchior to provide the *7th Planet* story idea with a fully developed plot, characters and incidents, and, as well, define the alien's abilities, powers and Achilles Heel. He decided that instead of some kind of robot woman why not make this a recreation of a real woman from the mind of one of the crew members—his ideal woman. And if the alien created a woman for one of them, why not the others? And not just create *any* women, but women who represented something significant in their lives. Past lovers, infatuations, childhood sweethearts and—in the case of one of them—his wife, as his mind's eye saw her as a radiant beauty. Likewise monsters would arise from their own internal images of things they irrationally feared—insects in one case, snakes in another.

Melchior decided that the landscape created for them by the alien should have some significance as well, and had it originate from one man's childhood memory of a forest he had played in as a youngster. And in this wooded garden, thoughts and wishes come true: An apple tree appears next to a crew man who loves apples. At another point, the commander recalls Skaane, the village he grew up in Sweden, and two big birch trees and an old windmill that had been visible from his room. At the same time, behind him, they come into existence exactly as he describes them. In a reverie, he imagines a certain vision of perfection, recalled from a festival on St. Lucia's Day held in his childhood village, when the "Queen of Light"—the prettiest girl in the town— would appear, wearing her gown of white and a crown of candles, to give the other children of their village her special cakes. He thinks she was the most beautiful thing he's ever seen. Later, he visits the materialized village and encounters the adult incarnation of this childhood icon, Ingrid—a literal "dream come true." The captain is shaken by feelings he has never allowed himself to have before.

Melchior had drawn upon his own memories of rural Scandinavia in writing the scene. Osa Jensen, Melchior's childhood friend, recalled just such scenery in their native country:

> There were several villages with thatch-roofed cottages and windmills, and houses with grass on the roof, though many of them don't exist any more. And birch trees were quite common... In the spring when the tiny, bright green leaves came out, everyone would go into the forest and gather branches and say, "See, spring is coming now"—because we had such cold, cold winters.

Melchior added:

> Of course I knew what all that might look like, so I created the blacksmith shop, the birch trees and village and all that from living there.

Interestingly, the story is a science fiction version of the kind of seasonal changes that occur in parts of the world, like Denmark: a cold, frozen land in winter that briefly experiences a summer thaw. In the film, of course, it is the alien intelligence that sweeps away the winter landscape and creates an oasis of artificial spring—complete with its birch trees and apples. It is also a perhaps subconscious reflection of Scandinavian and Anglo-Saxon literature's emphasis on the ephemeral, the transient nature of all things. The changing of seasons...

Melchior imagined an invisible wall extending around the forest—like a sectioned-off area for animals in a zoo. It separated the recreated forest from the actual, frozen landscape of the real planet. His version of the alien planetscape, with its deep crevasses, caves, winding passageways, glacial vistas and ice-crystal forest may have drawn some inspiration from Jules Verne's *Journey to the Center of the Earth*. One of its characters almost drowns in a cavern full of salt: On Uranus, one of the men is almost lost in a pit of quicksnow—frozen ammonia crystals so cold its particles lack cohesion.

But Melchior conceived his world as a far more dangerous place than that of Verne's fantasy. Razor-sharp ice crystals capable of slicing open the crew's vital pressure suits

A rare shot from *Journey to the 7th Planet* as astronauts battle a giant serpent represented here by a full-sized prop. The sequence was re-cut in U.S. and new effects generated.

hinder them at every turn; and they must continually cope with temperatures, at -200°, capable of freezing them solid in seconds. In the course of their struggle, the explorers also encounter exotic creatures, including a giant mole-grub which they bury under tons of rock, and the intelligence itself—a nasty mass of brain cells that ultimately eats away one man's legs with expelled corrosives.

An oblique reference is made to the story of *Beowulf*, in the latter encounter: The men approach the alien intelligence in its lair—the science fiction equivalent of a dragon in his cave who menaces, traditionally, the entire village—armed with their "sword," an oxyacetylene torch. In *Beowulf*, the dragon destroys the hero's sword and burns him: In Melchior's tale, the monster brain makes the "sword" disappear and burns away his legs with its atomic fire.

It is at the force-barrier that the space travelers discover the planet's true nature. One of the men foolishly thrusts his arm through the barrier—not knowing what is on the other side—and screams in agony as his arm turns white, instantly frozen. In actuality, Melchior himself had the unusual opportunity to experience nearly the same thing himself—to actually step into a chamber that maintained the deadly cold temperature of outer space—without a space suit. He explained:

> At Eglin Air Force Base in Florida they had a huge experimental hangar. And part of that was the special environment where they had lowered the temperature to that of outer space. The reason they'd

Karl (Peter Monch) sticks his arm through the force field on Uranus and has it nearly frozen off as John Agar, Carl Ottosen, Ove Sprogoe and Louis Miehe Renard try to help in *Journey to the 7th Planet*.

done that was because they were getting ready to send a capsule around the moon which they had to fire by remote control on the dark side, and they weren't sure it would work in the extreme cold. So they had to experiment with those exact conditions. While we were there they said, "If you'd like to see what it is like, you can go inside, *but*, when you get in there, do *not* breathe, stay in there only for a count of five, and don't touch *anything* because you'll stick to it and you will freeze. Just go in there and feel it, and come right back out again." So we went in, and immediately, I could feel the cold going "SSSSH-K" [indicating the cold traveling through his body]... and we stepped out, and in less than a second we were white. We were so cold the moisture in the air condensed on us. I actually experienced what that guy in *Journey to the 7th Planet* did when he stuck his arm through the force field. The feeling of it you can't describe. Imagine being dreadfully, dreadfully cold and having that travel up and *inside* of you in a split sec-

> ond. There was no pain because it was so fast. We were pale when we got out. If we'd stayed in there a moment longer we would've frozen to death.

Unlike the character in the film, he hadn't stayed in long enough to feel the burn of being frozen to the core—but he at least knew how frightening such cold could be.

In Melchior's initial draft, dated November 21, 1961, there are seven, not five, astronauts that are dispatched to Uranus. Soon after, he did a little trimming and eliminated Norwegian Ensign Olaf Bjornson and Italian maintenance engineer Anthony Minelli, a caricature of ethnically clichéd comedy relief. In addition to reducing the character roster, he also deleted one of his script's quirkiest scenes—in a barn in the village, Olaf meets a lonely girl, Helga, dreamed up for him by the alien. He is shy and confused, unsure of what to do. Under pretext of showing Olaf how to milk a cow, Helga takes his hand. He is still unsure where to go from there. The cow sees this and kicks him over. He tumbles with Helga into the hay—and into her arms. As they kiss, the cow watches them, obviously acting as another pair of eyes for the alien. An alien able to induce romance—through the actions of a farm animal—introduced an odd element that lasted only as far as the first draft.

Two nice touches were also, unfortunately, deleted by Pink: first, the appearance of astronaut Svend Viltoft's plain-Jane wife, who is recreated by the alien as Svend lovingly sees her in his mind—as a radiant beauty; and, second, the entire reason for their trip in the first place—a threat to the safety of the Earth. The latter entailed a 15-page sequence that detailed the hurried gathering of a crew assembled to seek out the source of a potentially Earth-destroying bombardment of pulsar radiation emanating from the seventh planet—a radiation that mysteriously ceases upon their landing. With Pink's deletion of this opening sequence, several references to this radiation, still left in the film, are a bit puzzling. The deletion also reduced some of the story's urgency, although the characters continue to track the creature, often visible in a haze of blue light. Considering the limitations of his budget, Pink probably had little choice but to make the deletions

Throughout the script the alien's radiation is monitored by Geiger counters. Melchior had gained extensive knowledge of radioactivity and atomic power via dozens of documentaries he'd written and directed for Leo Handel and the Atomic Energy Commission in the 1950s. He was accurate to the point of insisting that every time the alien made use of its atomic radiation it would be accompanied by the kind of blue glow witnessed in real life when unstable matter releases neutrons. Melchior was familiar with the dangers of exposure to such radiation. At least two weird and horrifying atomic accidents had occurred in the late 1940s at Los Alamos that could have served as a prototype for scenes in the film. In one, a technician grabbed two hot halves of a nuclear device in a laboratory in order to prevent a catastrophic explosion. The proximity of the halves released a burst of neutrons visible, according to witnesses, as an intense eruption of blue light. The burst was centered near the man's stomach, which immediately began to blister. Within a short time, his entire body began to disintegrate, and he died soon after.

Melchior mixed quite a few mythic elements into what might have been just a monster story on another planet—the men find a Garden of Eden forest, complete with the proverbial apple tree. There is a formidable barrier to cross, a virginal guardian who may be a guide or sorceress, an underworld with dragons for the hero to slay, the use of amulet-like radiation counters to guide the men, the climactic destruction of the land of youthful innocence and the gained knowledge that the greatest enemy may just be one's own self. There are also several Hollywood-style Eves in the form of beautiful women from the astronauts' past lives who try to tempt them into giving up their mission, while their minds are being probed for weaknesses by a force that dwells, like the devil, in a place hot and below ground. And, as if under the devil's spell, they quickly decline in morale and discipline, falling prey to what they know is in actuality just a material illusion. They finally realize their folly in falling for the false manifestations, and cross into the underworld to face and destroy their demons.

A giant serpent added further archetypal reference, as described by Melchior:

> It is coiled around the rocks, a huge, fearful serpent-like creature with a hideous head fully three feet across. There is one large eye in the center, two stubby deformed horns and a double set of curved, scimitar-like mandible fangs... The body is covered with slimy, sickly gray-green scales... the reptilian slit pupil of the eye expands and contracts rhythmically... [It] seems to be devouring time and space itself.

This actually marked the return of the one-eyed serpent: It was originally a creature—later deleted—that the space travelers battled after encountering the batratspidercrab in early versions of *The Angry Red Planet*. Melchior thought the creature—originally dreamed up by Pink—made more sense in the new film with its obvious link to the story of the Garden of Eden—even though Melchior had no fear of snakes himself. On the contrary, he found them to be fascinating creatures and had handled them often.

As with *Reptilicus*, the entire script was Melchior's, not Pink's. Pink did, in fact, trim the first 15 pages, and rewrote the first few pages aboard the spaceship to some extent to cover the deletion. Otherwise, the script was pretty much shot as written by Melchior, except for the kind of minor changes that normally occur in shooting a film. Surprisingly, Pink was to claim and receive co-screenwriting credit on both *Reptilicus* and *Journey to the 7th Planet*, though no evidence whatsoever exists that would support an assertion of co-authorship on such a grand level. Pink had merely come up with a premise and several elements—monsters, women, etc. Melchior, though aware of the shared credit, let it slide. He kept records of all of his work filed away to satisfy any possible questions about his creative contributions to the Pink films, as well as all of his other collaborations:

> Sid came over to the house several times. Just to talk. I don't think I showed him anything until I was completely done. He wasn't coming over with ideas—no. No. None at all.

Melchior decided the world in *Journey to the 7th Planet* would be filled with caves, ice-flows and this crystal ice forest.

Pink must've had faith in the writer: At least he never expressed anything to the contrary, according to Melchior or any others at the time.

THE MAKING OF *JOURNEY TO THE 7TH PLANET*

The film was shot in Denmark on a budget of around $74,000. According to the film's cinematographer, Aage Wiltrup, it was shot at Palm Garden, an unused ballroom where the sets were all built, and not at Saga Studios as with *Reptilicus*. Pink used some of the same actors he'd employed on *Reptilicus*—Carl Ottosen as the commander of the Explorer 12, Ann Smyrner as his love interest and Mimi Heinrich as one of the Uranian girls, Ursula. John Agar and Greta Thyssen were the lone recognizable names to American audiences.

For Agar it was to be his second acting assignment in a space-related story, having at the time recently starred in the unaired pilot for a Paramount TV series titled *Destination Space*. It was also the second time he would be encountering a giant alien brain in a cave, the first being Howco International's infamous *The Brain from Planet Arous*.

Of *Journey to the 7th Planet*, Agar recalled:

> I didn't read for the part or anything like that. I got the script and it was okay by me. I wasn't at the peak of my career, so I listened to what my

agent had to say, and he advised me to take it. The budget was very low, well under $100,000, and... was shot in about six weeks. I don't recall much about the sets or the monsters... I just shut those things out to concentrate on my performance. Acting is using your imagination.

Agar made fast friends with his Danish counterpart, Carl Ottosen—affectionately nicknamed "Lil' Bro" by his acquaintances—and enjoyed sharing, between takes, the small shots of schnapps the Dane would bring with him to the set. It certainly took the chill out of the cold stages and blustery Danish weather. On the other hand it also forced the crew—again according to cinematographer Wiltrup—to put the space helmet on the actor in such a way as to hide his face from the camera when he'd had a little bit too much of "Lil' Bro's" brew!

The space housing all the sets was a mere 2,000 square-foot area divided into two 44-by-25 foot spaces, practically a garage operation. The film, consequently, had an extremely cramped feeling, alleviated only by one exterior location—representing parts of the forest—shot in an area called Sealand. Unfortunately, the frozen surface of Uranus, which cried out for big production values, was entirely shot on the small stage. Melchior's original suggestion to shoot some of the alien exteriors on location in coastal Greenland with its fantastic, snow-sculpted mountains, went unheeded. Melchior explained:

Ove Sprogoe is pleased to be served by one of the Uranian dream girls in this posed shot from Journey to the 7th Planet.

> I thought that Greenland icescapes would be great for the locations in the film... inasmuch as the film was shot in Denmark, and there are close ties between that country and Greenland. Almost any countryside close to a city or town would have been acceptable, and would have made a spectacular contribution to the scope of the film.

But location travel turned out to be unaffordable, and Pink was unable to find such a locale near the shooting stage. The area was too flat.

The budget restrictions taxed whatever resourcefulness Pink brought to the project, and took their toll on the film in numerous ways: A giant, insect-like mole-grub monster described in the script proved beyond the means of the prop department. Approximately 12 feet long, the grip-operated monster featured non-articulated eyes on stalks, giant claws and an obviously papier mache skin painted lobster red—hardly convincing. Then Pink found his ice-crystal forest constructed of bits of metal pointers apparently lifted off of street signs in the city. And the sets were tiny. The earlier-mentioned serpent monster, according to witnesses, also turned out poorly.

Pink, undaunted, was able to hastily revise his crystal forest, replacing blatant metal work with ice-blue painted tree branches. His cameraman, Wiltrup, struggled valiantly to create wider vistas by backing up on a wide lens and shooting from the studio rafters. Wiltrup also employed low-key illumination, strangely colored lights, shallow-focus photography and anything else in his power to mask the seams.

The actors were dressed in space suit costumes which showed a fair amount of imagination. They were based somewhat on a space card illustration of the time, and provided a colorful visual counterpoint to the film that also helped set the human figures apart from the drab planet sets. The suits came with the ubiquitous, military surplus high-altitude pressure helmets used in so many science fiction films of the late '50s. In this case they were painted a bright yellow to match the trim on the otherwise blue suits, and given odd, box-like face plates of plexiglass fastened to the helmet fronts. Wiltrup wisely saw to it that the reflective face plates, which were always a photographer's nightmare in space films, were designed to be angled *downward* to minimize light and crew reflections. He also utilized polarizers on the lenses for the same reason. This had the added effect of giving the colors a very saturated, completely flat look. John Agar recalled that the suits "weren't the greatest things in the world to wear, but they weren't too uncomfortable."

Melchior's concept for the brain-thing was a colossal creature whose entire mass was so large it was never fully visible, it's unseen body winding its way deep into the underground caverns. What was visible was to be almost 12 feet tall and 30 feet long. His description lent new meaning to the word colorful: "like a huge, monstrous brain, oozing into the cave from the archway... the big, unblinking, bilious green eye set in the convoluted, glutinous mass of motley gray, colored through with sickly yellows, slimy blues and angry reds, glares at the intruders—the jet black slit pupil devouring them like a fiendish pit to hell itself." The on-screen result?—an oversized human brain all of four feet tall with a thinly disguised headlight for an eye. Not the worst prop ever made, but not at all what it should have been.

Many eerie touches in the script did in fact manage to survive—barely—in Pink's production—an astronaut plucking an apple from a tree that but a moment before was not there; bushes pulled from the ground revealing no roots; the ship's commander relating memories of his childhood village, sitting by a campfire in an imaginary forest 500 million miles from Earth.

In spite of Pink's attempts, when the film arrived in the U.S., AIP found it unreleasable. The production problems were one thing. Worse, some of the actors exhibited the same stiff speech pattern AIP found unacceptable in *Reptilicus*, and would have to be dubbed. John Agar recalled:

> We came back and re-dubbed it because the accents were so thick. Yes, the actors spoke English,

A Cyclopean dinosaur is blinded by gun fire. This sequence was animated by Jim Danforth under the supervision of Melchior and editor Anthony Carras for *Journey to the 7th Planet*.

but not real clearly, which is why we did it over. Greta Thyssen lived in Europe, so she didn't dub her part in the U.S... Somebody else did. We also reshot some close-ups in the States.

According to Melchior:

I remember several things. The film was not cohesive... It lacked something in the beginning. And the special effects monsters were so bad, so amateurish it became unusable. Literally, in one of the monster scenes you could see they were built of chicken wire... If Pink *didn't* see it, I don't understand. And if he *did* see it, that I also don't understand. He had nothing else to show for it. It hadn't been covered properly. I wasn't there, so I wouldn't know. [The snake] was so amateurish... We did the opening which, at the time, had some novelty to it, though now it's old hat. I did the whole front montage.

They asked me to fix it up. I gave them a list of what we could do with it and a budget for the work. I remember doing [that] montage at the opening and recutting it. The montage I did myself. I'm not an editor, but I can edit. And we redid the monsters and re-dubbed it. I did several voices myself. J. Edward McKinley did one of the voices [Carl Ottosen's part]. I was on this fix up only two or three weeks, maybe spread out over a couple of months... working as post-production director within the limitations of the original film.

Certain scenes shot for the film were entirely eliminated, including some mild love scenes in the forest. One of the sequences occurred just after the men return from their first crossover to real Uranus and the encounter with the giant serpent: A half-dozen girls await them by a small pool in the woods—one of them Ingrid, who sits on a rock combing out her long fair hair "like a gorgeous Nordic Lorelei." The men avoid getting involved at this point. The entire encounter is summed up in the American version with a brief montage of previous encounters with the girls, a testimony to how bad the original material turned out. The men eventually find an excuse to pair up with their various dream companions—while the captain is unconscious from his leg wound. The scene was shot as written, but deleted by Anthony Carras and Melchior, though—at least in one of two slightly different versions made for U.S. release—a couple of cuts sans dialogue were left in:

> There were parts of it that were so bad they had to be cut out altogether... It may be that we just couldn't fix it. We had very little money. That's why we used stock shots.

Surprisingly, the effects created by the internationally recognized Danish animation expert, Bent Barfod, and talented miniature cinematographer Ronny Schoemmel, proved unusable. According to Pink, they'd employed a type of claymation to actualize the metamorphosis of the creatures. But it may have been that the very abstract nature of these effects, as Pink described them on several occasions, made them unacceptable for a commercial film. Or perhaps they simply didn't cut in well. Short pieces of the original film offer glimpses of what appear to be close-ups of a real reptile's eye, used, apparently, to represent the eye of the monster serpent.

The serpent creature was the first to be scrapped. Project Unlimited, a company already doing special effects patch-jobs on some of AIP's then-current films, was hired to produce a new monster. The final product—a kind of one-eyed dinosaur—was primarily the work of young animation genius Jim Danforth:

> I was working at Project Unlimited and they had sort of a loose arrangement with AIP... When they were trying... to upgrade [*Journey*] for U.S. release, they wanted new creature shots. Project Unlimited originally did them, I think, with a Kinkajou they had obtained from an animal man. They'd

> built up a little cave, then tried to get him to do the various things that they wanted. They squirted him in the eye with freon and so forth... I guess nobody bought it... I just know that every once in a while I'd go in on that particular stage and there'd be some of the people squirting freon at the Kinkajou and I sort of wondered if this was going to work.

Melchior angrily stated if he had known this was going on he would have put an immediate stop to such abuse—if he didn't kill somebody first. Danforth continued:

> The next thing I knew, we were building a—well, we dubbed the thing the "furry uni-optic" because it had one eye. We took the armature from the harpy that was made for *Jack the Giant Killer*.
> Then I took the wing armatures home and built hands over them, brought it back and then Wah Chang covered it with fur. They shot the whole thing once in this furry version and AIP didn't like it. They thought it looked too cute... when they saw it on the screen it wasn't what they wanted. So we had to do it all again. We stripped all the fur off and Wah made up some latex skin with scaled, reptile texture on it, covered it over and did it again.

By this time, however, the film had already been dubbed with a reference to the creature as being a rodent, as it had been originally intended in the fix-up process.

Next, the mole-grub with its visible chicken wire framing had to be replaced with even less money. Initially re-tinted scenes of the batratspider from *The Angry Red Planet* with a double-exposed spiral pattern was tried. This proved a bit too mercenary, the source film too recent. A second, final attempt utilized blue-tinted scenes from Bert Gordon's *Earth vs. The Spider*, in which a giant tarantula scuttled about a Carlsbad-for-Uranus cavern.

Another scene almost entirely cut: One of the men has his legs burned away by a freezing cloud of blue energy roiling out from the brain creature. The only remaining evidence of the sequence would be several stills of a space suit lying on the ground with skeleton feet protruding from the suit's torn open legs. Two different attempts were made to salvage the scene. One employed a miniature made of tripe roughly in the shape of the brain swelling up as if it had just absorbed something. This version was only seen in some release prints. Another version, the more common one, utilized a quick shot of the amoeba from *The Angry Red Planet* absorbing Jack Kruschen. In both versions, Carl Ottosen's original line "burned... burned away...." was re-dubbed, and replaced by the words, "buried... buried within it...."

In an odd twist, *Journey to the 7th Planet*, although it was shot after *Reptilicus*, was to be repaired and released first, in February 1962.

John Agar is almost done in by a giant mole-grub in a sequence cut from *Journey to the 7th Planet* when the creature's papier mache origins proved too hard to disguise.

Mimi Heinrich recalled:

> We played [our parts] without ever seeing any of the monsters. I think at the time we were shooting, they hadn't even finished making any of those. They were in a critical period because they didn't know how to do them. I think that's why they were made [over again] in America, because they couldn't make them here [in Denmark].
>
> It was Ib's script, and I was ready for anything he had written. It was a fun time, but I must say Sid Pink was not really my favorite. I can truthfully say I don't think he was much of a director. He was not very good. The script was good and it could have been a much better film than what came out of it... People were laughing when they saw the monsters and everything. I will say that it was not the best film in the world. What really was wrong was that Ib should have been there during the shooting. Things would have been much different. It was such a stupid idea not to have Ib in Denmark. First of all, he is a Dane and could understand the people he was working with. Sid

didn't understand anything. Ib had been ahead of time in his thinking about movies. Not so much with *Reptilicus* but with *Journey to the 7th Planet*. I think many films after that have been made in those patterns.

Melchior commented:

> I think the Danes had relied on Sid Pink, who must have told them he was a special effects expert, that sort of thing. They relied on him, and that was probably their biggest mistake. What his purpose was in doing *Journey* by himself in Denmark, I don't know... Both [*Reptilicus* and *Journey to the 7th Planet*] *did* have possibilities. Had I the chance to direct them... I hope I would have done a better job and avoided the dilettante feel those films achieved under Pink's direction... I think Pink would have been better off had he allowed his Danish partners in the film a little more say-so. But, since I was *not* involved in the production of either film, I really have no direct knowledge of what went on.

As to Pink's suggestion that Don, the character played by John Agar, was in reality supposed to be a repressed homosexual overcompensating by flirting with every girl around, Melchior simply sighed: "That's the first *I* ever heard about it!"

The film was imaginative enough—and fixed-up enough—to attract some favorable reviews: For instance, *The Los Angeles Herald Express* in its review of February 15, 1962 stated, "put *Journey to the 7th Planet* on your show-going list. It is a fanciful effort, highly imaginative in theme and mixture of mystery and horror." "There are some montage effects in the color process that are technically skillful," offered *The Hollywood Reporter*'s James Powers. And "Tube" of *Variety* noted: "Among the capable physical contributions to a film highly dependent for dramatic interest upon abstracts, miniatures, opticals and special effects are those of Montage Director Melchior."

In advertising the film, American International had in-house artist Albert Kallis create a copycat version of the poster art for *The Angry Red Planet*. Kallis, who confessed that he never actually saw most of the films for which he designed campaigns, created a crab-clawed spider creature much like the batratspider critter, chasing astronauts across an alien landscape complete with a futuristic city—all elements featured in *The Angry Red Planet* campaign. AIP clearly hoped to cash in on the success of the earlier film.

Hour of Vengeance

Melchior had a chance to act as associate producer on the film *The Case of Patty Smith* in 1962, working with his old friend, Leo Handel. He also continued to develop his epic story about survival on the red planet, *Robinson Crusoe on Mars*.

More importantly, from a very personal creative standpoint, he finally finished writing a stage play that was close to his heart: Titled *Hour of Vengeance*, it was a dramatization of the ancient Viking legend of Amleth that was the actual source for Shakespeare's *Hamlet*.

As a former actor and certainly as an author, Melchior had always been attracted to the works of William Shakespeare, but primarily to *Hamlet*. Aside from the inherent fascination with the melancholy prince as a figure of the theater, *Hamlet*—rooted in Danish lore—connected Melchior with the rich history of his Danish ancestry and their Viking heritage. Melchior's interest centered around the original Viking story that had provided Shakespeare with the foundation for his, arguably, most famous tragedy.

Melchior traced the play's origins to *The Chronicles of the Danish Realm* written by the Danish monk Saxo Grammaticus in about 1170. Grammaticus had, for the first time, set down the record of Danish history, culled from rune stones, from word of mouth, from ancient writings, from song and so forth. Melchior explained:

> In his 3rd and 4th book, Saxo had recorded the story of Amleth, a Danish prince who formed the basis of Shakespeare's tragic figure. Others before me had already made this connection to the famous *Hamlet*. I was interested in how much and why and how it came to be.
>
> Shakespeare's *Hamlet* came by way of, first, Amleth, then a French author who wrote a version of it. Later, a British playwright, Thomas Kyd, wrote *The Tragical History of Hamlet*—and so on. Shakespeare's *Hamlet* was actually version number four. The interesting story to me is how it evolved.

Melchior's studies came to a head in the early 1960s when, between his popular science fiction screenwriting, he began work on his own retelling of the Amleth legend, culminating in his well-received play *Hour of Vengeance*. The play was a new take—actually the old, *original* take—on the well-worn Shakespearean tale. In *Hour of Vengeance* Melchior recreated, as accurately as possible, the cunning and suremindedness of the first Hamlet that made this very real historical figure the antithesis of the tormented and melancholy Dane. "[He is] the *intrepid* Hamlet," observed Cleo

Baldon. "He's out to trick his uncle and become king. Not at all the Renaissance prince we know. It makes a much more understandable story." Melchior was interested in this "alternate-Hamlet" who is not at all confused, but the creator of confusion, a man who runs the machine of fate guided by one principal—that truth be served.

The Grammaticus story background is quite similar to that incorporated into the later plays, including Shakespeare's, but has many fascinating differences. Melchior explained the intricate dilemmas presented to the characters of the original story:

> By Viking law, Amleth had to kill his uncle, the king, Fenge, because the uncle had killed Amleth's father. Uncle knows that, and so now *he* has to kill Amleth. Amleth vows to kill uncle, and he vows to do it *without ever telling a lie.* Now his entire life manifests two meanings—the real one, and the one that *seems to be* real: Everything he says has two meanings. Therefore, he sometimes sounds like a totally demented person—a madman. He does that on purpose because *he* knows that *his uncle* knows that if one kills a madman, the demon that possesses that madman will fly into his slayer. Therefore, the madman becomes inviolate. *But*—is the madman really mad? The king has to find out, is he or isn't he? And Amleth has to bide his time and not do anything wrong. He has to find a way to say, "yes," for instance, that seems like "no." He speaks in riddles.

So Amleth, though suspect by Fenge the King of plotting, maintains his cover. He speaks the truth in a manner that seems mad. Amleth is asked by the king about his romantic tryst in the woods with the Queen's beautiful maid, Alfhild:

FENGE: And I am further told you carried off a maid into seclusion.
AMLETH: Into the thicket, Sire, there to be alone, with my Familiar Spirit—and with her.
BOLVIR: And did you—ah—embrace her?
AMLETH: Aye! In truth I did; and in our ardent rapture we rested on a horse's hoof and on a cock's comb. And also upon a ceiling.
FENGE: His ill-devised behavior. His filthy, shabby rags! His mind cannot be sound.

But others are wary:

BOLVIR: Strong hands are often hid beneath a shabby cloak.

Bolvir then points out that a cock's comb and horses' hoof are both types of *wildflowers* in the forest, and thatching straw—of which ceilings are made—also grows there in abundance! So is he mad—or clever? "Aye, my Lord," observes

Dennis Patrick as Amleth in Melchior's first presentation of his play *Hour of Vengeance* (1962). Melchior was so impressed with Patrick, he cast him in *The Time Travelers*.

another character later. "Tis oft-times convoluted to wend the vennels of Prince Amleth's mind!"

Under his stepfather's gaze, Amleth prepares bent hooks he claims are "straight spears." The king and his men laugh at this senselessness, not realizing the hooks are part of Amleth's grand plan: They figure in the climax when, once the men are in a drunken stupor, Amleth drapes their sleeping forms under a great cloth—ensnaring them with the bent hooks they'd laughed at—and sets the sodden mass of them on fire! Caught in the cloak entangled and tied by the hooks, they all die; the deaths as sure as if by the spear Amleth then uses to slay the king.

All along, this Hamlet is steadfast, not the vacillating, unsure, melancholic of Shakespeare's *Hamlet*. He is truthful every step of the way, and clear in his goals:

AMLETH: And so it is with me! Assumed to be a filthy fool—a witless madman,
I, too, abide the fitting time.
Yet, neither you nor I hold forth a falsehood;
Those who see not the rigid spear,
Within your crooked form,
Or find the wroth avenger,
Hidden in my wretched figure,
Look only on the surface ripples,
And do not detect the deeper currents well below.
But never falsehood shall be thought or spoken!
A trick is fair; A lie is foul!
And I am loathe of lying,
And wish to be held stranger to untruth.

A play that had to be written to make sense and nonsense at the same time, was not far out of line with the kind of thinking that might try to unravel, for instance, the riddles that nature repeatedly lays at the feet of scientists; the riddles of birth and decay, of the butterfly and the moth. And *Hour of Vengeance* could be seen as not out of line for Melchior, fascinated as ever with riddles, codes, scientific mysteries and other forms of mental explorations. A case could be made for the link between the riddles of the play, and the cryptography and code-making Melchior learned during the war—both means to say things under the guise of another. Both forms of communication that might look like one thing, but actually mean another—if one correlates the relationships. It was also exciting to introduce modern audiences to Viking culture: Most people probably did not know that the popular Scandinavian toast "Skoal" referred to the Viking practice of toasting from cups made from the skulls—or "skals"—of the enemy: What does one have to worry about when one is, after all, drinking from the skull of one's enemy? *Hour of Vengeance* allowed Melchior to have some fun with those traditions in the service of his tale.

Hour of Vengeance was initially staged at the Professional Theater Center in June 1962 under the direction of Melchior and Bill Hellinger. Happily, Melchior and Hellinger had discovered and cast a strong young actor named Dennis Patrick in the Amleth role. Patrick would later be cast, based on the intensity of his performance in the play, in the role of the iron-willed Willard in Melchior's *The Time Travelers*.

Amleth was rich and challenging for any actor: He gets to make speeches, babble, make riddles—and commit murder. Even after killing a plotting henchman of the King, he is clean of conscience. He has slain the treacherous Bolvir before his mother, Queen Gerut, and speaks of cutting him into pieces:

AMLETH: Now I must hew this serf up small. And simmer him,—and swill him to the swine.
GERUT: He merely served his King, my son, And now his soul is dead, and killed by you...
AMLETH: You cannot kill a soul except your own, And not it with a second stroke! I only tore his spirit from his fellow flesh; His heart trots after no wrong master now.

Future *Night Stalker* vampire, Barry Atwater, was also cast, here as Ethelbert, the King of England. Though the staging was in the minimalist style, the performances and language were greeted with warm reviews and standing ovations. The Danish newspaper commented:

> The drama itself is effectively expressive and well-written, The vigorous and distinctive Viking language has been retained despite the fact that the Vikings speak English in this version. The lead [Amleth] was impressively portrayed by the actor, Dennis Patrick.

The play *Hour of Vengeance* and its great reception was a highly satisfying boost up for Melchior from the disappointment of several unsold science fiction projects—and the less-than-ideal version of his *Journey to the 7th Planet* script.

Within two months, Melchior would go from *Hamlet* to fix-up work on the least successful film version of any of his scripts. It was time to face—a monster.

REPTILICUS RETURNS

Reptilicus was not, from American International's standpoint, releasable in the condition in which it had been presented to them by Sid Pink.

On August 17,1962, Melchior was called in to AIP's offices to discuss how the film could be repaired for U.S. release. Jim Nicholson, Anthony Carras—AIP's editorial expert—along with AIP executive Lou Rusoff and legal representative Barnett Shapiro were in attendance. Melchior and Carras worked out a plan of attack to fix the film. Carras represented AIP, and Melchior represented Pink. All parties, including Pink, came to terms as to the "work to be performed."

Melchior and Carras quickly deleted all the stilted flying scenes of the Reptilicus puppet. A number of the remaining shots of the creature were either deleted altogether, or cut shorter, as had been originally intended by the technical crew. Almost all of them were double-frame printed—slowed down—to add a sense of scale, and optically reprinted slightly out-of-focus to hide the wires. Melchior and Carras also took pains to optically add larger-scale plumes of smoke and fire burning in the foreground of a handful of shots. The improvements to those shots were significant. And since there were almost no shots of people and Reptilicus in the same frame, an additional effect was optically added—a kind of green acid slime to create a bit of interaction between the creature and the fleeing humans, tenuous though it might be. Melchior wrote additional dialogue to explain the creature's new talent, and had it dubbed into the revised soundtrack.

Due to the severely limited post-production budget, AIP had contracted with the cheapest optical house available at the time to produce the work, the Ray Mercer Company. They were not known for the highest quality matte work, and the slime effect, in particular, while a definite improvement over no effect at all, left much to be desired.

Again, to provide a bit more interaction between humans and the monster, Melchior and Carras decided to add a farmer being tossed into the air by Reptilicus fairly early on in the action. Melchior needed an actor for the part, but the budget couldn't really afford one. His third way out, as it were, this time, was his own stepson, Dirk. Recalling his screen debut, Dirk Baldon, a junior high school student at the time, explained how it came about:

> I knew something was up when [Ib] came up to me with a well-worded question: "Do you have anything important at school tomorrow? Any tests?" Well, not really. So I got called in to be eaten by Reptilicus.

The bluescreen element was photographed at a small insert stage in Hollywood by a small crew from Mercer. Dirk continued:

> I was replacing a smallish farmer in the film. They put tape around my wrist to duplicate his watch, gave me matching clothes and put me on a blue ladder on a lazy Susan-type device that was mounted on the top of it. They spun me around on it, controlled me with a blue wire. I was up about five feet in the air—and they were shooting from about the same height. There were three or four people in the room doing this. I was curled up, on my side holding onto the [disc] of the lazy Susan, as they rotated it. We did it over and over... I'd been shown clips and photos [Ib] had of *Reptilicus* to explain the shot and what was needed. It was shot at various speeds from different angles.

In the film, Dirk is seen for a split moment tumbling about inside Reptilicus's mouth. The people at Mercer were barely able to create a matte for the bluescreen shot—it was a costly process at the time. It, to say the least, turned out to be a shot best not lingered on. It wasn't.

As with *Journey to the 7th Planet*, the film was almost entirely re-dubbed, with J. Edward McKinley supplying the voice for actor Carl Ottosen. Because of legal disputes between AIP and Sid Pink over the film's quality—or lack thereof—it wasn't until November 1962 that *Reptilicus*—shot in 1960—was finally released.

Melchior's opinion of the final film in general? Merely that it is the one project of his he has most tried to distance himself from:

> In a way I'm glad that I wasn't around when it was being made—although I get all the blame for it. In Denmark it is now called "Ib Melchior's *Reptilicus*," not Sid Pink's.

He sighed, perhaps unable to repress his innate generosity:

> You must realize that the people in Denmark had never ever made special effects of that sort. They *did* try.

Cleo Baldon remembers his attitude toward the project when it came back to him:

> As far as *Reptilicus* was concerned, for Ib it was just another problem that had to be solved. It was like taking a job at the Five and Dime.

A "Five and Dime" job that soon made an awful lot of money for American International Pictures!

THE TIME TRAVELERS

By this time, in 1962, Melchior had begun a correspondence via Forrest J Ackerman with a young man from Nevada named David Hewitt who had aspirations of making science fiction movies. The two were destined to work together on Melchior's next film, *The Time Travelers*.

Winner of the Silver Spaceship Award at the 1964 Trieste Science Fiction Festival, *The Time Travelers* has often been described as a minor but well-made entry in the genre, exhibiting "spirited flashes of imagination" and a truly unique ending. If the critics hadn't exactly raved over *Journey to the 7th Planet* or *Reptilicus*, they more than made up for it with the release of Melchior's new film in 1964. Richard Davis, in *Films and Filming*, commented:

> Through sheer audacity the whole bag of tricks works... Ib Melchior who directed it has done a good, well-paced job. Welcome dashes of humor... the special effects are imaginative and clever... I liked too the uncompromisingly tough ending. In fact I like *The Time Travelers*.

The Los Angeles Herald-Examiner opined that,

> [Melchior] has managed to dress events in such a bright, entertaining package that the result is entertainment.

Produced in 1963-64, *The Time Travelers* was an ambitious little film with production values far beyond its meager $250,000 budget, highlighted by a wide array of visual tricks—in some cases literally magic tricks—mixed with opticals, miniatures, makeup and editing tricks. The classic idea that to a primitive being differences between technology and sorcery would be indistinguishable, is carried to its literal extreme in *The Time Travelers*. While its story is another in the *World Without End* vein in which a post-atomic culture survives underground, the film introduced plenty of new twists to give it its own unique identity.

The Time Travelers begins with a view of the awesome Andromeda galaxy complemented by the simple but evocative score by Richard LaSalle, then quickly moves into a prosaic research laboratory that soon becomes a gateway to another world. Melchior catapults a group of four scientists to the other side of an accidental time portal—a window to the future. The four become trapped in a devastated world 107 years into the future, inhabited by a group of people living underground who are constantly defending themselves against the mutants who roam the surface.

The people of the future nurture technology and information as their sole means of survival in this wasteland of a world. Science produced the atomic weapons that put mankind in this predicament. Now the human race is reliant on the same science to feed itself, provide shelter, maintain its robots and, ultimately, design and construct a starship to escape to another planet.

The four time travelers—Dr. Eric von Steiner (Preston Foster), Carol White (Merry Anders), Steve Connors (Phillip Carey) and electrician Danny McKee (Steve Franken) exchange information with council leader Varno (John Hoyt), who treats them with fairness and extends any help he can to his stranded fellow human beings. He offers to take them on the journey to their new home in the Alpha Centauri star system. Another council member, Willard (Dennis Patrick), finds the newcomers a dangerous imposition: Considering the added weight of four more bodies, they would be a risk to the safe launching of the carefully calculated space mission. Varno's offer is overruled, and the time travelers' only recourse is to try to rebuild their time portal.

The rocket must be launched in one month, hardly enough time to complete the task. Also manpower is short as the starship must be completed and launched at a very precise time, and the mutants are increasing the intensity of their attacks.

With only hours to spare, the last adjustments are made to the time portal. Just then, the mutants attack in full force, destroy the starship and massacre many of Varno's people. The few remaining survivors manage to escape back through the rebuilt portal with the original scientists, and destroy this new window behind them to avoid being followed into the past by the mutants.

Having returned to their own time, the travelers face an even bigger challenge: It appears that they came back too soon and are out of synch with the flow of time. Everything appears frozen and immovable, since these returnees are existing at a much slower rate than the rest of the world. The time travelers rush to their lab to find *themselves* frozen in the exact positions they were in just before they first stepped into the time portal, a literal case of "this is where I came in." They have come back a few moments too early and thus are ahead of themselves.

They also realize that even though they seem to be outside of time, they are aging rapidly. Action needs to be taken immediately.

Joined by the few survivors from the future, they theorize that the original time portal now in front of them may still be open and decide to go through it again. They emerge in a far-distant future Garden of Eden, in a year accessed briefly by sheer accident just before they first left. All would seem well, except that they have now completed a kind of time loop in which their other selves will continue on as before, entering the time portal, going into the future, going through the entire story in the future, escaping back into the past, stepping back through the portal again... all of which will lead them to stepping back into the portal again, going into the future.... etc., etc., on and on through infinity.

Aside from telling his story with a firm hand, solid performances and refreshing clarity, the film has—everything considered—strong production values. It showcased ambitious sets augmented by the use of foreground miniatures, an assortment of novel props—the Matter Transmitter, the Lumichord, android skeletons, etc.—and a fairly spectacular scene of starship destruction. It was one of the earliest films to use blood packs for battle scenes, and stands as one of the best film examples of editing being used to demonstrate a story concept—becoming, in a sense, a film loop by repeating the story over and over, the plot literally depicting the circularity of the space-time continuum.

The various tricks and illusions used in the film were a definite asset in depicting a science-based society similar to that of *Things to Come*. Melchior's background in documentary work as well as features may explain the film's blend of science lessons and fiction, though there is not a handy word-hybrid to pigeonhole it. It plays like a cross between Hollywood feature and an industrial science film that, during its 83-minute running time, alternately reminds one of a magic show, an assembly line gone weird, a science lecture, a Frank R. Paul painting, the films *When Worlds Collide* and *World Without End*, an aberrant government documentary and a trip film that offers a peak into an emergency room and a visit to a World's Fair. While it's not really any of the above to any extent—and not the pastiche that the above list might suggest—it certainly gave pre-2001 audiences a lot to see along the way.

Melchior's depiction of the future encompassed labyrinthian caves wherein science and the exploration of other worlds barely, but heroically, struggles on. The science is a logical extension of present day research. The people still use hand tools and perform physical tasks. Presumably civilization was destroyed before computers had become commonplace. Great strides have been made in simple, practical inventions: The prognostications are pretty plausible. Even equipped with the tools of science, however, survival is a daily struggle. But in the end, the last remaining civilized people on Earth either are destroyed when their space ark is blown up, or become lost in the neverending time trap.

It was an unusually grim ending for the time.

THE MAKING OF *THE TIME TRAVELERS*

The Time Travelers owed its origins to a young man named David Lee Hewitt who loved science fiction and magic tricks, and wanted desperately to get into the movies. His situation was similar to that of Melchior's as a child in Denmark wanting to become a director in far-off Hollywood. To Hewitt, having moved as a young teenager to Winnemucca, Nevada, from his native San Francisco, and having no connections to the business, Hollywood seemed as far away as the moon, but was a goal as fascinating to pursue. He was a young man barely out of his teens at the time. His fascination with illusions motivated him to run away from home at the age of 13 to join a traveling magic show.

Being both extremely practical and resourceful, Hewitt decided to make a movie on his own. He first made a few quick calls seeking to buy a script. He learned his first lesson: In Hollywood, everything is *expensive*, including screenplays. So he wrote a script himself. It was titled "Journey Into the Unknown," a time travel story, a subject barely touched upon in motion pictures up until late 1959 when he wrote it. Hewitt revealed:

> I'd always liked time travel, I don't know that at the time anything had been done about time travel.

> My script was written before *The Time Machine* came out. [*Beyond the Time Barrier* had not been released yet, either.]

By his own admission, his story was intended as an homage to all the films he had grown up with and loved through his teenage and childhood years. Not surprisingly, many moments recalled these earlier films.

"Journey Into the Unknown" told of a group of four scientists, Steve Mansfield, Dr. Eric von Steiner, Louis McGraw and secretary Carol Martin, who, working together at an unnamed, unidentified facility, have constructed a matter transmitter. It consists of a clear cylindrical tube into which an object or organism is placed to be disintegrated prior to being transmitted; a locator, which is used to select a transmission target area anywhere on the Earth; and a large, built-in viewscreen on which is displayed an image of the target area.

In trying to work bugs out of the system, they cause a short circuit. In repairing it later, Steve finds that the system has been transformed into something far beyond its original intentions, for the viewscreen now displays images of prehistoric animals from an era 75 million years ago.

By matching frequencies with that of the Locator Screen and combining a matter transmitter and various technologies available to them, they devise a means of literally stepping into the picture into whatever time they choose to select and to whatever area of the Earth they target. All they have to do is enter the matter transmitter tubes. In an intriguing aside, they conjecture that perhaps what have become known as UFOs may actually be other people like themselves, possibly from the future, who've projected themselves into our era.

They embark on a series of adventures, starting with an excursion into the prehistoric past. Steve and Louis don special suits and travel back in time. They are chased by a dinosaur through a jungle, and observe wild geological volcanic activity. Dr. Steiner has warned them not to tamper with or take anything from the past lest it change the future. But Louis looses all control when they venture into a cave and find a vast deposit of fantastic gemstones.

Louis carelessly chips a few gem crystals away from the area against orders, producing a hole that quickly becomes a raging torrent. The water pours into flowing lava, and the meeting of fire and water causes a huge explosion. Steve just makes it out and is returned to the present.

In an impressively eerie sequence, the scientists next send out the signal to retrieve Louis who has gone out of the viewing area. They turn on the matter transmitter. It flashes with light. Then:

> They stand near the unit, tensely watching for Louis to reappear. The tube fills with more vapor than before. The pulsating light is stronger than before and the humming tone has reached a shrill, vibrating pitch. There is a piercing whine and a brilliant flash in the tube that lights the entire laboratory with a blinding flash. The three start toward the tube as all activity suddenly halts and the unit is

silent. Through the thick vapor a form is barely visible... The tube unlocks with an audible click, and slowly raises. There on the base is the crumpled skeleton of Louis. His suit is in shreds, torn and burnt, with some parts still smoldering. Glistening through the folds and shreds, his bones are seen. The camera comes in close to the skull with its gaping jaw frozen in terror. The camera follows down to his hand. The bones are holding something clenched, and then suddenly relax. The hand falls open and a number of sparkling gems scatter on the floor.

Dave Hewitt during the filming of *The Time Travelers*.

Having traveled into the past, they decide an attempt at a journey into the future will reveal the machine's full abilities. Rather arbitrarily they select a nice round number, 5,000 years into the future. The vicinity: New York City.

The machine works like a charm. They see "barren terrain... flat rocky plains, reddish and smoldering.... steaming crevices... steaming mud pots... and no form of life—either plant or animal."

Eventually they see a moving shape in the sky—a rocket. They track it to a mountain which opens up to reveal a landing pad and launch area. This is a place they want to check out and, now, all three make the time jump.

The threesome lands at the launch pad and look about. They see giant cement ramps running to the base of a mountain, huge concrete reinforcements that remind them of ancient Egyptian art and construction, and gigantic *doors*.

Within a short time they are met by strange, humanoid robot creatures that "resemble humans closely in shape and movements," but have bald heads and "two large, round black spheres" for eyes, no nostrils and "large, round, fairly flat protruding nodules of skin with a slight indentation in the center, similar to the ears of a bullfrog" for ears. These humanoids lead the group into an underground complex where they meet Dr. Varno, the distinguished leader of what is known as Atlantis II. This is but one of a number of such cities on Earth, all that remains after a great war. Varno explains:

> Many years ago—it is not permitted to tell you when—the Earth was destroyed by a great war, a war of weapons of a type that you could not imagine. The Earth was a flaming sphere for centuries. A small number of humans were able to find shelter under the Earth. The will to live won out, and

> over the centuries we have advanced our civilization to its present stage. There are a number of cities like Atlantis in the Earth now, and through time we have been able to establish transportation and communication networks.

Varno explains that the three were brought into the city quickly to protect them from the high level of radiation on the surface. Also to protect them from a race of mutanthropoids, creatures who live in a radiation-saturated jungle nearby. They are half-men, half-apes, creatures who've regressively evolved and pose an ongoing threat to the existence of the inhabitants of Atlantis II—a situation similar to that in one of Hollywood's only other time-travel movies until that time, *World Without End*.

The time travelers learn that the city is divided into regions by colors. The food center is the green zone. There is also a red zone, a blue zone, etc. Each is assigned a particular function in supporting life in the city.

The climax takes place when one of the mutanthropoids breaks into the city and abducts Carol. Steve manages to rescue Carol, pulling her from a cage in a deep pit. With the discovery of the close proximity of the dangerous creatures, Varno decides it is no longer safe to live in Atlantis II. The creatures have begun to infiltrate the city. His solution is rather extreme: complete evacuation and relocation to another world, possibly even an asteroid. The plan is set in motion, and spaceships are quickly loaded and begin to be launched.

Dr. von Steiner, meanwhile, who has become friends with Dr. Varno, has decided he will join the migrating humans rather than return to the past.

Steve and Carol return to the present and watch the last spaceship depart for the stars.

Hewitt's script was clearly fed on an array of the colorful old science fiction movies he enjoyed, including, besides those mentioned above, *When Worlds Collide*, as well as E.C. comics and other meat and potatoes sci-fi sources. In spite of its oversimplifications and unrealized dramatics, it was quite an accomplishment for a 20 year old writing in an era in which no information was forthcoming about how movies were made—this being long before *Entertainment Tonight* or behind-the-scenes magazines like *Cinefex* made specialized information readily available. What it lacked in sophistication it made up with its color and ambitions—and its unabashed love of earlier films.

The script repeatedly plunged into exacting detail to describe each piece of equipment, revealing Hewitt's obvious love of gadgetry: The Locator consists of two vertical and two horizontal bands that "form a small two-inch square in the center of the locater board... a large flat map of the world [which is] softly lighted from underneath." The viewscreen reveals images through a wash of colors that "blend in a mottled effect" that recalls the interocitor screens in *This Island Earth*. Likewise the Matter Transmitter's clear tube chamber is obviously inspired by equal parts *This Island Earth* and *The Fly*:

> Dr. Eric gets up from the desk and walks over to the disintegrator-reintegrator unit. The unit con-

Melchior strikes a classic director's pose on the set of *The Case of Patty Smith.*

sists of two clear tubes descending from heavy chrome bases on the floor. Each tube is approximately four feet in diameter and is controlled by a panel at the side of the unit... The lights above each tube cast an eerie effect on that part of the laboratory.

Another interesting detail is that travel through time also involves travel through *space*, in which the human body may encounter great pressures and hostile conditions. It is mandatory that they don high-pressure space suits before entering their time machine.

Hewitt, unlike a zillion other kids with big imaginations and a lot of plans but no stick-to-it-inventiveness, made repeated efforts to get his dream project off the ground. He wrote letters and did research, spending all the time that other kids might've frittered away drinking and going to parties in order to realize his goal. He planned to shoot his film in and around his home town which had, among other interesting geological formations, the caves he needed for the prehistoric scenes. For the time-travel suits he intended to buy and paint the pressure suits that were sold, at one time, through *Famous Monsters of Filmland* magazine. And, of course, he corresponded with that magazine's famous editor, Forrest J Ackerman, who announced the project in its pages.

But Hewitt's plans didn't see fruition until he was introduced by Ackerman to his friend, Ib Melchior. Melchior, with a track record in the business and a lot of experience as a writer, saw a diamond in the rough in the script as well as a kindred spirit in Hewitt, as he later recalled:

> David Hewitt was my special effects director on *The Time Travelers*, and was an extremely clever and imaginative young man...

Hewitt's story had caught Melchior's attention with its scientific gadgets, basic time travel concepts and adventures into the Earth's prehistory and journey 5000 years into the future.

Hewitt explained how the rest of it came together:

> On one of my visits from Nevada, I visited Ib when he was working as associate producer on a black and white film called *The Case of Patty Smith* out at Republic. He had already done *The Angry Red Planet* and he let me read some of his other scripts—*The Multiple Man*, etc., and he said, "Let's make this movie together. We'll take your screenplay and use it as the basis for the story and we'll share story rights." And I agreed with him. He restructured it, and added all sorts of side plots like the mutant caught in the caves. He really rewrote the story. It was an Ib Melchior script when it came out.

Hewitt recalled with amusement just how different his story read once he got it back from Melchior: "Well, some of the character *names* stayed, and there were still *people* in it." he laughed. "I wrote the cliché-riddled version, and Ib put in all the drama and character development."

Melchior retained the basic plot device of a window in time, but greatly streamlined it. The device is initially just a viewscreen meant to allow scientists to gain a look into the immediate future—just a couple of days—along the lines of the experiments with predictor instruments being conducted at the time by the Rand Corporation, with which, ironically, Melchior was totally unfamiliar. He simplified the transformation of the window into the future into a bona fide doorway: An electrical short in an overloaded circuit does the trick, and simply stepping through the portal—minus any cumbersome suits and procedures—does the trick.

Melchior then deleted the entire episode in the Earth's past. It existed as another story altogether. Too much for one film. He focused on events in the future, which, in essence, were not too dissimilar from the Hewitt version. In particular, the Melchior script became far more detailed, and full of dramatic conflicts between the newly arrived travelers and the more conservative members of the futuristic council. Ultimately they are given the almost impossible task of rebuilding their time portal in a ridiculously short time if they are to escape death—a situation resulting from the conflict between the time travelers and a council member.

Melchior knew the secret of making all the ideas work was in creating a *chain of conflicts* that becomes a *chain reaction* of events that, like falling dominoes, all starts with a simple, single push—in this case just stepping through a time portal that is unstable due to lack of funding. This tact led to an entirely new climax from the one in "Journey Into the Unknown." Now, a whole series of dovetailing events force the time travelers to return to their era with incorrect time calculations. This created not only the bizarre encounter with slow-frozen time, but caused the survivors to enter into an endlessly repeating time trap—the film's original title—that provided a disturbing and rhythmically thrilling wind up.

Melchior's very first draft was titled *The Timemasters*, but because the characters really hadn't exactly *mastered* time after all, he retitled it *Time Trap*. Very few changes were made between his first handwritten draft and the completed film. In the first draft, the science laboratory came equipped with a wall of cages housing small animals needed to test the safety of the portal's laser beams—an extremely rare example of Melchior suggesting in a story any kind of treatment of animals other than love and care. The ending, too, varied from the completed film: In the first draft, the scientists and several of the future people escape from the mutant attack through the time portal into a Garden of Eden world 90,000-plus years in the future—and the story simply ended there. Fortunately, Melchior continued to work on the ending, striving for something different.

Melchior dressed the film in visually varied images: The Earth 107 years in the future is a burnt-out cinder in space, landscaped by swirling, long-cooled lava beds. The surface is populated by mutants that are "man-like, yes, but hideously distorted, deformed, misshapen, each in its own monstrous way—like diabolic, evil gnomes from hell itself..." There are vast rooms full of planetary monitors revealing images being transmitted from all the planets and moons of the solar system by orbiting satellites; a rock-domed council chamber in which the time travelers review the atomic destruction of the Earth on viewscreens; a battle between humans and mutants in which they arm themselves with "axes, iron pipes, knives—anything that can kill!"; and the destruction of a mighty starship as it struggles to take off amid threatening flames and titanic eruptions.

Melchior held onto some of the ideas from Hewitt's script, including an experiment with a matter transmitter in the world of the future, and the *When Worlds Collide*-inspired spaceship launching pad.

Melchior built on the idea of the humanoid robots in Hewitt's script, turning those creatures into cyborgs—which, unlike robots, are technically augmented *humans*—that take on dangerous tasks and make up for the shortage of manpower in the depopulated future world. Before production started, Melchior reconsidered the cyborg idea and changed them back to nonhuman, mechanical robots, called androids. The androids would actually become the fall guys for the host of visual gags he peppered throughout the story—heads being removed, bodies torn open, etc.

Melchior's script was at least as ambitious, if not more so in some areas, than the Hewitt source material. But there were a few cuts he decided to make in his script before production began. They included deletion of an elaborate in-camera sequence in which a model of the starship being tested in a meteor-deflection test tunnel goes out of control; various bubbling liquids filling up in an android stamping press to create a new plastic body; a mutant cut in half in the collapsing time portal as it tries to escape; the visual aging of Varno's hand as he is caught in the time limbo; and the appearance of tiny dawn horses and exotic cranes in the climactic New World of the future. At one point, in another scene deleted before filming, one of the time travelers, Danny, watches an android being cut open and operated on in full view of the camera without any cuts. A cigarette drops out of Danny's mouth, as he leans in, and falls right into the interior workings of the android. It causes a short that makes the android kick up its knee. Danny is admonished by the creature, who is active throughout the procedure.

In August 1963, with the first draft of the script in hand, Melchior and Hewitt began to map out the production and special effects requirements. One thing they'd decided early on was the use of magic tricks and illusions to represent aspects of the future. According to Hewitt:

> It turned out that Ib also had this great love for magic. He was into magic. When he found out I'd traveled in an illusion show and I built illusions he said: "We could use magic tricks. We could use *illusions*... Shots could be done with no camera stops, so it would be obvious to the viewer if they were a fan of special effects that they would say, 'Jeez, there's no trick camera work there!...'" So I told him that I could take a person's head off and put it back on in one shot. He asked: "Is there any way we can do a test of this?" I said yes, let me hustle up the money and I'll shoot a test.
>
> I had met a man named Ray Storey at Alpha Omega Studios and I went to him and said, I want to shoot this test. Ray said, "Okay, you can use the studio." He worked a deal that would make him part of the project: Everybody liked the project.
>
> So we shot a test out there of the special effects. Melchior supervised the test.... We created a seven-minute reel. Some actors came and devoted their time. We did all the set construction, and made this terrible little rubber mask for the promo film. It took two or three months. How I did it was I ran an ad in *The Times* and I said to actors, "Do you want to have a part?" When actors came to see me, I said, "I have no money to pay you. All I can say to you is if this thing is made into a feature, we'll work you in somehow, maybe just as an extra"—I couldn't guarantee a speaking part. And these people put up part of the money. We said, "You'll get a film clip and some stills." I didn't take investments, because I couldn't do that. So they did it, and it helped finance the test. I put in some money. A man, a friend of mine, Gary Heacock, also put in money. He worked on the test, and through the entire film—I want to stress

his contributions through the whole thing. We worked together on *everything*.

So we promoted it, and the first guy that looked at the finished film that Ib showed was a producer named Bill Redlin. I remember that I had to take it over to a little screening room down in the basement of Bob Clampett Productions on Seward Street. I think there were three seats in this little room. And I stood up against the wall in the back—and then they *laughed* when the film ran. I remember standing by that wall saying to myself, I'll *never* do this again. I felt like I had a fever, and the heat just rushed to my face and I knew I was glowing red. But I couldn't get out of there. Then the guy asks, "Can I keep this film?" I said, sure, and I got the hell out of there. The guys had just *laughed* at my film!

Later, Ib called me up and said, "We've got a deal cooking here; [Redlin] really loved the film." [It turned out] they were *enjoying* the film, that's why they were laughing!

Bill Redlin made a deal with American International. They told him real quick, "If you can do a whole feature with these kind of effects, the way Ib's written the treatment—and of course AIP loved Ib—then we can work this out." So we got the deal. Redlin had been a producer for Disney, as an independent. He formed a company called Dobil Productions with a group of doctors from Lodi, California. We met with Bill and it was real simple. I was going to do all the special effects; Ib and I had designed a lot of things, although a lot of the things we'd designed I hadn't conceived exactly how I was going to do them... Redlin met Ray Storey and he [Storey] became part of the team, and it just went together like clockwork. It went very fast. [The test film worked because] it was visually all there... We did seven minutes of *visual effects*, which people had *never* seen! We did a [disembodied] hand grabbing the guy by the seat of the pants; we did a head on the shelf that came to life. We did a test where we changed the robot's head—took the head off, put the head back on. For that test we used a double-jointed guy who could bend his head way back, almost 90 degrees. His name was Wayne Anderson, and he's the same guy we used in the film itself.

I think when these producers saw that they realized, "Now here's something that's fresh and new."—And commercial as hell. So, Redlin showed it to AIP and they turned around and said, "Yeah, if you can do this for the budget you say you can do it for, you have a deal!"

Ib and I then got together and spent a lot of time discussing what we'd do [in the actual film]. Ib developed the story and said, "Can we do something in the Hydroponic Gardens?"—I had a scene in "Journey Into the Unknown" where people were picking oranges off trees in an aquarium. So I designed an orange tree that grows... I got my idea from the old Blooming Rosebush which magicians have... And I took an old illusion called A Tent in the Desert and changed it totally into the Vibra-Transporter. We built all that stuff, or we bought magic tricks and modified them. Like when Forry Ackerman [guest-starring in the film] squares the circle, that was a dollar trick—just a metal band that does that. The Cut-Restored Rope Trick is what we used where it looked like they were hooking ropes together. We just modified it.

For the next few months, Melchior and Hewitt had their hands full preparing for production. While Melchior made drawings and fine-tuned the script, Hewitt hired longtime friend Gary Heacock and two other assistants to help him build the illusion-props, as well as full-sized android skeletons for use in factory sequences, plus the spaceship, gantry, fuel tanks, service compounds and launch ramp required for the starship scenes. The establishing shots of the starship would have to be filmed before principal photography since they were to be rear-projected into the sets behind the actors in several scenes.

Ray Storey became the film's art director. He faced the daunting task of designing and building a long list of sets for very little money, including the Android Factory with its full-sized android stamping press, and racks of arms, legs and hands; the TV Monitor Surveillance Room, for which he installed numerous small television screens with backlit transparencies representing the surfaces of many planets and moons; the scientists' laboratory, complete with rows of computer equipment; the Council Chamber with large windows overlooking the starship launch platform; a cave; and many small chambers and various intersecting corridors and hallways.

Aside from designing the sets on a modular plan with interchangeable units, Storey extended some of them with foreground miniatures: an upper level to the Android Factory using a model which featured a motorized conveyor belt; a rock-domed ceiling for the Council Chamber; and a lofty, star-studded dome for the top of the Surveillance Room. The latter two sets and foreground miniatures were redresses of one set. The upper factory level was a six foot wide miniature built in forced perspective, but it

The first starship nears completion in David Hewitt's driveway.

proved less successful than the other two. It had been built with a much wider camera lens in mind and, therefore, did not exactly match the full-size set's perspective.

A deal had been struck with Helen Miles to shoot the bulk of the feature at the Carthay Stage on Pico Blvd. in Los Angeles—a relatively small stage better suited for the kind of commercials that would be its primary clientele in later years. Due to the impracticality of shooting the entire film on one small stage, a deal was also made with the studio where the initial test reel had been shot, Alpha Omega Studios. Located in Pasadena, it normally attracted producers of small religious films. While scenes were being shot on the Carthay Stage, additional sets were under construction at Alpha Omega, namely the Ray Bath Chamber, the Matter Transmitter and the Lumichord set. As the production company moved from one studio to the other across town, old sets would be taken down or redressed, and/or new ones built. It was only with careful planning and strict adherence to the shooting schedule that so much work could be done in so little time.

Bill Hansard's process projection team was brought in to rear-project images into the time portal window of "nuclear wasteland"—actually lava fields shot near Barstow, California—and the miniature of the starship and launch facility. Hansard, who was the principal independent process man in the film business since the 1940s—with credits on everything from *The Angry Red Planet* to *The Abyss*—was in an especially tight squeeze on *The Time Travelers*. The Carthay Stage was so small the Council Chamber and laboratory sets had to be laid out diagonally on the stage to get enough projector throw. But even this was not enough. The image of the starship only partially filled the projection screen. It had to be added to on the sides by a cave-like vignette.

The Android heads were designed and cast by Don Post Studios. The actors hired to play the human robots had to wear thick body makeup and pasties to give them a smooth, rubbery look. They also had to have all of their chest and body hair shaved off every day. They reportedly weren't too happy about that.

Melchior also had in mind to dress the Android Factory with highly detailed pieces of machinery, specifically to show off their supposed inner mechanical skeletons. Several were constructed for the film, their sophistication far beyond what one would expect from a low-budget feature: Most industry people assumed them to be rentals from some other film, but they were, in fact, created by Hewitt and Gary Heacock. Hewitt explained:

> To create those android skeletons, I went to downtown Los Angeles to mannequin companies until I found a company that had a couple of young, real neat people running it. I told them what I was going to do. I had to have some robot bodies and I wanted to buy some mannequins and I wanted to see how mannequins were made. They gave me a tour of the factory. I saw they were made of overlays of paper mache—not paper pulp paper mache, but overlays of this cardboard material—and wrapped using their own techniques.
>
> The other thing that was really interesting about it is when their mannequins were done, these wrappings were *not* smooth. So I asked, "How do you get that smooth look?" They showed me the paint that was used, this thick paint that was used in a spray gun, and they would spray the mannequin body and it would fill grooves that were as deep as an eighth of an inch. It would flow and level itself out. The guy said it was a silicone-type thing. I said I wanted x-number of bodies and I'm going to take them out in their raw stage and cut them up, cut holes in them. I asked, "When you spray them, will it fill in all my cut lines?" He said, "Yes."
>
> So, we took them out and sawed them up and did the breast plate pattern and all the holes in them with a sabre saw. We took them back and the guys sprayed them with this flesh-colored stuff and filled them in as smooth as glass.
>
> We went to C&H Sales and bought fan motors that we plugged in; we put in screen door springs—that's what you see rotating inside—and fish aquarium pumps with colored liquid bubbling up in them. Everything worked inside. There were

> bellows that moved. I just designed it because that's how I thought these things should look. I just did it as I went along. I made no sketches. I was never very good at blueprints or drawings. I just had a mental image of it.

One other big-ticket item which needed to be built and photographed prior to the start of the production proper was the giant starship in its crater launch pad. The job also fell to Hewitt and Heacock to construct: Melchior's scene was ambitious, in spite of the small budget. His description of the starship, in keeping with his belief that filmed science fiction needed to be visually awe-inspiring, was classic genre imagery:

> The huge, steel wall in back of the dais silently, majestically begins to draw apart—opening from the center, and gradually an awesome, mind-staggering sight is exposed... A huge opening through the 10 foot-thick mountain wall is revealed behind the steel doors, apparently covered over by a heavy glass pane... This immense window looks out upon a breathtaking scene... It is the inside of a gigantic crater, the sheer rock walls reaching seemingly towards space itself... Several tunnel openings gape at the base of the crater sides; one of them appears to be very much larger than the others; from this tunnel mouth stretches a mighty, massive concrete runway with several thick iron rails running its length, and a walkway along its side. This ramp runs to the center of the crater, and here—in the colossal intricate steel web of a towering rocketship launching gantry—stands a gargantuan spaceship, a starship, its slender, graceful lines gleaming silver... The crater floor is broken up with enormous concrete blocks and steel beam structures; there is a maze of power lines and pipes; a network of drainage ditches; row upon row of heavy transformers; a huddle of squat fuel storage tanks... Like busy ants, men in radiation suits and machines can be seen working on the crater floor and around the base of the titanic starship itself...

The model had to be constructed ahead of time in order to accommodate plate photography. Hewitt described the project:

> We started building the props and miniatures maybe a couple of months ahead of time... There was a lot of preparation time because I had to build the

spaceship and the launch pad and go out to ordinance places and try different explosives... We decided that I build this big miniature for the spaceship. Originally Ib wanted to do it actually in a crater in the Pisgah Lava Crater. We went out and looked around and there were some huge bubbles where the lava cooled that were 20 to 30-feet across, but there was so much vegetation we couldn't do it. It wasn't cost effective. And the heat was *terrible* out there.

We got detail parts—railings and so on—from Engineering Model Associates. They sold miniature parts for model refineries. I got all these parts from them—great stuff. And the gantry was made from a kind of construction toy that was out back then. The ship was about a five-foot-long model. The launch ramp resembled the one from *When Worlds Collide*. That was something that impressed me—the *massiveness* of the ramp. But I couldn't make that curved track on the budget I had.

I had a crew of only three or four. It was myself and Gary Heacock. Basically we built just about everything... I had another fellow help on the space platform, named Don Russel.

That launch pad cost maybe a few thousand dollars. The ship was made of steel I got at an auto body shop around the corner from me. I went to a sheet metal fabrication shop and had them roll the tube for me and make the cone. I then cut the wings out myself. And then I had them weld it and sand it and went to an auto body shop and had them paint it.

We tested the spaceship on the launch pad standing up and all of that at Alpha Omega Studios, then we took it over to the Carthay Stage. Ray Storey... built the crater, the walls and the platforms for the ground, and we brought in the rest and dressed it. We had motors under the set, and people, and a track. There were a lot of people behind that work.

We were [originally] going to go to the Pisgah Crater lava field—which we did shoot in anyway—and shoot some extras running, but we didn't get that shot. We were also going to shoot lock-offs of people and androids running along the L.A. River or the Hansen Dam and matte them along the top

Ib Melchior directs a mutant on the set of *The Time Travelers*.

of the launch pad: The gantry pulls away; the missile rolls up; it stands up; the gantry comes up; then you now figure they're loading up people, or whatever; the gantry moves away, and so on.... That was the idea. But it got canceled.

The live-action portion of *The Time Travelers* was shot in a total of 18 days, including one pre-production day to shoot process plates of the lava fields, the campus location of the lab and a Ray Storey miniature surveyor moving on a miniature landscape of Titan to be later matted into a Planetary Surveillance Screen. Various shots of the miniature starship were also shot separate from the main unit.

The shooting also included two post-production days to film optical elements such as the time travel survivors entering the far future world's Garden of Eden, and additional shots of the miniature starship.

The director of photography was none other than William (later Vilmos) Zsigmond, later to become one of the industry's most acclaimed cinematographers. His operator on the film was Lazslo Kovacs, a cameraman who would later achieve great fame. Melchior stated:

> As for William Zsigmond, he is absolutely the most terrific guy I ever worked with. There was noth-

Waiting on the sidelines on the Carthay Stage, athletes turned mutants line up to attack *The Time Travelers*... **and others!**

ing he would not do to get the shots that I thought would be the good ones. At one point he was hanging on a rope out over a ravine shooting down into it.

Shooting of the principal photography began on Monday, November 4, 1963, with 49 scenes—including the stranded scientists being attacked by mutants—shot on location around the lava fields near Barstow. Melchior recalled that day:

We had a rather amusing occurrence. [We had] the huge mutants who were kind of deformed human beings, in fact the biggest one was 7 feet, 6 inches tall. We had recruited them from the L.A. Lakers basketball team and they were made-up and looked quite gruesome. We took them out to a location where there were a lot of dead trees that looked kind of other-worldly and strange, to have them run through this terrain for a chase sequence. Through this terrain there was a side road, and as we were rehearsing, our camera being out of sight,

> some of those monsters came running up as a car was just driving on this little road. The car came to a sudden halt and a petrified lady leaned out of the window and looked at these monsters. Well, this was something that these guys could not let go, and one of the monsters went over and very politely asked, "Ma'am, would you please take us to your leader?"

The first strenuous day on location was followed by 14 more grueling days full of ambitious set ups, and onset gags. In spite of sagging energies about halfway through production, everything went off without any major hitches.

The filming went very smoothly for Melchior. He had the support of a good producer in Bill Redlin, and none of the inexpert second guessing he had experienced with Sid Pink during *The Angry Red Planet*. He recalled:

> *The Time Travelers* was one of the films I enjoyed doing most. Many of the effects were [those] illusions altered by David to look science-fictiony. The hydroponic orange tree was a tree that does exactly that. It has petals on it that fall off, and you can see little buds that grow, then it grows an orange and you can re-rig it and shoot it over and over. We had a magician who then picked the fake orange off the branch and did a palm-swap with a real orange so they could eat it.

Melchior described how he setup one of the film's most impressive tricks:

> In one scene we had an android, which was simply a young man with a head mask who was naked to his waist and wearing tights, who had been in an accident, his head having been laid open. We see the little wheels turning inside him, and so on, and he is brought to the factory for repair. Now, mind you, we did not cut away, we stayed with this one shot of the man coming in, lying down on a table, while his collar is loosened, his head pulled off, a new head given to him and screwed in. And then the android gets up and walks away. This was done without ever taking the camera off the scene, and we had many things like that in the film.
>
> These tricks took no more time than an ordinary shot. Sometimes we'd get it in one take. The head swap worked fine. That was nothing. We had a special boy (Wayne Anderson) for that set

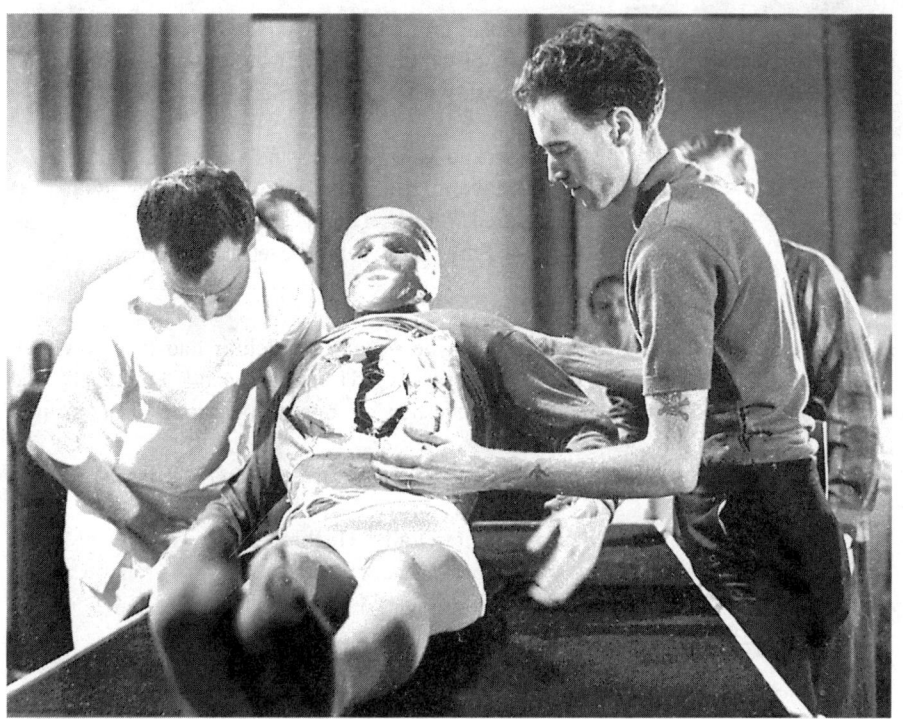

David Hewitt prepares a mock-up android for open heart surgery during production of a seven-minute test reel made to convince investors of the project's feasibility.

up, who could bend his neck back at a 90 degree angle so that his neck would become a straight line. We painted his chin and neck black, so if it became visible a little bit during the shot when he put his head down into the table, it wouldn't photograph—it would blend into the darkness. The other actors in the shot weren't even magicians. It was a tricky shot that worked.

Here again was another case where Melchior's years in live TV with its real-time, no-mistakes-allowed experience came in handy on a motion picture sound stage.

Melchior coaxed fine performances out of the personable, better than average cast: Versatile Preston Foster, in his first fantasy role since the 1932 film *Dr. X*—made up with a Morbious-like beard and manner—invested his character with kindness and intelligence. Phillip Carey brought real intensity to his first-ever science fiction movie role, scoring particularly well in a showdown with Dennis Patrick. Patrick was especially effective as the hot-headed Willard, delivering the same strength Melchior had drawn from him in *Hour of Vengeance*. Steve Franken exuded a sweet charm as the electrician inadvertently caught up in the adventure, while John Hoyt brought dignity to his role as the leader of the scientists fighting against all odds to preserve a dying civilization and Merry Anders brought beauty, charm and genuine believability to her part. The charisma of the main cast also minimized the impact of some of the rather shy-looking background extras—many of whom were, in fact, nonprofessionals,

Melchior was delighted with his cast, with very few reservations:

> I loved Preston Foster and Merry Anders and Steve Franken. They were wonderful. Also John Hoyt. Merry and I had already met. Dennis Patrick I knew. I didn't cast Philip Carey, but he worked out fine.

At one point, not getting the cooperation he needed, Melchior had to take Carey behind the set and—according to one witness—"read him the riot act!" Presumably the extra prodding paid off, for his performance became one of the strongest in the final film.

Merry Anders recalled the otherwise smooth camaraderie on the set:

> We met at Ib's apartment initially. He threw a bash with pastrami, corned beef, Aquavitj and Carlsberg beer. It was quite a jolly time. We had a blast and got to know everybody. By the time we got on the set we were very comfortable with each other. Ib brought about all of that. He's really gifted at forming an agreeable alliance, and he treated his actors extremely well... I had worked with Ib before, when I did *The Case of Patty Smith*... so when *The Time Travelers* came up, he remembered me and decided that he wanted to use me. Ib was always very encouraging, very helpful. There were certain things that he wanted done a certain way, and he didn't say, "Damn it, do it my way," he said, "Let's try it this way," or "Let me give you some thoughts on this." He was a wonderful director... It was a fun group to work with, which takes an awful lot of the pressure and the stress out of working on long, difficult scenes...
>
> We worked at the Pisgah Crater and Lava Flow, a lava field 40 miles east of Barstow. We flew up there and did a day's location. There was a group of... the mutants chasing us across the field there, and we were told to wear shoes that we didn't care a great deal about because they would get cut up by the lava rock, which was razor-sharp. We had to run and run, and, of course, I was huffing and puffing, but Phillip Carey and Preston Foster were doing just fine. Of course, their legs were longer than mine!

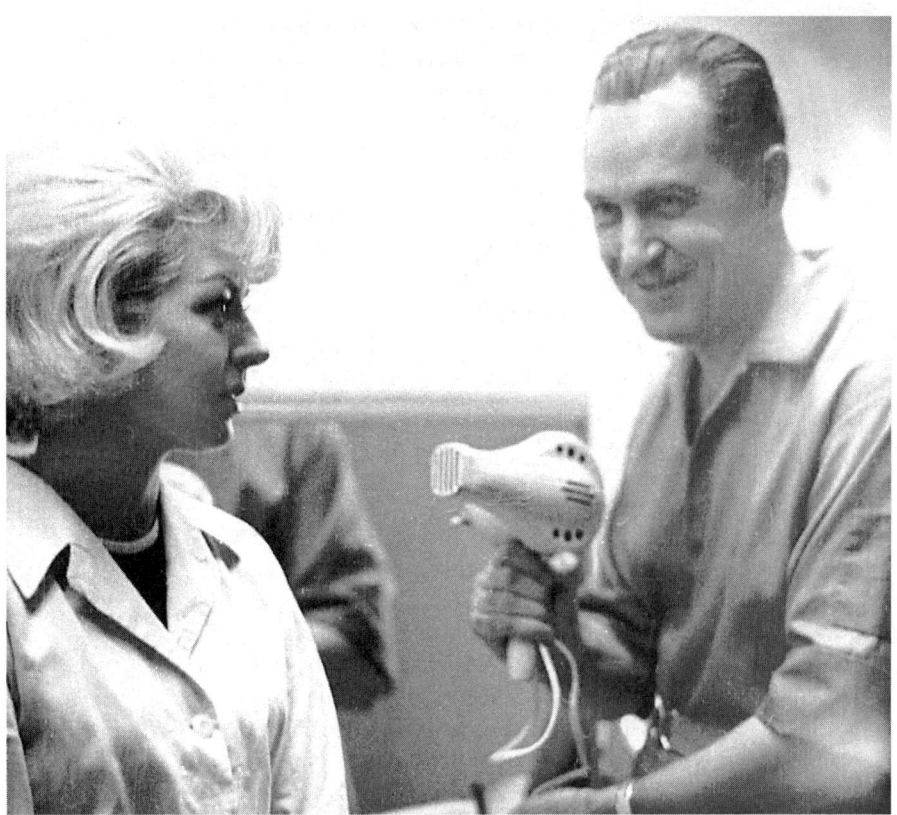

Foremost fantastic film authority and perennial cameo actor, Forrest J Ackerman wields his raygun hairdryer at Merry Anders between takes on *The Time Travelers*.

Anders particularly remembered those giant mutants, all young men she believed were cast from the USC football team, as opposed to the L.A. Lakers:

> They were such good sports. They had fun. When they came running up to the porthole, in full costume, and tried to step through the porthole... Ib handled it very well. He said, "Think ferocious." He told them to "think of your opponent who you want to put away."

Melchior also saw to it that his main female character was no shrinking violet: At no point in all of the action, including direct attack by the mutants in the scene just described, does she ever scream. She deals with the problem as cooly as the men—very much atypical of the times. Anders recalled:

> I was never really great at screaming and doing heavily emotional scenes. I was more apt to—which is the way my mind works today—be more

logical than emotional. You know you always look at a performance afterward and think that you could have done a little more—I could have played that a little stronger. [But] still I felt that if I was playing a scientist my reactions would be controlled, rather than emotional.

Ib allowed us to rehearse enough so by the time the takes came up, it was primarily whether everything worked with the special effects, timing, exits and entrances and that sort of thing. Everyone's timing was pretty well engineered by Ib, and it came across well. The film was well-paced. He came to me when we were going to do the ray bath scene and said, "You will be wearing a bathing suit. We will have ripple plastic across the most important parts." And of course some of the women who were in that particular scene were au naturel. I was the only one who had a bathing suit. It was a skimpy bikini. He'd give you little tips—not to worry. Like in the ray bath sequence—"just let the warmth let you feel comfortable and very relaxed. Don't feel nervous about it" ...He'd give us little things to think about at the time. When we were doing a scene he'd give us directions to go with certain reactions, and things of that nature and make it come together.

One part in the film—that of a forlorn outcast known as a deviant—was a case of casting someone with no prior acting experience whatsoever. Melchior remembered:

I cast Peter Strudwick. He'd written to me: "I'm a monster. I was born a little different from people." He had "lobster claws," but made of flesh and blood. On his left hand he had just pincers, and on his right hand he had nothing, just a knob. The same thing with his legs; he had no feet. And his cheekbones were very high, and he looked a little strange. I immediately wrote in a part for him.

As a child he realized he was not like others. He thought about what was the one thing he absolutely could not do, which was run a marathon—and that is exactly what he decided to do. And did. He ran many marathons, ran against Marines and beat half of them.

It was interesting when he first came to the door he just stuck out this knob and said, "How do you do?" Either you react or you just shake it. After that everything else is fine." [Melchior had Strudwick's pincer hand cast in rubber to provide a right hand for the character.] He did very well for an amateur, I thought. He did the part without the benefit of any lines, just the look in his face. It came out very well.

It is one of the scientists, Merry Anders' character, who, in the film, bravely comes to the rescue of the outcast, making a strong plea for people to try to understand those who are different than others. It was a pertinent message, especially since racial prejudice was beginning to tear the country apart. Merry Anders remembered Strudwick with fondness:

> Peter... had the most whimsical sense of humor of anyone I ever met. Just had a charming way about him. And he was so good in the part—that's the one thing we were razzing him about at the wrap party. We kept saying, "Are you sure you haven't had any experience before? This is too good for a first shot out." His reactions in the film were so honest—and that's so important. I think Ib found a way to capture that.

Anders recalled the difficulty of staying still for scenes taking place in the time limbo:

> We had the sequence where the time clock was moving forward. It was [shot] slow and stop action. We had to stand frozen in a spot. And we had to effect [a pose] that was comfortable to hold so it could be frozen on film... It takes an enormous amount of control not to move. You can't have your hand shaking. We were actually posed for a period of time—I think it was 10 or 20 seconds... And then we'd pick up and start to move again. A lot of it was done with different camera speeds—they had to test that. And it was very effective.

Anders also remembered the outlay of scientific equipment put together for the laboratory set. It had come, as in *The Angry Red Planet*, from the Burroughs Corporation:

> A lot of the equipment that we worked with on the set were actual computers. I was told they had

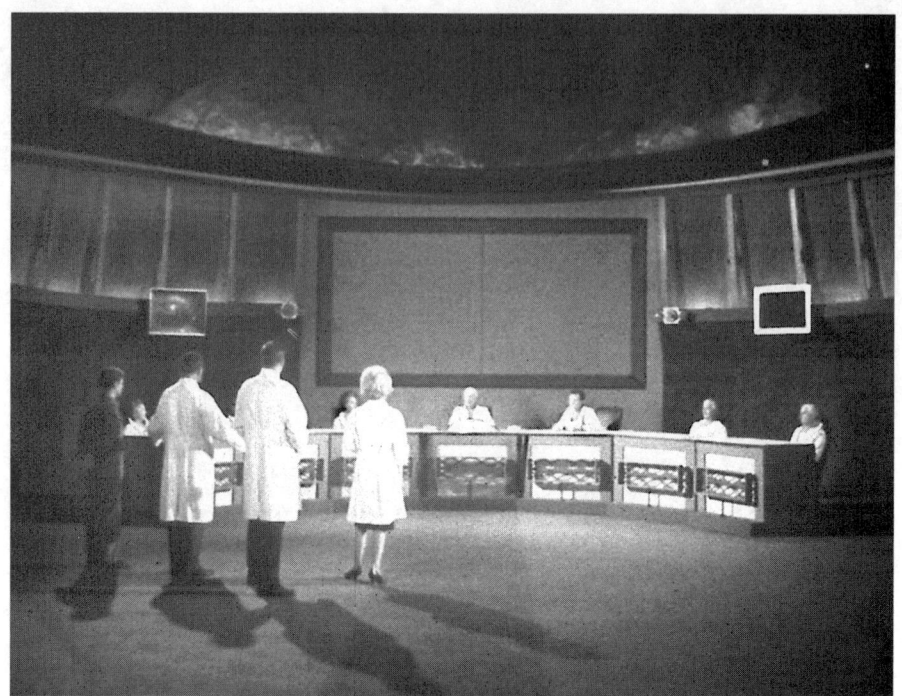

The four time travelers confer with people 107 years in the future. Foreground perspective miniatures, such as the domed ceiling here, helped give the film a bigger look.

>been used to plan the John Glenn flight, and also had had a large bearing on the [subsequent] flight into space... I was so amazed.

And then there was *that* day during production. It was Friday, November 22—the last day of principal photography—the day of the Kennedy assassination. It was not an easy spot to be in for the producers and director. Merry Anders remembered the way it happened:

>We were filming at the Carthay Studio the day that John F. Kennedy was assassinated. I had a transistor radio upstairs and heard the original broadcast. They were filming downstairs. We stopped for a brief moment and Ib led us in prayer... [It] was unique because there isn't too much emotion or religion on a set. We managed to get through it, but it was quite traumatic. It was like someone hit you in the stomach. Of course, you go home and all you can do is watch the TV set to watch the news to see what happened.

Melchior recalled:

Another crisis, the most serious crisis I ever had on a film, was the [JFK] assassination... If I had shut down and lost a day we would have been in trouble, because of our very tight shooting schedule and budget limitations. So one of the most difficult things I had to do was ask my cast and crew what they wanted to do. And they unanimously elected to stay with it and do as much as they could.

Once live-action was completed, there was still the matter of the remaining special visual effects, principally the destruction of the starship. David Hewitt worked out the details of the sequence from Melchior's vivid description and prepared the model after extensive pre-planning:

> For the big explosion at the end where the ship and launch pad are destroyed, we got some capacitors that were—I forget what the exact ratings were—but we hooked them up and sent 110 volts through them and it caused them to explode and pop open with an electrical charge. We did it by testing. A fellow in a surplus warehouse told me if I overloaded these, they would explode. I asked, "How much of an explosion?" He said, "Naw, they just pop open with a spark." So we got one and tested it and it looked *great*. So we bought all they had. They were a dollar apiece, and we used them for the big power transformer trailing out. And on the 4th of July we bought a lot of fireworks that were the snakes—the black pills that you light—and we ground them up and made a big pile of them and set those off because they were supposed to look like lava was flowing. [Note: This effect ultimately wasn't used in the final shooting.]
>
> For the big round oil tanks, we used large Christmas tree ornaments that we bought from Stats and Pacific Coast Ribbon in downtown L.A. I used thermos jar liners for the rocket engines on the wingtips and inside the main body down below, so that when I blew them up, you saw silver fragmentation that looked like metal. We had big CO_2 tanks—the great big ones—four or five-footers—manifolded together to be the jet vents that blew out the bottom of the ship. I copied that effect from what I saw from missile launch footage, knowing that when the missile fired, smoke came out the sides.

Miniature starship undergoing modification for the explosive sequence in *The Time Travelers*.

The bright light at the bottom of the ship when it was trying to take off was created by what are called stars. They almost look like a piece of dog food. They're compressed charges and I put them in florist's clay and stuck them to the ship's bottom, in the thermos jug [I had mounted in there] and put enough of those charges in it so that when they glowed that hot and so intense, you felt that the ship actually had lifted off. But it actually didn't lift, it was just that the glow *increased* as it burned. I had noticed that lifting effect when we did our first tests—that it got bright and it really looked like it was going to lift off. I was familiar with that from the old illusion show I traveled with... And then we detonated it right at that time.

Melchior explained:

> We built that big spaceship and crater miniature, and we had this long firing board that we ran a contact across for all the explosions and so on. Well, it all goes up, boom, boom, boom!—and everything goes, the spaceship falls, the whole thing. We shot it but we got *nothing*—the cameraman had forgotten to put film in the cameras. So, we had to reshoot it—of course with a new cameraman. We didn't have to start completely from scratch, but it was a big deal.

The ending—still one of the most unique in the history of films—in which all the events begin to repeat themselves again over and over, faster and faster, required special handling. For a while Melchior could not get an editor who would make the hundreds of minute cuts necessary to create the time trap—a technique unheard of at the time of the film's production—and wound up doing much of it himself. There was also a question of whether it would work or not:

> The idea was that our characters come back too soon and they have to do it all over again. So it simply came down to a question of how do you show that? And the only way is to show the movie again, but shorten it. And then again, shorter yet. What I did was use 40 or 45 master scenes, just a few feet of each scene. A few seconds. And then I cut the number of frames down to two, then finally, the last time around, it's just single frames.
>
> So I was working with the editor and he said, "It'll never work! It'll be just a blur. Nobody can see one frame." So what I did was take one frame of the old Aunt Jemima character from the television commercials, I took just one frame of that and I put it in the middle of the sequence and ran it for the editor who didn't know it was there, and suddenly he goes "Whoa! What was that?!" "See," I said, "you saw it!" Your brain can pick up something that quick. It registers. This ending got a great reaction. Many reviewers picked up on it. After that we saw a lot more of this type of fast editing.

And it certainly was a different notion for a Hollywood-type film.

One of Melchior and Hewitt's disappointments was the later editorial decision to delete a lengthy sequence occurring early in the story in which the soon-to-be time-traveling scientists are confronted by their funding committee. Put on the spot to explain their progress to the three committee members, Raymond (J. Edward McKinley),

Preston (Berry Kroeger) and Miss Hollister (Margaret Seldeen), they are completely frustrated in their attempts to justify further investment for their research. These bureaucrats seem unable to grasp the simplest concepts about the need to continue, much less the nature of time. The scientists discuss a promising Department of Defense project in the works which "looks down [from orbit] and reflects moving images of people and objects not then present, but that were there on the previous day... It is used to gather information on missile bases in Cuba. The TV-like eye somehow picks up reflections of activity and things from some time before, referring them to an observation screen. For instance, the eye may pass over an empty parking lot to capture pictures of the spot when it was filled with cars during the day."

These scientists here are following a similar but much more ambitious route, which, if they are successful, probably will result in thousands of civilian, industrial and military applications. But the committee's reaction is myopic: "Taking pictures of parking lots as they were a couple of days ago strikes [us] as the height of useless occupation. Hardly worth thousands of dollars."

With little time left before the proverbial plug is to be pulled, the scientists press on with their tests. They experience a few spectacular, but unstable, breakthroughs, including a quick glimpse of the distant past of a dinosaur in a jungle (unidentified rear-projected stock footage). Ultimately their experiments lead them to an inadvertent breakthrough in the opposite direction, the future. This is where the edited film picks up, just as electrician Danny McKee shows up to cut the power at the funding committee's request.

The sequence was shot and the actors are still credited in the opening of the film, but not a trace of it remains. Melchior regretted losing that first reel; in it he explained his hypothesis of time travel. He had a theory of why it was eliminated:

> Pete Strudwick was a Mensa, his IQ was very lofty. He worked for the Rand think-tank in Santa Monica, and one day during post-production he came to me and told me that there were two men who wanted to talk to me. We had lunch. The two men—long in the face—gravely asked me from where I had my knowledge of time travel. I told them that I'd made it up, that it was conjecture, but logical conjecture. It turned out that the Rand organization was working on a project for the Air Force called a Predictor Instrument, a device that could foretell the future for a few seconds, long enough—for example—to give a pilot time to take steps to avoid a possible disaster, to change the future as it were. My time travel explanation had come so close to the workings of that device, that they thought Pete had spilled the beans. I often wondered if that had not influenced some cautious individual to cause the whole reel to be eliminated.

Among *The Time Travelers'* weaknesses are a few overly cute music cues in the Android Factory, a tendency toward flat lighting and snail-paced camera moves in the factory. Another slow down: A montage whose images, meant to convey urgency, are undermined by the slow pace of the cutting and the actors in the scenes themselves. In the case of the music, Richard LaSalle's otherwise effective original score suffered from his decision to utilize stock music from the Bob Hope feature *Call Me Bwana* for the Android Factory, containing "funny" music complete with a sliding trombone.

The Time Travelers showed Melchior to be a versatile director, able to keep everything moving evenly—effects, physical adventure and dramatic interludes—although the film shifts sometimes uncomfortably between the main storyline and the often humorous wonders of the future. The removal and replacement of the android's head and the blossoming tree worked well, even if others, such as the endless glass of water and linking chains, looked like the tricks they were. The time screen, the Council Chamber and TV Survey Room perspective shots, the slow rising of the

DR. VON STEINER'S LABORATORY

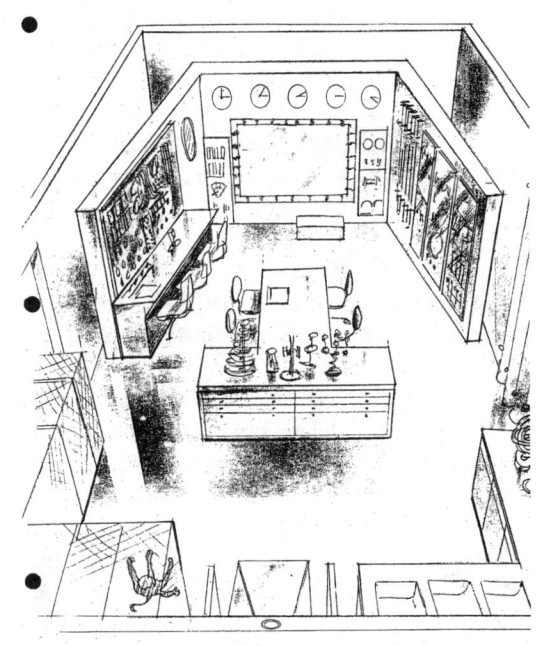

Above: the actual lab for *The Time Travelers*, and below, the design sketch by Cleo Baldon.

starship on its pad and the iris-like opening up of a cave wall, however, belied the film's low budget and short shooting schedule. His best work in the film took place near the end as atomic-scarred mutants lay siege to the underground fortress, sweeping viciously through its inhabitants. The sequence is unusually frenzied and bloody for its time, with violent mutants spearing and hacking androids apart, while humans slash back into the marauding creatures with axes, clubs, broken bottles and guns.

Merry Anders remembered:

> That was the movie that I probably enjoyed making the most. There were so many good people on

Ib Melchior: Man of Imagination

that, such good performers; I just loved working with everybody. Preston Foster was a delight. He brought his guitar down on the set and he played all sorts of songs... and Dennis Patrick... had learned some Irish street dancing, and he was doing clog dancing on the set as Preston played the guitar and sang... It was a fun group to work with...

It takes a great talent and gifted mind to think of these things and put them down. But to convey them on screen or in book form is another talent. A lot of people have a mind like Ib, but not many people can convey it. I'm very grateful I had a chance to meet Ib and know him as a warm and kind person. He never talked down to you; he'd teach you and share with you and explain things so you could understand them.

I just think that Ib has a great heart and a wonderful mind, and great ingenuity and great, clever ways to present things in the most effective way possible.

Anders praise was matched by that of Preston Foster who commented in a *San Francisco Examiner* interview in 1964, "Ib Melchior—directed the film. He is a brilliant man."

The Time Travelers went on to receive many excellent reviews and decent box-office returns. Melchior's experience making the film had proven very satisfactory, and encouraged him, in conjunction with David Hewitt and Bill Redlin, to continue pursuing such projects as *Space Family Robinson* and *Columbus of the Stars*.

After completing *The Time Travelers*, Melchior and Hewitt tried, without success, to build a TV series based on the film. While they were not able to get a commitment for a series, the film's concept was strong enough to have surely inspired the Irwin Allen TV series *Time Tunnel*, based on a similar time portal idea. The show gave no acknowledgment to either Melchior or Hewitt.

Many years later, a TV movie, *The Langoliers*, based on a Stephen King story, featured sequences of a frozen time limbo that also seemed as if they might have been inspired by *The Time Travelers*.

ROBINSON CRUSOE ON MARS

"If Ib was cast onto an island, he would *be* Robinson Crusoe."
—Cleo Baldon

The early 1960s continued to be an especially productive time for Ib Melchior. His personal interest in science and space exploration coincided with the public's fascination with the subject. He'd dusted off and finally finished a script which bore the working title *Robinson Crusoe on Mars*, a project he actually had begun work on in 1960.

According to comments in a letter to his friend, Leo Handel, on March 7, 1960, Melchior intended *Robinson Crusoe on Mars* to be the first of what could eventually become a series of family-oriented space age updates of perennial classic adventure tales: For instance, *Treasure Island* and *Gulliver's Travels*, would yield, respectively, "Treasure Asteroid" and "Gulliver's Space Travels." *Robinson Crusoe*, the Daniel DeFoe novel of a shipwrecked man surviving and growing in stature on a small island, was so popular at the time of its writing in the early 1700s that it eventually inspired a sub-genre of its own called "Robinsonnades" all dealing with the survival theme. Johann Wyss' *Swiss Family Robinson*, would be another entry in the category—years later. *Robinson Crusoe*, the first of three books DeFoe was eventually to devote to his noble survivalist, served as the basis for the first in Melchior's projected series.

Melchior's script for the film was the basis for probably the best known and highest regarded, critically speaking, of his screen collaborations. At almost one and a half million dollars, it was a relatively big-budget project, cast clearly in a big-studio commercial mold and featured the finer dressings afforded by a less restrictive budget and shooting schedule. Trim, inventive and straightforward, the completed film paid tribute to the strength of the human will, and was not ashamed to acknowledge a power greater than man's.

It would retain its Disneyesque temporary title right to its final release. In retrospect, the title probably discouraged more serious critical examination. At the very least, a list of the memorable entries in the survival movie category would have to count *Robinson Crusoe on Mars* among them. As a matter of fact, *Robinson Crusoe on Mars* was selected to be included in the book *Twenty All-Time Great Science Fiction Films* by Kenneth von Gunden and Stuart H. Stock (Arlington House, 1982).

The film was released in June 1964, only a few months before the November release of *The Time Travelers*, but four years after he first sat down to write it. Melchior explained:

> The inspiration for *Robinson Crusoe on Mars* came about when I first saw Death Valley. I was absolutely astounded by the look of it. It looked to me

like another world. And I said to myself, this has *got* to be a film. That was in the 1950s. So I decided that some astronaut would be marooned there. And I decided it would be Mars.

Melchior worked on the lengthy script between other projects for over two years, finally completing his 177-page draft in 1962. Paraphrasing Defoe's classic at times and at wide variance with it at others, the story starts out with a bang:

> A searing, blinding jet of almost solid fire and flame
> is spewing from the rocket exhaust, thundering with
> a bone-rattling roar directly into the camera...
> Gradually [a] big graceful spaceship draws away,
> revealing the huge disc of the red planet Mars...

The ship is the Mars Probe One, piloted by Captain Dan McReady and Captain Robin Cruze—Melchior here remaining stubbornly faithful to the Robinson name dictated by literary precedent. Their mission is to orbit and scientifically survey the planet. McReady is in the process of transmitting a description of the fantastic sights below when "a horrible grating sound, as of viciously scraping, gigantic sandpaper" fills the cabin. They have encountered a magnetic storm that forces them to abandon ship.

Robin's emergency capsule works perfectly, sending him parachuting down to the hostile planet below. McReady's capsule malfunctions and, failing to eject, plummets down to destruction in the Martian desert, carrying the pilot to his death.

With that, Robin's odyssey of survival on a hostile planet begins. Through Yankee ingenuity and a tenacity born of sheer necessity, he begins to solve his immediate problems. He rigs a sand clock—an hourglass-type device that triggers a recorded noise—which prevents him from accidentally sleeping through oxygen tank switch-over time. He finds he can breathe the Martian air for limited periods of time, aided by short spurts of oxygen from his tank. To facilitate this, he builds a booster breather rig.

His continuous tape recorded messages bear out his progress:

> The temperature during the day is pretty much like
> a Boston spring. At night it's more like an Arctic
> winter.

To help get through the freezing nights Robin burns a yellow coal-like rock he discovers, a rock that apparently has a built-in oxygen supply. He notes:

> The vegetation is sparse and appears to be mostly
> lichens, hardy mosses, and some shrub-like plants...
> I've come across some kind of eggs in the sand.
> Look like turtle eggs and don't taste too bad, although I hate to contemplate what kind of creatures they are supposed to turn into. I've got to

> experiment with native foods, however repulsive they seem to me. I can't afford to be squeamish.

Later:

> My cave has now all the comforts of home. I've got a nice work table—and the contour chair from the capsule is, of course, very comfortable. And I've graduated from sleeping on the sand to the luxury of a bed. Steel frame and legs, and the fine roots of a leather-leaf plant turned out to be quite flexible and fully as tough as the leaves.
>
> I've figured out an easy way to keep track of time... A system of calendar stones. A red stone for every day... a blue one for every week... a yellow one for every month... That's as far as I need to go as of now.

Robin's next great problem is water, which he is unable to locate. One late afternoon Robin hears strange scraping noises in the darkness of his cave. The source turns out to be a strange, but cute little animal with big ears, banded markings and a spiked collar. This friendly creature, native to the planet, becomes Robin's "dog" which he names Marsa. It is Marsa who eventually leads Robin to underground water, but not before Robin suffers a horrible, poison mushroom-induced hallucinatory dream of water deprivation. The dream takes him back to Earth and the rigors of the astronaut training program, which blend with a distorted memory of a pre-launch party.

The lone man has learned to take care of all his physical needs. But, ultimately, he must conquer the toughest enemy of all: loneliness.

Finally he meets his man Friday in the form of a noble, three-fingered humanoid who has escaped alien captors who are mining ore on the planet. The slave is a man, but although humanoid, obviously not an Earthman. He towers over Robin and is "unusually handsome and impressive-looking in an alien way, with no hair and large, intelligent and expressive eyes." He is clad in a simple metal suit. The most amazing thing about him is that he has only three fingers on each hand, each of those fingers equipped with suction cups. [Melchior anticipated the question of how any civilization could advance to a high state with so few digits; the suction cups aid in manual dexterity, each one finger able to do the work of two.]

The slave becomes Robin's faithful companion. Together they explore the surface of Mars, with Friday learning English when his native tongue proves too difficult for an Earthman to speak. Friday has oxygen pills that enable him to breathe the Martian air and these he shares with Robin. He also has a communicator device by which he tracks his masters who will eventually return to find him. These miners have enslaved Friday's people.

Robin and Friday build a raft and navigate an underground river, aiming to elude Friday's pursuers. Along the way they fight their way through rapids, escape a valley of an almost living whirlwind, get blinded and then lost in a huge prismatic cave of ice.

Finally, they emerge in the "Green Area Plain of bushes and cacti and many-hued lichens." There they are attacked by a giant multi-segmented centipede. Robin destroys it by setting its oily skin afire with his acetylene torch. Huge smoke clouds billow up into the atmosphere from the flaming carcass. The encounter proves serendipitous: The smoke from the creature that almost killed them attracts a rescue ship from Earth that has been cruising the planet in search of the stranded astronaut.

Robin records one last message: "I am coming home... and with me comes a man from another world. Friday, my friend. The realization of man's greatest dream ever since he first looked up into the sky at the stars and the planets and wondered... contact with a new, a great alien civilization in friendship."

Melchior wrote his screenplay as detailed and as scientifically as he could, without sacrificing high adventure. His tale bore a streak of space age romanticism, evidenced by scenes of Robin and the alien rapturously recalling their loved ones back home. In one touching scene, compassion trumps logic: As their raft plunges wildly out of control, both a tool box and little Marsa begin to tumble overboard. Robin can only save one, and disregarding their dire need for tools, he rescues Marsa instead.

During the course of the story Robin battles the formidable forces of nature on the red planet, including a giant Martian "ant-lion" equipped with scimitar-like mandibles; hallucination-invoking poison mushrooms; a 12-foot-long mole-insect with its ferocious brood; aquatic and flying reptiles; and gigantic "puff-balls" that explode with suffocating clouds of spores. Another encounter brings Robin and Friday face to face with the ultimate image of nature at its most frightening—an almost living, screaming whirlwind existing in a Daliesque, valley of surrealistic, wind-sculpted rocks.

The polar landscape of Mars from *Robinson Crusoe on Mars*.

The screen story was both epic and personal, scientifically accurate and yet full of fantasy. It is not unlikely that *Enemy Mine*, a large-budget film made decades later, was directly inspired and derived from not only the completed version of *Robinson Crusoe on Mars*, but elements of Melchior's script—such as the giant ant-lion—which were *not* filmed.

Melchior often wrote in a lushly descriptive manner, especially those scripts, like *Robinson Crusoe on Mars,* he intended to direct. His writings increasingly tended to read like novels rather than scripts. It was important to him to capture fully the specific details and mood of each scene to aid him in their recreation during the actual shooting. His description of a fungus forest is atmospherically tinged with a taste of the old *Weird Tales*:

> Robin is cautious, apprehensively making his way through the weird growth. It is a fantastic place... eerily quiet, ominous, menacing in its gloom... Giant deformed, slimy fungus plants vie for space in every crag and crevice with huge, twisted tufts of long moss hanging like demoniac curtains from every rock outcropping. Grotesquely distorted

> saprophyte weeds gleam luminously with decay from dark recesses... Wisps of gaseous fog float from toadstool-covered bog holes... Huge mucous mold weeds reach from the ground toward the fungi hanging from above. It is quiet except for near-silent rustlings and night-secret whispers...

In other scenes a reverential tone foreign to most science fiction screenwriting provided an inspirational respite from the terrors of the planet:

> [Robin] stops... and looks solemnly out upon the Martian landscape... The alien land lies before him in all its weirdly wondrous beauty; the distant sun is setting in a riot of deep red and purple colors; the dark shadows are long on the sand... He looks up into the sky, then slowly bows his head...

The Mars that Melchior wrote about was based on what was known about it in 1963. Temperatures were estimated to be between 50 and 75 degrees Fahrenheit near the equator at midday, with temperatures falling to 20 degrees below zero at night. Atmospheric pressure was thought to be equivalent to that on Earth's highest mountains—approximately 29,000 feet above sea level. The U.S.'s leading space scientist at the time, Dr. Werner von Braun, stated at the time: "A man can stay alive longer on Mars than a native of the tropics could exist in the Arctic."

New information was discovered shortly thereafter that readjusted the figures to less-hospitable levels. The new facts, in part, accounted for some rewriting Melchior's script underwent at Paramount. By the late 1970s, scientists concluded temperatures only occasionally reached a high of 60 degrees Fahrenheit and only at certain latitudes. Generally temperatures were much lower, and at night dropped to as much as 125 *below* zero. Furthermore, the atmospheric pressure at an average of 7.7 millibars, as compared to the Earth's—around 1,000 millibars at the surface—meant conditions on Mars were actually similar to those 20 *miles* above the Earth. However, Melchior's depiction of running water on Mars was to be borne out by Jet Propulsion Lab satellite photos that clearly revealed the extensive presence of dried river beds and tributaries.

The red planet turned out to be a much more hostile place than that depicted in either the film or screenplay. Mars would present an astronaut stranded there with a nearly impossible survival challenge.

Melchior was greatly interested in the actual surveys of Mars done 14 years after he'd written his story:

> I was intrigued with the photos and reports from Mars. My greatest fascination was the statement that the scientists found that oxygen could be extracted from the rocks—a device I used in my story.

Interestingly enough, the red skies depicted in this film as well as *The Angry Red Planet*—which seemed at the time one of their more extravagant touches—proved to be, essentially, correct.

The overall tone of Melchior's *Robinson Crusoe on Mars* was more *Seventh Voyage of Sinbad* meets NASA than *2001*. Its themes and fantasy, though, presented within the context of a scientifically accurate trip to another planet, were more important to Melchior than too faithful an adherence to dry reality. Nonetheless, even with these fantastic elements, he sought to build a foundation of scientific reality before venturing into the purely fantastic. Hence the two years spent developing the project. With the help of Cleo, Melchior sketched out on paper all the devices, characters and creatures, including mechanical details, camera angles, special effects and set designs. He made several trips to Death Valley to search out actual locations he intended to use, then referenced them into the script.

Cleo Baldon recalled the designing phase:

> Ib just said, "I need some drawings." The drawings for the film were really made-to-order for him. I wasn't really designing much of anything myself. I take no credit except that Ib was using my hand... I did get intrigued, though, by those three-fingered hands that had the suction cups on them. I think I got emotionally involved with the hands because they really were a case of industrial design, so I was that much involved—to figure out what the communicator would look like if it had to fit into a certain type of hand.

Melchior also created a series of color storyboard paste-ups comprised of location photos and artwork blended together to illustrate the achievability of such seemingly difficult locations as the wind-sculpted valley and the Prismatic Cave. Melchior commented:

> One of things I have always tried to do was to combine what you could do in a studio with locations that have the sweep and the grandeur of other worlds. I have a whole file of such weird and fantastic looking places close to Hollywood... I believe in doing a lot of pertinent research and making every concept appear plausible [which is why] for *Robinson Crusoe* every location was selected by myself, described and pinpointed as to location in the shooting script in order to achieve the look I had in mind.

The astronaut's survival techniques were lent authenticity by Melchior's World War II training:

Storyboard illustrating the climb through miles of Martian canals that forms the climax of *Robinson Crusoe on Mars*.

Of course, my own experiences both in the war and at other times influenced my creation of both characters and action in my writing this. [*Robinson Crusoe on Mars* had a] favorite theme of mine—Man's indomitable spirit which makes it possible for him to overcome seemingly insurmountable obstacles. That was true during the war, of course, many times.

I wrote *Robinson Crusoe on Mars* as a huge film. A three-hour roadshow picture with an intermission from the very first. I took the script to producer Howard Koch at Paramount. Koch liked the project but said, "Unfortunately, I have two other projects already. I couldn't do this for some time. But, I'm working for a guy looking for something big to do"—and that was Aubrey Schenck. After reading the script, he called me into his office. He asked me if I was actually the author of the script; I said I was. He pulled open a drawer and took out a script, *Robinson Crusoe on Mars* was the title. It was my script, word for word, only the title pages were different. The author was now another writer—

one Freddie Gebhardt—who had simply substituted *his* name for mine and attempted to sell the script as his! Having registered the property with the Writers Guild and by other means, I had no trouble convincing Schenck that the script was indeed mine, and he bought it from me. But it had been a close call; I might have lost the property in a way that is not uncommon in Hollywood. I went to him and gave him my script—it had been around to a few studios. He called me back and said he'd like to do it. And he did.

THE MAKING OF *ROBINSON CRUSOE ON MARS*

Paramount had become very excited about Melchior's script and had presented it to Schenck with the order to get it into production as soon as possible. The timing for Melchior, however, was a little bit off: It was now August 1963. He had a deal for *Robinson Crusoe on Mars* in place, but, ironically, would be unable to direct it himself since he was now tied up with pre-production chores on his own film, *The Time Travelers*. The downside to this turn of events was that by allowing another director to take over the film, he would be unable fully to protect his script.

Aubrey Schenck recalled:

> I just read two pages or so of the Melchior treatment and I thought, here's a hell of an idea. I knew I wanted to make this picture. But my idea was to go even more directly to DeFoe's story and then make it as scientific as possible.

Having said this, Schenck then proceeded to delete the creatures and replace them with "realistic" threats like flying fireballs! The producer said,

> Paramount in London had suggested shooting the film there because the special effects would be cheaper to produce. We dropped all of the monster[s]... and rewrote the script [because]... I wanted to do the film here.
>
> My experience with Paramount was one of the best experiences with a studio I've ever had. It was the first film I did there and they gave me a free hand and all the support I could need. They were leery of the fact that we wanted unknowns for the parts. They wanted a name of some sort, but I fought that. I didn't want audiences to see someone playing an astronaut who they'd just seen

> the week before in a Western. That would destroy the realism we were going for.

Unfortunately, in spite of Paramount's initial impulse to produce the Melchior film exactly as he wrote it in its three-hour roadshow format, they caved in to Schenck and allowed him to par the project *way* down. Melchior stated:

> I was all set to direct the film. But when Schenck decided to go into production, I was in the midst of preparing to shoot *The Time Travelers* and was not able to perform the needed work on the script, which had to be condensed to normal size—the super-length having been abandoned—and to direct the production. Another writer, John Higgins, was brought in to shorten the script, and another director, Byron Haskin, was set to direct. Byron had done other science fiction films, such as *The War of the Worlds*, *Conquest of Space* and *From Earth to the Moon* and seemed a good choice.

Together, Haskin and Higgins edited Melchior's screenplay, reducing the scope and cost, while making a few updates based on some newly obtained information about the planet. They eliminated all the native creatures, ice caves, windstorms, exotic jungles and a few other elements with the goal of producing a far more conservative script. Gone were many of the very things that'd made the script the "ultimate sci-fi thrill ride" circa 1962. Perhaps scientifically more accurate—although it took no great leap of faith to imagine water and plants on Mars at the time—but somewhat drained, the final shooting script now featured minute details of rock and geological formations in place of exotic life forms. This was not surprising, since the new writer—Higgins—was a self-described rock hound, an amateur geologist, able to bring a certain amount of reasonably accurate geographical information to the project. At least in those areas he complemented the location planning done by Melchior. Haskin too was concerned over the look of the film, and, in early September 1963, spent considerable time conferring with Melchior, reviewing his notes and design concepts. Melchior commented:

> Byron spent many hours with me in my home during the time between shooting *The Time Travelers*. We went over every location in Death Valley, which had been preselected by me, and discussed the approach to the story.
> They brought in John Higgins, whom I'd never met. As far as I'm concerned he didn't really contribute anything... and he reinstated the one thing I *really* didn't want, which was this master-slave relationship between the astronaut and the alien. I

Robinson Crusoe on Mars producer Aubrey Schenck whips Friday (Vic Lundin) into shape. Inadvertently, the gag pose illustrates Melchior's dissatisfaction with the presentation of the alien as a slave to the Earthman.

> wanted it to be about beings from totally different cultures who found out they could work together. I was *so* angry about that... I wanted to show they were equal and avoid this whole bigoted concept of master and slave. I said okay, if you're going to change things change them, but don't change *this* idea. It's central to the whole theme of the picture.

The film had gone into pre-production in September. Higgins continued his work on trimming the script from that point on into November. In early December, Haskin and Schenck began scouting the Death Valley locations indicated in the script. Locations like Stovepipe Wells, Devil's Golf Course, Mammary Mound, Sandy Swale and Ubehebe Crater. Places more Mars-like than terrestrial. Work, meanwhile, began in earnest on the film at Paramount Studios. Sets were in preparation on two separate soundstages under the supervision of art director Arthur Lonnergan. Assisting him on special technical designs such as the astronaut's suit, the interior of the ship and the very hi-tech, highly miniaturized—for its time—Omnicom transmitter-camcorder unit, was art director Al Nozaki.

The art department went wild designing the scientific equipment required for the story, as well as suggesting by means of hundreds of sketches the many items the stranded astronaut could make on the planet out of space capsule wreckage as well as from natural sources: baskets, blankets, mattresses, etc., woven from the long fibers of the poi plants he finds—created by the art department using eel grass; the same plants, drained and ground into edible mush for pancakes and bread, or dried and used to make candles (forgetting perhaps momentarily that candles probably wouldn't burn without oxygen); natural stones strung up to make chimes, or hollow flutestones used as a musical instrument; oxygen cylinders cut in half for serving trays; a sighting tube made of metal tubes from the space capsule; and many other typically Crusoesque implements and tools. If the studio had any reservations about the title, it wasn't apparent, as the art department made dozens of sketches of possible costumes for the astronaut, including a pointed husk hat and other garments woven out of fibers found on the planet—designs all taken right from old illustrated editions of DeFoe's book. Melchior's sketches were also utilized as design sources or springboards for ideas.

All the film's sequences were storyboarded in excruciating detail: It was Haskin's usual method, having come to direct motion pictures via the special effects department at Warner Brothers.

Haskin's main collaborator during actual production was his cinematographer, Winton Hoch. Winner of Oscars for Best Cinematography for *Joan of Arc* (1948), *She Wore a Yellow Ribbon* (1949) and *The Quiet Man* (1952), Hoch was a physicist who'd begun in the industry as a Technicolor consultant in the early days of color cinematography. His contribution to *Robinson Crusoe on Mars* was considerable.

Haskin's relationship with Hoch extended back to their initial meeting when Hoch was doing aerial photography on *Captains of the Clouds* (1942). Their friendship survived the years and made for tight creative control over the *Robinson Crusoe* shoot. His scientific background was a special aid during the location photography. According to Haskin:

> He was helpful in divining which of those funny-looking stripes in Death Valley were made by water erosion, telltale signs of Earth we were trying to avoid. We could accept wind erosion, but not water erosion. He could quickly tell you what the strata of the rock were caused by and so forth.

Ironically, JPL photos later revealed distinct water-erosion formations on Mars similar to those Haskin so painstakingly tried to avoid. The assignment would turn out to be a real learning experience for Hoch in that the film was shot in the then-new Techniscope process. Techniscope was a system that allowed the normal four sprocket-high 35 millimeter frame to accommodate two rectilinear images—one atop the other. The two-to-one aspect ratio image was later optically enlarged to fill the standard full frame format and printed through a squeeze lens. The resulting image was then ready for release projection as an anamorphic—wide screen—film. The advantages of Techniscope were twofold: Economically, the process used half as much film as a conventionally shot feature. And, on the technical side, it eliminated the use of bulky anamorphic lenses on the camera.

Shooting began within weeks, with Academy Award-winning Winton Hoch behind the camera, and relative unknown Paul Mantee in front of the camera as stranded astronaut Kit Draper. Friday—or Kosmos as Draper first calls him—was played by Vic Lundin.

Haskin's entourage clambered their way up into Suicide Ridge, at times having to manually dig out the roads, widening them for the heavy vehicles. Block and tackle and thousands of feet of rope helped in hauling tons of camera equipment up cliff sides. Eventually even the trucks became useless. All along the way the crew stripped out all the weeds in sight. This was Mars as envisioned by Haskin: Nothing alive was to be seen. Cold. Dead. Mars on Earth.

Robinson Crusoe on Mars was only the second excursion into science fiction for the New York-born former architect and illustrator, art director Lonnergan, though his earlier genre credit was the considerable *Forbidden Planet*:

> Aubrey Schenck came to me and asked if I'd be interested in doing this picture. I was fascinated by the idea of a Robinson Crusoe up there with his man Friday. So I came onto the film from the beginning, from its very conception when we were just playing around with various abstract ideas. I think the film had a better story than *Forbidden Planet* which, I felt, was a little bit too contrived. This had a better flow, but we did have that problem of just one man on the screen most of the time. For that reason a lot of people at the studio kind of wrote it off as being another picture that would just get made and go down the drain.
>
> We had the limitations of what we could do on the Paramount lot with the facilities there, and the limitations of the budget... We did have one major thing going for us; we had Death Valley. It had kind of a look that might be Mars. That's a location we didn't have on *Forbidden Planet*.
>
> There were several Death Valley locations that I had to reproduce in detail on the stage—such as the sand cave—so I had to be on location during shooting... as they got into areas I was involved with. I commuted back and forth.

In all, 13 sets, many quite extensive, had to be constructed on stage: two crew cabins aboard the Mars Gravity Probe 1, the capsule crash site, Kit's cave home, a warm springs spa, the mining crater, an inner chamber, various areas under the Martian canals, the interior of an obsidian mountain, an underground pool and the polar cap.

According to Lonnergan:

> Subterranean cliffs and ledges were [made up of a] series of rock formations, maybe 25 feet high each. They were on rollers which allowed us to

Kit (Paul Mantee) and Friday at the rock pool in *Robinson Crusoe on Mars*.

put them together at different angles and change them as we progressed along them so you never knew where they were. The actors were always going along a continuous wall as far as the audience was concerned... All of this was custom-designed and built for this picture. I sketched them first, then modeled them in clay—in drawing it's very difficult to indicate exactly what you want. I modeled them in one-half-inch scale, and these were cast in plaster. By slicing the model up we had a section every five or ten feet. In clay we were able to imitate what our full-size pieces would be.

The sections were primarily used for extensive scenes of the characters fleeing from Friday's masters through a vast network of underground tunnels. Nozaki stated:

They had this idea that the surface of Mars was characterized by these crevasses that'd been formed when the planet was younger. With time, they got covered over with a layer of a certain kind of rock— I can't remember what it was supposed to be—so now there were these tunnels extending all over the under-surface of the planet, and the characters would later use them as an escape route.

Lonnergan recalled:

> The ravine with the water spa was made of these same rock formations. These were built on wire and mesh atop framing which was sprayed with a type of plastic fiberglass that would give it character. The texture of the rocks we got by using actual skins taken off real rock formations—you get a sense of surface realism that way... I had the paint department rough it in, then I got scenic artists to work the final detail in.

To simulate the vari-hued phosphorescence described in the script, cinematographer Hoch had the art department use fluorescent paint which he lit with ultraviolet light for an eerie effect.

It had been decided early on that Mars would have a red sky which was to be added optically. Haskin had come up with the ingenious idea of using the skies above Death Valley as a blue screen to produce mattes. The deep blue winter skies provided their own mattes into which orange and red-hued skyscapes would be inserted later by Lawrence Butler's optical printer. A dozen years later, Viking Lander photos revealed the accuracy of this aesthetic choice.

Hoch felt that some special lighting effect on the actors would help sell the idea of red sky ambient illumination. Bulky clusters of red fill lights were out of the question because of the precarious locations. Hoch's solution—red foil reflectors that would kick just enough warm fill light back at the actors to visually tie in the sky color. The reflectors, cut into circles, eliminated angular, unnatural reflections from Paul Mantee's helmet visor.

Another factor: working conditions that would try the patience of a saint. Arthur Lonnergan recalled:

> It was *hot,* but none of us really folded. We walked down a huge crater above Stovepipe Wells that was so steep we had a helluva time getting back out!

Another perilous location was Ubehebe Crater, the site for filming the astronaut and Friday emerging from the inner volcanic regions of Mars. For these scenes, the crew descended into the great crater itself where thick, powdery ash aggravated climbing and made camera maintenance a hopeless task. Working from within the abyss, the mechanical effects crew planted powerful red-hued smoke pots in and around the crater. On cue, a hellish wall of smoke was instantly created, synthesizing the spoutings of an active volcano.

It proved to be a rough shoot for the cast and crew: In a way the behind-the-scenes experience proved how difficult survival in such an environment could be.

Robinson Crusoe on Mars **featured strong performances—Paul Mantee as Commander Kit Draper and Adam West as Colonel Dan McReady.**

One of the best things that had emerged during principal photography, somewhat to everyone's surprise, was the strength of the performances of their two leads, Paul Mantee and Vic Lundin. Mantee projected a compelling sincerity as the stranded astronaut, indulging in neither theatrics nor method. His honesty as a performer brought the proper focus to the story even during its more fantastic moments. Scenes of Draper learning to play his bagpipe, wearily watching an out-of-date training film and quantifying his chances of survival with heroic resignation gained their strength from the very directness of his approach.

Lundin as Friday, with less screen time, and far fewer lines, developed an equally attractive character, a feat again arising from a sincere performance completely devoid of cynicism. Both Lundin and Mantee amplified each other rather than competed, with a resulting truth in acting rare in motion pictures, much less motion pictures in the science fiction genre. Melchior had developed a complex and highly authentic alien language for the Friday character drawn upon his extensive knowledge of linguistics. Melchior related:

> I had our hero teach Friday little by little. Why would this guy come out and speak English? I had a whole vocabulary, a mathematical system all worked out. Since the man had three fingers on each hand, their mathematical system was Base Six.

The alien ships for *Robinson Crusoe on Mars* were built to resemble the ships from *War of the Worlds*.

Unfortunately, all this work was deleted by second writer John Higgins. This turn of events was yet again reversed when director Haskin allowed actor Lundin to devise his own alien language for the part, which he based on Mayan language patterns.

The miniature and effects photography on *Robinson Crusoe on Mars* went into production in December 1963 just as, across town, Melchior was in post-production on *The Time Travelers*. The effects work continued on through March 1964, by which time Melchior's more complicated but smaller film was already in the can.

Although special photographic effects occurred throughout *Robinson Crusoe on Mars*, they were to be entirely subservient to the story and characters. The effects included dozens of orange-sky mattes; insert matte shot of the South Polar ice cap; the Mars Gravity Probe-1 approaching Mars; several fly-bys above Mars; three views of the lander's descent; Martian aurora borealis; crevasse matte painting; Draper's spa matte shot; alien satellite fly-bys; alien ray blasting cliffs; planetoid orbiting above Mars; fireballs; alien mothership landing; Omnicom-screen views; scanner screens; underground fire plume and climatic matte shot of a polar cap meltdown and the rescue ship landing.

The single involved miniature built for the film was that of the Gravity Probe, designed by Al Nozaki, known to genre fans as the key creator of visuals for *The War of the Worlds*. The two-foot-long metal construction was supported by a hidden armature, animated frame by frame, then double-exposed and/or matted atop background paintings and starfields. The same approach was taken in shooting the three *The War of the Worlds*-like manta-ray satellite models built for the film. These were mounted by supports from above, then animated. They were given eccentric maneuvering qualities—rushing vertical moves up and down in frame, abrupt stops and forward rushes directly into the camera.

The spacecraft sequences had an artificial quality—the subject of some criticism. Screenwriter John Higgins recalled:

> What I really didn't like were those saucer ships. Something about the way they moved was wrong.

> They looked like cartoons. I don't really know whose idea it was to do them that way. I had something different in mind. My idea was that they were small radio-controlled ships sent out from a mother ship—like a whaling ship with its dories. When I saw the rushes I thought they should change it somehow, or cut it shorter, which is what they did.

The distinctive look arose from an after-the-fact decision to accelerate all of the shots via skip-frame printing—i.e., the printing of every other frame of film. The technique tended to exaggerate the strobing—or blurless—effect inherent in noncontinuous motion photography. Nozaki explained:

> The special effects director felt that if these ships were traveling at, say, 15,000 miles per hour, maybe they should look like they were going that fast, rather than what they'd actually look like. In real life [in space], of course, they'd appear to be moving slowly. But he decided to speed the whole thing up for dramatic effect.

Upon its release the film attracted extremely favorable reactions from the critics, both in local papers and the trades. Critic Eugene Archer of the usually guarded *New York Times* remarked that while survival in hostile territory had always been an effective grabber as plot devices go, the combining of the DeFoe saga "with a science fiction setting... turns out to be a surprisingly good idea." *Los Angeles Times* critic Kevin Thomas gave the film one of the best reviews ever accorded a science fiction film up to that time:

> The film's overall design and careful composition of each scene make it a work of art... *Robinson Crusoe on Mars* is that true rarity, a multiple-run masterpiece... A triumph of technique, it has superb effects and strong performances by its space age hero... Ib Melchior brings to the conquest of space a universal and timeless appeal.

The trades were equally favorable: "An enthralling screen experience," raved *Variety*, "an outstanding achievement of its genre, a class science fiction film that is a tribute to the creative and cinematic ingenuity of all who toiled on it." "A genuine effort to use the theme in modern terms, not just another interplanetary cheapie," remarked *The Hollywood Reporter*. Ray Pickard, in his *Companion to the Movies*, called the film "vastly superior to others far better known of its kind."

The film continued to weather the passing of time much better than others of its era. Serious and less wild-eyed thinking behind the scenes produced an unusually realistic, sober space adventure. Unfortunately, the ubiquitous budgetary restrictions

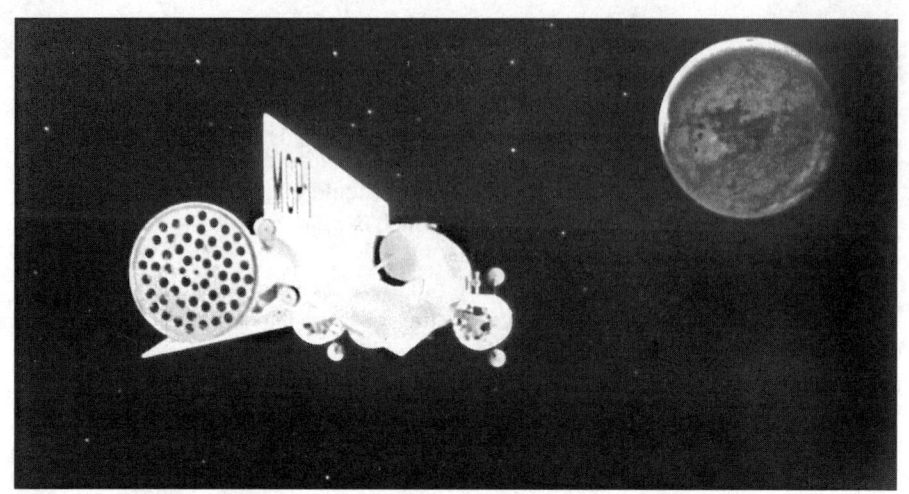

Little do the brave astronauts know what fate awaits them as they approach Mars in Robinson Crusoe on Mars.

and some careless thinking hurt the production. Certainly Friday's alien masters, clad in *Abbott and Costello Go to Mars*-type suits were grotesquely out of synch with the overall production design. Melchior's designs for Friday's captors were far more interesting: Cleo Baldon had sketched squat, armored alien miners and guards far superior to the suits seen in the film. She commented:

> I loved our alien spacemen. Underneath these suits, they had a brutish, no-neck quality. [We were thinking of] that line in *Cat on a Hot Tin Roof* when she talks about "the kids with no necks."

Baldon also aided in the design of alien weapons, complete with curvilinear stocks contoured to fit the guards' brutish shoulders.

Although Melchior remained extremely pleased with Haskin's film for the most part, he was disappointed with some of the director's choices:

> He did some things I did not like. I would've used Death Valley even more so than he did. Then he used the same ships he had in *The War of the Worlds*. That wasn't in the script. I thought it would look like we crimped from that film, and that wasn't my intention.

The choice is all the more perplexing since the producers weren't necessarily trying to save costs by reusing existing models: The alien saucers, in fact, had to be custom built for *Robinson Crusoe on Mars*, and could've been conceived in any shape or design. Al Nozaki himself had no idea why Haskin made the choice to use the old design.

Melchior also felt let down by the use of a monkey—Barney, the woolly monkey, as Mona—the astronaut's companion. This had already become tired in countless jungle films. His own concept for a Martian pet, Marsa, "could've been done with an armadillo altered with a rubber collar, coloration, and so on..." Likewise, Friday, who Melchior had described as a striking, metal-suited man evocative of another world: His three-fingered hand, Melchior pointed out, could easily have been created by grouping the fingers together and covering them in a simple rubber prosthetic, as he had done to create the deviant's second hand in *The Time Travelers*.

His biggest complaint was that his concept of Friday as a being of nobility and intelligence who was to be greeted with *equality*—was altered to the project's detriment. In the process, his theme of racial equality beyond petty, Earthbound prejudice was diluted by the astronaut's standard assertion of Yankee superiority over all beings—human, animal or alien.

Al Nozaki, having read Melchior's original epic version, ultimately found the completed film a disappointment. A full-blown epic on Mars would've been more to his liking. He would've been up to the challenge: After all, he had worked for Cecil B. DeMille for years, and had art directed one of the biggest films made up to that time, *The Ten Commandments*:

> This was cheaper than *The War of the Worlds*—we cut corners everywhere, so when I saw it, I'd just see the things I didn't think worked. At first this [*Robinson Crusoe on Mars*] was going to be a really big film, but they kept cutting it down, kept cutting the script. I didn't really like it by the time they were finished, I was sick of it. This process went on for months. They kept rewriting it. It was better to start with.

Producer Aubrey Schenck recalled:

> That was both Paul Mantee and Vic Lundin's first film. They've done a lot of things since then, but those were their first roles. I think they did a good job... I received good feedback on the film. When it came out, the critics liked it. New York said they finally have made a good science-fiction film. But the studio didn't know how to sell it and it didn't do as well as it probably should have—not that it did that bad. We also may have lost some of the adults because of the Walt Disney appellation of the title, which the studio insisted upon.
>
> I was very active in the production of this film and am proud of it. I had an idea for a sequel which would have taken him to another galaxy [*Robinson Crusoe in the Invisible Galaxy*] and actually was

ready to implement it when there was a change in the upper echelon at Paramount, and it was dropped.

Byron Haskin had guided an earlier excursion to Mars—*Conquest of Space*—on a much shakier ride, both technically and dramatically. *Robinson Crusoe on Mars* was based on much stronger material, even in its edited-down form. "I consider [that film] one of the best things I've ever done," Haskin declared in later years, "because it had basically one of the soundest stories ever written: a man conquering a hostile environment, but finding, when the pressure's off, he can't conquer his own loneliness... "

Arthur Lonergan pretty much summed it up with an equally satisfied note: "It's a strange thing in this industry, but once in a while everything comes together nicely. Everybody's happy, and you know it's going to be a good picture."

If the film had been shot as originally written, *Robinson Crusoe on Mars* might have resulted in a space epic in the modern *Star Wars* mold. Nonetheless, it is one of the best science fiction films to come out of the space-age era—a reflection on the realities of existing in and of itself. The story of a man's survival on a hellish world was near mythic—the myth being that of the eternal man enduring against all odds. *Robinson Crusoe on Mars* came at a time when its character's persistent faith in his ability to conquer the unknown coincided with the Kennedy-era belief in Man's ability to survive and explore the "new frontier" for the benefit of all mankind.

What the film did achieve was a sense of the authentic—on both technical and human terms. It showed audiences Martian red skies and rocks that discharged oxygen long before the Viking Lander showed them for real. It predicted accurate advances in miniaturization—as exemplified by the Omnicom video system—and projected a far off, yet believable, world into the viewers' imagination. It did many things good science fiction pictures are supposed to, but rarely, do.

"I consider *Robinson Crusoe on Mars* to be probably the best [of my films]," stated Melchior. "It had a story which had more fact to it. I tried to make it as scientific—for its time—as I could."

Cleo Baldon stated:

> Survival is an important theme for Ib. His own ability to survive is very good. He had a tough way to live—if he'd thought of it that way—when he was a child—although I don't think he did: His mother was ill all the time and he was released into the streets of Copenhagen. At age 11, when his mother died, Ib's father put him in a boarding school... they had to raise their own crops and raise the animals and so on. And there was a certain quality to that that was actually perfectly suited to him... The intrepidness of the man—was already there in this little boy. He was born with it, I think.

SPACE FAMILY ROBINSON

On a personal note, 1964 had been a landmark year for Melchior. On January 18 he'd married Cleo Baldon. It was a relationship that brought together two creatively centered people who shared a rich variety of similar passions. It was truly a melding. They helped each other with their various projects, co-developed design ideas and traveled together extensively.

Professionally it was also a banner year for Melchior. In February, having completed the direction of *The Time Travelers*, and with *Robinson Crusoe on Mars*—the first of his proposed updates of adventure classics—nearing completion at Paramount, he decided to strike while the iron was hot: He quickly put the finishing touches on a 38-page treatment he'd been developing since March 1960, when he first hit upon the idea of updating adventure classics, a science fiction version of *Swiss Family Robinson*. Little did he realize what an odyssey of frustration had begun with his registration of *Space Family Robinson* on February 28, 1964.

Melchior's fascination with the planet of choice of the 1960s—Mars—was side-stepped with this project as the inadvertent landing site became a distant moon. Set in the year 1997, it told of the trials and tribulations of a family of five when their Mars-colony bound ship, the Alpha, is struck by an asteroid, forcing passengers and crew to abandon the vessel. The Robinson family—three teenaged boys and their parents—plus a single crewman, are ejected in an escape pod. Uncontrolled acceleration propels them to a crash landing on Titan, one of the moons of Saturn. The crewman dies in the crash, and the first task the Robinsons face is a burial service for the brave man.

The moon world proves to have a life-supportive environment, and the family begins the arduous process of survival, including setting up fortified living quarters in a cave, establishing a radio rescue beacon and planting a garden.

A series of novel adventures follows, oft-time spun directly from *Swiss Family Robinson*. The youngest boy, Jimmy, encounters an armadillo-like creature—an idea not used from Melchior's version of *Robinson Crusoe on Mars*. They take it in as a pet and name it Teeta. Later, suspicious sounds around their camp motivate them to seek shelter in a valley of demonically shaped stone pillars carved by erosion. Here they set up their tree house amongst the stone.

Later one night they observe a *light* in the distance. The boys sojourn to discover the light source culminates in discovery of a cave before which lies a giant alien skeleton. The cave itself is full of alien artifacts, including a technological archive, strange glass tubes which revive a fearsome creature, a vat that gives birth to a monstrosity and a machine that causes Jimmy to disappear. After a series of these adventures in which all seems lost, the boys are reunited and escape.

Back at the rock treehouse, the family discovers that the source of the earlier sounds around their first camp was caused by a young girl named Jane Winfield who also crash landed on this world in an escape pod. Some distance away her brother Edward awaits her return with food. He was injured in the crash and has become ill.

The boys mount a rescue mission. The going is tough. They almost get sucked down into thick layers of unstable dust-powder—but Teeta shows them the way to safety. Finally they endure a tremendous tide-storm while transporting the fever-wracked Edward back to the safety of their home.

In the end, a rescue ship comes for them. But having gained great strengths and endurance while living here, they decide to stay permanently on Titan. The strange world has become their new home. The ship's captain does the honors of marrying the oldest of the Robinson boys and Jane, a happy, far cry from their first line of duty—burying a dead man—upon arriving on this world.

Melchior's treatment seemed a natural: pure space age family entertainment built on elements that had proven popularity. He had an agreement with his *Time Travelers*-collaborator David Hewitt to produce visual illusions along the same lines of that film, an approach Melchior now christened Technimagic. As part of the package, Technimagic would be used to create in-camera effects, such as the disappearance of one of the boys, the creation of an alien monster out of a glass tube and a lava effect to destroy the creature. And, as usual, Melchior worked out detailed budgets, and locations to prove the viability of every one of his concepts.

The script treatment was passed on to a number of potential investors, producers and distributors, including Hunt Stromberg, Jr. at CBS, Sam Arkoff at AIP, Jim Allen Trudeaux of Jata Productions, Louis M. Heyward at AIP, Helen Miles of Carthay Studios (the studio used for filming *The Time Travelers*) and producer and longtime friend William Redlin. Ads in both *Variety* and *The Hollywood Reporter* appeared in July 1964 announcing that *Space Family Robinson* was "in preparation."

It all sounded great. The project had tremendous momentum and seemed a shoe-in for actual production.

Enter Irwin Allen.

Ten days after the advertisements in *Variety* and *The Hollywood Reporter* appeared, producer Allen, known for films like *The Animal World* and *The Lost World*, announced his own pre-production of a project called *Space Family Robinson*.

The announcement was for a TV series that supposedly had nothing to do with Melchior's development. A rather surprising state of affairs, since a careful going over of Melchior's fastidious records established a rather intriguing paper trail of mutual contacts, to say nothing of an extremely similar updating of the classic novel. Eventually Melchior and producer Redlin were able to put together a list of 42 points of similarity between Melchior's treatment—which was registered months before Allen's first draft teleplay. These included story ideas not present in the original novel, virtually identical descriptive passages, and specific details of a number of gags and props—the sudden blossoming of a plant, the presence of five-foot-tall alien remains in a cave full of archives and artifacts, a valley of colossal sculpted rocks, etc.

Several people associated with the Allen project who were also acquaintances of Melchior assumed, because of the numerous similarities between the projects, that, of course, they were working on Melchior's *Space Family Robinson* project. But they were curious why Melchior himself wasn't working on it. And when David Hewitt visited the Irwin Allen production offices during the early stages of the project by invitation of Allen associate, director Felix Fiest, he viewed storyboards and idea sketches that almost identically paralleled work done by himself and Ib Melchior.

Melchior suddenly found himself fighting an uphill battle to get his original version of *Space Family Robinson* off the ground in spite of much initial interest. Had it been appropriated by another producer? As he began to contemplate some type of remedial action, he was quickly advised that taking on the big boys when you're new in town could prove not only fruitless—these guys after all had very deep pockets—but a bad career move. He was still establishing himself in the business and could ill afford to find forces working against him behind his back. It was a setback for himself as well as all the others in his camp, including his special effects creator, Dave Hewitt. But he didn't give up hope for the project. For the moment he could only wait for further developments, keep records of all his dealings on the project and seek advice.

Lost in Space **emulated films such as** *The Angry Red Planet* **and** *Robinson Crusoe on Mars* **down to the strange landscapes and monsters.**

Along with *Robinson Crusoe on Mars* and *Space Family Robinson*, Melchior invested some time developing his third updated classic, titled *Gulliver's Space Travels*. An out-and-out adventure story aimed more at a younger audience than any of his others, the main character—unabashedly—is Gulliver Mace, an Earthman who, along with his companions, has been forced to crash land their ship, Nomad, on a small moon of Jupiter. Gulliver is separated from the crew and presumed lost. The Nomad departs, leaving Gulliver behind. In short order he is discovered and taken captive by giant beings engaged in a colossal mining operation on the same moon. In search of vitally needed uranium, the giants probe Gulliver's mind and discover that the element can also be found on the Earth—a less hostile environment. They begin preparations for an assault on the Earth, armed with vast, super-advanced weapons. The climax details Gulliver's quest to sabotage the aliens' murderous mission.

For the project, Melchior intended to experiment with the idea of mixing a perfectly proportioned midget actor for Gulliver with unusually tall actors for the giants—certainly not quite as extreme as the giants of Brobdingnag in Jonathan Swift's episode in *Gulliver's Travels*.

During this time, Melchior took advantage of the long delays between meetings and responses to keep his idea hopper full of other new projects. Among these creative efforts was a projected one-hour science fiction adventure series detailing the voyages of heroic Captain Christopher and the crew of his huge starship into deep, uncharted space to seek out new worlds. *Star Trek*? No. This was July 1964, two years *before* the Roddenberry show. This was *Columbus of the Stars*.

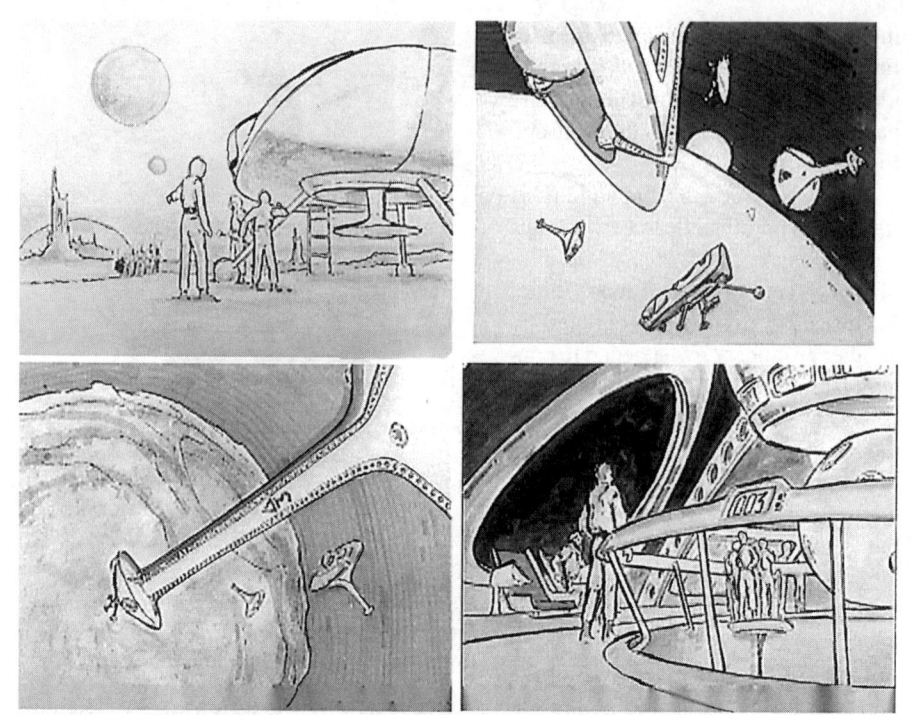

Melchior and Vic Lundin had these illustrations created to help sell their proto-*Star Trek* project *Starship Explorers*.

Melchior had developed the idea for the series, which was also known as *Starship Explorers*—in conjunction with actor Vic Lundin, who had portrayed his character of Friday in *Robinson Crusoe on Mars*. Their concept was inspired by the voyage of Columbus. It was to feature three interplanetary ships, each with a crew of 20 traveling the vast gulfs of space by means of an "advanced space/time warp drive." The premise was set in the year 2077, a time when the Earth is suffering from the problems of overpopulation. New inhabitable worlds must be found to house the ever-growing millions.

The space fleet is under the command of Captain Christopher, a "brilliant, forceful, imaginative young space captain in his early 30s," who pilots the flagship. Also on board the flagship is the "Chief Scientist, a mature man perhaps 45 years of age. Because of certain basic differences there is a conflict between this man of science and the young Captain, although at the same time the two men hold one another in great respect. This man will also be a continuing character."

In addition, there is a young "Astro-Engineer" who is "hot-headed, but a genius in his vital field"; a female officer under whose command the women spacecrew serve; and lastly, a forerunner of *Star Trek: The Next Generation*'s Data, a "fabulous, highly complex Servo-Android, who is one of the running characters." The Melchior treatment elaborates that the Android is a "robot made approximately in the image of man, [and] is designed to perform duties patterned for the size and build of a man. An interesting and unique relationship develops between Christopher and this android—almost a friendship, certainly an attachment such as most people form for a faithful car or boat. This android also serves many unusual functions—for example taking chances no human could take, and surviving in environments no human could tolerate. All an unique, fascinating addition to the cast, whose presence lends opportunities for unusual story lines, and startling special effects along the lines of Technimagic."

The vast panorama of space and the exploration of "solar system after solar system" with these characters aboard the "fabulous, awe-inspiring ships, outfitted with the most weird and wondrous equipment of a totally novel technology" was to be the background for what could've been both highly a successful series as well as the kind of visually exciting science fiction that appealed to Melchior. The story possibilities seemed virtually endless considering the wide variety of alien cultures and creatures, environments and outer space phenomena that would present itself week after week.

One of the first story outlines Melchior developed for the series had the flagship become magnetized and nearly buried in a cloud of ferromagnetic particles, then narrowly avoiding a plummet into the sun of a distant star. The planets of the star system one by one prove inhospitable to human life. But, finally, on the second planet from the sun, they find a beautiful, lush world. Captain Christopher and his crew land and discover great abandoned cities, totally lifeless, but once apparently peopled—based on artifacts found—by a magnificent race. Life has been wiped out: Long ago the planet had passed through the tail of a comet that killed everyone. Christopher and his crew find themselves confronted by powerful, self-maintaining robots that, even after eons, still fight to protect their long-gone masters.

Other stories for the proposed series included "A Good View From All Seats" about an attempt to rescue an inherently evil civilization; "Stimulant" in which lab animals are "taken too far" in their physical and mental development and become a menace to the ship; "Regeneration" in which the starship crew works together with an alien civilization to save it from a growth process gone wild; and "Amok" in which an android exoskeleton is tampered with and attempts to destroy the ship. Throughout, the stories provided constant setbacks for the crew, even as news of the Earth's situation worsened and put increasing pressure on them to find a New World for humankind. Melchior also outlined a variation on the TV series idea, called *The Outworlders*, conceived on an epic scale, for possible motion picture development: *The Outworlders* was to relate the adventures of 20 specialists who cross light years of space in suspended animation to colonize a planet in the Alpha Centauri system. Their journey, the building of the colony and all the challenges they encountered were to be the film's subject matter.

But alas, completely unknown to Melchior and Lundin, a format very similar to *Columbus of the Stars/Starship Explorers* was in the works at Desilu Studios: The soundness of Melchior's concept was brutally demonstrated by the tremendous success of *Star Trek* as it proved to be one of the few truly international cultural phenomena created by the entertainment industry in the 20th century. One could imagine an "alternate world" version of the show in which *Columbus of the Stars*—or *Starship Explorers*— filled that same cultural niche. For Melchior it was, unfortunately, another case of what might have been.

Melchior felt validated, as well as deeply frustrated, by the similarities between *Star Trek* and his concept. His own project would have to be filed away. He was, however, intrigued enough to put together notes for several potential *Star Trek* episodes. Thirty-five years later, however, he would be unable to recall whether or not he ever actually pitched them to the story editors. "The Attendant" told of the Enterprise crew finding one lone man living on a planet. Beaming down to meet this mystery man, members of the exploration party inexplicably *vanish*. Probing further, light and sound diffractions are detected on the planet's surface, giving rise to speculation that some kind of complex actually exists there, which is being cloaked. Spock discovers that the mystery man is not a man at all, but a humanoid robot. It turns out there was a civilization on the planet, but the entire population had themselves cryogenically preserved when their world became unlivable after passing through a comet's tail. They are housed in a vast complex made invisible to protect them from discovery. Their minds are all hooked into a mental stimulator that provides adventures for their quiescent minds—a state that is so satisfactory that the humanoid attendant has not awakened them. As a matter of fact, he just put some of the Enterprise crew into the same state!

Another story dealt with the Enterprise encountering another, *identical* Enterprise with the exact same crew—with slight and puzzling differences. The Enterprise has slipped the space/time continuum where two near-identical universes are in touch.

For a time in real life it was as if two intergalactic starships—the ones from *Starship Explorers* and *Star Trek* had entered the universe at the same time—with "slight and puzzling differences": The crew of the Enterprise entered this universe and stayed... while the crews of *Starship Explorers* veered off into a far more distant alternate universe where go all unrealized dreams.

THE OUTER LIMITS

A few months after putting together his *Starship Explorers* proposal, while awaiting word from potential interested parties, Melchior pitched some ideas to the second season producer of *The Outer Limits* TV series, Ben Brady. Brady had stepped into a conspicuous hole left by the departure of the show's originators, Leslie Stevens and Joseph Stephano. In filling that creative void, he had steered the show away from non-genre writers. His idea was to utilize authors firmly established in the realm of science fiction: people like Harlan Ellison, Jerry Sohl and Clifford Simak. Melchior was a natural. According to Brady in *The Outer Limits Companion*, "Ib is a science fiction freak... He did the most 'science fictiony' stories I'd ever heard of." He later confessed that he'd been open to many of Melchior's ideas—if only the show had continued.

Melchior discussed some ideas with the producers, including a variation on one of his *Time Travelers* concepts, outlining a story about a man, a woman and the woman's daughter caught in a terrible paradox in frozen time as the result of an Air Force experimental flight. Brady liked the story enough to commission a script from Melchior. It became story number 67 in the series. After several redrafts the story, originally titled "The Gordian Knot," became "The Premonition."

The story literalized the ticking clock metaphor integral to the best of suspenseful plotting, and time's arcane intricacies themselves became the centerpiece—the Gordian Knot of Melchior's mythically referenced original title—that must be untied to save three lives.

Test pilot Jim Darcey, in trying out a daring new maneuver in an experimental plane, slips ahead of time into a frozen limbo in which he can move about while the entire world appears motionless. He awakens in the wreckage of his plane on the ground and, looking around, sees a flying hawk apparently frozen in flight about to catch its prey, a fleeing jackrabbit frozen in stride, technicians at the air base absolutely motionless and even his own plane stuck in the air heading earthward before the crash. His wife Linda, who had raced to the test sight in her car to meet the descending plane, has been caught up by the cone of the plane's sonic time boom and joins her husband in the time limbo.

Soon it becomes apparent that time itself has not actually stopped, but is moving forward relative to them at a vastly *reduced* speed. It will eventually re-synchronize with them. They are in fact wandering about in a very near past that is slowly *catching up to them*. They calculate how long they have until they must return to the exact place they were in when they jumped ahead of time in order to re-synchronize with the normal time flow. In Jim's case that would be in his just crash-landed jet. Linda must take her place in her careening car. Complicating matters is an encounter with a trapped shadow creature who faces a meaningless eternity in this limbo unless he can exchange places with one of them. More urgently, they discover that their daughter will be run over by a truck far from where they need to be if the course of events plays out without their intervention. But how can they be in two places at the same time?

The drama takes place in moments between seconds. The creature is foiled and the necessary time differential calculations are worked out. Their daughter is saved by clever use of seat belts taken from Linda's car: Jim ties them into a length and wraps one end around the hub of the threatening truck's wheel and ties the other end to the hand brake. The belt will pull the brake to stop the truck just as soon as it begins to move forward.

Jim and Linda return to their positions before the time jump and re-synch with real time. Back to normal, they now have no recollection of the events in the time limbo, only a vague premonition that they should immediately check up on their daughter's safety.

The series' signature "control voice" concludes:

> Man is forever solving the most perplexing problems as he ventures ever further into the unknown. But where are the outer limits of his ingenuity? Will he ever encounter a problem—a Gordian Knot—which he cannot ultimately cut?

Melchior's earlier draft of the story prior to edits and rewrites was longer and more complex: "The Gordian Knot"—the title reflecting a theme retained throughout rewrites—not only showcased the kind of events that might occur in the "molasses world," as Melchior referred to it, but sought to remain absolutely faithful to the rules of logic dictated by the premise.

In "The Gordian Knot," Jim Darcy is not married to Linda. Linda is Linda Austin and is recently divorced. She has a daughter, Janie. Events unfold in the beginning very much as they do in "The Premonition." Darcy is testing a new plane. He makes his high-G maneuver creating a shockwave time-displacement in which he and his plane and Linda, driving her car near the test range, are all catapulted forward in time 27 seconds. Time is, for them, advancing at the rate of one second *per day*. Everything is frozen in the moment, absolutely motionless.

Linda is angry with Darcy, blaming the test for their situation. She lives at the base with her daughter and mother and insists upon looking into their condition. Darcy and Linda split up; Darcy goes to check on conditions at the air base control center; Linda goes to her house.

Along the way—more often than in the episode itself—the two help delineate the weirdness of the frozen world with their unsuccessful attempts to jostle and move objects around them. They struggle to lift a pair of earphones; fail to budge the branches of a simple plant—it feels as if it were made of steel—and cut their hands on blades of grass that act like razor-sharp, green-colored needles. At her house, Linda is terrified to find her mother in a frightening tableau:

> Bent awkwardly over the sink is an elderly woman; her head is forced under the faucet; her hair is frozen in a grotesque mass of tangled clumps flecked

In "The Premonition" a time jump produced weird anomalies such as frozen time and the occurrence of the same car in two places.

and streaked with a slimy-looking white matter; her head and face are engulfed by a transparent, frozen-flowing substance, which runs and drips from her in a motionless, glass-sculptured cascade; behind it and through it—turned directly towards Linda—the woman's face can be seen... CAMERA Zooms in to a CLOSE UP: The woman's eyes are screwed tightly shut, her features hideously distorted and tortured, as if in great strain, mouth half open in what seems to be a desperate, vain effort to breathe through the clinging, engulfing mass. It is a frightening, harrowing, marrow-freezing sight—even though the woman, in reality, is merely in the time-frozen process of rinsing out her hair.

The scene is one of many frozen details that the producers elected to cut either for reasons of time or budget.

"The Gordian Knot" develops similarly to that of "The Premonition," though with intriguing differences that give it more the scope and texture of a feature-length motion picture: Since time is moving slower than in the series, Linda and Darcy must survive for 54 hours in this immobile world. Darcy comments, "We might as well be marooned on another planet—and a blasted hostile one at that." They are able to nourish themselves with candy bars and a couple sticks of chewing gum they have between them. But water is more important, and sorely lacking—until Darcy realizes his plane is equipped with two experimental fuel cell batteries. Darcy explains: "They use hy-

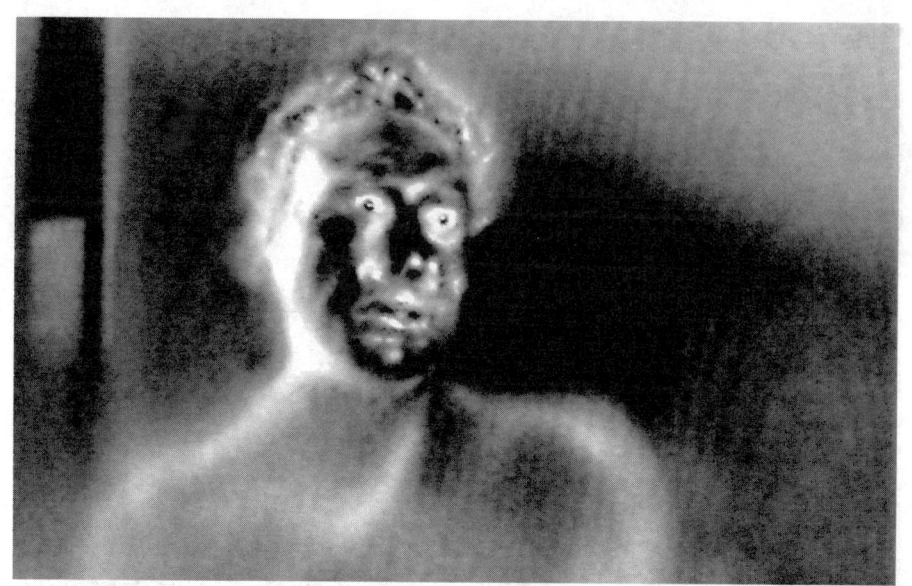

The Limbo being, a creature stuck in time, from "The Premonition." Melchior's original creature was a more nebulous entity.

drogen and oxygen gasses to convert chemical energy into electrical power and, as a by-product, they combine the hydrogen and oxygen in the ratio of two atoms to one. H20.... *Water*. As much as 30 gallons a week." Darcy puts the batteries to work to produce drinking water.

But other challenges face them: Young Janie is found to be riding her little red wagon down the driveway at the house. A big, non-moving moving van parked in the street blocks her view of an oncoming car. As Linda and Darcy find evidence that time here is not at an absolute standstill but creeping ever-slowly forward like the hands of a clock, they see that Janie—if allowed to continue on her way—will be struck and likely killed by the car.

They also catch a glimpse of a strange gaseous being lurking about the air base. It is tenuous, and—like some Lovecraftian entity—"it seems to flow and undulate with monstrous, alien lights and shadows and shapes," and raises "shadow—dripping arms" as it stalks them. At various points "it carves an unearthly face out of its shadows and light." Unlike in "The Premonition," the Limbo Creature makes attempts to kill them. At one point it tosses a heavy piece of the engine taken from the plane down upon Darcy and Linda from a rooftop at the base, almost killing them. It also sets a spring-loaded metal shaft inside the cockpit of the plane that almost spears Darcy. As they go from one crisis to another, their characters are given time to develop. Darcy must constantly reassure himself that as complex as the problems are, there *has to be* a solution—Melchior's third way out. And he and Linda begin to work as a team. She loses her anger and begins to admire the seemingly indefatigable pilot who is constantly drawing on his imagination as the problems stack up.

They fend the creature off with flares. It is afraid of fire as in the show itself. The Limbo Creature is, like them, limited to using only those things on the plane or in the car that came through the time-jump. Nothing else can be moved. They also figure out that they will synchronize with time, and when that happens, anything—*any* piece of matter taken from the car or plane, as well as themselves—will cease to exist at that point unless within the close proximity of the time-jump zone.

The creature is trying to take their place—as in "The Premonition"—in order to escape the time limbo. And it will do anything to escape. "It's the old kill or be killed," muses Darcy.

As events unfold, Darcy and Linda come up with a plan to save Janie. The actual means for doing this were hotly argued by Melchior: As far as he was concerned, the premise of the story by its very nature precluded the use of *any object from the plane or car by itself* as a means of saving the girl, since it would simply cease to exist at the most critical time of re-synchronization. Melchior argued and dispatched memos to the *Outer Limits* story department begging them not to use the seat-belt idea—which was being foisted on him in the rewrite.

But arguing proved useless. The seat belt was used anyway, if not entirely logical: They felt the idea of tying together seat belts segued nicely into the notion of a Gordian Knot, even if that wasn't the final title.

Melchior believed that the only thing that could be used by Darcy and Linda would be something that was created *while within the time limbo itself*—which was the *water* from the batteries. Darcy works out a plan: He removes the inner-tube of one of the car tires and fills it with the battery water. He hangs it off the moving van's mirror in such a way that when time re-synchronizes and the tire itself ceases to exist, the water will splash out into the street in front of the oncoming car. The gamble is that the driver will see the spray of water and veer away from it, not only as a natural reaction, but doubly so because the car is a convertible with its top down.

In fact that *is* what happens in "The Gordian Knot" and Janie is saved.

In the end, Linda and Darcy do *not* forget everything that has happened to them in the time limbo. Instead, the 54-plus hours spent together has resulted in a deep bond sure to develop into a relationship. As Darcy puts his arm around her, Linda reacts in put-on shock: "Mr. Darcy. Please. We've only known each other 27 seconds."

The quality that really would've distinguished "The Gordian Knot" from "The Premonition" was the much greater exploitation of the frozen-time world's inherent novelty. Water, in the original, is seen in mid-motion, along with other falling objects—if only the bullet-time photography seen in films like *The Matrix* existed at the time the episode was filmed!—and numerous objects such as a doll and a piece of cellophane are felt, kicked, stepped on or otherwise shown to be un-liftable, immovable and locked in place.

One of the most effective sequences was an inspired nightmare. At one point, Darcy must hide out in a windowless side room whose sole entrance—a door—is partially open. It's just wide enough for Darcy to squeeze in. He slips into the room. In the darkness he fails to see a simple wad of paper on the floor and steps on it: The frozen-solid paper edges are like a piece of razor-edged rock, and Darcy trips and falls unconscious. When he awakens after a while he finds, to his horror, that the door opening is smaller now—too small for him to fit through. Something must have happened while he was unconscious. And no force on Earth can open the door. With Linda's help on the outside, she is able to tell him that a man is standing outside the door with his hand on the knob. He may be in the process of opening the door—which had just drifted shut—or, to their horror, shutting it. Tense time goes by before it becomes clear that the man is indeed opening the door, and Darcy is able to slip back out.

Another quality in the earlier draft is Melchior's use of the Limbo Creature as a true dramatic element. In "The Premonition" it does little to pose a real threat. In "The Gordian Knot" it plants traps, even moves out across the desert in its gaseous form. In the earlier draft the creature is still used as a source of information as in the completed show, though the information is conveyed only when it engulfs Darcy in its shadowy body:

> Suddenly the creature moves; slowly it begins to advance towards Darcy... The creature is almost upon him—when suddenly Darcy strikes out with his razor-sharp weapon directly at the being... He almost loses his balance and his mouth is wrenched open in a silent scream of horror, as his deadly weapon *goes right through* the creature, as if meeting no resistance at all—and with not the slightest effect.
>
> There is not even time for the sudden terror that wells up in Darcy to grip him firmly; the Limbo being raises his arms; the weird, unearthly lights and shadows seem to cascade all around him—and with a sweep he is upon Darcy, *enveloping him*, surging about him—actually engulfing the man with his very mass.... Darcy's weapon clatters to the floor; frantically, he struggles with the tenuous form enfolding him. He fights to breathe... For Darcy it is like being inside a heavy, syrupy gas, which shuts out all air and literally begins to choke and asphyxiate the man. Savagely he battles, but he is getting weaker...

He manages to free himself just in time.

The creature has told them that they will face the same fate as the Limbo Creature if they are not at the crash site at the proper time; they will become two nebulous, nonentities forever roaming this silent, motionless void. There are a few creatures such as itself. They are former humans who've for one reason or another, slipped out of synch with time and are now living in this realm.

In the climactic moments, two Limbo Creatures bear down on Linda and Darcy and they prepare to fight them off with flares—but are sucked back into the normal time flow at that very moment.

With a bit more development "The Gordian Knot" could've become a small feature. As it was, it greatly expanded the frozen-time idea of *The Time Travelers*, developed an interesting relationship between its characters, introduced what could have

The crash of an experimental plane upsets the flow of time in "The Premonition."

been one of *The Outer Limits*' most interesting "bears" and provided a whole host of problems and obstacles for the protagonists to overcome. And while "The Premonition" hinted of a source for "premonitions" as encounters all but forgotten in a space between moments, "The Gordian Knot" suggested something about the nature of lost spirits—possibly what people call ghosts—wandering in a timeless void, looking for a way to get "back into the world."

As an interesting side note, the earliest idea for "The Gordian Knot," was a story Melchior had toyed with called "A Good View From Any Seat," developed for his *Columbus of the Stars*: A pilot undergoes circumstances much like those in "The Gordian Knot" wherein human ingenuity is taxed to the limit. However, in "A Good Seat... " the concept was that of an evil alien race which had created the time-limbo for their amusement in a colossal, other-worldly "Pleasure Dome." He later reworked a variation of the idea as a possible story for *Star Trek*.

After working out a revised version of "The Gordian Knot" with story editor Seeleg Lester and writer Sam Roecca, Melchior turned in his draft of the teleplay on October 22. "The Premonition" went into production on a tighter than usual budget for the series. Gerd Oswald, director of other episodes in the series such as the highly regarded "Forms of Things Unknown," was assigned to handle the show. Jim Darcy was played by Dewey Martin—a last minute replacement for actor Don Gordon. Linda was played by Mary Murphy—the same actress who'd starred in Melchior's earlier *Live Fast, Die Young*. The Limbo Being was actor Kay Kuter shot through a distortion lens and printed in negative—a popular technique on the show. Kenneth Peach, a man with many years of experience lighting miniatures for Jack Rabin's Studio Film Service—including *Kronos* and *The Giant Behemoth*—was the director of photography. The episode premiered January 9, 1965.

Melchior's revision still featured some interesting variations of his time limbo idea, including clever time calculations, as well as several imaginative, if unambitious, ways to illustrate frozen-in-time reality. In one instance inspired by his first draft, but unfortunately deleted before filming, Jim Darcy pushes against one of the time-halted technicians and pierces his hand on the frozen, needle-like hairs of the man's crewcut, causing dozens of pin-prick holes in his palm.

The notion of motionlessness was a theme Melchior visited frequently in past films. In *The Angry Red Planet* an entire planet appeared to be held frozen by a controlling power. *Journey to the 7th Planet* found astronauts in a world encased in ice where one slight movement in an underground crevasse is the only indication of life. The creature in *Reptilicus* returned to life only after having been removed from a frozen state that had held it "outside of time." *The Time Travelers* featured a time-limbo of non-moving people and countryside in which nothing could be budged, much like that of "The Premonition." A later project, *Planet of the Vampires*, revealed a three-dimensional rendering of an alien family preserved as if in a block of glass, a domestic moment in time captured and held fast. Maybe there was something still lodged in the back of Melchior's mind about those eggs he'd seen dipped into liquid glass before the war, a means of slowing the decaying processes of time—frozen, in a way.

In "The Premonition," only a few of his "Gordian Knot" frozen tableaus remained. One was the plane itself:

> High above in the clear sky, its distinctive design plainly recognizable, hangs the experimental plane, hovering completely motionless, as if glued to the sky.... [It is] Darcy's own ship, unmistakably the unique craft, which at the same time lies crashed only a short distance away. And silence—silence everywhere.

Melchior ultimately chose unusually fast-moving animals, a blinking light, an undulating American flag, etc., rendered absolutely motionless to illustrate the frozen time phenomena rather than the pouring water and hard plants of his original. Even then, the seemingly simple ideas on paper far exceeded the execution. The non-moving running jackrabbit, hawk, etc., were simply—too simply—created by freeze printing the motion picture frame—a desperate budgetary technique at best that illustrated a certain poverty of directorial ingenuity. A posed taxidermy model of either or both animals suspended on hidden wires would've added immeasurably to the illusion, or use of rear projection or simple split screen to combine the actors with the frozen hawk or plane.

The Limbo Being remained throughout the rewriting phase. It *had* to be there, if for no other reason than that the producers expected it. One of the basic rules of the series—and the basis which helped sell the show to the network in the first place—was that each episode feature a "bear," some type of unearthly physical threat, or monster. In "The Premonition," the idea was to keep the Limbo Being monster as simple as possible. However, by the time Melchior's story had been simplified, its relevance to the drama itself had been minimized. As aired, it seemed to have been created mostly to provide the characters with all-too-convenient information at critical times.

The Outer Limits as a series was rapidly drawing to a close as "The Premonition" went into production. The looming shut down of the operation no doubt stifled the episode's creativity. That, combined with Gerd Oswald's indifferent direction—he made little attempt at varying camera angles or striving for mood in spite of a wealth of possibilities—lent the episode a somewhat dispassionate atmosphere. Signs of carelessness—the actors ran across the desert in the supposedly frozen world and bumped and jostled plants that were supposed to be unmovable, and the sunlight could be seen to have changed its position during the course of the show, contrary once again to the idea of an unmoving world. At least, Oswald was careful not to shoot when any wind blew through the area.

While working on the episode, Melchior also developed another potential concept to pitch to *The Outer Limits*, titled "The Trawler"—about a "mousy Wally Cox-type" character who is trapped in a kind of test cage set down in a wooded area by an alien race. The man, who'd always been insulted due to his lack of brawn, would more than prove his manhood through his intelligence. Unfortunately, no new stories were being commissioned for the show by that time.

In spite of some contrivance to put all three characters in imminent jeopardy, Melchior's central idea and general development of "The Premonition" proved intriguing. The strong concept helped make up for deficiencies in the production, and it was to remain among the best of the underproduced later episodes. Seeleg Lester recalled:

> That second season was a real piece of work. We were all proud of it... I had done a lot of the *Perry Mason* shows—where one of the two types of stories was "there's a mystery, a puzzle of events that is slowly put together"— and this episode ["The Premonition"] sort of fell into that category... We were very happy with that one.

During all this Melchior kept an eye out for any developments on the *Space Family Robinson* front. The proceeding months had been full of letter exchanging and legal inquiries. He was not particularly happy just to hand over his time investment in the project to another party. But ultimately, the reality sunk in: Irwin Allen indeed was off and running on his version of the same material for 20th Century-Fox TV. Physical production of Allen's *Space Family Robinson* got underway January 6, 1965, under its new title, *Lost in Space*. The rest is history. But the story wasn't quite over.

Melchior explored his options. An independent production company named Drummer Boy Productions took out an option on *Space Family Robinson* early in 1965, bringing the project back to life. He found further support with Sam Arkoff who expressed real interest in distributing the proposed film. That became a real and potentially fruitful option. In the meantime, Arkoff and American International were to provide Melchior another interesting project. A trip to a purely imaginary planet—a haunted planet.

PLANET OF THE VAMPIRES

Within the space of a few short years, Melchior had already made two speculative journeys to the red planet, landed on the moon, visited the frigid giant outer planet Uranus, traveled to the future and conjured up deep-range journeys across the galaxy in his two proposals for TV. This next cinematic voyage initiated by AIP eventually became *Planet of the Vampires*. It was to be an excursion into the stellar and funereal, a sepulchral, low-budget arabesque of vampirically themed though not literally vampiric—space adventure made in collaboration with one of cinema's greatest impresarios of the macabre, Mario Bava. It was a collaboration that veered Melchior away from the world of straight science fiction into almost Lovecraftian horror-fantasy.

Planet of the Vampires began when, in the spring of 1964, American International Pictures was contemplating a co-production deal with an Italian production company for a series of five science fiction films, the first of which was to be based on a screenplay variously titled *The Shadow World*, *Warlords of the Outlaw Planet* and, for a long while, *The Haunted World*. Bava, famous for his earlier and financially successful films *Black Sunday* and *Black Sabbath* for AIP, was to direct the new project, and hopefully the others as well.

A script for a space-terror film had been written by the Italian screenwriters Antonio Roman and Rafael J. Salvia and presented to AIP by a young, ambitious producer in Rome named Fulvio Lucisano. Roman and Salvia had based their script on a short story by well-known Italian science fiction writer, Rene Pestriniero, titled "The Night of 21 Hours," which had been published in the Italian magazine *Oltre Il Cielo* in June 1960.

Referring to it by its original *and* final Italian title, Fulvio Lucisano, elaborated:

> *Terrore Nello Spazio* was a story that Mario Bava brought to me. Mr. Arkoff and Mr. Nicholson of American International had come over and brought a picture of Bava's called *Mask of the Demon* or *Black Sunday* in the United States. They were looking to make another movie with Mario. So, Mario came to me with this project and I discussed the matter with Nicholson and Arkoff and we decided to make the picture as a co-production.

As soon as the Roman/Salvia script was delivered, Jim Nicholson and Sam Arkoff called in their frequent screenwriter/troubleshooter/problem-solver Louis M. (Deke) Heyward for advice. According to Heyward:

> Sam sent me the script with a note attached, "Please evaluate." It was by these... Italian writers. I read it and was aghast. It was totally unshootable. Wanting to be positive I said, if this is supposed to be a *comedy*, then we might have something. It was so full of holes I told them "This script has nothing for us." For instance, the lady astronaut comes in behind the pilot and she is naked. We called Fulvio Lucisano in Italy; "What's her motivation, what's going on?" He says, "She's naked because she wants to have something to do with the pilot. She wants him."
>
> So we talked about who could completely rewrite the script and Ib's name came up. Jim suggested it. I had heard of him and knew of his family. He had such a sweet nature. Very sweet. We talked about some various ideas, then he went to work on it.

To try to make sense of the screenplay that had been handed him, Melchior asked to see the original Pestriniero story. He quickly read it and made an evaluation: It was a story about transformation, specifically the loss of Ego and triumph of the Id on a strange, unknown planet.

The story picks up after two ships have attempted landing on a featureless, fog-bound planet. Although one ship, the Vega, has landed safely, its sister ship, Orion, had gone out of control and crashed, killing the entire crew. Few of its much-needed supplies have survived.

The crew of the Vega face certain doom. Their situation seems hopeless. Apprehension and fear grows with the onset of night. Crewman Pat Weaver gives voice to their tensions:

> Millions of years have passed since man was born, and with his capacity and ingenuity he has dominated all the universe he knows. But leave him alone in an abandoned house, by himself, at night, and he will find himself completely indefensible against the assault of a thousand enemies: Incubi, the fear of the unknown—which we continually create and deform according to circumstances—[and] the untouchableness of the dark, which can house anything...

The men bury their dead, then alternate guard duty every four hours through the long night—even though, some of them argue, the planet appears absolutely lifeless and should therefore pose no threat.

Throughout the night shadowy sounds and sightings occur, including the shifting and crunching of sandy ground. Two crewmen wander as if in a trance through the ship at night, ready to sabotage valuable equipment. Finally, the maimed bodies of the dead crew members of the Vega are glimpsed: *The dead have returned to life*. They, however, act very strangely. Like the "materialization of a lunatic's dream," the dead are seen to hold hands and dance and shout in merriment.

The Vega's survivors, quickly reduced to two under mysterious circumstances, conclude that the men who have returned to life have become infant-like:

> They're having a good time, like kids... What do you think makes the difference between a man and a child? The repression of the Id by the Super Ego. There must be some unknown force on this planet that acts on our psyche and removes our inhibitory Ego, letting the Id fire up to full control of the mind.

The last man alive, with seemingly no other recourse, puts a gun to his head in order to join his celebrant friends.

"The Night of 21 Hours," lacking in any visceral power—conceptually or visually—and devoid of any real scope, served as the merest springboard for Melchior in his effort to adapt it into a new screenplay. To help him prepare for the task, he first familiarized himself with Bava's previous work by viewing *Black Sunday* and others of the director's films at Sam Arkoff's home screening room. These screenings set a mood for the screenplay— atmospherically aggressive, mysterious, grotesque.

According to Melchior:

> I had had a very good working relationship with Jim Nicholson and Sam Arkoff at AIP. They called me in for what became *Planet of the Vampires*. They had, I think, just a bunch of writers who'd worked on this damn script, and it didn't work, didn't work, didn't work. It's possible Bava had tried to do it and couldn't make it work either, I don't know... So I took that one over and wrote a new script for them... I got paid in full *before* I ever put pen to paper, it was such a good relationship. I was given no input, no special requests. I knew Bava was going to direct it. I had seen his work. [As I wrote] I was thinking absolutely along the lines of Bava.
>
> The script I received had a lot of ideas from those first writers, but it just didn't work and we ultimately threw everything out and started over... So it was myself, then finally Louis Heyward, who worked on it...

Melchior started with basics: He made a breakdown of crew members for the two space ships, and a list of possible character names—Comal, Iola, Lanark, Drake and Merek were some names considered—and rankings. He played with the names of the ships—the *Argosy 1* and *2*; the *Corsair*, etc.—finally settling on the *Argos* and the *Galliot*. ("Galliot" is a type of Mediterranean galley. "Argos" is a variation of the name of the ship Jason set sail on in search of the Golden Fleece.) Then he completely restructured the story in the form of a four-page continuity outlining the flow of the action. Next, he wrote up the continuity as a 39-page treatment that described the story's action, dialogue and—most importantly—mood. Along the way, he did some research into the actual beliefs of certain primitive peoples regarding the ability of spirits to enter and reanimate the bodies of the recently dead—one of his story's key horror elements. He found literature describing these beliefs that did actually exist.

His new title was, appropriately, *The Haunted World*. It was the title under which the trade publications originally announced the film.

Melchior's treatment turned out to be a feverishly foggy, "long night of the soul" piece set on the anguished surface of a vagabond planet—Conundra or Nomad at first, then Aura, to suggest a ghostly luminosity—whirling about a wandering star that has invaded our solar system. (The theoretical existence of such planets has recently been proposed.) His rewrite—in his characteristic novelist style—hammered the reader with word-vistas of a twisted, final-resting-place world where every shadow and cloud hid waiting dead eyes and rotting threats. He even imbued the treatment with a mad, Poe-like rhythm, an obsession with death-related events and gave the threats themselves a distinctly Lovecraftian texture. If ever a science fiction script sought to production design the look and feel of a film, this was it—one of the most insistent—and ultimately most successful—attempts. Commented Melchior:

> Normally the details I wrote would be left for the director. But since I was a director myself, I wrote it as I thought it should have been done on film. I'd write that into the script, [meaning] what I saw, how the people moved, what they did and so on. I wrote this as a director, and not everybody likes that. A director may not like that because he wants to make up his own mind, but I felt... if my script read more like a novel than a script... it would give the right flavor.

The Melchior version was sent to Bava for his reaction. His comments on the 39-page treatment were sent to Sam Arkoff, who passed them on to Melchior on June 22, 1964, with the following letter attached:

> Dear Ib,
>
> Here are the comments of Mario Bava on *Haunted Planet*, which he persists in calling *The Shadow World*, for some reason.

> As you will note, Bava's comments about your abilities are so laudatory, that I am frankly a little remiss to send it to you, lest you feel that you have no further goals to achieve and simply stop work[ing].
> Sincerely,
> Sam Arkoff

Indeed, Bava's reaction to the material was one of great enthusiasm with very few suggestions:

> Great compliments to Mr. Melchior. The subject is really fine, full of surprises, suspense and situations. It is obvious that he knows what cinema is all about. The finale where we suddenly learn that the two leads are possessed by the [Aurans], Reed's death by his own hand and not through the work of Mark is excellent. The very final scene of the protagonists becoming Adam and Eve is extremely well done... Again vivid compliments to Mr. Melchior, and let's hurry up with it because it seems just the right time for a Fantasy-Science-Terror-type of idea.

Bava's notes set forth several suggestions, specifically the idea that "being possessed by the Aurans means possessing something spiritually internally that permits life to be looked at with different eyes." That suggestion was a bit odd considering Melchior's treatment already expressed that very idea. In fact, Melchior had utilized the theme of beneficent alien symbiosis several years earlier in his unproduced screenplay, *The Micro-Men*.

Bava also requested burials of the dead in order to set up the sort of rising from the grave sequence he'd excelled at in *Black Sunday*. He was eager to, in his words, "see the dead ones walking out, one by one, with their ghostly faces." Bava's suggestion to make more of the burial scenes was not surprising. He was probably already imagining the staging of what was to become one of the film's—and cinema's—most macabre resurrection sequences.

With very little else in the way of input, Melchior sat down to write the actual script. The Melchior final was dated January 18, 1965—his first wedding anniversary to Cleo Baldon. Whereas "The Premonition" had taken place in familiar territory and concerned time limits, Melchior's new film script was set in unknown realms and concerned bodiless beings for whom time meant very little.

The Haunted World—now officially titled *The Outlaw Planet*—began far out in unexplored space: "Swimming serenely against the fabulous beauty of the cosmos is an unfamiliar planet. It nestles in space like a beautiful opal ... on a jewelers velvet. This is Aura."

Two ships approach Aura, the *Galliot* and the *Argos*, the latter commanded by Captain "Mark" Markary. As in *Journey to the 7th Planet*, men have been sent here to investigate a mysterious, regular pulse-signal. Descending from orbit, a strange power seizes the ships. The *Galliot* crashes, killing all on board, including Markary's brother. The *Argos* lands with minor damage. Apparently some tremendous planetary force has dragged both ships down to the surface. Was it a deliberate, intelligent act, or just a force of nature?

Markary dispatches a land crawler, a kind of six-wheeled, all-terrain vehicle, to the *Galliot*. There they proceed to bury the bodies of the dead crew, then begin the challenging task of repairing their own ship.

It isn't long before Melchior's survivors start to discover weird, spectral forces at work on Aura, along with sightings of gape-wounded, grievously injured dead bodies from the *Galliot* wandering about. Coruscurant, flitting lights are spotted, which are visible—as in supposed real-life supernatural encounters—*only* out of the corner of the eye. These are the bodiless inhabitants of Aura.

In search of answers, Markary and Baia—Sanya in later drafts—discover some kind of ghostly alien apparatus—colossal in scale and visible only in their peripheral vision—obviously a construct of the other-dimensional Aurans. They also find wreckage of an immense alien spaceship in which they become trapped and barely escape.

Eventually they learn the Aurans plan to take over the bodies of the *Argos* crew and steal the ship for themselves. It is their only means of escape from this doomed planet, since they do not possess physical bodies.

Captain Markary defies them. He will fight such an invasion to his dying breath. The aliens offer another option, suggesting that the Captain and his crew volunteer to share their bodies *symbiotically* with the Aurans rather than fight. Perhaps this type of arrangement could even prove beneficial... perhaps even give both races an added dimension.

When Markary refuses, the aliens attack, using the revived bodies from the wreck of the *Galliot* along with the ghastly, half-decayed bodies of a myriad other, long-deceased aliens whose ships have also crashed on Aura in eons past. Melchior wrote:

> They move inexorably towards the pitifully small group of defenders, every one of them dreadfully, horribly maimed and disfigured with gaping wounds and mind-staggering injuries... and behind the hideously mangled humans comes a demoniac array of monstrous creatures, the non-dead crews of other-world spaceship wrecks, the utterly alien specters of long-dead, unearthly beings, led by the coppery-hued humanoids from the alien wreck in the shallow valley.

In the end the *Argos* manages, narrowly, to lift off, escaping the ghoulish horde. But, in a twist it turns out that Markary and Baia, the sole survivors of the attack, have, in fact, been taken over by the Aurans. Not only that, but, even though they are human in appearance and we've assumed they and the others were all from the Earth, they are actually beings from the planet Mars. All the human characters in the story have been Martians.

Markary and Baia watch helplessly as their ship misses Mars. Now their only other choice is the Earth. In yet another twist, this turns out to be the Earth in prehistoric times, the time of the ancient mammals. This story then, has taken place over 100,000 years ago.

Markary and Baia crash land on the Earth. In the final twist the reader realizes—*not* just the obvious that they are Adam and Eve, which they probably are—but that the cohabitation of their bodies by the Aurans has provided these creatures with *souls*: The human race is founded by symbiotic composite beings, part Martian, part Auran. Is it a good thing or is it the source of human evil?

Melchior had retained some of the ideas from Pestriniero's short story, such as the fog-shrouded planetscapes, the crash landings, the complete destruction of one of the ships, the wandering dead and the takeover of a crew member in his sleep in order to damage equipment. But he totally discarded any notion of an Id-liberating force—too similar to *Forbidden Planet*—and invented the ghostly, other-dimension Aurans. He developed an entirely new conflict, and embellished the whole project with wonderful touches, including the enshrouded bodies rising from the dead, batteries of light beacons used to repel the dark-dwelling ghouls, discovery and exploration of an alien derelict ship, the peripherally visible Aurans and their technology, the *Night of the Living Dead*-like siege—years before that film—and the notion of alien entities providing mankind with a soul.

His characters are strong, seasoned space travelers: Markary is depicted as a man who will not give up, who refuses to let his crew fall prey to the Aurans. An iron-willed man, he is an effective symbol of the powers of light against those of the enveloping darkness. His adversary is the planet itself, the elements of which form an atmosphere of doom. The Auran fog, in both Melchior's script and the eventual film, assumes a personality of its own—a kind of Nth presence over all that blurs the lines of definition between the familiar and the unreal. It accentuates the gnawing fear of the enclosing darkness and the disquieting effect the unknown can have upon rational men.

Melchior's story covered a lot of terrain on the planet as the surviving crew must travel repeatedly to and from the wrecked sister ship. To cut down on shoe leather, he envisioned travel by a land rover, and had Cleo create a rendering of it. He suggested how the six-wheeled vehicle could be simply constructed over the body of a Jeep, its four real tires hidden behind six oversized dune-buggy-type wheels. Cleo observed that the vehicle did, in fact, resemble a large version of the Mars Land Rover that captured worldwide attention in 1995. She was not surprised by her husband's plan to use a real Jeep redressed by the art department:

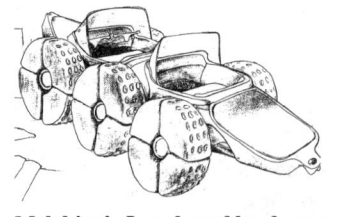

Melchior's Jeep-based land-rover

> Ib's always been mad about Jeeps. A friend of ours had a World War ll Jeep in his front yard and Ib

The briefly seen crew of reactivated dead at the helm of the *Galliot*, in *Planet of the Vampires*, provided one of the film's eeriest moments.

> was just crawling all over it. He wouldn't come in and join us.

She long ago grasped the appeal such a vehicle might have for a man she regarded as the living embodiment of something she calls "The Intrepid Man":

> Here again, the Jeep is just about the most intrepid vehicle in the world—a hardy little vehicle that anybody in the world can start up and use at any time.

A machine, solid, direct, dependable, that gets the job done, no matter what.

As far as Bava was concerned, Melchior's story was exactly what he had been aiming for. He'd been most impressed by the shadow world's all-pervasive mood, and would let the complex descriptions in the script guide him in creating the look of the film. He also had, as usual, numerous pet ideas and motifs stuck in the back of his mind that he intended to introduce into the project's story and texture as he went along. It was not unusual for him to improvise with the materials on hand during principal photography.

Bava's vision would, unfortunately, be compromised by the looming realities of his limited budget. Two new writers, Callisto Cosulich—a professional movie critic—and Alberto Bevilaqua—later to become a famous novelist—were brought in to rework Melchior's script. Bava involved himself in the rewrite sessions. Cosulich recalled that Bava encouraged them to write as if money was not a factor because he—Bava—would see to all the special effects himself. In spite of that, the writers essentially made more cuts and simplifications to reduce the budget than additions. They did run with Melchior's images and further tailor the film to Bava's style.

Back in the States, Nicholson and Arkoff were becoming aware that changes were going on with the screenplay they weren't sure were in their best interests. Since AIP had been very happy with Melchior's material, they sent Louis Heyward to Rome to insure that the screenwriting process didn't get out of hand. Heyward's job was to see to it that the film remained faithful to the original intent of the project as approved by AIP. According to Heyward:

> Fulvio Lucisano apparently wasn't happy, perhaps because there wasn't any nudity, or there wasn't enough horror, I don't exactly remember. Sam and Jim sent me over there with Ib and told us "don't let them do anything stupid."

Heyward had also been dispatched to Italy to help maintain control in the event of any international clashes, including potential competition between other participating countries eager to give more screen time to their own particular star. He arrived amid the babble of various competing languages and completed sets in time to deflect any of the above subterfuge. Heyward put most of his efforts toward reigning the producers into a middle ground between American and foreign market tastes, and protecting the screenplay from overzealous changes. Heyward stated:

> Bava had his own take on this, and he did change *some* things. He had two in-house Italian writers [Cosulich and Bevilaqua]—the script had been translated back into Italian for them—and they were coming up with things.

Heyward perhaps began to feel he wasn't protecting Melchior's material as much as he could have:

> It was a question of either Ib fighting for what he believed in, or me fighting for what I believed in, but I've got to say—ethically and morally—Ib was stronger than I. He was much more honest about what he wanted in the film than I was.

Among the changes that the script underwent either during the rewrites or as production problems arose were the deletions of the discovery of quasi-visible alien technology and the land rover. While the writers slightly expanded Melchior's events inside the derelict ship, they cut Markary and Tiona's discovery of a crystal-encased 3-D image while rummaging through the ancient wreckage of the derelict. The image discovered—a kind of snapshot of the nonhuman wife and child of one of the ship's former occupants—would've been one of the few moments in the genre in which the traditional bug-eyed monster ever receives any sympathetic character background. Instead, Bava took Melchior's description of oversized, skeletal alien corpses and shifted them from the end of the film to the derelict ship sequence.

Additionally, they rewrote the script so that *neither* of the arriving ships crashed. This avoided the need for redressing the *Argos* sets to represent the damaged *Galliot*.

That single change would later make events in the story harder to follow, as two groups of identically dressed characters would move from one ship to another one exactly like it: The loss of visual geography in the story was significant.

Another truly unfortunate move was the deletion of the alien resurrection sequence featuring hordes of extraterrestrial corpses laying siege to the *Argos*. It was rewritten to feature only the revived dead of the *Argos*' crew—and a few *Galliot* victims—to avoid costly prop and prosthetic construction. In retrospect, it was a disappointing compromise.

Louis Heyward, continued to work with the writers, offering suggestions that cut corners without significantly altering the story or blunting Melchior's sense of wonder. Heyward had proven an expert in this area over the years.

Together, the little group eventually turned out a 200-plus page revision in a European script format that allowed vast amounts of white space per page for text translations.

For his work, AIP rewarded Heyward with a co-writing credit on the film. He reflected on the merits of that credit with, for Hollywood, unusual candor and honesty:

> Here again, I was a hired gun on this film, and, looking back on it 35 years or so ago, I would say that the Writers Guild would *not* have given me a "co-written by" credit today. I don't think my written contribution was that great. I think, frankly, I probably got in the way of Ib, and may have even hurt him creatively. Maybe I made the script more shootable from a cost standpoint, [but] I have the feeling that Ib was overwhelmingly more creative on this thing than I was.

THE MAKING OF *PLANET OF THE VAMPIRES*

The film went into production in March 1965 at Cinecitta Studios in Rome. It was a truly international effort, with production funding from the U.S., Spain, South America and Italy all involved. A partial list of participants included, aside from American International Pictures, Fulvio Lucisano's Italian International Films in Rome, and Castillo Cinematografica from Madrid. As Lucisano explained:

> We put the film together as follows: We shared 50-50 the cost of the picture with American International and I kept the rights in Italy and Spain, with us [doing] a co-production with Spain... And AIP distributed the picture all over the world.

Barry Sullivan had been cast to play Captain Markary. He was the sole name recognizable to American audiences. Susan Hart, who'd recently starred in AIP's *War-*

Melchior took this snapshot of Barry Sullivan and Mario Bava on his brief trip to Rome to help finish *Planet of the Vampires*.

Gods of the Deep opposite Vincent Price, had been initially cast in a lead role of Sanya. That bit of casting did not last long, however. Louis Heyward explained:

> [Casting Susan] was a bit of friction between Jim and Sam. Susan was not an actress; she was a dear, sweet lady who was Jim's girlfriend. But he constantly tried to promote her as an actress. It became a question of which producer at AIP would "win her" for their next picture... Finally, Sam got off a memo that was permanently posted, that went something like "No members of or relatives of AIP will *ever* appear as performers in *any* AIP production—in the U.S. *or* abroad."

And that ended Hart's involvement on the picture.

The Susan Hart situation was over and done with before the film was even fully funded. She was replaced by the Brazilian actress Norma Bengell while the film was still in the deal-making stage. According to Lucisano:

> We took a Spanish female... because we were wanting that co-production with Spain.

Bengell was also a good choice as far as the AIP's South American investors were concerned. Louis Heyward added:

> Once there was a completed script, Fulvio would go around—it would maybe take a month, or a couple months—and raise the money for his end. [To his advantage] he had Bava, who was going to direct this—*and* he had Norma Bengell. I asked [one of the producers] what she had to contribute to the picture, and he said, [accompanied by appropriate melon-handed gestures]— "She is-a so-o-o-o-o *mama*."

Aside from Barry Sullivan, Lucisano added, "the rest of the casting was done here [in Rome]." Lucisano provided a little insight into what they felt was a basic problem with the film right from the start:

> The casting, unfortunately—I don't really want to say unfortunately because I don't want to hurt the actor—but from [the standpoint of box-office] we had to rely on the American actors—particularly on the judgment of American International—because *they* selected the names that were salable in the United States. Well, to be honest, we had other actors in mind [for the Sullivan role]. As a matter of fact, Bava was not really sold 100 percent on Mr. Sullivan, because he thought he was not young enough for the part. Not that he wasn't good—he was a *wonderful* actor—but because the idea at the end of the story was that they were going to be repopulating the world, and to have an actor that was mature was something that was against his point of view. Which I agreed with. And that is nothing against the actor. He was okay. In fact, when we finally saw him, we agreed [he would work out]. But, in principal, the idea was to have a *younger* actor.

The entire film was actually shot for under $250,000 in six weeks, with an additional two weeks with a small crew—one would be tempted to say a skeleton crew—to pick up some of the special effects shots. Throughout, practically the entire production was shot in a foggy environment using simple backlit cutouts and a collection of fiberglass rocks that were used repeatedly to redress the exterior sets. Bava's frequent special effects associate, Geofredo "Freddy" Unger—who worked for three days staging the stunt fights in *Planet of the Vampires*—explained the particulars of their fog:

> There were two types of smoke—interior and exterior smoke. For exterior shooting, [fog] was created with fumone, an incense-type material. It's the same stuff used by soldiers [for camouflaging]. Today it is no longer used. For the interior, [Mario] used church incense. It was a good smell. The smoke that was needed for interiors was a thin, soft smoke.

Heyward remembered Bava having very idiosynchric ideas for handling and dispersing the fog during filming:

> Bava had two huge fans on the stage that he somehow alternated to fit a vision in his own head—where the mist is materializing above the gravesite. He used [those] two fans to achieve that... It was a personal thing with him...

Heyward did point out, however, that "the idea of those gravemarkers not being crucifixes but pieces of metal—which I thought was very cerebral—*that* detail came from Ib's script. It's to *Ib's* credit, not Mario's."

Perhaps inspired by *This Island Earth* or the then-recent Czech film *Ikaria XB-1* (known in the U.S. as *Voyage to the End of the Universe*), Bava created unorthodox, Olympus-sized spaceship interiors; the giant landing legs—which surely must've inspired the much later *Alien*; long circular corridors; and the darkly chortling intergalaxial skeletons. His planetary terrain consisted of incessant fog, moodily garish lighting and occasional in-camera perspective and mirror shots. Also contributing were the costumes of Gabriele Mayer, whose scuba-like, high-velocity crew-suits—bat-black, wing-collared and warning-yellow striped—anticipated the crew's deep dive into a sea of planetary fog.

The film's memorable art direction was, obstensively, handled by young Giorgio Giovannini, who'd worked imaginative budgetary wonders on Umberto Cottifolvi's *The Giant of Metropolis* and many years later handled design chores for Terry Gilliam's Italian unit on his *Adventures of Baron Munchausen*. But few who worked on *Planet of the Vampires/Terrore Nello Spazio* credited the visuals to the young man: Mario Silvestri, the film's production manager, who was on the project from the very beginning to the very end, felt the art direction was entirely under Bava's and not Giovaninni's control:

> Mario Bava would make all the suggestions for design. Giovannini, at the time, was not a well-known designer. If he had been a well-known designer, he would have been calling all the shots,

not Bava, and there would have been no discussion. And this is [actually] the reason he used Giovannini. He was young, unknown, but very clever. Bava would send him off to do a design, and then comment, "Maybe you should change this or that"... Going back to the space suits, you can see the design of Bava even in the suits. The hand of Mario Bava was in the costumes, set design, the lights, in the makeup... in everything.

Bava's grandson, Fabrizio, who'd lived with his grandfather for some time, recalled his elder's thoughts on the *Planet of the Vampires* sets:

> He wanted things *simple*. For the ship he said, "Everything should be *hidden*"—meaning the controls and mechanisms. "You have to open things up, pull things out of hidden panels in the walls, the floor, and so on. Otherwise," he said, "too much detail reveals the time the film is made."
>
> He didn't ask for sets so much as a lot of *space*, and built the sets right up to the studio walls. He'd build the sets from a piece he found here, a piece he found there and so on. He was always more interested in the *visual*.

The film's costumes were no ordinary flight suits, but another exotic Bava touch well-attuned to the story. According to Mario Silvestri:

> [Our costumer], Gabriele, was never wardrobe. He was an owner of a tailoring shop who rented costumes to films. Mario Bava did not want a wardrobe person who would do the designs and then have to find a tailor to run them up. This was a much more direct approach. Gabriele was a specialist in costume design for movies, but because he was also a tailor, it cut out an extra person.

Gabriele Mayer was only 25 years old when the film was made:

> I was called upon to create the costumes for the film by director Mario Bava and I remember what I agreed upon with him regarding how to create these aliens. My initial idea—my favorite one of all the designs—was that the costumes should resemble the bodies of insects; the seams should mark the segments of the body of the animal, like

that of the mantis. The idea was accepted and taken forward to completion, even though the time at our disposal was very short—at most about 20 days, plus one week for conception. And the budget was very tight, so much so that we had to do somersaults to get it all finished.

In this case, to create these costumes, I used a very simple cloth. The base was a jersey covered in a plastic material which resulted in what looked like the polished, luminous skin of certain insects... The material used at that time was essentially a... material that succeeded perfectly when we had to ruin them [later, for the story]. I am sure that today, with modern cloths and techniques, it would be possible to make very detailed things.

As in Melchior's story, the trick was to suggest that something weird was going on as far as the human characters were concerned, without tipping the audience as to their true nature. Bava's notion gave the actors a look that at once was off without being obvious.

If Bava wasn't fully able to match the original script's tight concept and development in his own reworking of the material, he truly did excel in the visual areas of the story—those areas of art direction and lighting that he was to be remembered for. His vision of the haunted planet drew inspiration from the script as well as his own obsessions in creating a sometimes color-saturated, sometimes gray-black-indigo pastiche of sculpted rocks, rolling fog, looming steel hulls and bubbling liquids. The completed film showcased mournful, 10-foot-tall alien skeletons moldering in an interplanetary wreck, a volcanic swamp, hi-tech graves that lure Auran ghosts and strange otherworld technological colossi. The latter included giant, beetle-shelled spaceships whose sinister female ports beckoned to crewmen standing diminutively beneath the ship's sleekly outstretched insect-claw landing legs. It was a credit to Bava's ingenuity and imagination that, in the face of an extremely tight budget, he was able to retain as much of the physically ambitious phantasmagoria that was Melchior's original treatment, as well as its gloomy tone.

Perhaps his affinity for the macabre, embodied in the ancient skeleton, was in his blood after all. Such images—artifacts dusted and injured by pitiless time—had surrounded his formative years. Bava's father, Eugenio, used to sculpt the heads of Saints and other ecclesiastical things, for a living, while Mario's sister had made, according to Unger—"the mummies of the saints for the churches—[like] Saint Catherine in New York. She made the mummy of Saint Catherine." In the alien skeleton Bava found again a form of mummy—an ancient, powdery guardian—while the ship was its sarcophagus. To create the scene, Bava had the inspiration to move one of the skeletons lying about outside the ship into a chamber of the derelict itself, thus trapping his characters with it, as if in a tomb. It was entirely an improvisation on the set built around Melchior's cemetery-planet concept—and stands as the film's purest blending of the two sensibilities—director's and writer's.

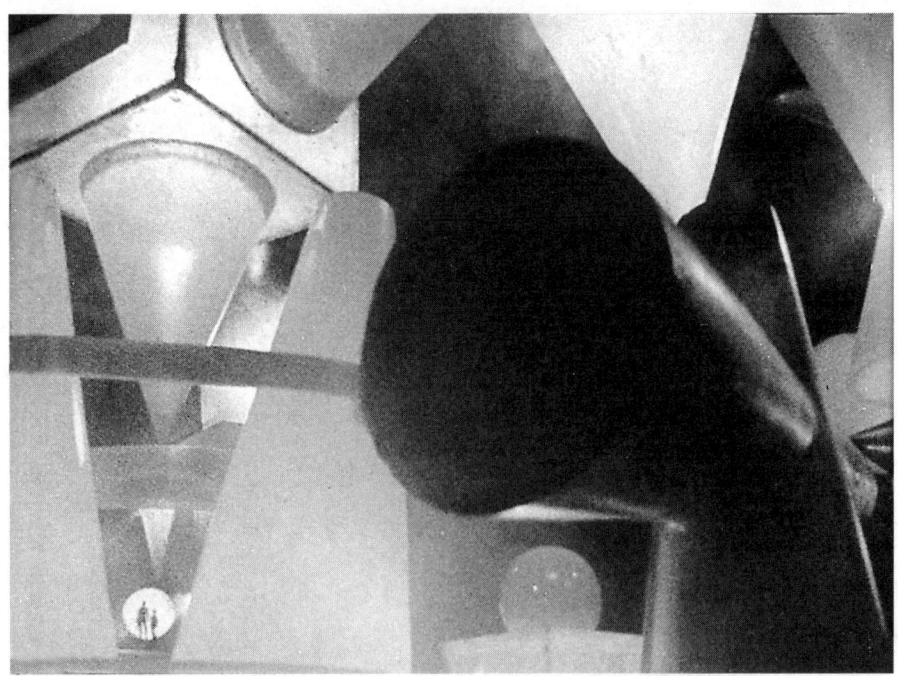

Perspective shot of strange abstract shapes deep within the alien derelict ship as depicted by Mario Bava.

The macabre extended to the sound work as well. Scenes on the planet's surface were filled with sounds that suggested rolling fog, the movement of shrouded beings or the hushed shifting of atmospheres—and were simply created by slowing down the sound of ocean waves; likewise, the slowed sounds of an oil derrick fed into an echo chamber provided the throbbing oscillations of alien machinery suddenly come to life deep inside the derelict ship.

Callisto Cosulich, one of the last writers to work on the film, commented:

> I was never on the set of *Terrore Nello Spazio*. I have only seen the film one time... To this day I remain surprised that it has become a cult movie. [But] all that time I remember, above all, Bava's personality. I remember his modesty and his irrational fears, such as his fear of being left alone in an office during the daytime. Only after meeting him did I understand why he was so good at making horror films: In order to make a movie that frightens an audience, the movie had to first frighten its creator. It was the only way to create complicity between the director and the audience.

But for his macabre tastes and inner demons, Bava, like Melchior, could charm people, and enjoyed his work immensely. Geofredo Unger recalled:

Ib Melchior: Man of Imagination

Norma Bengell as Sonya and Barry Sullivan as Captain Markay rehearse their scenes. Notice the cigarette in Bengell's hand.

> To Mario, these things that seemed very complicated, he would have fun doing them. He didn't want to be a director. He was a man that when he made a film, he would surround [himself] with people he liked, that he could work with. If not, he would not do it. When he arrived on the set he would remove his shoes and put on slippers. He would work in slippers because it was more comfortable. I can tell you that from him you could learn a lot, [but] he wasn't a man who gave himself a lot of importance.

And, while the filming was often, according to Heyward, chaotic, everyone got along well. Unger remembered:

> Barry Sullivan was wonderful. He was the only one speaking English. Everyone there spoke their own language. Norma was speaking Portuguese. They were not speaking phonetic English: They'd wait for somebody to speak their line, then they'd

speak... [But] there were a lot of amusing things that happened on the set during shooting because Mario was a practical joker... He would arrange for food to come down to the set, but only for certain people, in other words, "Barry Sullivan can have some food today—if he's acting good—but not Norma Bengell. Norma Bengell can have some food it she puts on a dressing gown" ...and so on.

To which Silvestri added:

> Bava was very simpatico [charming] and mischievous... He had a great relationship with everyone on the set. He would consider himself a worker—one of the guys—opposite of management. A very sweet character.

The miniature effects were handled during the regular shooting schedule, with Bava personally setting up and filming most of the work himself. Silvestri commented on Bava's approach to special effects:

> You can make special effects in cameras practically or optically. Almost all the effects Bava did were done in-camera, and very little was done optically. Everything was very homemade. This is a fundamental concept of his work, compared to how it's done today. He was a genius; that is, an inventor of small effects that he would create himself, because he knew the camera so well. For example, in *Terrore Nello Spazio*—which will make you laugh—at a certain point, the spaceship lands on an unknown planet. We had to make the surface, a piece of the surface. And what did Mario Bava invent? He had his crew construct—how can I say this?—a giant frying pan. I don't know, 15 meters in diameter—[about] 45 feet—which we put in the studio at Cinecitta. Very big. Underneath he lit small gas canisters. And what did we put inside this great big frying pan?—Polenta [cornmeal]. We acquired hundreds of kilograms of yellow flour. And this was his genius, to create the bubbling surface of the planet—bloop-bloop... This polenta story should give you insight into his thinking.
>
> To make the spaceship, he called Carlo Rambaldi, who, at the time, was an unknown. He made this spaceship. It was a very, very small

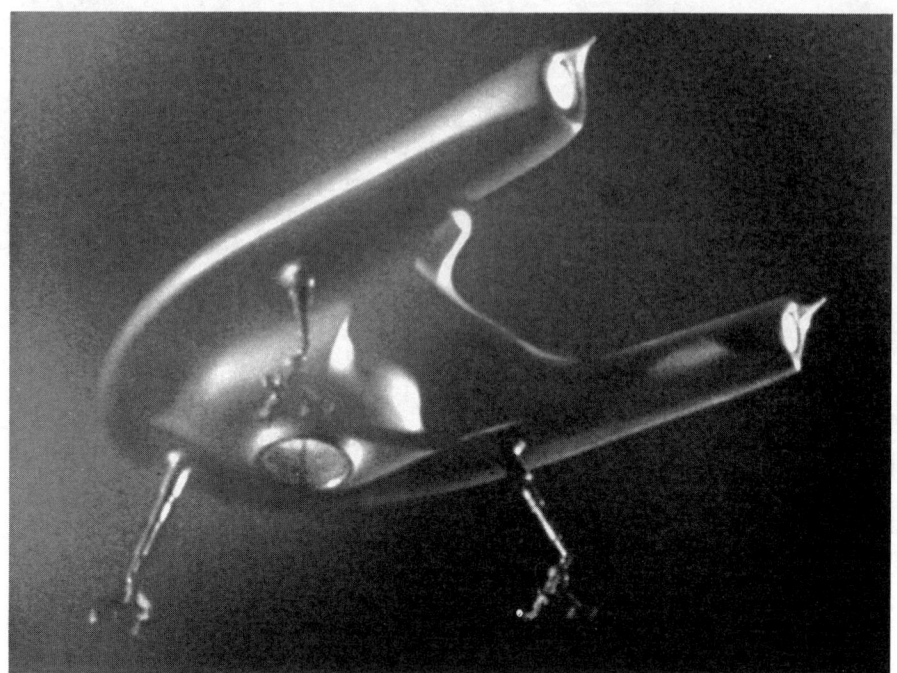

The boomerang ship captures the strange tone of Melchior's script while being wholly inventive. The ship and derelict sequence most likely influenced *Alien*.

> model. To make this spaceship take off and land, Bava constructed a giant fish tank full of water. At the bottom of the tank there was a layer of sand, [so] as the spaceship would take off or land, sand would kick up in apparent slow motion, thus giving the illusion of mass and size. The water would also soften the movement of the spaceship while in this water tank [so it wouldn't jerk].

For this landing sequence Bava also fed an airline into the two-foot-long model of the *Galliot* and forced air out under pressure, backlit, to create bubbles to simulate the glow of braking engines. For other shots, Bava relied on shooting in a partially silvered mirror to reflect the small image of actors standing far from the camera into darkened areas of the miniatures—again in lieu of optical composites. Lucisano shook his head:

> A lot of the things he tried to explain to us were very difficult to understand, because he could visualize it—he saw it through the lens in his mind—which *we* were not able to do.

Unger recalled Bava's use of foreground miniatures:

> Mario had a fabulous mind. It's not that he used a lot of [full] miniatures, he had special lenses made that had two different focal lengths. Half of one focal length for shooting the miniatures and half for the actors, since they were both at different distances and shot simultaneously.

One of the impressive opening shots in the film—a tilt-down from an overhead dome of stars to the Galliot's control room—was accomplished by means of a foreground miniature of the dome set in front of the full-sized control room set. It had actually been inspired by almost identical shots Melchior had created in *The Time Travelers*: A print of the film had been sent to Rome to familiarize Bava with Melchior's work, and the director took the opportunity to simply duplicate the shot. But he also added to the idea a nodal tilt—the camera mounted in such a way to prevent shifting between the background and foreground—to make for a more interesting shot. The very nature of making a move, however, also prevented the use of his split-focus lenses, and he was forced to share the focus between the foreground and background.

Silvestri remembered:

> We left all these effects until the end of the shooting. The actors were already finished. There were four or five crew members left to shoot the effects in a corner of a small studio of Cinecitta. It was Mario, me and a few workers, including [cameraman] Antonio Rinaldi.

Most of the shots worked well for their time. Others suffered the curse of fast-moving, miniature smoke. The slow exposure rating of the film didn't allow for high-speed/slow motion photography. Some of the effects betrayed the size of the miniatures in their lack of depth of field—primarily in scenes of the spaceship flying in space with stars blurred out in the background. When the script called for distant Aura to be shrouded in fog, Bava was forced merely to throw the image of the planet out of focus in an attempt to achieve the illusion. However, his use of large circular cutouts and foreground miniatures to create the impression of an alien ship interior revealed cinematic inventiveness at its best. These scenes still stand as a real tribute to Bava's creative powers. (Although why the art director chose to place within easy reach an air-siphoning vent in the derelict ship that threatens to suffocate Markary and Sanya rather than in the unreachably high ceiling, as in Melchior's original script, is perplexing. The characters appear rather stupid as they make no attempt to plug it.)

In actual fact, the film ran into a few story and production problems along the way—at least from AIP's standpoint. According to Heyward, Bava had begun to diverge from the written page, and alternate versions of many scenes were shot, some of which required explaining, others which hit dead ends. Scenes were shot, for instance, involving a subplot of the crew attempting repairs of the ship, which turned out were not to be needed. Heyward began to raise concerns, and summoned Melchior to Rome to help get the film back in line. During his brief stay, Melchior viewed the dailies,

Kai (Rico Boido) makes a getaway with the critical meteor rejector in *Planet of the Vampires*.

suggested ways to improve what they'd already shot and worked on a new ending. Melchior recalled:

> I did go to Italy for a few days and worked on a rewrite with Bava and Louis. I got along famously with Bava and the Italian producer, Fulvio Lucisano. It was full up in production, but they had had some difficulties with the ending in particular. So we sat down and looked at the rushes. I came up with some ideas and out of that came what wound up in the film.

Melchior was pleased with what he saw being filmed, and felt that Bava had remained faithful to the tone of his writing:

> Bava paid attention to what I'd done, very much so. This writing was [all] a deliberate effort on my part to pre-direct the film... to the extent one could [on a written page]. Mario Bava was a very nice guy. I liked him a lot.

Lucisano looked at the project more from the standpoint of box office. Again, he felt it came down to a casting problem:

> I'm afraid, to say that if the picture had a younger actor like Mario wanted, it would have been a big success in Italy. It did okay, but not enough to write home about. [Mario didn't do more science fiction] because the film didn't do that well here. It did okay in the United States—it did better in the U.S. than anywhere else.

Melchior, upon viewing *Planet of the Vampires* many years later, commented:

> It was nothing from an acting standpoint, and I didn't like all those zooms, but I very much liked its mood. It was very atmospheric, and it was all just done with fog and lights and shadows.

The film, released in November 1965, though occasionally confusing and hurt by some of its weaker effects, emerged as one of the most visually arresting and atmospheric "B" science fiction films of its time. As well, it introduced a number of influential thematic and visual motifs to the genre. Melchior's derelict scene, combined with Bava's improvised skeleton and design sensibility, were to inspire some of *Alien*'s best-remembered scenes. The film's sense of wonder was perhaps best encapsulated by Melchior's thesis on the first page of his script:

> The unknown can only be questioned in terms of the known. There are no magic words to talk about the totally alien, nor any magic ways to understand it—nor will there be until it has been experienced. And what provocative vistas may then not open?

Strangest of all is how two such sweet personalities like Mario Bava and Ib Melchior could have worked together to produce such a macabre motion picture.

CYBORG XM-1

Cyborg XM-1 was another project Melchior wrote and developed in 1965. Perhaps his most ambitious science fiction screenplay, it detailed the creation and testing of the first biomechanically re-engineered homo sapien. Its ultimate mission—Mars.

Set after the year 2000, the story began in a vast, underground science laboratory where vertical accelerators, attitude control simulators, tilt tables and the Multiple Axis Space Test Inertia Facility provide the requisite whirl of big space technology. Various space-related tests are underway, including extreme human-endurance tortures and an experiment to utilize algae to maintain breathing balance between a man and a monkey housed in the same restrictive environment. Long before *The Abyss*, a hamster is seen living underwater amidst an aquarium full of fish. There's also the Marsarium, a large-scale simulation of the surface of the planet Mars, complete with rocks and exotic plants.

The major breakthrough work-in-progress, however, is Project Cyborg XM-1. The design team is lead by brilliant Dr. Borksenius. As in *The Time Travelers*, there are long uninterrupted shots where attention lingers on a Cyborg-to-be named Mark Fleming as he is opened up surgically while fully awake, then added to and subtracted from. Organic parts are deleted, enhanced or reduced, reconstructed in alloys, replaced by rubber arteries, metal and plastic. Hormones and vital chemicals are worn on his belt. As scripted, the effect was to be gruesome-awesome:

> The surgeon takes a sharp surgical knife; he places it in the middle of the Cyborg's chest just below his throat. CAMERA MOVES IN and slightly UP to get the best possible view of the Cyborg. The surgeon makes a long, deep incision all the way down the chest... almost to his naval. The surgeon folds back the two large skin flaps, exposing a plastic plate beneath, about 8 by 10 inches big. Borksenius turns an inset locking device with a small tool, and the surgeon lifts the entire plate out, handing it to the nurse... It is a fantastic, impossible sight... The *exposed chest cavity* of the fully conscious Cyborg lying on the operating table is like a vision from a haunting nightmare. On one side, encased in clearly transparent plastic, the *Cyborg's heart* can be seen rhythmically pumping his bright red blood through an intricate network of clear tubes connected to his own arteries and veins. But where his lungs should be there are, in-

stead, *rows of plastic racks*, holding several small transparent containers with liquids of different colors, and tiny tubes running to a complicated, automatic valve system. Other strange-looking pieces of tiny, compact equipment are secured inside the chest cavity and connected in various ways to the very life forces of the Cyborg himself. Assisted by the nurse, Borksenius and the surgeon place two small flasks with a greenish liquid missing in the exposed racks and make the delicate necessary connections...

Borksenius explains:

> As you can see the Cyborg's lungs already have been removed. Oxygen is being fed directly into his bloodstream along with other vital chemicals and nutrients... We are now adding the last two boosters located interiorly—an immunizer and an adrenaline-based energizer...

The bodily reconstruction moves on to a second stage where questions of grisly vivisectional violence versus inspirational human striving become meaningless amid an array of the anticipated Technimagical tricks:

> The skin on Mark's face has been laid open and folded back to expose the actual bone of his upper and lower jaws. All his teeth have been removed... As we watch, one of the surgeons moves the lower jaw down, while the other doctor places a form-fitting, double-grooved piece of metal or plastic onto the upper jaw line; the first surgeon then firmly presses the lower jaw into position in the appropriate groove... The first surgeon has picked up a thin piece of equipment—much like a slender fountain pen flashlight with an electric cord attached. It is a Laser Beam Surgical Welder. He points it at the joint of the Cyborg's jaw and the metal-plastic reinforcement piece; a hairline beam of intense light shoots from the instrument—and a thin wisp of steam rises from the point of impact, as the Laser actually is welding the joint together.

The Cyborg is vital to help solve one of the monumental problems this future age faces—the search for new fuels to replace dangerous nuclear power plants and the nearly-expended fossil fuels of our planet. A tiny fragment of an incredibly efficient new type of fuel has been sampled on the planet Mars. A few thousand pounds of the material could potentially supply most of the Earth's power requirements for a century. But it has proven impossible to locate any other deposits of it, even with the combined resources and technology of a group of scientists who have built a colony on the red planet. There is one hope left unexplored: a small group of natives—strange, coppery-hued beings from a distant star system who long ago abandoned their civilization to take up residence on Mars. Apparently they know the location of these elusive fuel deposits. But they are a distrustful race of esthetes, and communication with them has proven difficult. The Cyborg, the scientists believe, may be the means of bridging the gap:

> The Martian natives are a strange, enigmatic race... evasive, primitive, yet with a certain ancient sophistication. They are still being studied, but it seems to be increasingly difficult for our Base personnel to make contact with them.

Borksenius adds:

> It is imperative that the Cyborg goes to Mars as soon as possible... He can establish a much more efficient contact with the Martians than the clumsy Base personnel who are forced to bring a bit of Earth with them to Mars just to be able to live. The Cyborg can *join* the natives, *live* with them as an equal—*teach* them, *learn* from them, learn their most precious secret... how to find the fuel deposits.

With this in mind, Cyborg/Mark Fleming spends time in the test track—the Marsarium—learning how to live in the hostile environment with his new life-support body.

If science alone were involved, that would be the end of it, but the human personality is not an innocent bystander: An agent from NASA's Security and Intelligence Agency arrives to investigate the experiments, and to deliver some very bad news: Their Cyborg may be a troubled man. Records indicate he'd experienced a terrible trauma in his past. On one of a series of mercy missions to a region of the Amazon he was captured by the dangerous Auca natives along with his wife who he'd invited for the first time. The exact events aren't known for sure, but apparently she was taken away, never to return. He was beaten, but managed to escape somehow. A review of his psychological profile has lead to certain likely conclusions:

> Fleming is apparently blaming himself for the fate that befell his wife—whatever it was. He volunteered to be a human guinea pig not because of his dedication to serve mankind, but out

> of a deep sense of guilt... a deep desire for self punishment.

Government agents want to close down the project as unsafe, until they can sort this all out. Borksenius refuses, pointing out how close they are to completion, how long it will take to produce another Cyborg and how dangerous it would be abruptly to stop the medical work Fleming is undergoing. But the agents insist the program be halted. Borksenius manages to stall them and have them escorted off the grounds.

Matters become even more complicated: Cyborg/Fleming's wife, Susan, turns out to be very much alive, although she is suffering from a type of amnesia about what exactly happened to her in the Amazon jungles. She has tracked her husband down to this lab. Her inquiries to learn the whereabouts and fate of her husband are evaded. Borksenius suggests she come back the next day when she may see her husband. But secretly he has prepared a ship for launching to Mars—space travel is relatively commonplace in the world of Melchior's story—for both he and the just-completed Cyborg. He sets out for the red planet to prove his experiment a success before either the agents and/or his wife throw a wrench in the works.

Days later, Susan hooks up with the agents. Using sodium pentothal, they are able to uncover details of her terrifying ordeals and escape from the Auca Indians. Together with the agents, and accompanied by a group of scientists, she pursues Borksenius to Mars. Upon landing, new problems arise: True to the warning, the Cyborg went amok, stole a laser weapon, plus additional survival chemicals and stimulants, and escaped the compound. He headed for the hills shortly after his arrival on the planet, apparently in search of the natives of Mars: He now seems to confuse them with the Auca Indians who tortured him and his wife in the Amazonian jungles.

A whole series of adventures leads up to a dramatic climax: The Cyborg stalks and kills one of the natives, then falls into and barely escapes the cave-pit lair of a gigantic burrowing insect; the dead native is brought to the tribe by the colonists, with the tribe driving a symbolic staff into the ground as warning of impending retribution; the Cyborg's wife, Susan, goes it alone in search of her husband in the Martian desert and is inexplicably saved from suffocation by one of the natives when she looses the oxygen supply for her spacesuit; a search party, attacked by a giant serpent in a cave, manages to escape by setting off a lava-like chain reaction in the oxygen-rich lavox mineral deposits embedded in the rock; the Cyborg returns to the base and attempts to destroy valuable equipment. At the same time the natives launch their attack, armed with mysterious staffs that generate protective force fields while projecting their own *thoughts* as explosive, hemorrhage-inducing telekinetic firepower.

All would appear lost when the entire compound erupts in destruction as the colonists watch from their fortified base:

> [On the screen] a horrifying, hellish sight confronts them... A blazing fire is burning fiercely from one of the huge tanks; the flames lick greedily towards the other tanks, and suddenly one more gigantic tank explodes and another.... It is an unparalleled display of pyrotechnic turbulence; fireballs of many

> hues, streaked with black smoke, billow and swirl in burst after burst of explosive, searing blasts... Towers and tanks topple and explode; the gantry at the great gleaming space ship crumbles and collapses... scene after scene of infernal holocaust washes the screen with the furious colors of destruction...

The colonists try to barricade the complex, but the assault continues unabated. Their laser weapons are completely useless against the natives' force-shields:

> At once a thin, high-pitched WHINE is heard, so sharp and piercing that it seems to penetrate every fiber of the body.... [The men's] faces are contorted in anguished grimaces, and some of them claw at their helmets... More of the defenders are falling lifeless, blood oozing from their noses and ears... A man stumbles on the verge of madness...

In the final scenes, the Cyborg has been restored, his crazed behavior explained as the result of an intolerable mixture of chemical nutrients. He is sent out as an ambassador to the natives to restore peace. Accompanying him is a *second* Cyborg, his wife, Susan, who had agreed with Borksenius to undergo the transformation in order to rejoin her husband. It was the only way, and she was glad to do it. A truce is drawn, and, with real communication now established, the natives use their telekinetic powers to reveal the source of the wonderful new fuel.

Cyborg XM-1, written during the heyday of the spectacle film, was planned as an epic tale, with lots of extras, numerous sets and changes of locale—including a huge laboratory, space ship launching pads, technological catacombs, otherworldly terrains and a vast array of gadgets—in a bookishly complex storyline told in multiple episodes. The base on Mars, for instance, provides a spectacular background:

> Mars Base One is built in what appears to be the sandy, rock-strewn bottom of a huge meteor crater... Far in the background is a fabulous, awe-inspiring installation—a great, sprawling space port with a couple of launching-landing pads and gantry towers; with great, squat, vari-colored tanks and chunky power plant structures; with oddly constructed control towers and the... reaching bowls of galvanized steel mesh that are the radio-telescopic guiding systems... The Martian atmosphere is saturated with the roar of power-spewing rockets... A big space cruiser is slowly descending on a pillar of white-hot flame onto one of three launching-landing pads. As it nears the solid concrete pad, the fury of the fire-thrust is catapulted out-

> wards in a huge, orange-red inverted mushroom cloud of steam, smoke, dust and pure, raw power...

The spiritual presence of Melchior's early inspiration, E.E. "Doc" Smith, is readily apparent in such scenes.

There are also Leinster-esque scenes of the trapped Cyborg fighting his way out of the insect lair, plucking disgusting root tendrils to form a rope:

> The sandy bottom is strewn with the white bones and skeletal remains of wholly alien, unidentifiable creatures. The putrid refuse of other unimaginable things lie torn and noisome against the walls, revoltingly fed upon by huge, fetid, maggot-like slugs. Long, rope-like tentacles from a saprophytic vegetal-organism are embedded in the... cadaverous mass draining a foul nourishment from it... He ties the organic rope to a grapple hook made up of a chunk of alien skeleton bone and narrowly evades the monster in the pit.

Cyborg XM-1, with the above scene, was another in a line of Melchior scripts featuring revolting insect encounters: A mole-grub had made an appearance in *Journey to the 7th Planet,* and an ant-lion in *Robinson Crusoe on Mars.* It was not by accident. Insects had held a special fascination for Melchior for many years:

> I'd always been very interested in insects—especially in *beetles.* But in all kinds. At one time, between jobs and the theater, I worked for the Museum of Natural History in New York classifying 5,000 beetles from South America. They were all similar, but they were of different types. So I sat there pulling them out one at a time classifying them. Fascinating. As a kid I had a beetle collection—and I still have a few of them.
>
> An ant-lion—I used one in my original *Robinson Crusoe on Mars*—is a strange-looking creature. It has a large body, and it has a head with huge pincers on it. And it sits down into the ground in a big pit of sand. And an ant will tumble down the slope and *crunch*—the ant-lion takes him...
>
> The thing with insects is, you can *not* describe anything that even comes close to the *horror* of some of them and what they look like. I mean, every once in a while you see a picture layout and you can see they are absolutely monstrous. Monstrous. And all you need to do is exaggerate their size.

Melchior, however, is quick to point out that a story built entirely and only on monster insects is very limited. And, if the monster is not within the realm of reason, the story itself is undermined. He found himself for a while, ironically, writing on the outer edges of plausibility with some of his films, films that stressed such monsters:

> I prefer plausibility over bug-eyed monsters. However, bug-eyed monsters is what sells, or at least did when I was in the business. So, of necessity, I had to write things like *The Angry Red Planet* and stories with big monsters in them. But what I much rather preferred was a picture like *The Time Travelers*, where there are monsters—if you will—but they are monsters which are *plausible*. There are no other weird creatures in it.
>
> The original *Robinson Crusoe on Mars* had big monsters in it, because that's what they wanted in it at that time. But I tried to make them logical. The television shows—*Men into Space*—they were all *possible*. *Cyborg* was plausible. You take something *known*, and you go way into the future with it—and that, to me, becomes interesting.

Melchior could move away from this logic if the premise *itself* allowed for it—for instance, *Journey to the 7th Planet* with its mind-robbing conjurer of irrational fears, and *Planet of the Vampires*, with its ghostly aliens able to raise the dead.

Cyborg XM-1 would've been a sister film to *The Time Travelers*, although much larger in scope, combining elements from it and other Melchior moments and ideas that were, in some cases, not fully realized in his earlier scripts. These moments, motifs and images underline and define a self-consistent, invented universe not dissimilar to the coherent world constructs of writers like Lovecraft and Edgar Rice Burroughs. A review of *Cyborg XM-1*'s elements provides a basic litany of sequences, gadgets, gimmicks, themes and wow moments—including the educational-science film-styled demonstrations he'd toyed with in *The Time Travelers*—that serve to illustrate a few of his favored tableaus: There are lone-survivor elements spun off his 1957 script *The Savage Trap* as well as *Robinson Crusoe on Mars*; various hi-tech medical procedures that elaborated on the Android Assembly Plant in *The Time Travelers*, as well as a tunnel-like underground complex and rocket launch site similar to those in the same film; a gigantic sand-pit creature that recreated the underground insect threats in *Journey to the 7th Planet* and *Robinson Crusoe on Mars*; coppery-hued alien natives that may have been distant ancestors to the living dead aliens in his early version of *Planet of the Vampires*; discovery of a cave-hidden treasure trove of alien artifacts imbued with seemingly magical properties—including metal cubes that meld together, revivable glowing plants and instant x-ray photographs that are extensions of moments in both *The Time Travelers* and his unrealized *Space Family Robinson* project. Even the use of narco-synthesis as in *The Angry Red Planet* is brought to bear in trying to restore Susan's memory of things she's buried in her subconscious.

Cyborg XM-1, at least in first draft form, contained enough plot complications, characters and action to fill a good-sized novel, and, coming on the heals of a series of frustrated projects, suggested a kind of ultimate sci-fi, techno-pulp grand finale. It touched on everything from Frankenstein themes, to the Belyayev's *Amphibian Man*, to Conrad's *Heart of Darkness*. It bore colorful echoes of the near legendary Winston Science Fiction Series that made the rounds of many a baby boomer's library in the 1950s. With further refinements it might have become one of the classics of the Golden Age of filmed science fiction.

Like Melchior's *Columbus of the Stars/Starship Explorers*, the project, unfortunately, never saw fruition. Melchior prepared notes, conferred about the effects with David Hewitt and attended endless meetings with producers in Los Angeles and New York. Eventually he wound up working on further developments of the project with well-known science fiction author Frederick Pohl. But the deals all fell through.

A new wrinkle to the *Cyborg XM-1* saga cropped up in the mid-'70s, when Frederick Pohl based an entire novel on the same ideas and situations depicted in Melchior's script. The book, titled *Man Plus*, went on to receive a Nebula Award for Best Science Fiction Novel in 1976. Melchior received no credit. He was, however, awarded an out of court settlement.

More frustrating news arrived around the same time about his *Space Family Robinson* project: Melchior received a letter addressed to him from his friend and potential distributor, Sam Arkoff, in August 1965. In it Arkoff regretfully explained he had learned of the similarities between Irwin Allen's *Lost in Space* TV series and Melchior's project, and expressed doubt that he could go forward with any plans for *Space Family Robinson*. It effectively terminated one of Melchior's most dedicated efforts to launch a project.

The unaired pilot for *Lost in Space* seemed very much like an also-ran TV version of an Ib Melchior movie. Before the show aired, alterations were made to the pilot, including the addition of two new characters—the infamous Dr. Smith and the Robot—and a lighter musical score. The changes mitigated, but did not completely erase the obvious similarities the show bore to Melchior's property.

Melchior reflected:

> I felt *Time Tunnel* was another steal. It was the time portal from *The Time Travelers*. The problem with that for me was that I didn't own *The Time Travelers*. I had sold my rights to it to AIP. [When I saw the show] I just knew that the man had stolen my stuff entirely. I mean it was so *obvious*. He later on did a show—a remake of *Time Tunnel*—which was even called *The Time Travelers*... But I think, in the end, the people in Hollywood who are in the know knew him for what he was. He had a reputation for taking other people's ideas and not creating anything by himself.

It was not encouraging that a man whose every association with science fiction films had resulted in strong box-office returns, and whose ideas were proven sound by the tremendous popularity of the likes of *Star Trek* and *Lost in Space*—both shows based on concepts virtually identical to Melchior's—should find it so difficult to get his projects financed. He seemed to be continually running up against the proverbial brick wall.

Perhaps times had changed and movies that spoke about the aspirations, great successes and strivings of humankind suddenly had less appeal. Perhaps it was because the motion picture business was undergoing basic changes in style and content at the time. Movies were beginning to focus on such pervasive cultural concerns as the Viet Nam war and racial injustice. And, amid a sea of turbulent news, the traditional hero was quickly being replaced with the antihero. If nothing else, space travel at the time was about heroes and courage, qualities that may have begun to seem abstract or even naive. The American public was also losing its infatuation with the space program, an erosion that continued to eat away at funding for exploration of the next frontier. And, of course, Melchior's science fiction films were principally about space travel. The immediacy of the nightly news itself may have swept away a certain type of optimistic adventure film and interest in far-off worlds. With that change, plus several other failed attempts to launch ambitious science fiction projects fresh on his mind, Melchior turned away from work in the genre for the next decade, leaving projects like *Cyborg XM-1* to gather dust.

Osa Jensen commented:

> In a way it was a surprise he got into science fiction considering his background, but on the other hand not really, because I knew he was a very good student at school: [For example], he did a lot of studying on the old signs we have in Denmark called runes, which are not letters but picture-graphs. So he studied that and gave a seminar on that: A serious sort of person. He was always a *deep* thinker, so it wasn't so much a surprise. He was a visionary—he was very ahead of his time. And *special*.

The end of Melchior's science fiction projects marked the end of a tremendous amount of work and effort. In the wider picture of his entire life this work actually comprised but one *small* portion of his life's experiences, interests and accomplishments: It was a life in which many of his professional works where created almost as an outgrowth of his personal passions and hobbies, and were thus tinged with the same sort of playfulness and disregard for the commonplace that H.P. Lovecraft had displayed in his writings.

Were his science fictions days all over? Had the fat lady sung the end of that saga? Or had she developed a case of laryngitis?

FROM LASER BEAMS TO VIETNAM

> [It] was one of the most fascinating things I've ever done. You open the person up, you stop the heart, you operate on it—and then you restart it. If you *can*. I observed the whole thing. I could see the man's heart in his open chest. The doctor asked me, "Have you ever felt a human aorta?" I said, "Not recently," and he put my finger on it.
>
> You know what a cat feels like when it's purring? That's what the human aorta feels like... The very next day I talked to the man on the phone...

Filming open-heart surgery—and touching the inside of a living human being—was just one of many unusual experiences Melchior acquired while working on a variety of documentaries over several decades. Between assignments following *Cyborg XM-1*, Melchior returned time and time again to directing a wide range of documentaries as he had in the 1940s and '50s. His subjects put him in contact with experts on everything from rocketry and drug addiction to Vietnam cargo drops and laserography.

He co-produced and directed dozens of these shorts and educational films, and won a number of national awards for his work:

> I have found that in making documentary films the best result is obtained if one does not know too much about the subject *going in*, but emerges an expert. At first they explain and you don't understand a word. After that, you ask them all the idiot questions—"What happens when you put the key in the car? What happens then," and so on. And with that you get the full picture and then you can write the script. You do become an expert—for a while.
>
> Making the documentaries gives you knowledge that you would not otherwise get. Where else would I get any direct knowledge of open heart surgery as a normal person? By *doing* it, it's much more interesting.
>
> I loved documentaries because I got to do things otherwise I'd never do—or be able to do—work with nukes, laser beams, animals, surgeons and so on.

Among his documentary films over the years were a series of nearly 30 films about nuclear physics and atomic energy for the government in the 1950s, then, later, a series of projects with titles like *The Two-Legged Spaceship*, *Alcohol and Red Flares*, *Keep off the Grass* and *The Laser Beam*, the last of which won an award from the U.S. Information Agency.

Hot Run was the fascinating true story of a young boy who developed a new type of rocket:

> A young man—a 16-year-old—had developed this new rocket with significant design differences. He'd made it in his garage out of scrounged things, and he got several patents on it along the way. The Navy became interested, and decided to bring the young man out to test it at China Lake Bed [California]. And the first one crashed—it never got off the pad. So, he took the whole thing apart and he found there was just this little *ten cent* gasket at fault. And he put it all together again and it flew. It was very impressive. The U.S. military purchased it from him.

Hot Run was, in reality, a kind of mini-*October Sky*.

> I did a couple of films for the Air Force: *LAPES*—Low Altitude Parachute Ejection System—and the other *PLADS*—Parachute Low Altitude Delivery System. With *LAPES*, you deliver a fully loaded three and a quarter-ton truck from a *low* altitude: five feet. The plane comes down within five feet and then the load is pulled out with a parachute where it drops to the ground and skids to a halt. And it could be done precisely enough so that you could draw a line in the dirt and it could be put right there. And the other one—Parachute Low Altitude Delivery System—they could put a load right on top of virtually anything—my own head, if needed—from an altitude of 250 feet.

The work was very confidential, and a film of the procedures was vitally needed to train troops in Vietnam. Melchior and documentary producer-cameraman Sid Davis were contacted by the military. They flew down to Eglin Air Force Base in Florida and met with the base commander in his office. They presented their proposition to the general who assigned them a Project Officer, a colonel named "Slaughter" Mimms. The military had estimated the films would take six months to make, but he needed them much sooner. Melchior asserted the two of them could get both films done in two months. With that, the general said, "Slaughter, give Melchior *whatever* he wants."

And he literally meant it. If Melchior had needed 10 planes flying upside down painted purple, he'd get them. But, the only way to get the project done in time was if there truly was *no* interference; so the first time the colonel questioned why they were shooting out of order, Melchior handed him a script and walked away. And *that* was the last problem they had. The prints were delivered wet to Vietnam—each film had taken only a month to do—which allowed the *LAPES* and *PLADS* techniques to be quickly taught to the troops. The Parachute/Drop Systems were soon to be extensively employed in the Tet offensive.

Melchior directed a documentary about drunk drivers at one point and decided he wanted to know what it might be like to be arrested:

> So, I made an arrangement with the police department, and they arrested me. They take your shoes and give you paper ones and so on. Everything in the process is very demeaning... But now I was able to *describe* it. I always feel that you have to *know* what you are writing about.
>
> All the documentary experience helped the features. Obviously when you do a film like *Hot Run* everything has to be accurate. When you get into fiction those things stay with you, so if you want to talk about something scientifically, the authenticity that you have learned obviously becomes part of it. You don't have to make it up.

It is then not surprising that projects like *The Time Travelers* and *Cyborg XM-1* linger a bit on those science film moments—discussions of laser beams, open-heart surgery on androids, etc.—moments of documentary sciential-fiction.

There was a truly sad observation Melchior made in regards to several anti-drug films he directed:

> We made a lot of films about drugs, or law enforcement. But the films we made for high school were much too late. The ones for junior high, much too late. For grade school—again too late. The final one we did was called *The Two-Legged Spaceship*, where we likened the human body to a spaceship which you cannot pollute. We made that film for kindergartners. That's where you have to start.

REAL MONSTERS AND WEAPONS OF DESTRUCTION

Science fiction would be hard-pressed to top the extremes of man's invention, destruction, strategy, improvisation, endurance or creativity during World War ll. Mankind had been given carte blanche to do whatever was necessary to destroy the enemy. Consider some of the lesser-known strangeness of the war effort: German experiments with cannons over a thousand feet long; pilots sent up in veritable death jets—the volatile ME 163s—planes barely capable of landing without exploding; attempted construction of flying saucers; German experiments with atomic energy and the atomic bomb; the first large-scale rocket launches; the creation of Schornsteinsfeger—a stealth paint that could make planes invisible to radar; guns that could shoot bullets around a corner; planes designed to cut bombers in half; push-me/pull-me planes that could perform outrageous maneuvers; chemicals intended to turn the ocean into giant churning Bromo Seltzer. And then other amazing feats: New York completely covered in seconds by clouds of super-expanding fog shot from planes, to hide it from attack...

And impossible daring: When the Germans couldn't figure out what was going wrong with their V-1 buzz-bomb rockets, Hanna Reitsch, a tiny daredevil test pilot, voluntarily strapped herself onto the hull of one of them and flew it for the Germans in order to check out its steering problems first hand. She said, "Okay, I'll ride it"—and off it went. Once she figured out what the problem was, she jumped off—and parachuted to Earth.

And then there was destruction. Beyond comprehension. Unheard of. Unequaled in human history...

Ib Melchior had been there, and came away with close-up memories of what happened—and ideas on how these fantastic, real-life events could be told to those who hadn't been there. Ambush *Bay*, a 1966 United Artists release starring Hugh O'Brien, Mickey Rooney, Harry Lauter and James Mitchum, marked Melchior's return as a writer of war movies. A medium-budget production with decent performances directed by Ron Winston, it was something of a departure for Melchior as it took him away from the European Theater of Operations of his own experiences and into the Pacific Islands. The plot: U.S. Marines, landing secretly at night on a small Philippine island, attempt to get through to a Japanese-held village where they are to contact a Japanese who has important information concerning General MacArthur's planned invasion. They have only 96 hours to complete their mission and return. They encounter Japanese resistance and, when they finally reach the village, they learn that the enemy knows of MacArthur's planned route and has mined the entire area with explosives anchored on the ocean bed. The Marines' radio is destroyed and they must make their way to a Japanese control center where the mines may be detonated prematurely in order to save the invasion.

Melchior worked on *Ambush Bay* with producer Aubrey Schenck. The film was a tale of war in the South Pacific and earned good reviews.

The script had been handed to Melchior from another writer. He did a complete rewrite—and it worked. The film received good reviews.

> *Ambush Bay* packs the type of war action which is well-received in both the general and outdoor market. Striking color photography and realistic treatment give meaning to this strong World War II melodrama. Forceful acting and mounting tension hold to its effective windup.—*Variety*, August 31, 1966
>
> *Ambush Bay* [is a] taut World War II film. A straightforward, old-fashioned, well-made war film. [It] is as good as any... done in taut documentary style... exciting to watch. The script was by Marve Feinberg and Ib Melchior...—*The Los Angeles Times*, September 29, 1966
>
> *Ambush Bay* is a very good picture, taut absorbing and individual... done without clichés and, in fact, with a good deal of original thought and enterprise... The screenplay by Marve Feinberg and Ib Melchior is extremely well-done. It is neatly constructed and developed with sparse speech and meaningful incident... character is achieved but without stereotypes. The dialogue is a great deal of help, in part possibly because it is thriftily em-

> ployed, with emphasis on action. It makes its points well, too, often with a wry observation, a laconic comment that displays character while advancing action.—*The Hollywood Reporter*, September 1, 1966

The film was a clear indication of the direction Melchior's career was moving in:

> [As a writer] I was very, very interested in military intelligence operations, particularly my own experiences during the war. I had done *Ambush Bay* and that had gotten me into thinking about the war again. I had written accounts of my own experiences and so on, ad infinitum. And I had one about the Nazi 'Werewolves' which I rather liked...
>
> If things had gone differently, I probably would've stayed with science fiction. Let me put it this way: I was doing my films but I was deprived, obviously, of what I could've done by Irwin Allen. [Otherwise], I would've done *Space Family Robinson*. Remember, what I created was *Robinson Crusoe on Mars* from *Robinson Crusoe*, *Space Family Robinson* from *Swiss Family Robinson*, *Columbus of the Stars*, which was essentially *Star Trek*—before Roddenberry—and *Treasure Asteroid*. These are all things that I [probably] would have done had I not been robbed by Irwin Allen. But then, my books might never have been written. I might've been too busy with other things.
>
> As it was, when Cleo started nagging me—I might as well say it—to "write a book, write a book." I was in a position that I *could* take off a couple of months and write a book. When it became a bestseller it came down to, why not do another?—then another and another, and so on? Had I not been able to take that two months because I was in production on these other things, I might never have written any of those books. And I'm kind of glad I did because I think they're a good record of a particular kind of intelligence operation that went on during the war.

On top of that, it all happened with relative ease—and ease isn't a word generally used in Hollywood. Melchior found this writing rewarding in ways that the films, with their politics and compromises, seldom were:

> With my first book the kind of thing happened that almost never happens: Within a week of submission I had a *check*. It was immediately published by Harper and Row and became a bestseller. I was so lucky. So it wasn't just a matter of my interest that I moved away from science fiction toward war stories. My books sold well, and have been published in 25 countries.

While Melchior had stopped writing bona fide science fiction, his interests did not lie in stories of ordinary people and everyday events. His new writings were stories about people who'd employed the faculty of the imagination in pursuit of extreme goals, as often for evil as for good purposes: The human imagination could be put to work as a tool for *any* conceivable goal. Altogether, the new series of writings comprised a kind of storytelling that might be called ultra-fiction, for the people and events they described ranged, almost unilaterally, well beyond normal human experience.

The first in his series of war novels, *Order of Battle,* was published in 1973. Melchior went on to write a total of 14 books, ending with his purely autobiographical, *Case By Case,* written 20 years after his first book. A look at the these stories reveals a kind of uniquely talented, intrepid human being who is repeatedly thrown into challenging, sometimes exotic environments not dissimilar, in some ways, from the worlds encountered in science fiction.

Order of Battle was based on one of Melchior's own exploits when working as a U.S. Counter Intelligence Corps agent in World War II. It concerned the locating and destruction of the fanatical Nazi "Werewolves." The terrorists planned to survive the Allied's final drive by hiding out by the hundreds in underground bunkers built beneath the Black Forest of Germany. The novel takes place during the 19 days between Roosevelt's death and Hitler's suicide, and ends a few scant hours before the "Werewolves'" planned assassination of General Eisenhower. Melchior:

> Writing my first novel came very, very fast and very, very easy because I was writing about things I had lived as a CIC agent. I was just remembering and putting it down on paper. I did it as a fiction novel, even though it was my own case, because I wanted to tell it from the German side also. Fiction—although fiction based on fact, because it all did happen.

Cleo Baldon admitted:

> I really did nag him to write that book. I pushed it at him because it was such a great story. When he told it, there wasn't anyone who wasn't fascinated about these "Werewolves" [and that] this young kid at 24—he was a man grown, but really still a

young kid—could go in there and have the imagination to know what to do, and as an actor, go in and kick open the door and play the scene as if it had been *written* for him....

Sleeper Agent came about when Melchior learned of the existence of agents of the enemy who enter their foe's territory and come to live there as ordinary citizens, living a life of apparent total normalcy, but with the ultimate goal of becoming an active force of sabotage when called upon to do so—even years or decades later:

I was talking to someone in New York who was discussing the *S.S. Normandie*—the French liner that capsized on fire in the harbor and was destroyed. And he said that it had been done by a sleeper agent. I said, what the hell is a sleeper agent? "A man named Fritz Scheffer is the one who caused the fire, and *he* is a sleeper agent." Now I said to myself, this is a hell of a story, but I didn't want to do that particular one. I started to look into the whole sleeper agent thing, how they were trained, what they did and so forth. And I wrote my own story, but wrote it set in an area which I was very familiar with: Germany and Denmark. The idea of *Sleeper Agent* was a fascinating idea because we didn't know how many of them were sent out after the war and where they were today. When I wrote it in 1974 they were still around...

The book suggested some disturbing parallels with the behavior and desires of the so-called skinheads of today—the notion of an *idea* living on quietly in the populace, just awaiting the right time to be activated once again for the cause, in this case white supremacy and Nazism.

[My next project] *The Haigerloch Project* came about when I got interested in the fact that the Germans had attempted to make an atomic bomb. In one of my own cases, I had to go in behind the lines and get one of the German scientists out of Germany, and he was one of the scientists who supposedly had worked for something called the *Degussa*, the organization manufacturing uranium for use in their atomic bomb. He was involved in the production of heavy water. So with that little bit of information I started researching how far they had gone with this, and I found out a lot. I wrote the story which was strictly fiction, except the atomic pile in Haigerloch did malfunction, and nobody knew—or knows—why. In my book, I explained why.

The Haigerloch Project told the story of a team of brilliant scientists and top Nazi Party leaders who feverishly labored within a hidden labyrinth of caves in Germany to manufacture this ultimate weapon in an attempt to turn the tide of the war. The action took in a wide swath of territory, and featured a dramatic climactic death scene involving a collapsing stage of burning, tumbling props and Nazi officers in a Wagnerian setting turned into hell.

After the book came out, I got a letter from a scientist, who said, "You are so right on the button about this [the atomic bomb]. We were *there*. How did *you* know about it?" He actually was part of the team that infiltrated Haigerloch and found out about the experiments. How did I know? I don't know. I just made it up. I figured, logically, this will happen and, logically, that will happen, and when you put it all together—wrapped in a bit of imagination—then you get something that *could* be.

Melchior used logic and facts as tools to build a virtual reality version of what happened without actually having been there.

Melchior had also proven not only to have been historically correct, but darn close to perfectly correct on the *science*. He received the following letter from Samuel Abraham Goudsmit, a renowned physicist:

> Dear Mr. Melchior:
> I finally obtained a copy of your book *The Haigerloch Project*. I read it carefully, in one long session. I could not put it down. I greatly admire

> your creative imagination, combined with strict logic. If you had studied with Niels Bohr, you might have made valuable contributions to physics also. However, I must admit that I am glad that reality was a lot tamer than your fictionalized version.

The physicist included a few minor corrections:

> I want to make two very minor remarks about factual statements in the book. On page 244 you mention Cadmium metal to control the neutron flow. However, there were no Cadmium controls at the Haigerloch reactor. This was a serious oversight and it was fortunate that the reactor did not go critical. The German project was dominated by theorists, who had erroneously concluded that the reactor would be self-controlled when the temperature reached a certain height.

Melchior was gratified for the acknowledgment about his overall accuracy, but hidden in the comments on the German failure was a greater and ironic satisfaction:

> My delight, in all of this, is if it were not for Adolf Hitler's anti-Semitism, the Germans *would* have had the atomic bomb long *before* we did, and they would've won the war: When the German scientists went to Hitler and said, "We have the possibility of developing an explosive device thousands of times bigger than anything ever seen," and they started mentioning who was involved—and they were all Jewish—Hitler said he would have nothing to do with Jewish scientists. So for two years they did *nothing*. It was really because of his anti-Semitism. But, if they *had* started two years earlier... [The pause is ominous.]

The Watchdogs of Abaddon focused on the Nazi's long-range plans to regain power beyond the immediate war and traced the seeds of Nazism into contemporary Los Angeles. Its title derived from the mythic hounds that guard the gates of hell. Melchior recalled:

> I found out there were many rumors of Hitler's children that actually existed. As a matter of fact, some of them were listed on a number of SS documents, where the mother was getting a certain

> amount of money for support. That set me off on the idea: What if there was a son who was being groomed to take over...?

Watchdogs gave Melchior the opportunity to conduct some of the most exotic research of his career: He needed to know something about *prostitutes*—the Hollywood Boulevard variety. As with his deliberate arrest for drunk driving, he arranged with detectives from the Hollywood Police Department to give him a note stating he was doing research for a book. He picked up a cute 19-year-old:

> I was not interested in her services, *of course*—but when she found out I was researching a book, she got very excited and interested and said, "Oh, I can tell you all *sorts* of things."
> One of the things I thought was funny is when she pointed out a bar that was a meeting place for all the streetwalkers. She said, "I will go in first, then you come in afterwards. Now they won't know you, but what will happen is this: The bartender will take a look at you and he will go to the cash register and ring up *no sale*. That means don't approach this guy, I don't know him." And that is exactly what happened. Now, how else do you find out about such things except by doing them?

In writing *The Watchdog of Abaddon* Melchior had used Karl Malden, whom he admired, as his prototype for the hero, and when the book was published he took it to the actor, hoping he might like to appear in a possible film version of the book. Malden liked the property, and agreed, and together they went to a major studio and made a deal. But before it could get off the ground outside forces once again came into play. The Writers Guild went on strike, making it impossible for Melchior to go to work. When months later things went back to normal it was a whole new ball game, and the Watchdogs would not be playing.

Melchior's next novel, *The Marcus Device* was written simultaneously as a motion picture screenplay titled, at least initially, *The Seven Inch Wilderness*. The script title (sited in the first pages of this book) was a reference made by a doctor, to the diameter of gray brain matter in the human head by which all life is perceived and understood. The book/screenplay dealt with one man's attempt to survive the dark forces that are brought into play to destroy someone who is experiencing his own mind purely as a wildland. The plot details what happens to a test pilot who has a vital piece of military information, but due to a brain injury suffered in the crash of his experimental plane, has been robbed of all memory, all special and learned skills. He experiences total retrograde and aphasic amnesia and is reduced to the level of an animal. He must survive in a hostile terrain, while being hunted down by government agents. The agents appear as dangerous monsters to him and he is forced to combat them solely on an instinctive level.

The chase becomes one of technological knowledge pitted against pure animal cunning. But it is actually a lot weirder than that. Much of the story takes place from the amnesiac's point of view, and that perspective is of an alien being who has crash-landed on a strange, incomprehensible planet. Melchior explained:

> *The Marcus Device* really goes back quite a while. I was in Death Valley and I said to myself, if someone from another galaxy landed on Earth in Death Valley, he would say this is a barren world. There is nothing here. It is like another world. Then I got the idea of someone being [stranded there]... *Robinson Crusoe on Mars* came right out of that same experience. It was the reverse of the situation in *The Marcus Device*; Death Valley inspired both of the projects. This was in 1960.
>
> The main character doesn't know where he is or who he is, or *what* he is. Or anything. It is one of the most unusual *love* stories written. I originally wrote it as a script, then turned it into a book, then wrote a new script based on the book. I checked out the medical condition with a friend who is a psychiatrist, Dr. Elliott Markoff. He said it's not common, but it certainly is possible. Aphasiac amnesia. You can't even talk. All *learned* knowledge is gone. You are like a newborn. You have your intelligence. You can learn. You can reason, but when the hero sees the sun go down, he has no idea it is going to come back up again. It is simply *gone*. All he has is instinct. He's dying of thirst, and he comes upon one of those drums of water they have in Death Valley scattered about if your car runs out of water, that say, "Water: Not for Drinking Purposes." He has no idea what it says, even though it's right there—*water*—and he's dying of thirst.
>
> The very first version was called *The Animal*. It was done for a producer who did short films and he suggested we try to make a feature together but with no sound, just voice-overs. It was very weird. Unusual. Very undoable actually. But, I did it for fun.

The notion of a man without knowledge—a mass of sentient flesh capable of hunger and pain, thirst and fear but lacking the database as to where these things come from or why—becomes all the more startling when the primal survival instincts kick in. While *The Marcus Device* reads a bit more like a transcription of a screenplay than a pure novel, it is rife with horrors all the more disturbing because of their innocent mindlessness: The once-civilized human throws himself upon a lizard in the desert, cracks its back and gnaws on its still-struggling body. Hungered again, later, he vacantly reaches for a curved shape scuttling in the sand, ready to make a snack of a scorpion with its stinger up. Cars roar by—and are perceived to be block-like monsters. Someone opens the door to a trailer at night, and the shaft of light that shoots out becomes ghostly tentacle reaching for him.

Throughout, the pilot sees things—every *thing*—as phenomena, as a series of merely inexplicable shapes, motions, temperatures and sensory facts. The book is told through his senses and point of view, leaving the reader in the same position as the character. The world is full of strangeness that Melchior backs the reader into understanding. In the course of the story, it becomes apparent that a man reduced to reliance merely on his instincts would not even be on equal footing with most animals, since man's senses and physical endurance are far inferior: His situation would be more like that of a handicapped or injured animal.

When the novelty of seeing the world through uncomprehending eyes is just about used up, Melchior sets up a new and emotionally unsettling situation: The man on the run captures his own wife, but she is now merely an entity whose body is different than his. The difference creates reactions in his body that are incomprehensible to him—arousal—as well as uncontrollable. His wife, Randi, who has been frigid for some time in their relationship, is now faced by a being who is, at one and the same time, her husband, a complete stranger and an animal. A being whose sexual instincts have awakened, and who no longer possesses knowledge of morality. That she is willing to consider this encounter raises issues that have no easy answers.

Melchior stated:

> To me, that was one of the most fascinating things
> I've ever attempted—trying to put myself into the
> mind of a man who does not know that you cannot
> walk on water.

Novel number six was an international thriller based on a *Life* magazine feature article by Melchior. In the OSS he had studied cryptography—the art of secret writing—and cryptanalysis, and in one of his textbooks a famous cipher was depicted as an example of an unsolvable cryptogram because it was unique and too short. It was the inscription on the tombstone on William Shakespeare's grave, which it is said Shakespeare himself composed and designed. The original carved quatrain, replaced in 1831, looked like this:

> Good Frend for Iesus SAKE forbeare
> To diGG TE Dust EncloAſed HE.Re,
> Bleſe be TE Man Y ſpares TEs Stones
> And curſt, be He Y moves my Bones

Through the centuries cryptanalists the world over had tried to decipher this inscription; they had all employed one of two approaches to find the hidden cryptogram in the plain text either by detecting different fonts in the carving, which was patently impossible on a carved stone, or by transposing the existing letters according to a system. All had failed. Melchior thought of his third way—there had to be a third way. He found the answer in the obvious mixture of upper and lower case letters in the inscription; found the hidden cryptogram and deciphered it. He says:

> I don't like when people say something is impossible. So, for *seven years*, I worked on this cipher—and I finally solved it. I took my solution to the Black Chamber in Washington—that's the Army Cryptographical Unit. And they looked it over and they said that it was correct. I took it to the New York Cipher Society, and all their members spent an entire night trying to find a problem with it. Finally, the president said it was okay. I next took it to Rosaria Candela, who, at the time, was the foremost cryptoanalyst in the country, who said "that *is* what it says."

What it said was *startling*. It stated that the original manuscript of *Hamlet* was buried in the dungeons of Elsinore Castle.

Melchior and a team from *Life* magazine were off to Elsinore in search of this prize. They did not find it, someone had been there before them, but they did find what is believed to be the wrappings of the treasure. Anyway, *Life* devoted 17 pages to the piece.

Eva, his seventh novel, was spurred by a note Melchior saw in the *London Times* in 1981 that quoted scientists' belief that the supposed body of Eva Braun found in Hitler's bunker was, in fact, not her. In his book, Melchior took the Nazi's hopes for continuance after the war in a different direction. This time Hitler launches an elaborate plot to save Eva Braun, pregnant with his child. An American agent is determined to prevent the escape of the Fuhrer's bride, who carries the dangerous seed of one of history's vilest monsters.

V-3, novel number eight, concerned a terrifying secret weapon—developed by the Nazis and about to erupt in today's world, a world seemingly far removed and safe from the horrors of World War ll—deadly nerve gas. Melchior recalled:

> I'd read in the paper that a group of fishermen had been poisoned by poison gas while they'd been fishing, because certain poison gases had been thrown into the Baltic Sea, and over the years the drums deteriorated and came up through the water and poisoned the fishermen. In one of my CIC cases, I had investigated a plant that had manufactured poison gas. We found drums, but never found the gas. Now I thought, suppose that that deadly sort of thing was lying someplace for a reason. I built a story about a submarine and Hitler's final

> scheme: He loaded that submarine with poison gasses and had it lie off the coast of Ireland. The prevailing winds would engulf all countries in the deadly gas if it were released, wiping out all life in both Ireland and England. Everything. So he would deliberately release some of the toxic gas so some people would die, and then say "Now, give up—or you're wiped out."

The V-3 of the title, by the way, was an invented designation not used in the war: Only the V-2 and the V-1 were bona fide designations.

For his ninth excursion into World War II storytelling, Melchior explored the fragile threshold at which real life and make-believe blur together. In *Code Name: Grand Guignol*, horror elements of a fictional nature—as staged by the Grand Guignol, the legendary French theater that specialized in the masterful illusions in the theater of gore—are mixed with Nazi atrocities. The story of the famous troupe's brave efforts to sabotage a giant gun almost 500 feet long capable of firing and striking targets a hundred miles away results in a startling blend of horrifying stage tricks and real-life atrocities. Hitler actually came frighteningly close to completing and using this super-science device—two batteries of 25 guns each had been built at Mimoyecques in Belgium, zeroed in on London and all the English Channel ports where the invasion fleet was assembling.

The novel relates how members of the Grand Guignol get involved with the underground, find out about the weapon and seek a way to destroy it. Although they are not trained infiltrators, their special talents make it possible for them to get to the site and sabotage the weapon before its final test. Along the way, the inexperienced infiltrators witness horrors of a very real and distinctly *un*-theatrical nature. Melchior based one of their encounters on his own experience getting bombed by a test firing of one of the Nazis' giant guns:

> A violent fire storm raged through the street. Blazing liquid fire seeped inexorable through drains and down stairs to the shelters below. And from the doorways, flaming figures—their mouths wrenched open in screams, unheard in the din of the conflagration, their hair and clothes ablaze—emerged to dance a macabre, frenzied dance of doom before being swept into the holocaust and consumed—grisly marionettes on strings manipulated by a puppeteer gone mad. Every window in every building popped out and shattered, raining shards of glass into the street, and an asphalt patch sizzled and bubbled in the intense heat—little puffs of flame dotting the rolling surface.
>
> Suddenly, they saw a small figure, dragging a bicycle, running down the street. It was [the boy]

> Helmut... he was frantically trying to run away from the fiery nightmare surrounding him. As they watched in shock, they saw him run into the street... The boy fell, his feet stuck in the melting asphalt. His bike flew from his grip. Quickly covered with steaming asphalt, he writhed in agony to free himself from the burning embrace. He struggled to his feet; his arms flailing in slow-motion frenzy at the sticky, searing mass that engulfed him. All at once a little flame licked at him. And another. And in a sudden flash, the struggling figure flared up in fire and collapsed in a spasmodically jerking heap.

Viewing the performances of the Grand Guignol was perhaps a cathartic experience for those who attended the shows, Parisians and occupying Germans alike, as the real world around them grew more depressingly intolerable every day.

Melchior explained:

> The Grand Guignol was a theater that opened in the 1800s. In all those years it only closed once—a day at the end of World War I when they honored someone. All those years, they did five one-act plays each night. Three horrors, plus two farces. The farces were absolutely ridiculous and very funny. The horrors, well, they were something else.
>
> They had their own little infirmary in the theater because people would faint and faint and faint. In fact, they used to say unless six people fainted it was a flop. I knew the stage manager—the Grand Guignol was not that far away from the English Players—sort of off a little alley. So, I was quite often backstage, and I saw all the tricks. Most of the actors there were what they called specially endowed, meaning they had an arm missing, or a leg, or they had a glass eye...
>
> One of the most gruesome shows I ever saw was a story that took place in a suburban home, and the family there had a gardener who was mute. Late at night, for some reason, the gardener gets into the house, and the owner upstairs hears this intruder. The owner takes his shotgun and goes downstairs, and as he goes down, the mute gardener goes behind a door to hide. But, the guy with the shotgun notices the door still moving a

> little bit when he gets down the stairs and he fires, *bang*—and the whole door disintegrates. And the guy behind the door suddenly steps out and comes up to the footlights—and from his nose on down, his face is *gone*. It's tattered. Just bloody tatters. And, of course, some of the people in the audience actually faint at that point.
>
> What it was, was that the man had had cancer of the jawbone and his entire lower jaw had been *removed*, and he'd had a prosthesis put on, so his face looked all right. But what he did was he took that fake jaw off behind the door, and you could see the flaps of flesh with all this blood on it—and it looked absolutely *horrendous*.
>
> Another guy had an arm missing and they made him a special prosthesis. They took a real bone, wrapped real meat around it, and saturated it with a special blood—nobody knows how they made that blood—and put it all into this prosthesis. And then, in the show, they sawed it off. So when the saw goes through it, you'd see pieces of meat and bone coming out. It's not just a prosthesis, but real bone and tissue.

Of course, again, people fainted. In his novel, Melchior found fictional use for this real-life endowment: To fool a witness in his story, Melchior had his heroes trick a child into believing the man with the fake arm was, in fact, a Martian. They filled the prosthetic arm with green blood, and cut it—revealing the unearthly blood—to prove they were not enemy agents but beings from another world.

To illustrate many of his novels, Melchior had made up intricate, three-dimensional shadow boxes—featuring tiny plastic figures, set pieces, backgrounds and realistic lighting—which he'd put on view at various book signings. These quickly became a fascinating new hobby. By acquiring plastic toy figures and through various quasi-vivisectioning techniques of sawing, sanding and gluing, he was able to impart a wide range of poses to the diminutive humans. Houses, bunkers and various paraphernalia were also made by hand, with Cleo painting the highly detailed backings. Melchior's shadow box for *Code Name: Grand Guignol* was a view from the back of the theater's stage looking out at the audience. On stage, a scene described in the book—a typical gruesome show at its peak moment of horror—is in progress. Melchior described the backstory of that particular scene:

> The shadow box depicts a show about a guy who's murdered a little girl who had blue eyes. So then he is locked up in an insane asylum, and one of *his* eyes is gouged out by the inmates. Now he wants a new blue eye. When a new inmate comes in—

A shadow box in the wings of the theater Grand Guignol used to illustrate *Code Name Grand Guignol*.

one with the most beautiful blue eyes—his eye is then poked out by the friends of the murderer.

What they did to create this on stage, was they put a bench about three feet from the front row, and the guy would be laid out on this bench with his head hanging over, and the actors playing the inmates would pin him down, take out a screwdriver and *thunk*—stick it into his eye—and the eye would pop out, and the blood flowed everywhere. He actually had a glass eye, and behind it they had put a special pouch with blood in it, and when that was ruptured... .

And, of course, people fainted...

Quest was Melchior's first collaborative book venture, having been written in conjunction with a young man named Frank Brandenburg. It told the true story of Brandenburg himself who, having just seen an American television film broadcast in Germany describing the Holocaust, found himself profoundly appalled and unable to accept it as fact. He set out to track down and win the confidence of those people still living who had actually been closely associated with the Third Reich in order to discover their perception of the war and their plans for the future. Some astounding revelations came to light which opened up new insights into that terrible chapter of human history—a chapter whose horrors will likely remain forever ungraspable by all. The book was highly praised by Simon Wiesenthal.

Melchior's last war book was *Case By Case*, an autobiographical retelling of his hair-raising training and exploits with the Counter Intelligence Corps. It brought into focus how truly extraordinary, catastrophic and disturbingly unearthly the events of World War II actually were. The insanity and sheer genius that was indulged in by power-mad leaders toward the goal of earthly human destruction is vividly revived page by page, case by case. There is, for instance, a letter of such arrogance as to define the very essence of human evil—a letter the Mayor of Munich wrote when corresponding with the camp commandant at Dachau:

> [Regarding] the Jewish cadavers in your crematorium ovens... it is intolerable that good German citizens, who must breathe that smoke, should endure being contaminated by such Jewish filth.

In 1961 Dachau was opened as a museum. Melchior went there, and described his reactions to this museum in *Case By Case*:

> In 1990 I finally revisited Dachau. It was an experience that left me shaken, angry, and frustrated.
>
> What angered me most was what had been done with the camp itself, a place that I remembered stank of death, a bleak and filthy place, a place of horror. All the barracks had been razed; the gravel-covered rectangles bordered with concrete foundations marked where they had stood. But one had been restored—as a showpiece. Clean, spacious with spotless wooden bunks and a fine wood floor, the barrack had individual lockers for the inmates, a communal area with game tables and chairs for cozy relaxation, a separate washroom and toilet facilities. There was no mention, no hint of the overcrowded conditions in a barrack built to house a maximum of 300 inmates into which *3,000* had been crammed—the sick, the starved, the exhausted—three inmates to a bunk. No inkling of the unspeakable hardship—the horrendous filth caused by the issue of the ever-present dysentery that oozed and dripped from the top bunks through the lower two to the floor, the victims too weak to move. Should anyone die, his corpse would lie with his bunk mates until the prisoners were herded out in the morning to stand formation.
>
> Instead, the walls in this showcase barrack displayed large, nicely framed quotes from the writing of various famous authors, extolling a strict

> adherence to cleanliness and order. To the uninformed, all this said, "Well, this is not so bad"—and, in fact, I heard these very words spoken as Cleo and I stood in this miserable misrepresentation of the truth.
>
> Dachau had been sanitized and sterilized: Everything had been scoured off—including the truth.

Of the crematoriums, Melchior described how they were still standing at the far corner of the camp. The bleak spot was now a lovely *garden* area with flower beds and lush green bushes and trees.

> When I had stood before this building, years before, there had been naked, emaciated corpses stacked high all around me. A couple from Estonia asked what it had been like on that spot. When I told them that where they were standing now, there had been a stack of dead bodies six feet high—they moved away.
>
> Although I realize that it would have been impossible to show Dachau as the camp had really been, I was resentful and bitter at what it had been made out to be. My frustration threatened to choke me. I had to do something.

Melchior then went to the building that had housed the camp administration offices and SS guard rooms through which ran the entry tunnel to the main gate.

> There was no one about. I opened the gate and went through to the other side. I looked at the neat, well-kept building, the clean, whitewashed wall and I *urinated* on it.
>
> It felt good. Damned good.

Of *Case By Case*, Richard Thorpe, author of *Die Hard,* aptly commented:

> Novelists and screenwriters will be stealing from this book for decades: On every page is an anecdote, a moment, or an insight that makes World War II in all its fury blaze to life again.

Writing novels did indeed bring Melchior much of the satisfaction he often felt wanting in the movie business. He commented:

> Every time you make a motion picture, there is one governing word that permeates everything:

> *Compromise*. Compromise. You *never* get exactly what you want. You compromise. When you write a book, you don't have to compromise, you create exactly as you want. The publisher cannot change it. He can say "I don't want to publish it," but he cannot change it without your okay. That is the one thing I liked about writing books. Whatever I did was mine. I took the blame for it, I took the credit for it —and that's it.

Another perk of writing—the ability to create and enter a virtual world of the imagination:

> Everything that I write I *see*; I'm looking at it, I'm *seeing* it... and I simply describe what I'm seeing... and it becomes—it *is*—very real to me. Once, I had just written a big scene with a character named Jane. And when Cleo came home, I said, you won't believe what *Jane* did today. Jane was a real person to me. And she had actually done something as far as I was concerned. Then I thought, what am I saying?—I *wrote* her. Then I thought again, no I didn't—she *did* do something.
>
> So, very often my characters take over and do things *on their own*. This sounds crazy, but it's true. I was writing a scene in *V-3* that took place in Bonn, and my hero had been involved in all sorts of things. He'd been in an office and now he comes out. And he has just found out that he has got to go to England within hours, or the most terrible things will happen. He comes out of the door and there are two men waiting for him and they say "You are under arrest." I said, "What? It *can't* be. You don't understand—he's *got* to leave!" I was stunned. I myself had had *no* idea that these people were going to arrest him.
>
> I was living this moment. I was with this man and I'd already figured out how he was going to travel and, suddenly, here come these two men say-

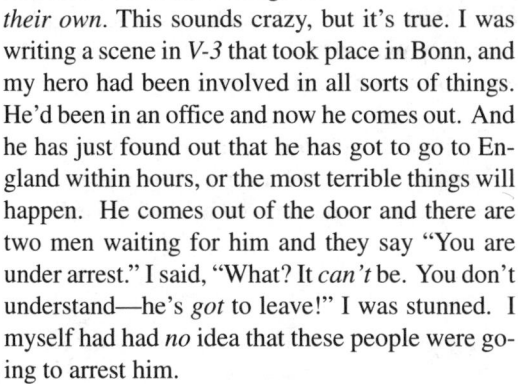

ing he's under arrest. Now, of course, I had to come up with one hell of a way for him to get out of there.

Every single one of his books have been optioned for motion picture production, one of them—*Eva*—14 times. However, for a variety of reasons, none has made it to the production phase. *The Marcus Device* came, perhaps, closer to production than the others. It had been announced for production by Dimension Pictures in 1978 as *The Seven-Inch Wilderness*. Optioned by Larry Babb, former commissioner of motion pictures and television for the state of Massachusetts, he and Melchior were to be co-producers.

Cleo Baldon related:

> I think Ib was very much more in the war than any veteran I knew. I think he had quite a time during the war and he was glad to be able to write about it... I don't think he ever really said good-bye to science fiction. He was still telling imaginative stories. And even though he'd really wanted to be a director, directing *other* people's ideas, it turned out *he* was really the idea man, and *he* became a storyteller.
>
> At a Danish club meeting after he'd written *Order of Battle* and had given a copy of it to his father, his father clinked his glass and stood up and said, "I want everyone to know that my son has written the *best damned book*." And that was a very good moment for Ib... To Ib and to me, we were both pleasantly surprised that he became such a successful author. It had not been in his master plan, but after one success, he just turned out another, then another. He had a good relationship with the publisher, and a very good, specific audience—like with science fiction...

And, most importantly, it gave Melchior the opportunity to tell not only fascinating stories, but provide, for those who would never wish to have been there, a mind-camera view into the terrible chapter in human history he'd witnessed.

STORIES AND HISTORIES IN A BOX

An interesting life often brings with it an amazing collection of souvenirs, both mental as well as physical. Melchior's home, like his work, would become heavily invested with its creator's personality, memories and inventions. Actually, in the case of his Hollywood home, the personalities of both Ib Melchior and Cleo Baldon would become not only invested in it, but festooned within its every available space. Cleo stated:

> Ib loves to make stuff like those little stage settings, those shadow boxes, for all of his books. There is a quality to them like a puppet theater. You get so intrigued you forget their size, then somebody's hand gets into it and it becomes a monster, and you're suddenly snapped back... I don't have that kind of patience to make them but I had the inclination to put them out, to display them. There is an intrigue about them. Each one makes you want to step into a picture

It certainly wouldn't be a stretch to imagine analogies between his shadow boxes and his time travelers stepping through a frame and entering a world that is more than a picture.

The shadow boxes took their place in a rapidly evolving home setting that housed a number of other impressive collections. Among them: A highly valued collection of Nurnberger-size classic military miniatures displayed in a variety of beautiful mini-shadow boxes featuring hand-colored scenic backings rendered by Cleo Baldon. These small boxes include a detailed scene depicting Marshal Ney's cavalry charge at the battle of Waterloo through a small village. With the flick of a switch, the houses and farms blaze, flames shoot up and water pours from a shattered water tank—all realistically animated by clever use of polarized light. In Melchior's words:

> If one must have war, what better place for it than
> on the living room wall—in miniature.

Baldon, as an enormously talented and influential designer of environments—along with the things within the environments—had conspired to exhibit her husband's miniature wars in a way that would not only make for a pleasant display, but cagily show

A portion of Melchior's shadow box built to illustrate scenes from his novel of German atomic bomb development during World War II, *The Haigerloch Project*.

up their very smallness. She mounted them within a mirrored wall in order that, while exploring the boxes, the viewer could not help but see himself, out of the corners of his eyes—looking gigantically down into these tiny worlds.

The Melchior military collection eventually numbered close to 9,600 figures, and included a number of five-inch-tall lead soldiers used as distant extras in the 1938 MGM movie *Marie Antoinette*, and a small Hittite warrior made of clay that served as a toy for some child 4,000 years ago.

Melchior has also collected rare historical documents and autographs. Among his hundreds of items are letters from P.T. Barnum, Queen Victoria and many U.S. presidents; documents signed by Thomas Jefferson and Alexander Hamilton by which the U.S. borrowed 12 million dollars from Holland to get back on its feet after the Revolutionary War; and a large collection of autographs, ranging from those of Fredric March and Errol Flynn to Wallace Beery and Natalie Wood, among many others.

Some of the old documents are reminders of the emotions as well as the facts of history: for instance, a father's heartbreaking letter relating the facts about his dying son, the last of the male line. The father was named Robert, the son, Jack. The family: Abraham Lincoln's. With Jack's death, the family line would come to an end.

One of Melchior's most beloved collections is a variety of items pertaining to various aspects of *Hamlet*. Among these is the first pictorial representation of the Danish Prince made in 1581—years before the Shakespeare play, and signed photographs of famous actors who've played the role on stage and screen.

Numbering among Melchior's other literary interests: the writings of a fellow countryman, Hans Christian Andersen. Melchior owns a pair of Andersen's actual spectacles—and no doubt has looked through them from time to time.

Melchior commented:

> I am a great fan of Hans Christian Andersen. He is one of my heroes. I think his writing is beyond brilliant. It is absolutely wonderful. The idea of *The Emperor's New Clothes* is so classic. Andersen really wrote for adults, not children. Many years

ago I wrote a story in the style of Hans Christian Andersen for my little niece and nephew when they were children. It was called "The Story of a Loaf," the story of a loaf of bread. I made inanimate things animate. It's just a little story, written in his style. Several years ago I was in Odense, Denmark which is the birthplace of Andersen. There's a big museum there and all his writings are collected there. And I gave them this story without saying anything about it and I got a call—very excited—"Where did you get this one? This is one we've *never* heard about. This is a new one." Well, I said, "*I* wrote it." They said, "Oh." Then they asked if I would mind if they could include it in their collection. So my little story is now part of their Andersen collection. It's flattering. But I got a kick out of that because it became a Hans Christian Andersen story written the way he would've written it, with the same meaningful story in it.

Melchior made an interesting discovery about Andersen: The storyteller had, surprisingly, in the middle 1800s, written one of the earliest science fiction stories ever, "1,000 Years From Now," about a sight-seeing trip in an airship of the future over Europe. Melchior translated the Danish text into English. The story was one of those magical things that linked the past to the future; in Melchior's home, the two were welcome to coexist comfortably side by side. Occasionally, they even seemed to trade places.

Between these hobbies, plus script and novel writing, and extensive traveling, Melchior somehow still found time to indulge his talents as a frequent magazine and newspaper feature writer; explore his interests in languages—he speaks six; ride an elephant and romp with lions and other exotic animals; act as a literary translator; solve cryptograms; function as gourmet chef and dinner host for the likes of many well known guests, including—over the years—actresses such as Eva Marie Saint, Ann Miller, Glynis Johns, Sharon Stone and Melchior's favorite, Susan Oliver, and actors such as Ernest Borgnine, Walter Slezak and Werner Klemperer, as well as Merry Anders, Naura Hayden, Dennis Patrick, Jan Merlin, Les Tremayne and others who'd acted in his films and TV shows. He once even appeared as the *real* Ib Melchior on TV's *To Tell the Truth*.

And the holidays were frequently a colorful time at the house. Cleo recalled how Ib's father in his later years would position himself next to the fireplace around Christmas, with one hand placed on the mantle and the other gesturing grandly, as he played classic songs from the operas. He knew a captive audience when he saw one, and couldn't resist performing. Cleo related:

> His father would lip-sync to his own records and, since we were really a social family, we'd be talk-

ing, so he'd announce in a great big, deep voice, "There will be *no talking...*" So [now] Ib has taken over the role and stands by the fireplace while we play his father's records, and he goes, "There will be *no talking.*"

Melchior's son Leif, lives in New York City. He is a psychologist with a private practice, so getting together on a frequent basis is not easy, but Leif and Ib's grandson, Torben, usually spend the Christmas holidays with the Melchiors in Hollywood, as well as making short visits.

Melchior liked to do something special for his family when they visited, and usually was able to come up with something interesting. But in 1996, when Torben was 11, he outdid himself. Telling Leif and Torben that he had to fly to San Francisco on business, he suggested they come with him and take in the city while he worked.

When they arrived at the airport in San Francisco they were met by one of Melchior's friends and a Navy limousine into which they all piled. Off they went to the Navy base. Torben's eyes grew round as the sentry at the gate smartly saluted Melchior's friend who happened to be Rear Admiral Paul A. Peck who was the commanding officer of Carrier Group Three. Melchior had met him in 1976 when he was a guest during maneuvers in the Pacific.

They stopped at the boarding ramp to the nuclear aircraft carrier, *USS Carl Vinson*. Torben was piped aboard and had lunch with the admiral, the captain and several officers, after which he was given a personal tour of the ship.

Melchior enjoyed coming up with such special treats. Once, in a restaurant in Santa Monica, Melchior and his wife had dinner with some friends in an upstairs room when he found that Mikhail Baryshnikov was having dinner downstairs. Melchior, knowing that Cleo was a great admirer of the ballet dancer excused himself, went to his car and got a copy of his current novel, signed it, dedicating it to Baryshnikov and had the maitre'd take it to his table. Baryshnikov asked him over and they chatted for a few moments. Then Melchior went back upstairs and told Cleo that there was someone downstairs who would like to meet her. As they entered the dining room, Baryshnikov rose from his table and met them halfway, graciously greeting Cleo who was absolutely delighted. He took her to his table and they had a short chat. Melchior was impressed that Baryshnikov had shown real class. Few stars of his stature would have been as gracious.

At about the time Melchior began working as a novelist, he also underwent a change of appearance: He and Cleo were invited to a costume party for which Melchior decided to go as a Viking. To achieve the proper look he grew a thick beard. His gray-white beard flattered his appearance enough that it became a permanent fixture, distinctive and distinguished. More than one acquaintance has attempted to pinpoint his visual pedigree, among the most apt being one writer's suggestion of a "cross between Freud and Hemingway," although Melchior, an animal lover, was no doubt far removed from the Hemingway macho/hunter mentality.

Maybe it was more like a pinch of Jules Verne.

DEATH RACE 2000

In 1974, Melchior suddenly found his name again linked with science fiction after several years' absence from the genre when producer Roger Corman purchased Melchior's first-ever written piece in the genre, "The Racer," for motion picture production. The film, *Death Race 2000*, was released the following year by New World Pictures and starred, among others, a very young and eager Sylvester Stallone. It was photographed by Tak Fujimoto, whom would go on to rank among the top of Hollywood's new crop of cameramen.

Melchior stated:

> Forry Ackerman, who was my agent, sold "The Racer" to Roger Corman, and Corman made it with Paul Bartel as the director... I was not considered for writing the screenplay for the film. It was actually a *fait accompli* by the time I even found out about it, and I had nothing else to do with it... But, even though the producers of the film of necessity added a lot to my original concept as well as its execution, they did keep my idea, using satire and outrageous exaggeration to bring the point across.

The opening of Melchior's story observes that, "the most popular spectator sports of the latter half of the 20th century were such mildly exciting pursuits as boxing and wrestling. Of course, the spectators enjoyed seeing the combatants trying to maim each other, and there was always the chance of the hoped-for fatal accident." It is in this worthless world that "The Racer" is set, a world in which the popular spectator sport of the moment is the Annual Transcontinental Road Race. Unlike other races before it, however, this one not only allows, but encourages, the scoring of points by having the competitors actually go out of their way to hit and *kill* as many innocent bystanders as possible. Driving cars customized to resemble sharks, tigers and other predatory animals, the racers must weigh going out of their way to run

A portion of the original *Escapade* magazine illustration for Melchior's story "The Racer."

over unsuspecting victims for extra points versus loss of position in the pack. At no point do the racers ever give a second thought to the fact that they are actually killing people.

Willie Connors is a top racer, a man with only one thing on his mind: winning. His car is The Bull, so-named for its durasteel horns and the streamlined bull's head on the front of the car, complete with "bloodshot, evil-looking eyes, and iron ring through flaring nostrils." Willie and his navigator Hank rocket across country running over dogs, elderly women and even children. No one is safe:

> Near Calvin College an imprudent coed found herself too far from cover when the Racer suddenly came streaking down the campus. Frantically, she sprinted for safety, but she didn't have a chance with a driver like Willie behind the wheel. The razor sharp horn on the right fender sliced through her spine so cleanly that the jar wasn't even felt inside the car... Leaving town, the racer was in luck again. An elderly woman had left the sanctuary of her stone-walled garden to rescue a straying cat. She was so easy to hit that Willie felt a little cheated.

Willie's fatal mistake occurs moments after his biggest score ever—hitting a group of off-guard theater goers. There is so much gore he is forced to use a special automatic spray to clean the blood from the windshield. Dying of curiosity about his potential score, he stops and gets out to take count. Suddenly he finds himself mingling with a crowd of people who, he figures, could only be fans. It's not what he expected. He now comes face to face with a young girl named Muriel bearing one of the victims—a little child—in her arms. She has one word for him: *Butcher*.

From that moment Willie is doomed, haunted by Muriel's eyes. He can no longer bring himself to make the cold kill. His navigator Hank, suspecting Willie has become an Anti-Racer, struggles for control of the wheel. There is an accident and Willie is seriously injured. In his delirium he is heard to murmur one word over and over: Muriel. The girl learns of this on the news and shows up at his bedside. Facing her, person to person, Willie knows he will no longer be a butcher—*or* a racer.

"The Racer" is a strong indictment of the human obsession with violence. It is the epitome of Melchior's approach to speculation about the future—taking what is now and leading it along to an outrageous conclusion, when latent problems of today become an absurd reality tomorrow. It suggests that while there is no redemption from such hideous crimes, there is still the possibility of change for the better.

Melchior had a peculiar talent for staging grisly events in unlikely places—like the woman getting wiped out while rescuing her cat in the garden. Cleo Baldon remembered:

> Ib writes great deaths. He'll take you through a beautiful meadow, and on the other end he'll kill you. I find those contrasts are brilliant.

Simone Griffeth navigates for ace racer-killer Frankenstein (David Carradine).

The sense of the placid everyday within which the story's deadly race exists is, in fact, one of its lasting strengths. Outrageous normalcy lies at the center of most satire. The biggest change to Melchior's story in translating it to the screen was the introduction of gallows humor, largely the contribution of the screenwriters Robert Thom and Chuck Griffith.

SOME NOTES ON *DEATH RACE 2000*

Griffith was certainly no stranger to the Corman fold. He had started to work with Corman at the very beginning of his career as a screenwriter—and sometimes production assistant, actor and all-around gopher—on Corman films like *Attack of the Crab Monsters*, *Not of This Earth*, *It Conquered the World* and the *original* version (or, as some critics would note, the *funny* version) of the now legendary $18,000 movie *Little Shop of Horrors*, along with many, many other genre projects. A wildly inventive, and often underrated, writer, his scripts are usually laced with a type of bleak, beat, out of left field humor. Typically, in the past, he had collided with Corman over the inclusion of this humor, and often Griffith had lost out to the serious side of the movie producer. However, with *Death Race 2000*, not only was Griffith perceptive enough to revel in the black humor inherent in the story, he was actually allowed to get away with it.

Griffith recalled:

> I had just returned from living in Europe and called Roger and he put me right on [this]. It was a bizarre, mad script and, I guess, unshootable. I asked

> him, "Why did you pick me?" and he said, "Because your scripts are mad and unshootable, too. So you fix it." So I was hired to rewrite it. I mean, [Thom's] script was pretty mad.
>
> It was a general make it work and do it again. It was pretty much done [all over] again, although the idea stayed the same. I went through five drafts of it myself, and went crazy with Roger... Francis Dole... and Beverly Gray worked on it too.
>
> The in-office version was hilariously funny. But Roger didn't want it funny. "This is a hard-hitting, serious picture." After we saw the cars, which were being built in the Cahuenga Pass, I said this has *got* to be another comedy—[but] he said, "Absolutely not."

Corman was intent on maintaining the realistic tone of Melchior's story, even if the satiric undertones did call out for a black comedy approach in the more literal realm of motion pictures.

Griffith had also been given what he felt were arbitrary rules that made the writing more difficult:

> Like you couldn't show any spectators. I wanted to show people watching [the race] on television, things like that. No reason given. Possibly because it would be more expensive. But not necessarily. There should have been people betting on it, all sorts of things.

Again, Corman was trying to maintain the same focus "The Racer" had—the race itself.

Griffith recounted:

> I worked with [Paul Bartel] on developing the script, and we'd have meetings. I liked his direction. It's quirky, and kind of fey, and funny.

And Paul Bartel turned out to be the idiosynchcratic—and perfect—director hired by Corman to move the story to the screen. Bartel, who later made a name for himself as director of cult-aimed films like *Eating Raoul* and *Scenes from a Class Struggle in Beverly Hills*, pushed the material in the script ever farther into areas of black humor, creating a fast-motion Keystone Kops comic book meld of humor and horror. Even in the context of his racing meets big-time wrestling goofiness, none of *Death Race 2000*'s violence is without a point. The violence is there, to be sure: decapitations, human-

Jack Rabin produced this matte shot for Roger Corman to add production value to *Death Race 2000*.

skewerings, high-speed crashes, etc. Bartel doesn't dwell on these flashes. They blink by with just enough impact to disturb the viewer in the midst of some really funny moments. By controlling the use of violence, Bartel and Corman avoid rendering a hypocritical treatment of Melchior's theme. There is no rationalizing of the human love of violence: The problem is how to gain control over it.

Adding to the tone of the film is the comic performance by newcomer Sylvester Stallone as Machine Gun Joe Verterbo, a gangster-styled racer complete with pin-striped suit and constant flow of demeaning invectives. A trim David Carradine as Frankenstein, the stitched-back-together protagonist clad in zippered leather, manages to ride the fine line between believability and farce, as does the work of custom car maker Dean Jeffries with his shark, bull and Frankenstein-inspired designs. Contributing further to the comic book feel of the film is an opening matte painting by Jack Rabin that places the southern California-based Ontario Race Track in the middle of a Jetsons'-redecorated New York skyline. The race cars themselves were buildups and modifications of existing cars, all handled by Dean Jeffries. Total cost: $5,000.

Melchior, at first, had been unprepared for the level of humor that was worked into the screenplay, but was pleasantly surprised at the outcome:

> They invited me to a screening, and I nearly died.
> I said, what have they done to my story.? But as

> the picture unfolded I realized what they had done. They had really *improved* on it. They made it a totally black comedy. And it hit home. And I thought they did a great job on it. It was something I had written one way that somebody else changed and made better.

Death Race 2000 is far from being a perfect film. It frequently shows its low-budget by attempting to emulate the production values of much larger-funded films; its treatment is often too glib; and at least one of its characters, Nero the Hero, seems to have stepped right out of an old AIP beach party movie. But it does avoid pretension and provide entertainment through the performances of its likable cast and bang-up race sequences. The critics—including even the reserved *Time* magazine—praised the film as a hallmark "B" film, preferring it by far to the then-current big-budget film Corman intended to cash-in on, *Rollerball*.

Melchior was pleased to experience a rare occurrence of generosity in the film business shortly after the release of *Death Race 2000* when Roger Corman actually paid Melchior additional fees that were *not* contractually required of him. This occurred when Corman produced a sequel to the film called *Deathsport*: Although there were no characters in the new film carried over from the earlier film, and the plot had nothing specific to do with Melchior's story, Corman felt he owed a debt to Melchior, stating that "I couldn't have made the first *or* the second film if it hadn't been for the inspiration of the original story," proving—against type—that even the normally hyper-frugal Corman could be generous given good reason.

By the actual year 2000, studios began to talk of a big-budget remake of the film. Tentative title: *Death Race 3000*.

Shortly after the release of *Death Race 2000* Melchior was honored by the Academy of Science Fiction with their Golden Scroll Award for his achievements in the genre.

In March 1982, Melchior's Viking, pre-*Hamlet* version of the same story, *Hour of Vengeance*, staged originally in 1962 by the Professional Theater Center, was restaged by the Shakespeare Society of America at L.A.'s Globe Playhouse. This time the actor who'd originally enacted the part of Amleth, Dennis Patrick, directed the production. The play was staged more elaborately than the first; it, likewise, received high praise from the critics. Along with praise, *The Los Angeles Times* reviewer made note of the play's special worth:

> It's interesting to watch a performance of *Hamlet* and not know how the story's going to turn out... Only once does Amleth waiver, and that almost seems a tribute to his Renaissance descendant. Usually, he plunges right in... Its [finale is] highly satisfactory... with the bad people dead and the good people celebrating. That's entertainment... We read [Hamlet's character] more clearly in the light of Melchior's reinstatement of the original theme.

> Oddly, this non-Shakespearean play may be the finest service that the Shakespearean society has ever done its master—certainly preferable to yet another run-through of *Hamlet*...

While the reviewer found the authentic Viking-era blank verse trying, he concluded *Hour of Vengeance* to be "a very vigorous play."

The now-defunct *Los Angeles Herald Examiner* was a bit snippy about this unwavering pre-Hamlet prince, but enthused about the play overall:

> [*Hour*] is entertaining enough on its own. Melchior keeps the plot boiling with the skill of a paperback novelist. Director Dennis Patrick fills the stage with booming voices and robust action.

And, though staged in English, the Danish newspaper *Bien* raved:

> The world premiere of *Hour of Vengeance*... was not just the opening of a new play, but a major theatrical event... Melchior's play [compared to *Hamlet*] has a style all its own. It is vigorous in its action, rich in its language and stirring in its drama... The beauty and imagery of the language in the play, with it's robust Viking flavor, are exceptional...

While the play was still running in Los Angeles, the Hamlet Society International proudly announced that the recipient of its prestigious Hamlet Award that year was Ib Melchior: He received the award—one of the happiest honors of a career filled with them—on April 18, 1982.

Melchior remained proud of the award and *Hour of Vengeance*, finding it more gratifyingly his than many of his other works, compromised as they often were by limitations in budgets, changes made by producers and co-writers, as well as the tunnel-vision the Hollywood marketplace more often than not imposed on the imagination.

HOW THE ROBINSON FAMILY GOT *LOST IN SPACE*

Ironically, the use of Melchior's *first* science fiction story, "The Racer," as the basis for the *Death Race 2000* certainly seemed as if it were destined to be, after two decades, his *last* association with films in the genre. A surprising turn of events occurred in 1995 that was to spin that notion completely around. Now, fully three decades after its television premiere, Melchior found that Prelude Pix, a production company associated with New Line Cinema, had undertaken a new motion picture version of the later *Lost in Space* TV series. In checking for the rights with Irwin Allen's widow, Prelude executive Mark Koch learned that years earlier someone by the name of Ib Melchior had made some claim to origination of the show's concept. And in a reaction that is as rare as it gets, Koch and other Prelude executives expressed a *moral obligation* not only to check the story out, but act on that same moral principal to rectify any past inequity.

They indeed took the time to look into the matter, checking out Melchior's background and accomplishments, aided by author/researcher/*Lost in Space* fan Ed Shifres' tireless and exacting investigations into the early history of the TV series. They soon began to realize Melchior was no crackpot, and his claims seemed based on solid fact. The details of what occurred not only *could* fill a volume, but *did*, in Shifres' revealing book, *Space Family Robinson: The True Story*. The book was later published under the title *Lost in Space, The True Story* (revised by Windsor House Group, Inc., Midvale, Utah). In the end, the executives came to several inescapable conclusions: namely, that Melchior had been unfairly treated; that he was, no doubt, the originator of the show's concept with his *Space Family Robinson* script first written way back in February 1960; and, as such, he was morally entitled to compensation for the inequity.

Simply stated, the impossible had happened. Melchior was not only offered compensatory fees by Prelude, but, upon learning how much knowledge and expertise, to say nothing of familiarity with the subject matter, Melchior could bring to the project, they offered him an ongoing role on the projected $50 million *Lost in Space* film. So, some 30 years after *Space Family Robinson* became a something that was not to be, Melchior found himself back in the science fiction saddle again, working on a project close to his heart. The film initially suggested a refreshing return to the space exploration format with a host of spectacular encounters and unearthly threats, now to benefit from the latest in visual effects technologies. Melchior commented at the time,

> I will work on the motion picture in a production capacity as a special advisor. I am very gratified by the way things worked out through the ethics and morals and sense of what is right displayed by

Mark Koch—a far cry from what happened earlier.

Melchior studied each version of the script as it came to him, analyzed it and sent in his observations and suggestions. A selection of his comments on one of the drafts, for instance:

> I feel that in the relationship between the Sheik and Smith the motivations are missing. *Why* does the Sheik want to sabotage the mission? What does he want to gain? Smith stands to make money, initially—but once that is no longer in the cards, why does he keep on trying to sabotage John's efforts? If they all fail and perish, Smith will perish as well. What is his motivation for keeping on being the bad guy? I presume there will be a *Lost in Space* II, III, etc., and that Smith will be the villain throughout. If so, I think motivations for that must be spelled out. First, the Sheik's motivation for sabotaging a venture which would benefit mankind, himself included, and secondly, why does Smith keep on with his treachery once the prospect of payment is lost, since his success in destroying the Robinsons would result in his own demise.
>
> You once expressed that you wanted a little more for the robot to do. This might be a spot.
>
> If it is deemed undesirable to introduce the carnivorous plant, the same scene could be played with a mechanical device, a futuristic trap set to catch unwanted marauders. Like a futuristic giant mouse trap.
>
> Maureen reading "More like spiders than bees"—implies communal relationships. It is the other way around. Bees are communal, spiders are not.
>
> From here on I feel the explanation for what is going on may be difficult to follow. Since the TIME WHIRLPOOL is the central theme of the story from here on to the end of the story, it should be made as understandable, plausible and acceptable in imagery as possible. I was not quite sure WHY portals occasionally opened up into the past and future. However, if the planet is located at the edge of a TIME RIFT in the universe—already a sci-fi accepted concept—the crash may have

> jogged it closer to the edge, creating a whirlpool in time with the planet seesawing precariously into the past, the future and the present. It is an image easily visualized, and it makes it understandable why the Robinsons find themselves sometimes dipping into the past or future as well as being in the present.
>
> Also, I think we may have to have some brief, pseudo-scientific explanation of how it is possible for someone, or some creature (i.e. the green monkey) to coexist in two time periods, physically meeting themselves. Without such an explanation it becomes difficult to accept; at least a question will always linger in the audience's mind. It probably should not be allowed to stay there...
>
> ...It should be explained that there are countless different futures possible. Every time we make a decision we create a future; a different decision would make a different future. Thus the future, seen in the time whirlpool (i.e. the graves of the Robinson women), is only *one possible* future, which may result from a wrong decision, if nothing is done to prevent it. In other words, it is not necessarily the real, inevitable future, but a future that depends on the actions taken in the present *now*.

Some of Melchior's suggestions addressed details as well as concepts, particularly those he felt to be illogical. He commented:

> I had one fight with them, which was a thing about the dog tags. At one point the adult Will is about to slide down into the time-pool and he snags on his dog-tag. I said that is so nonsensical. A dog-tag has a two pound test—Snap—and it's off. You mean this guy weighed only a pound and a half? They said, "Oh, nobody will know." I said, only several million people who had dog-tags will know that. They would not change that. It took me—you should see the correspondence I had, the telephone calls. I said you've got to change this. They finally did.

The film itself eventually ran millions over budget—and, in spite of hundreds of costly and impressive special effects—underperformed at the box-office. In the opinion of many, it lacked the simple charms, character interactions and clarity of the original show. The human element was not only overshadowed by the ubiquitous computer effects, but drowned in a sea of chip-on-the-shoulder attitude, forced conflicts and illogical progressions. Unfortunately, the impressive production values and a few exciting concepts couldn't overcome the story problems. Along the way, several scenes seemed to be a tip of the hat to Melchior: The characters cross a force-field barrier on a planet (*Journey to the 7th Planet*); there's a derelict ship explored and weird gravestones on another planet (*Planet of the Vampires*); a jump through a time portal and encounter with same selves (*The Time Travelers*); weird spider creatures (*The Angry Red Planet/Journey to the 7th Planet*); spores on another planet (the original *Robinson Crusoe on Mars*), among other Melchior-like motifs.

What had started out with a lot of promise in terms of recognition, remuneration and justice over his *Space Family Robinson* experience all crumbled when New Line Pictures became involved with the *Lost in Space* feature. Melchior's name, as it would turn out, wound up, more or less, buried in the end title crawl—a far cry from the promised single card credit that would have stated and/or strongly implied Melchior's work was the basis of the original series opener. In a letter of official complaint to the producers, he noted some of the pertinent points of the agreement as signed by the parties prior to the film's production:

> My Property, *Space Family Robinson*, was purchased by Prelude Pictures, the producers of the feature film, *Lost in Space*, to form the basis of this motion picture. In doing so, Prelude executives assured themselves of controlling the first and original such property, created and registered long before even Irwin Allen's *Space Family Robinson/ Lost in Space* program.
>
> My agreement with Prelude Pictures states the following [Note: These are excerpts only.]:
>
> Paragraph 6. Page 4: The Melchior parties hereby irrevocably and unconditionally *grant, sell and assign* (emphasis mine, IJM) to Prelude any and all rights in and to *Space Family Robinson* and the exclusive right to produce a feature length motion picture *based upon* (emphasis mine, IJM) *Space Family Robinson* in any and all media: etc...
>
> This feature length motion picture, titled *Lost in Space*, has now been produced, demonstrably using as its base my property, *Space Family Robinson*, bought by Prelude Pictures, the producers of the *Lost in Space* feature film, for that express purpose.

Whatever the final outcome, the *Lost in Space* experience proved a big disappointment to Melchior:

> They paid me. I obviously felt I should have had a better credit on the film, but since Irwin Allen's

company was one of the production companies that had to [eventually] say "yes" or "no" to the credit, it was quite obvious what it would have to be: It had to be *no*, otherwise Irwin Allen would have been shown up for what he was—and they couldn't afford that.... [All of this] just preserves the myth that Irwin Allen created the story, which he did not. [I feel] that it has been proven over and over that he did not.

There was nothing new, *imaginatively* new in the film... The production values were not bad, if derivative. When you spend so many millions of dollars you are bound to get some effects that are good.

As usual, Melchior refused to let the disappointment slow him down. Other projects, other travels, other life experiences were awaiting him. In the summer of 1999 he and Cleo went sailing on a full-scale tall ship in the Caribbean. He could be found helping to rig the ship—or lying on a vast deserted beach playing host to swarms of friendly iguanas who'd come out to greet this lone, brave human being. The two species apparently got along just fine. Possibly better than most people in Hollywood.

A THREE LETTER WORD

Melchior has continued his wide-ranging activities in many fields: In the last decade he has co-edited and written with Cleo Baldon two well-received coffee table books dealing with architecture and environment. The first one, published by Rizzoli and titled *Steps and Stairways*, reveals the tremendous variety of shapes, designs and materials that have been employed in this most basic of architectural features; the second, *Reflections on the Pool*, explores many of the shimmering permutations of the swimming pool.

Melchior has also been a frequent radio guest in Los Angeles, and has been sought out by magazine, television and newspaper interviewers on a host of topics. Of interest to his science fiction fans, Melchior contributed an extensive interview and material to a laser disc edition of *Robinson Crusoe on Mars*, and appeared on The Discovery Channel's *Movie Magic* series to discuss his past work in special effects movies, along with several other shows in a similar mode for audiences overseas. And remakes were in the works of *Death Race 2000* and *The Angry Red Planet*. And John Carpenter's *The Ghosts of Mars* would seem to owe not a little of its inspiration to Melchior's draft of *Planet of the Vampires*.

Another ongoing Melchior project, and one of his passions, revolves around the creation of an illustrated book version of the Amleth legend, utilizing hundreds of old engravings altered and reassembled to conform to the specific scenes needed for the tale. He traveled throughout Scandinavia for a month in 1998 researching the century of Scandinavian pre-Vikings history between 800 and 900 AD to procure the necessary facts. The project is massive, requiring the collecting of, sorting through and reassembly of thousands of images.

In March 1999 an event occurred which Melchior considered one of the highlights of his life. His native country Denmark and his countrymen honored him for his work. "It meant more to me," said Melchior, "than any other honor ever bestowed upon me."

Every year Denmark holds a film festival that lasts about a week, to which is invited two international motion picture personalities. That year they invited Maggie Cheung, the foremost Asiatic film star, and Melchior, as a science fiction pioneer. They had special screenings of Melchior's science fiction films and one of his TV episodes. Melchior introduced each one of them and was subjected to a question and answer period after each screening—in Danish—not an inconsequential feat since he had left the country 62 years before and had spoken English ever since. The Danish people folded him in their arms and there was not a day when he did not have at least a two-page spread in one of the Copenhagen Metropolitan papers. It became so pervasive, that when he would hail a taxi, the driver would address him by name.

Although it was not the first time he had been honored by his fellow Scandinavians—in 1995 he had been named Outstanding Scandinavian-American of the Year by the American Scandinavian Foundation of Los Angeles—he felt his nostalgic trip to him homeland "will never be forgotten."

Melchior continued to follow the latest developments in science, having maintained his long-held fascination with astronomy and space exploration. New discoveries allowed by new technologies enabled humans to glimpse something science fiction writers like Melchior had long imagined—planets outside the Earth's solar system—over 30 of them discovered by the year 2000. The idea of oceans harboring life on one of Saturn's moons, or possible fossil microbes existing on Mars were no longer purely in the realm of fantasy, but things debated by serious scientists, and reported in daily newspapers. Glass worms were found to exist in methane ice, and bloodworms in the pitch-black ocean depths. Weird life forms existing in previously-thought inhospitable conditions, without light and at dangerous temperatures, suggested that life may be more adaptive than ever thought before. New evidence and theories even pointed to the likely existence of outlaw planets much like the one in Melchior's *Planet of the Vampires* [originally titled *The Outlaw Planet*]. Science was beginning to weigh more in favor of the kind of fantastic universe once only the domain of science fiction writers. Melchior followed the latest developments with keen interest, though disappointed in the human reluctance to fully embrace the possibilities offered by space:

> Space exploration as far as we've gone with it has enriched our lives beyond anybody's understanding. A lot of what we now take for granted in our lives has come about only because of space: Miniaturization, new materials, among many things. People don't realize that.

With the all-pervasive fascination with computers and dot-com-ing rapidly growing, the biggest loss might be the loss of the spirit of adventure, the loss of physical as well as mental participation, as people begin to accept the idea of looking at cathode pictures of places, rather than actually going there—of simulating, for instance, space travel rather than actually doing it. Of living totally safe, but less-involved lives. Melchior views the interest in the technology, in and of itself, as a dead end, especially if all that is gained is information:

> Information can be wrong. Facts can be wrong. Knowledge and wisdom are more important than that. What is more important than the existence of the Internet, is what will be said on it.

Without him saying it, it is obvious that his incredible experiences could never had been lived on the internet.

As for Melchior himself, he and Cleo continue to make plans, travel and explore their shared creativity. And when they come home from their experiences, it is to a home that is an ever-evolving sanctuary from a perhaps less inventive, more turbulent world around. The tones are subdued, the sense of comfort thick but luminous. New niches are discovered, uncovered, created and become nurturing places for colors, vines, shapes and things from other times and distant places. Tiny spaces divide small spaces and seem to make new space where there is none. Stairways wind, rooms constantly fold around corners and interiors trade place with exteriors. Any meeting of walls, ceiling or floor space could and does become a lily-pond, sauna, bookcase or spa... Anything can and will probably happen. The Melchior home, like its inhabitants, is fertile with eventualities and expansions. Their living space is a state of mind.

Pausing for a moment in his office where on a shelf stands an Android head from *The Time Travelers* and a model of the batratspider from *The Angry Red Planet*, an office through which grows a couple of trees and flows a waterfall, Melchior feels he has one more thought to share:

> If you want to know my true science fiction belief, it is that I believe there is a tremendous, unplowed field in that seven-inch wilderness in our heads. I believe we have powers in there that we haven't ever even *dreamt* of. I *know* that they exist and that occasionally you can actually tap into them... It just requires an absolute, total, complete belief in them.

Leo Handel, his friend of over 60 years, offered the observation:

> If you asked me how I might describe Ib Melchior He is the most *positive* person in my life. When he encounters a big issue that's all screwed up, if there's one positive item in it, that is what he is going to talk about. With him, is the glass half-empty or half-full?—it is *always* half-full. He's about possibilities. It's just amazing how he picks out the *positive* of the issue. I mentioned that to him some time ago, and he wasn't even aware of it. Basically, a very positive individual.

Cleo Baldon stated:

> As you listen to Ib and read his stories, the theme is the intrepidness of one man: the self-contained unit who moves through the landscape and takes care of things. This is the theme of any one of his stories...

Imaginative. Positive. Intrepid. Three admirable qualities, any one of which most any person would be happy to possess.

We wondered if the early years of his life might indicate something about the future course his life would take. We asked Ib Melchior if he might know what his first words might've been. Possibly they offered a clue, though we held out little hope such an utterance could be retrieved from a time nearing a century ago. But, in short order, he had an answer:

> According to my mother's records in her Child's Book, the first word I uttered at the age of nine months, on June 6, 1918, was the word "Ja."

"Yes" in Danish.

Yes. Indeed.

ACKNOWLEDGMENTS

The author wishes to express his deepest thanks and gratitude to the following research assistants for their support and great help in compiling or contributing materials and/or conducting additional interviews:

Dennis Skotak
Anthony Mark
Giac Belli
Brian Anthony
Dorothy Fontana
Paul Taglianeti
Miller Drake
Tom Weaver
Jim Kroeper
Kip Doto
Lynn Barker
Anthony Evans
Ed Shifes
Stephane Bourgion

The author also wishes to thank the following individuals for participating in the making of this book by sharing their memories, agreeing to be interviewed, and for their contributions in time, information, and/or materials:

(In alphabetical order): Mort Abrahams, John Agar, Merry Anders, Howard Anderson, Dirk Baldon, Bob Baker, Bent Barfod, Fabrizio Bava, Lamberto Bava, Ben Brady, Anthony Carras, Callisto Cosulich, Oscar Cosulich, Sergio Cosulich, Billy Curtis, Roberto D'Amico, Jim Danforth, Paul Dunlap, Marie Rita Germani, Charles Griffith, Leo Handel, Naura Hayden, Mimi Heinrich, David Hewitt, John Higgins, Osa Jensen, Albert Kallis, Seeleg Lester, Warren Lewis, Fulvio Lucisano, Vic Lundin, Roger Mace, Joan Maurer, Norman Maurer, Leonard Maurer, Gabriele Mayer, J. Edward McKinley, Jan Merlin, Albert Nozaki, Sid Pink, Jack Rabin, Aubrey Schenck, Christina Schoemmel, Mario Silvestri, Curt Siodmak, Les Tremayne, Alex Toth, Herman Townsley, Geofredo "Freddy" Unger, Aage Wiltrup, Thomas Wiltrup...

...and especially Ib Melchior and Cleo Baldon!

APPENDIX A
Documents

Samuel Z. Arkoff				August 17, 1962

						Lou Rusoff

James H. Nicholson
Barnett Shapiro
Tony Carras
Ib Melchior

				RE: **REPTILICUS**

Following a conversation with Mr. Ib Melchior on this day, August 17, 1962, and following a meeting with Tony Carras, of our Editorial department, I am taking the following steps in regard to REPTILICUS.

The film has been turned over to Mr. Melchior and Tony Carras, for the finalizing and execution of the changes and deletions etc., to be made. All such changes are being made with full agreement of Ib Melchior and myself. Each of these changes will be initialed by the principal parties concerned.

In the physical execution of this work, Mr. Carras will represent American International Pictures and Mr. Ib Melchior will represent Sidney Pink. It is my understanding that Mr. Pink has given the necessary authority to Mr. Melchior to carry out and execute these matters pertaining to this project.

Should any discussion arise that cannot be resolved between Mr. Carras and Mr. Melchior, the matter should then be brought to my attention.

I do not anticipate any difficulties since major agreement was reached as of this morning. A step by step work report will be kept on the progress of this picture, each step being duly signed and notated by Mr. Melchior, representing Sidney Pink; by Tony Carras or Lou Rusoff, representing American International Pictures.

Mr. Melchior has been made aware of what our responsibilities and limitations are in regard to this picture. He has also been advised that should work be required other than specified in the overall agreement with Mr. Pink and A.I.P., additional provisions would have to be made for such expenditures.

						Lou Rusoff

LR/bh

MEMORANDUM OF AGREEMENT
between

Sid Pink, Producer, 1914 S. Vermont Ave., Los Angeles, California

and

Ib J. Melchior, Writer, 2050 Stanley Hills Place, Hollywood, California.

March 14, 1960

1. Ib J. Melchior agrees to write the following two feature motion pictures, "Journey To The Seventh Planet" and "Reptillius" from verbal story outlines supplied by Sid Pink. Both screenplays are to be written during the ten week period commencing March 14, 1960.

2. For the above mentioned services Sid Pink agrees to pay Ib Melchior the following:

    a. The sum of three thousand dollars ($ 3,000.00) to be paid in ten weekly payments of three hundred dollars ($ 300.00), the first such payment being due on Friday, March 18, 1960.

    b. One percent (1%) of the gross income of the two motion pictures after print and distribution costs.

Agreed:_____
Sid Pink, Producer

Agreed:_____
Ib J. Melchior, Writer

Journey to the 7th Planet interior spaceship set

```
INSERT SHOTS    (COLOR)
TV set in store window - for matted news 30A and on.
BLOCKHOUSE    ((COLOR)
         a.  radar scope for mattes - 8-10-21-25-27
STOCK  b.  instrument panel - working - 14-18
         c.  TV screen for matte - 48
AIRLOCK
pressure sign going on
NEWSPAPERS - 28-29    (COLOR)
HOSPITAL SIGN - 76A    (COLOR)
MINIATURE SHOTS AND SPECIAL EFFECTS    (B+W)
Space ship ramp opening - for matte 48 (mini)
X Rocket in clearing on Mars  171 - (242 int?)
                                          NIGHT   NIGHT    Cover with stock -
STOCK → Take-off - 249-251 (NIGHT)          light fires-rocket tail
   X Amoeba - 322 (see note)
   X Pseudopod - 303          X CL.SH. Part of Amoeba
                                 for Sam's dissolve 304 X
   81 - Universe - approaching meteor
   Universe - 85-348-378  ⎫
   Mars - 97-379            ⎬ (COLOR)
   Ship in Space - 110-352 ⎭

PICK-UPS   (COLOR)
   52 - vehicles racing across desert
   98 - magazine cover
MATTES FOR CONTROL ROOM TV/RADAR SCREEN    (COLOR)
   95    F & R   Earth & Mars (not as written in script
   100   F       Mars
   109   F       Mars (huge)
   111   R       Landing
   117   Landing on Mars
MARS P.O.V. SHOTS  (& PORT MATTE?)    (B+W)
119-120-122-129-139-(180 sunrise) (214 Lake)

322-Note = Shot for optical combinations.  ⎫
   a. Amoeba hiding ship.                    ⎬ 2 cuts
   b. Ship on black velvet.                  ⎭
```

Melchior's list of insert shots needed for *Invasion of Mars* (*The Angry Red Planet*), including his handwritten notes.

Below: A scene from the film as people on the street are updated on the fate of the Mars ship. (Portions of this scene were later deleted.)

The first page of Melchior's prescript treatment for *Planet of the Vampires*—known then as *The Haunted World*: The *Argos* and the *Galliot* orbit a strange world...

APPENDIX B
Photographs and Production Sketches
The Angry Red Planet

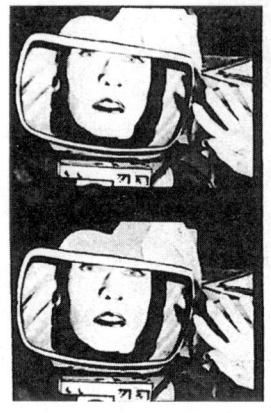

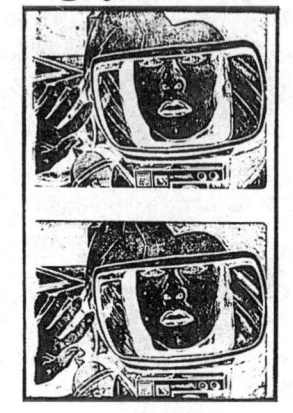

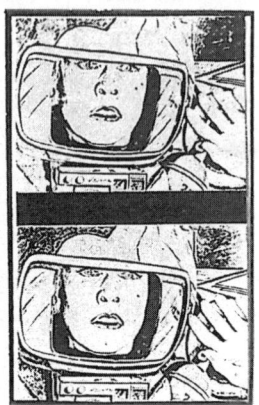

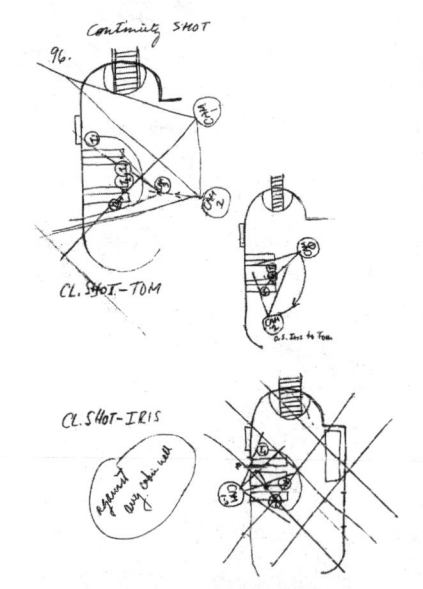

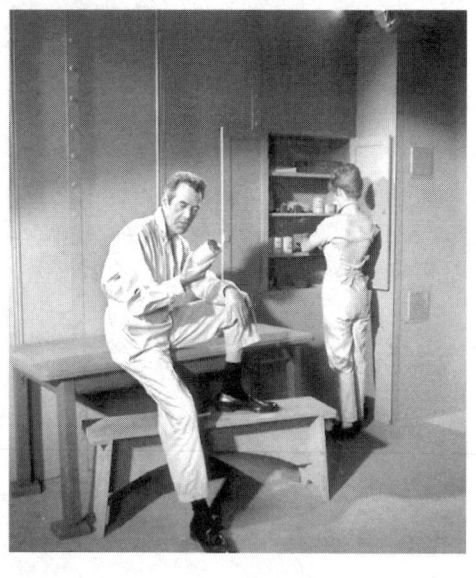

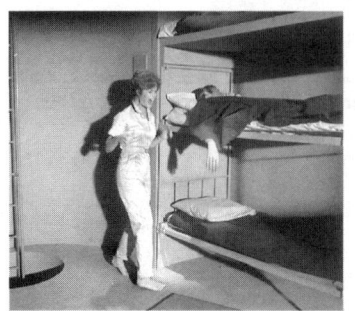

Top: A demonstration test strip approximating the intended look of Cinemagic.
Middle Left: Melchior's camera angle sketches for filming the upper deck sequences.
Middle Right and Bottom Left: Rarely seen upper deck of the Mars-bound rocket. The appearance of these photos in sequence with other proof sheet scenes from the film contradict producer Sid Pink's claim that the scene was written and directed by himself at a later date.

Top: Sammy reads a pulp magazine featuring situations much like those that appear later in the film. (The actual magazine contained a rendering of a three-eyed monster [see insert] that bore a resemblance to the one in the film.)

Right: The original magazine cover (left) and its modified version (right) used in the film.

Ib Melchior: Man of Imagination

305

A rare view of miniature photography in progress on the Martian lake.

Model kits now available of *The Angry Red Planet* monsters

Howard Anderson

J. Edward McKinley

Top: Rare Norman Maurer illustration for the porthole view of the Martian landscape cut from the film.

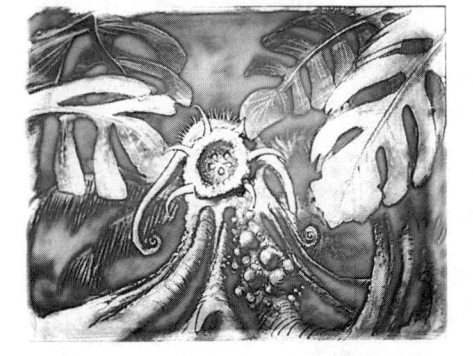

Above: Two examples of weird Martian plant life.

Italian poster

Ib Melchior: Man of Imagination   **307**

Robinson Crusoe on Mars

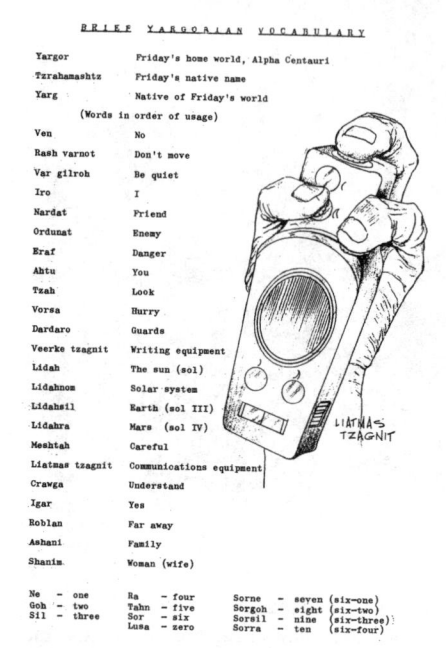

BRIEF YARGORIAN VOCABULARY

Yargor	Friday's home world, Alpha Centauri
Tzrahamashtz	Friday's native name
Yarg	Native of Friday's world

(Words in order of usage)

Ven	No
Rash varnot	Don't move
Var gilroh	Be quiet
Iro	I
Nardat	Friend
Ordunat	Enemy
Eraf	Danger
Ahtu	You
Tzah	Look
Vorsa	Hurry
Dardaro	Guards
Veerke tzagnit	Writing equipment
Lidah	The sun (sol)
Lidahnom	Solar system
Lidahsil	Earth (sol III)
Lidahra	Mars (sol IV)
Meshtah	Careful
Liatmas tzagnit	Communications equipment
Crawga	Understand
Igar	Yes
Roblan	Far away
Ashani	Family
Shanim	Woman (wife)

Ne	–	one	Ra	–	four	Sorne	–	seven (six-one)
Goh	–	two	Tahn	–	five	Sorgoh	–	eight (six-two)
Sil	–	three	Sor	–	six	Sorsil	–	nine (six-three)
			Lusa	–	zero	Sorra	–	ten (six-four)

Melchior devised an alien language and communication device for Friday in *Robinson Crusoe on Mars*.

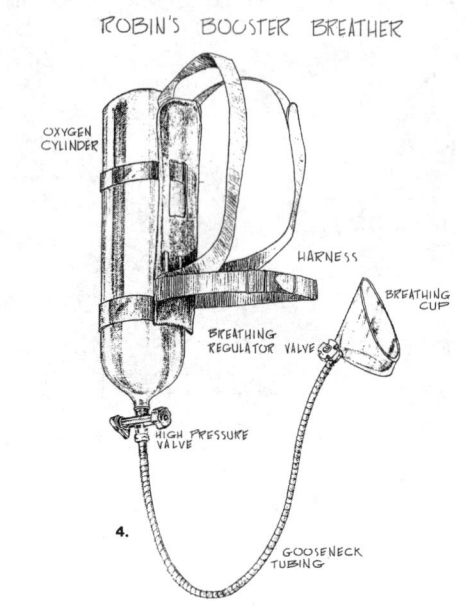

Melchior's original Booster Breather for *Robinson Crusoe on Mars*.

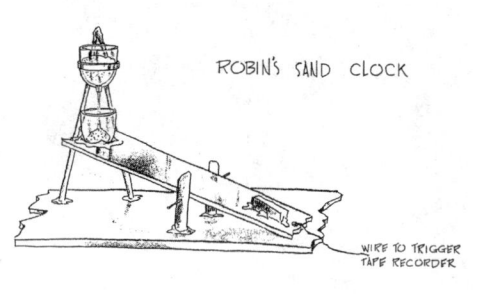

The Melchior-Baldon design for Robin's Sand Clock in *Robinson Crusoe on Mars*.

Art department illustrations for top: alien guard and slave, Kosmos; and bottom: alternative designs for alien weapons in *Robinson Crusoe on Mars*.

Storyboard of dangerous solo landing on Mars

Right: An Ib Melchior paste-up illustration of a shot of the earth rescue ship coming in for a landing.

Bottom: An establishing matte painting of the astronaut's natural "spa." (Optical and mattes were designed by the art department and realized by Larry Butler.)

Ib Melchior: Man of Imagination

Fiber glass construction of rocks is apparent in this still taken during photography of the underground canal sequence. Note the clothing tie-in to the Defoe novel.

Camera crew and grips work to film sequence of wrecked Mars Probe One capsule on Death Valley location.

Journey to the 7th Planet

Ib Melchior, accompanied by Greta Thyssen, (right) speaks to acquaintance Hanne Scheel. Melchior, for a short time, dated Thyssen.

Below: Carl Otteson, at a campfire, relates a story about his childhood, while, unknown to him, his memories are brought to life by an unseen power on the planet Uranus.

Planet of the Vampires

Wide, in-camera matte shot created by Bava to represent the *Argos'* sister ship the *Galliot,* which owes part of its origin to photographs of a large reflector telescope for a real observatory.

Below: One of the first of the modern era's unflinchingly grisly make-ups—dead crewman Sallis' uniform is accidently torn away to reveal ripped-open flesh and bones.

Above: An impressive full view of the control deck aboard the *Argos*, created via a foreground miniature.

Left: An encounter with the alien dead aboard the derelict ship.

Ib Melchior: Man of Imagination

Reptilicus

Top: Cinematographer Page Wiltrup lines up his camera on one of the miniature sets of Copehagen.
Bottom: Model builder Kai Doed (far left) and his crew at work with the Reptilicus marionette. Wiltrup stands on the far right.

The Time Travelers

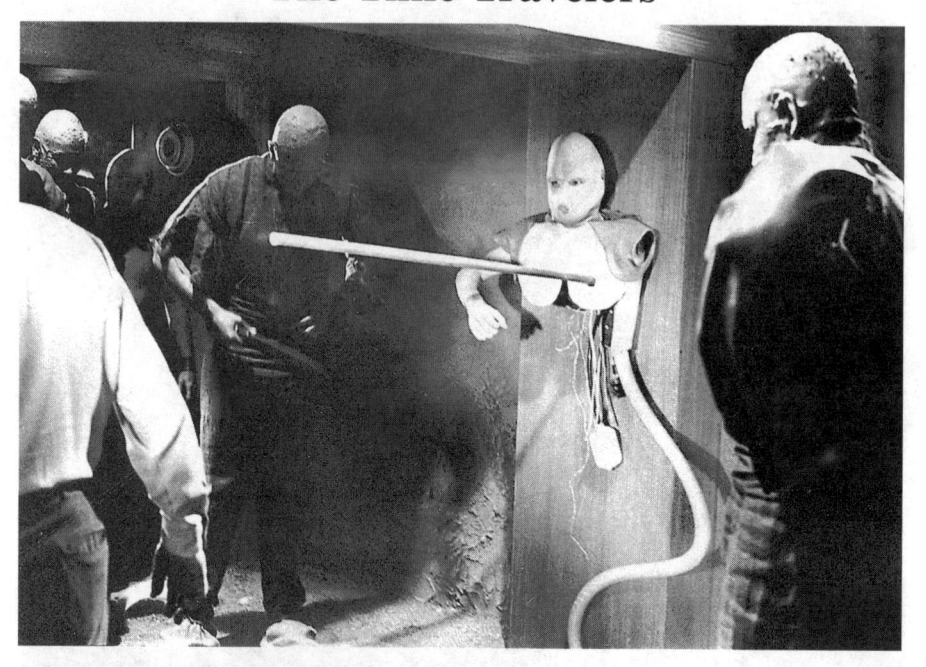

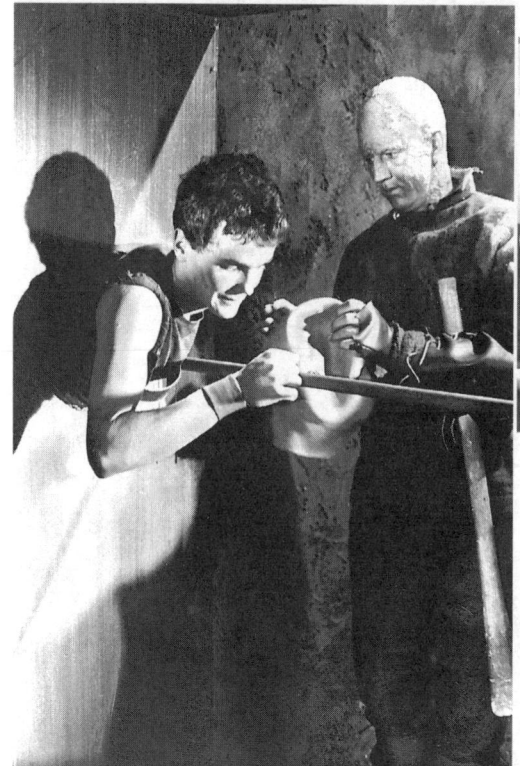

Top: David Hewitt and Melchior rigged an unusual number of visual tricks including hiding bodies in sets, tables and walls to chop, mutilate and sever.

Bottom left: A mutant comes to the aid of an android before killing him.

Bottom right: A deleted scene from the film.

INDEX

A Gift of Murder 122, 125
Abrahams, Mort 53-55, 60
Ackerman, Forrest J 8, 160, 166, 171, 181, 288
Agar, John 142, 145, 146-147, 152
Alcohol and Red Flares 258
Alcoholism: The Revolving Door 63
Allen, Irwin 190, 212, 225, 255, 262, 290, 293-294
Ambush Bay 260-262
American International Pictures (AIP) 94, 121, 127-128, 135, 147, 149, 150, 152, 158-159, 170-171, 212, 225-226, 233, 235-237, 245, 255, 288
American-Scandinavian Foundation of Los Angeles 296
Anders, Merry 161, 179, 180-181, 183-184, 189, 281
Andersen, Hans Chrisitan 14, 280-281
Anderson, Howard Jr. 118
Angry Red Planet, The 8, 12, 69, 88-89, 93, 97, 99, 100, 120-122, 127-128, 134, 137, 144, 150, 152, 167, 172, 178, 183, 196, 213, 224, 254, 293, 295, 297
Animal World, The 212
Argosy 62, 262
Arkoff, Sam 127, 212, 225-226, 228-230, 233, 255
Army Intelligence Service 38
Arnold, Jack 10
Atwater, Barry 157
Baker, Bob 111
Baldon, Cleo 8, 19, 30, 41, 62, 64, 126, 153, 159, 189, 191, 196, 208, 210-211, 230, 232, 262-263, 273, 276-279, 281-282, 284, 294-295, 298
Baldon, Dirk 158-159
Bang, Poul 131
Barfod, Bent 124, 149
Barison, Ed 73
Barstow 172, 177, 180

Bartel, Paul 283, 286-287
Bava, Eugenio 240
Bava, Fabrizio 239
Bava, Mario 226, 229-230, 233-234, 236-241, 243-244, 246-247
Bayreuth 18-19
Behrens, Marlies 133
Bengell, Norma 236-237, 242-243
Beowulf 15, 141
Bevilaqua, Alberto 233-234
BIEN 289
Black chamber 270
Black Nemesis 123, 125
Black Sabbath 226
Black Sunday 226, 228, 230
Blake, Carter 55
Blind Faith 87
Block, Irving 83
Blue Book 62
Bluebeard 111
Bohr, Niels 266
Bonestell, Chesley 9, 83
Boy Who Said Yes, The 19
Brady, Ben 217
Brain From Planet Arous, The 122, 145
Brandenburg, Frank 274
Braun, Eva 270
Braun, Werner von 195
Brave New World 11, 25-30, 32
Brodney, Oscar 74
Bronson, Charles 74
Bronze Star 41
Brown, Maurice 43
Bryce, Edward 55-56
Burroughs Computers 99, 105, 183
Butler, Lawrence 204
Candela, Rosario 270
Candidatus Philosophiae 24, 33
Captain Video 52
Carey, Phillip 161, 179-180
Carradine, David 285, 287

Carras, Anthony 135, 148-149, 150
Carthay Stage 171, 175, 177, 184, 212
Case By Case 37, 263, 275-276
Case of Patti Smith, The 166-167, 180
Center Theater 31, 36
Chaney, Lon Jr. 12, 122-123
Chang, Wah 150
Chronicles of the Danish Realm 153
Cinecitta Studios 235, 243, 245
Cinemagic 97, 100-103, 107, 116, 127
Civic Theater 44, 45-47
Code Name: Grand Guignol 271, 273-274
Columbus of the Stars 190, 213, 215, 223, 255, 262
Cookerly, Jack 117
Corman, Roger 283, 285-288
Cortez, Stanley 105, 117-118
Cosulich, Callisto 233-234, 241
Count of Monte Cristo 20
Counter Intelligence Corps. (CIC) 13, 37-38, 42, 263, 270, 274
Crane, Kenneth 74
Crater Base One 12, 77-82
Crosland, Alan 83
Curtis, Billy 113
Cyborg XM-1 248, 252-257, 259
Dachau 8, 37, 274-275
Danforth, Jim 148-150
Davis, Sid 258
Death Race 2000 12, 283, 285-288, 290, 295
Death Valley 191, 196, 199, 201-202, 204, 208, 268
Deathsport 288
DeFoe, Daniel 191-192, 198, 201, 207
Denmark 10, 14, 17, 21, 24, 32-33, 127-128, 131, 133, 140, 145-146, 151, 159, 162, 256, 264
Department of Defense 82, 188
Destination Moon 9, 52, 96, 110
Devil's Messenger 126
DeWitt, Louis 83
Dijon, Louis 23-24
Dobil Productions 170
Dolgrin, Sol 83
Don Post Studios 173
Dougherty, James B. 77

Dracula 44
Dunlap, Paul 116
Earth Vs. the Spider 150
Ed Sullivan Show, The 51
Eddie Arnold Show, The 49
Eglin Air Force Base 141, 258
Eisenhower, Dwight D. 74, 263
Elsinore Castle 67
English Players, The 21, 23-25, 28-29, 31, 272
Escapade 64, 283
Eva 270, 278
Fantastic Universe 69
Feinberg, Marve 261
Fiest, Felix 213
Fire Maidens From Outer Space 98
Fire Monster, The 73
Five 90
Foster, Preston 161, 179-180, 190
Franken, Steve 161, 179
Fujimoto, Tak 283
Garland, Margaret 55
Garnel, Lloyd ôGoldieö 113
Gebhardt, Freddie 198
Giant of Metropolis, The 238
Gigantis 73
Giovannini, Giorgio 238-239
Girls on the Loose 75
G.L. Enterprises 62
Globe Playhouse, The 156, 288
Godzilla 12, 72-73
Godzilla Raids Again 72
Gordian Knot, The 217-219, 221-224
Gordon, Bert 150
Gordon, Don 223
Gorgo 128, 132
Gould, George 53
Grand Guignol 271-272, 274
Griffith, Chuck 285-286
Gulliver's Space Travels 191, 213
Gulliver's Travels 191
Haigerloch Project, The 264
Hal Roach Studios 90, 103, 110
Hamlet 12, 67, 122, 153, 157, 269, 280, 288-289
Hamlet Award 289

Hamlet Society International 289
Handel, Leo 8, 35-36, 42, 72, 90, 119, 122, 143, 153, 191, 298
Hansard, Bill 105, 172
Hart House Theater 43-44
Hart, Susan 235-236
Haskin, Byron 199, 200-201, 204, 206, 208, 210
Haunted Planet, The 229
Haunted World, The 226, 229, 230
Hayden, Naura (Nora) 90, 93, 97, 108-109, 116-117, 119, 128, 132, 281
Heacock, Gary 169, 171, 173-174
Heinlein, Robert 54, 77
Heinrich, Mimi 132, 135, 145, 151
Hellinger, Bill 157
Here's Sport, Indeed 66
Hertz-Lion Productions 122, 125
Hewitt, David 160, 162, 164-167, 169, 172-174, 178-179, 185, 187, 190, 212-213, 255
Heyward, Louis M. (Deke) 212, 226, 228, 234-235, 237, 239, 242, 245
Higgins, John 199-200, 206
Hiroshima 43, 47, 81
Hitler, Adolf 263, 266, 270-271
Hoch, Winton 201, 204
Holocaust, The 274
Hot Run 258-259
Hour of Vengeance 12, 153, 155, 157, 179, 288-289
Howard, Moe 100
Howco International 145
Hoyt, John 161, 179-180
Huston, John 49
Huxley, Aldous 25, 28-29
Inside the Moon 122
Invasion of Mars 90-92, 94, 103, 110
Irwin, S. Leroy, Gen. 40
It Conquered the World 285
Italian International Film 235
Jack Benny Show, The 51
Jack the Giant Killer 150
Jefferson, Thomas 280
Jeffries, Dean 287
Jensen, Osa (Petersen) 17, 20, 140, 256
Jet Propulsion Lab 195, 201

Journey Into the Unknown 162-163, 168, 171
Journey to the Center of the Earth 140
Journey to the 7th Planet 13, 128-128, 136, 138, 142, 144-146, 148, 150-152, 157, 159-160, 224, 231, 253-254, 293
Kale, Harriet Hathaway 32, 36, 48
Karloff, Boris 126
Keep Off the Grass 258
Kelly, Grace 42
Killer Secret 122
King Brothers 128
King of Denmark 41
Klushantsev, Pavel 77
Knechtel, Lloyd 95, 113, 115
Knight Commander Cross 40-41
Koch, Mark 290-291
Koed, Kai 133, 136
Kovaks, Lazslo 176
Kroeger, Barry 188
Krueger, Paul, Gen. 40
Kruschen, Jack 97, 116, 150
Kubert, Joe 100
Kyd, Thomas 153
Lang, Otto 86
LAPES 258-259
LaSalle, Richard 160, 188
Lester, Seeleg 223, 225
Lincoln, Abraham 9, 280
Little Shop of Horrors 285
Live Fast-Die Young 74, 223
Lonnergan, Arthur 200, 202, 204, 210
Los Angeles Lakers 177
Lost In Space 12, 213, 225, 255-256, 290, 293
Lost World, The 212
Lovecraft, H.P. 256
Lucisano, Fulvio 226, 234-237, 244-245
Lundigan, William 82
Lundin, Vic 200, 202-203, 205-206, 209, 214
Main Street Undersea 62
Man From Planet X, The 111
Man From U.N.C.L.E., The 53
Man Plus 255
Man Who Laughs, The 21
Mantee, Paul 201, 203-205, 209
March of Medicine, The 63, 90

Marcus Device, The 267-268, 278
Markim, Al 55
Martin, Dewey 223
Mask of the Demon 226
Maurer, Joan 100-101
Maurer, Leonard 100-101
Maurer, Norman 89, 92, 94, 96, 100, 103, 105, 109, 112, 115, 118, 120-121, 127
Maximilian, Maj. 39
Mayer, Gabriele 238-239
McKinley, J. Edward 106, 109, 149, 159, 188
Medal of Merit 41
Melchior, Birte 15, 18
Melchior, Inger 15-16
Melchior, Lauritz 14-15, 18-19, 32-33, 45
Melchior, Leif 36, 282
Melchior, Torben 282
Men Into Space 82-84, 86, 88, 91, 254
Mercer, Ray 120, 158-159
Merlin, Jan 55-56, 58-59, 61, 81, 281
Metropolitan Opera 18, 33
Micro-Men, The 8, 12, 76, 81, 128, 230
Mimms, "Slaughter," Col. 258
Missle to the Moon 98
Mohr, Gerald 97, 109, 117
Monch, Peter 142
Monganga 63
Multiple Man, The 8, 12, 76, 80, 167
Murphy, Mary 75, 223
NASA 196
Nazis 13, 17, 37-38, 264, 266, 270
Nebula Award 12, 255
New World Pictures 283
New York Cipher Society 270
Newman, Joseph 70
Night of the Living Dead 232
Night of 24 Hours, The 226, 228
Night Must Fall 48
Night Stalker 157
Not of This Earth 285
Nozaki, Al 200, 203, 206-209
Office of Strategic Service, OSS 34, 37, 269
Oliver, Susan 281
Oltre Il Cielo 226
1000 Years From Now 281
Order of Battle 263, 278

Orleans, Vincenzo Abbate Castello, Prince 40
Oscar Wilde 23-24
Oswald, Gerd 223, 225
Ottosen, Carl 133, 135, 142, 145-146, 149-150, 159
Outer Limits, The 11-12, 76, 84, 217, 221-222, 225
Outlaw Planet, The 230, 297
Outstanding Scandinavian of the Year 295
Outworlders, The 215
PLADS 258-259
Pal, George 9, 10, 13, 110, 120, 11-12, 224, 226, 228, 233, 235-236, 238
Parsifal 18
Patrick, Dennis 155-157, 161, 179-180, 190, 281, 288-289
Perloff, Lou 121
Perry Como Show, The 49-50, 52, 90
Pestriniero, Rene 226-227, 282
Pine-Key Productions 77, 79
Pink, Sid 89-91, 94, 96, 98, 100-102, 105, 107, 116, 118-121, 127-137, 143-144, 146-148, 151-152, 158-159, 178
Pisgah Lava Crater 175, 180
Planet of the Apes 53
Planet of the Vampires 239, 246-247, 254, 293, 295, 297
Pohl, Frederick 255
Predictor Instrument 188
Prelude Pictures 290, 293
Premonition, The 12, 217, 219-225, 230
Professional Theatre Center 157, 288
Project Unlimited 149
Purcell, Pete 76
Rabin, Jack 83, 223, 287
Racer, The 64, 283, 286, 290
Rachmil, Lewis J. 82
Radio City Music Hall 31, 42
Rambaldi, Carlo 243
Rand Corporation 167, 188
Redlin, Bill 161, 170-171, 178, 190, 212
Reitsch, Hanna 260
Renard, Louis Miehe 142
Reptilicus 127-128, 130-132, 134-137, 144-145, 147, 150, 152, 158-160, 224
Rinaldi, Antonio 245

Rivkin, Allen 76
Robinson Crusoe in the Invisible Galaxy 209
Robinson Crusoe on Mars 12, 121-122, 153, 191, 194, 196-198, 200-203, 206-211, 213-214, 253-254, 262, 268, 293, 295
Rocketship X-M 52
Rockettes, The 8, 31
Roddenberry, Gene 213, 262
Roecca, Sam 223
Roland, Norman 43, 46-47
Roman, Antonio 226
Rooney, Mickey 260
Ross, John F. 63
Rusoff, Lou 158
Rybnick, Harry 73
Sabateur 87
Saga Studios 131, 145
Salvia, Rafael J 226
Satinsky, Vic 76
Savage Trap, The 76, 254
Saxo Grammaticus 153-154
Schenck, Aubrey 197-200, 209, 261
Schoemmel, Ronny 149
Schorr, Friedrich 19
Science Fiction Theater 11, 67, 76
Seeds of Violence 76
Seldeen, Margaret 188
Seventh Voyage of Sinbad 196
Shadow From Beyond 124-125
Shadow World 226, 229
Shakespeare Society of America 156, 288-289
Shakespeare, William 12, 32, 66-67, 122, 153, 155, 269, 280, 289
Shaw, George Bernard 24, 32
Shifres, Ed 290
Sigilla Veri 32
Silver Space Ship Award 160
Silvestri, Mario 238-239, 243, 245
Sinatra, Frank 50
Siodmak, Curt 32, 122, 125
Sleeper Agent 264
Smith, E.E. (Doc) 32, 243
Smyrner, Ann 132-133, 145
Space Cadet 54
Space Family Robinson 110, 190, 211-213, 225, 254-255, 262, 290, 293
Sprogoe, Ove 142, 146
Stag 62, 262
Stallone, Sylvester 283, 287
Star Trek 11-12, 52, 213-216, 223, 256, 262
Stars on Ice 32
Starship Explorers 12, 214-217, 255
Stenhus College (Boarding School) 16-17, 19
Stephano, Joseph 217
Steps and Stairways 295
Stevens, Leslie 217
Stirling, Edward 22, 24-26, 28-29
Storey, Ray 169-171, 175-176
Story of a Loaf, The 281
Stromberg, Hunt Jr. 212
Strudwick, Peter 182-183, 188
Sullivan, Barry 120, 235-237, 242-243
Summer Theater 42
Suspense 48
Sutton, Frank 55
Svensk Filmindstri 122
Swiss Family Robinson 191, 211, 262
Switzer, Herb 110
Terrore Nello Spazio 226, 238, 241, 243
Theatre De L'Oeuvre 25, 28, 29
13 Demon Street 12, 122, 125
Thom, Robert 285-286
Thomas, Frankie 55-56
Three Stooges, The 100, 120
Thyssen, Greta 145, 148
Time Machine, The 163
Time Trap 168
Time Travelers, The 12, 155, 157, 160, 162, 164, 167, 172, 176-178, 180-181, 186, 189-190, 198-199, 206, 209, 211-212, 217, 222, 224, 245, 248, 254-255, 259, 293, 297
Time Tunnel 190, 255
Timemasters, The 168
Tom Corbett, Space Cadet 9, 11, 51-54, 56, 58, 60-61
Tombstone Cipher, The 269
Toth, Alex 102-104, 120
Townsley, Herman 110-111
Treasure Asteroid 191, 262
Treasure Island 191
Tremayne, Les 107-108, 117, 281

Trieste Science Fiction Festival 160
Two-Legged Space Ship, The 258-259
Unger, Geofredo (Freddy) 238, 241-242, 244
Unidentified Flying Objects (UFOÆs) 70-71
University of Copenhagen 21, 24, 33
V-3 270
Verne, Jules 32, 43, 140, 282
Victorious Might, The 19
Vidiot, The 66
Vietnam 256-259
Vikings 14, 31, 67, 153-154, 156-157, 282, 288, 295
Visigood, T.L.P. 77
Vogt, A.E. van 77
Voice of Infinity 82-83
Volcano Monsters, The 72, 74, 80, 127, 130
Voyage to the End of the Universe 238
Waffen SS 39-40
Wagner, Richard 15, 18-19
Walinsky, Louis 25, 28-29
War of the Worlds, The 70, 110, 199, 206, 209
Warlords of the Outlaw Planet 226
Waste Product 67, 69
Watchdogs of Abaddon 266-267
Water Tank Rescue 84, 86
Watson, Ed 75
Weeks, Howard 110-111
Weil, Kurt 19
Wells, H.G. 32
Werewolf Organization 38, 62, 74, 262, 265
When Hell Broke Loose 74, 83
When Worlds Collide 120, 162, 165, 168, 175
Wiesenthal, Simon 274
Wiltrup, Aage 131-132, 134-136, 145-147
Wiltrup, Thomas 132
Windham Playhouse 48
Wings Over Europe 43-47
Winner and New...,The 12, 65
Wolf, Stanley 53-54
World War II 12-13, 34, 40, 52, 70, 74, 81, 196, 260, 263, 270-271, 274-276
World Without End 120, 160, 162, 165
Writers Guild of America, West (WGAW) 198, 235, 267
Wyss, Johann 191

If you enjoyed this book, check out Midnight Marquee Monsters magazine

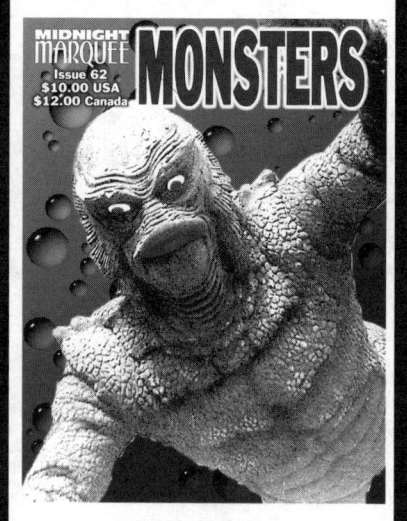

**Midnight Marquee Press, Inc.
9721 Britinay Lane
Baltimore, MD 21234
410-665-1198
Visit our website
(www.midmar.com)
for complete
back issue
information!**